D0722565

Managing and Accounting for Inventories

THIRD
EDITION
of
Inventories
by
Raymond A. Hoffman
and
Henry Gunders

MANAGING AND ACCOUNTING FOR INVENTORIES

Control
Income Recognition
and
Tax Strategy

C. PAUL JANNIS, C.P.A.
Partner, Price Waterhouse & Co.

CARL H. POEDTKE, Jr.
Principal, Price Waterhouse & Co.

DONALD R. ZIEGLER, C.P.A.
Partner, Price Waterhouse & Co.

A RONALD PRESS
PUBLICATION

JOHN WILEY & SONS

New York   Chichester
Brisbane   Toronto

Library of Congress Cataloging in Publication Data

Jannis, C. Paul.
    Managing and accounting for inventories.

    First-2d ed., by R. A. Hoffman and H. Gunders,
published under title: Inventories.
    "A Ronald Press publication."
    Includes index.
    1. Inventories.   2. Inventories—Accounting.
I. Ziegler, Donald R., joint author. II. Poedtke,
Carl H., joint author. III. Hoffman, Raymond,
1911- Inventories. IV. Title.

HF5681.S8H59 1979   658.7′87   78-31481
ISBN 0-471-05016-4

Printed in the United States of America

10 9 8 7 6 5 4

Preface

Almost a decade has elapsed since the publication of the SECOND EDITION of this book by Hoffman and Gunders. During the intervening period, certain aspects of inventory accounting and reporting have been examined by authoritative accounting bodies, the Internal Revenue Service, the courts, and the Securities Exchange Commission, with resulting changes in financial and tax accounting and reporting requirements.

The last decade has also been a period in which commodity prices have almost doubled. This dramatic increase in the inflation rate has directly affected inventory values and regenerated a strong interest in the use of the last-in, first-out (LIFO) method of accounting. The number of users of the LIFO method has increased substantially since 1973, and continues to grow. The increased cost of borrowing has also accelerated interest in this tax-saving technique. There is no question that LIFO can be a tax saver, but under the income tax law the method cannot be used for tax purposes unless it is also used to determine annual income for financial statement purposes. This book–tax conformity requirement continues to be a dilemma, because interpretative positions taken by the Internal Revenue Service since 1973 restrict what a LIFO company can say about the effect on income from its use of the LIFO method. Regulations proposed by the Service in July 1979, however, should help to alleviate many of these concerns.

Because of the effect of inflation on inventory values, the 1970's have also seen much greater interest in the subject by the Securities Exchange Commission in the form of a request for disclosure of the effect on income from "inventory profits." In a period of rising prices such as experienced beginning in 1973, the adoption and use of the LIFO method for financial purposes may very well improve the quality of reported earnings and minimize concern with so-called "illusory profits" in inventory which has been valued under the first-in, first-out (FIFO) method. The restrictive attitude of the IRS as to what a LIFO user can disclose via reports to owners and creditors has seemed at times to be irreconcilable with what is interpreted as an SEC-required disclosure. This apparent difference in the requirements of two important government agencies has introduced a certain ambiguity into the position of a LIFO user.

The mid-1970's also saw the IRS issue income tax regulations that made mandatory the use of full-absorption inventory costing by a manufacturer or processor. Several court decisions involving the income tax aspects of inventory valuation preceded such IRS action. In early 1979 the Supreme Court of the United States interpreted, in the IRS's favor, regulations relating to the determination of "cost or market, whichever is lower" for excess inventory.

Rising interest rates, an economic downturn in the mid-1970's, continued inflation, and present economic uncertainties have led to conservative inventory management policies, and these factors have contributed to new developments in the management and control of inventories.

Against this background, the present volume reviews in a comprehensive manner the entire subject of inventories and inventory accounting and emphasizes successful methods of planning and control. The book reflects the many developments in the rules for taxation, accounting and financial reporting of inventories, and gives careful attention to the effects of inventory policies and methods of accounting on income and taxes. It is a comprehensive guide to forecasting and quantitative techniques, costing (including full absorption), the "cost or market, whichever is lower" rule, the retail method, and the various methods of valuing inventories under the LIFO principle. The LIFO book–tax conformity problem is reviewed in depth.

In recent years understanding and use of up-to-date and cost-effective techniques for the control of inventories have become even more vital to the successful operation of every organization. This book provides a useful overview of such techniques, including material requirements planning, demand forecasting, and capacity planning and control. The effect of automated interactive systems is fully reflected.

The authors are deeply indebted to Raymond A. Hoffman, a retired partner and good friend, whose expertise, interest and dedication to inventory accounting throughout his career with Price Waterhouse & Co. were in large measure responsible for both the FIRST and SECOND EDITIONS, and form the foundation for this volume. We are equally indebted to Henry Gunders, the firm's Vice Chairman of Management Advisory Services, who contributed so substantially to the SECOND EDITION, and graciously afforded an opportunity to others to participate in the present undertaking.

The authors have sought and received assistance from numerous associates in Price Waterhouse & Co., and give special acknowledgment and thanks to the following: J. C. Everett, T. R. Hunter, W. M. Lehman, John J. Mullahy, W. T. Muir, Michael R. Redemske, and James O. Stepp. Special recognition is also due those who helped in preparation of the two previous editions: John B. Inglis, John G. Henderson, Michael F. Klein, Jr., Bernard Tecotzky, Jay R. Oliff, Paul Rosenfeld, and Kevin G. Weis for the FIRST EDITION; and Carl H. Poedtke and Donald R. Smith for the SECOND EDITION.

C. PAUL JANNIS
CARL H. POEDTKE
DONALD R. ZIEGLER

New York
January, 1980

Contents

ing Related to Inventories. Forecasting Related to Inventory Management. Nature of Forecasts. Nature of the Long-Range Forecast. Intermediate-Range Forecasting. Short-Range Forecasting. Inventory Planning and Forecasting. Developing a Forecasting System. Forecasting Methods and Techniques. Subjective Methods. Time Series Analysis. Combined Approach. Forecasting Errors. Forecasting and the Computer.

Identification of Inventory Levels. ABC Approach to Inventory Management. Inventory Data Requirements. Manufacturing Control Systems. Warehousing and Distribution Control Systems. Material Requirements Planning. Reorder Point Systems. Visual Review. Two-Bin System. Min–Max System. Reorder Point–EOQ System. Reservation System. Order Quantities. Inventory System Implementation. Summary.

The Accounting Function. Meaning of "Cost" and "Expense." Meaning of "Fixed" and "Variable." Factors in Classifying Expenditures. Recognizing Alternative Courses of Action. Suggested Classifications for Expenditures. Factors in Determinations of Product Costs. Applying Overhead on Basis of Activity.

Factors Involved in Determination of Cost Generally. Factors Involved in Determinations of Cost for Inventory Purposes. Treatment of Overhead by IAS 2. Treatment of Overhead in Federal Income Tax Regulations. Use of Specific and Average Costs for Inventory Purposes. Effect Upon Income of Cost Determination Procedures. Practical Aspects of Costing Procedures.

Chapter 11

Use of LIFO for Federal Tax Purposes   239

Chapter 12

Measuring LIFO Inventories by Dollar-Value Principle   261

Chapter 13

Retail Method of Computing Inventories   294

Chapter 14

Adapting LIFO to the Retail Method   309

Chapter 15

APPENDICES

Managing and Accounting for Inventories

ONE

The Significance of Inventories in Determining Income and Tax Liabilities

Everyone does not begin his/her experiences in the business world by selling homemade lemonade; but envisioning such an activity can be helpful to a discussion of the significance of inventories in the determination of income.

To the extent that the materials required for the product, that is, the lemons, sugar, and paper cups, were obtained by gift, or otherwise procured from the family kitchen without cost, no question is involved as to the amount of cash disbursed in acquiring an inventory. If the unused materials are returned and the product is completely sold or consumed, there will not be an inventory. Here the determination of income is easy. Although a technical question could be raised about the proper accounting for the contribution from the benefactor who donated the materials, as compared with the profit realized from the sales transactions, a practical solution adequate for the purpose can usually be found for that type of problem. If materials are held overnight, however, or if some unsold product is stored in the refrigerator, an inventory question exists in this most basic situation.

Beyond the simple venture, the question of inventories becomes increasingly important. Materials must be purchased, not just once but on a continuing basis. There will always be both materials and unsold product on hand. Furthermore, the enterprise will be managed on the assumption of an unlimited existence.

There are two distinct attributes of an inventory: the physical and the financial. The physical characteristics are factual, whereas the amount assigned to the inventory for financial reporting purposes is subjective. The inventory amount results from the exercise of judgment and the application of particular accounting procedures. An understanding of the different acceptable inventory methods is of increasing importance in dealing with the more complex business problems. However, regardless of which inventory method is used or what amount is arrived at, the true worth to the business of the articles on hand is the same.

The fact that the physical attributes of an inventory are not affected by the dollar amount assigned to it in financial statements is not always recognized. For example, corporate executives, investment bankers, business brokers, and others have been influenced during merger negotiations by the relative "book values" of two companies, even though such book values were not comparable because of different accounting methods having been used with respect to inventories. Attempts to explain the lack of comparability have not always been successful, and *adjusted* book values have been looked upon with some misgivings because of inadequate appreciation for basic accounting concepts.

WHAT IS INVENTORY?

The word "inventory" can be used to mean several different things. It can be used to refer to the stock on hand at a particular time of raw materials, goods in process of manufacture, finished products, merchandise purchased for resale, and the like, tangible assets which can be seen, measured, and counted. As a verb the term embraces the acts of weighing and counting the items on hand and preparing a list with appropriate descriptions. The word is also used to mean itemized lists of goods or property. In connection with financial statements and accounting records, the reference may be to the amount assigned to the stock of goods owned by an enterprise at a particular time. For present purposes, only the first and the last of these meanings needs be considered.

The significance of inventories in modern business is basically attributable to the need for measuring the results of operations for a particular period, such as a month, quarter, or year. If income were being computed only for the entire existence of a business entity and there were no taxes, there would be no necessity for inventories. The income would be determined after all property had been converted into cash available for distribution to the owners.

Corporate finance long ago developed to the point of expecting a determination of periodic income for even the largest of businesses. Management needs to know the operating results on a current basis, shareholders and potential investors are interested in earnings reports from time to time, and the Internal Revenue Code provides that federal taxes on income shall be computed generally for no period longer than twelve months.

The significance of reliable inventory determinations to statements of periodic income has been emphasized by the Securities and Exchange Commission.[1] Problems have arisen, particularly in situations involving the offering of securities of closely held corporations which have failed to maintain and preserve accounting records and data necessary to permit verification of financial statements.

In advance of any detailed discussion, it can be observed that (a) the optimum quantity of the numerous items needed in the conduct of the business is of basic importance to the over-all profitability of the operation, (b) the amount assigned to the inventory for accounting purposes is of primary significance in the determination of income, and (c) both the quantity of the physical inventory and the amount assigned thereto can have an effect upon the assessments made against the business for property, franchise, and income taxes.

It has been found that savings equal to 15 per cent or more of the cost of excess quantities can be effected by reducing the physical volume of the inventory in some situations. If the quantity of scrap at a foundry can be reduced 10 per cent, for example, without impairing efficiency, the business operation will be more profitable because, in addition to other factors, less storage space and a smaller amount of capital will be required.

The significance of the amount assigned to an inventory can be illustrated by the case of a retailer who purchased 1,000 novelty toys at 80¢ each and sold 950 at $1.00 before the demand slackened. A gross profit of $190 was realized from the sales. Should it be necessary to sell the remaining 50 units at 30¢ each (or for 50¢ less than cost), the gross profit realized from the entire shipment will be only $165. If a profit and loss statement is prepared when the last 50 toys are unsold, the computed profit to that date will be $190 if the amount assigned to the inventory is cost (50 at 80¢, or $40), but only $165 if the inventory amount is net realizable value (50 at 30¢, or $15). If cost is used for inventory purposes,

[1] Accounting Series Release No. 90 (Mar. 1, 1962).

a $25 loss will be taken into account in the period when the cut-price sales are made.

The effect upon taxes of inventory quantities and amounts has many ramifications. Ordinarily, the physical volume of the inventory will have no direct effect upon taxes based upon income, and the amount assigned to the goods on hand at the end of any tax assessment period will only have the effect of accelerating or deferring the payment of taxes. Unless there is a change in the income or franchise tax rate, the aggregate tax liability will not vary because the total earnings during the life-span of a business will be the same regardless of the amount assigned to any particular inventory. Minimizing quantities on hand and assigning the proper amount to an inventory have a more direct effect upon property taxes. Assuming a property tax rate of 1.5 per cent, ownership of a $400,000 inventory rather than a $500,000 inventory means a direct property tax saving of approximately $1,500.

HOW MUCH INVENTORY?

Inventories enter directly in the determination of income in the sense that the amount of earnings will be less if the quantity of goods on hand and the balance among the various components are not at the most economical level. If a larger amount of capital is required to operate the business because of improper inventories, this fact will have an adverse effect on profitability, in addition to the consequence of incurring unnecessary expenses.

The expense of storing and handling materials may be substantially increased if inventories are not kept at the proper level.

Furthermore, the larger the quantity of inventory, the greater the possibility of loss as a consequence of deterioration, obsolescence, and other factors.

Income will also be indirectly affected by inventory quantities if proper inventory management could free some portion of certain facilities for other uses.

Some of the procedures utilized to avoid inventory practices having adverse effects on income and taxes are discussed in later chapters. Decisions made by management as to when and in what quantities various required items are to be ordered will determine the number of units on hand at any particular inventory date.

A study of one company's inventories involved more than 6,000 items. With respect to a single item, the annual saving from determining the most advantageous buying practice by use of a mathematical formula was approximately $1,000. The total potential savings were indeed impressive to a management which had always been conscientious about its responsibilities.

ASSIGNING AMOUNTS TO INVENTORIES

The function of financial accounting is to reflect systematically, in terms of monetary units, the events which have occurred. This objective requires trained judgment in classifying the transactions and applying the accounting principles most appropriate under the particular circumstances. Each decision will have a bearing upon the amount to be assigned to the inventory and will represent in the financial statements the aggregate of the materials, finished products, and component parts owned by the business at a particular time.

The first area of judgment pertains to the factors to be recognized as the "cost" of the units on hand. Where an item is purchased at a specific price per unit delivered at the company's plant, the question of cost is simple. If the same item is purchased f.o.b. a distant point, the question becomes somewhat more complex. After work has been performed upon the item so as to change its physical condition, there are numerous decisions involved in arriving at "cost." Several equally acceptable answers can result from following alternative accounting procedures.

The preparation of general statements as to what factors should be taken into account in arriving at the cost of work in process and finished goods is comparatively simple, but considerable judgment is required in applying the general statements to any particular set of circumstances. As more fully developed in Chapter 5, there is a tendency among businessmen and accountants to consider all expenditures as "costs." Although a cash expenditure or a contractual commitment is required whether an item is a "cost" or an "expense," there are comparatively few expenditures which are obviously *costs*, and it is necessary to give careful consideration to the proper categorizing of *expenses*.

After determining the number of units to be taken into account in calculating the inventory and the cost elements to be recognized, the dollar amount to be assigned to a particular inventory will still be affected by the choice of concepts as to the flow of costs. These concepts are discussed in Chapter 9, and it will be noted that the selection of the procedure to be followed need not have relationship to the physical movement of the goods being inventoried.

AUTHORITATIVE PRONOUNCEMENTS
RELATIVE TO INVENTORIES

Before discussing the factors to be considered in determining what amounts should be used for inventory purposes in any particular type of situation, it is important to review the major authoritative statements on the subject.

Numerous articles have been published concerning various aspects of the "inventory problem" and the subject has been dealt with to some degree in books on accounting theory and practice. Few of these writings, however, specifically deal to any great extent with the matter of inventories in the determination of income. The amount assignable as "cost" to the units remaining unsold at the end of an accounting period and includable in inventories should be considered separately from a compilation of all the amounts expended in the conduct of a business which must be recovered in the proceeds of sales in order to make a profit.

Three authoritative statements on the determination of amounts to be assigned to inventories are reproduced herein as appendices and merit careful analysis:

Appendix A   "Inventory Pricing" by the Committee on Accounting Procedure of the American Institute of Certified Public Accountants (AICPA) published as Chapter 4 of Accounting Research Bulletin No. 43 ("ARB 43")

Appendix B   "Valuation and Presentation of Inventories in the Context of the Historical Cost System" issued as International Accounting Standard No. 2 by the International Accounting Standards Committee

Appendix C   United States Internal Revenue Code Provisions with Respect to "Inventories" and Related Regulations

A comparison of these statements is helpful when applying the basic principles to a particular set of facts.

The statement by the AICPA is summarized below, with cross-references to the paragraphs in the other two statements covering the same aspect of the subject.

As noted at the end of Appendix A, even the general statements on inventory pricing summarized above were not adopted unanimously and without reservation by the Committee on Accounting Procedure of the AICPA. The fact that it was not possible to obtain complete agreement among the twenty members of the committee is an indication of a lack of agreement among businessmen and accountants as a whole.

Para-graph in App. A		Cross-reference to related paragraphs in	
		App. B	App. C
1	It is necessary for adequate financial accounting purposes that inventories be properly compiled periodically and recorded in the accounts.	5	1.471–1
2	Conclusions are not directed to or necessarily applicable to noncommercial businesses or regulated utilities	—	—
3	The term "inventory" embraces goods awaiting sale (the merchandise of a trading concern and the finished goods of a manufacturer), goods in the course of production (work in process), and goods to be consumed directly or indirectly in production (raw materials and supplies).	4	1.471–1
4	In accounting for the goods in the inventory at any point of time, the major objective is the matching of appropriate costs against revenues in order that there may be a proper determination of the realized income.	32	1.471–2(a)
	The inventory at any given date is the balance of costs applicable to goods on hand remaining after the matching of absorbed costs with concurrent revenues, which is appropriately carried to future periods provided it does not exceed an amount properly chargeable against the revenues expected to be obtained from ultimate disposition of the goods carried forward.	—	—
5	The primary basis of accounting for inventories is "cost," which, as applied to inventories, means in principle the sum of the applicable expenditures and charges directly or indirectly incurred in bringing an article to its existing condition and location.	4 & 20	1.471–3
	In the case of goods which have been written down below cost at the close of a fiscal period, such reduced amount is to be considered the cost for subsequent accounting purposes.	—	1.471–3(a)

Para-graph in App. A		*Cross-reference to related paragraphs in*	
		App. B	*App. C*
5 (cont'd)	Under some circumstances, such items as idle facility expense, excessive spoilage, double freight, and rehandling costs may be so abnormal as to require treatment as current period charges rather than as a portion of the inventory cost.	11 & 23	—
	General and administrative expenses should be included as period charges, except for the portion of such expenses that may be clearly related to production.	12	1.471–3(c)
	Selling expenses constitute no part of inventory costs.	12	1.471–3(c)
	The exclusion of all overheads from inventory costs does not constitute an accepted accounting procedure.	4 & 21	1.471–11
	The exercise of judgment in an individual situation involves a consideration of the adequacy of the procedures of the cost accounting system in use, the soundness of the principles thereof, and their consistent application.	—	1.471–2(b)
6	The cost to be matched against revenue from a sale may not be the identified cost of the specific item which is sold.	—	1.471–2(d)
	Cost for inventory purposes may be determined under any one of the several assumptions as to the flow of cost factors (such as first-in, first-out; average; and last-in, first-out); the major objective in selecting a method should be to choose the one which, under the circumstances, most clearly reflects periodic income.	24	1.471–2
	Standard costs are acceptable if adjusted at reasonable intervals to approximate reasonably costs computed under one of the recognized bases.	27	1.471–11(d)(3)
	In some situations a reversed markup procedure of inventory pricing, such as the retail inventory method, may be both practical and appropriate.	—	1.471–8

Paragraph in App. A		*Cross-reference to related paragraphs in*	
		App. B	*App. C*
6 (cont'd)	The business operations in some cases may be such as to make it desirable to apply one of the acceptable methods of determining cost to one portion of the inventory or components thereof and another of the acceptable methods to other portions of the inventory.	—	1.471–2(d)
7	Although selection of the method should be made on the basis of the individual circumstances, financial statements will be more useful if uniform methods of inventory pricing are adopted by all companies within a given industry.	—	—
8	Cost is satisfactory only if the utility of the goods has not diminished since their acquisition; a loss of utility by damage, deterioration, obsolescence, changes in price levels, or other causes is to be reflected as a charge against the revenues of the period in which it occurs.	16	1.471–2(c)
9	As used in the phrase "lower of cost or market," the term "market" means current replacement cost (by purchase or by reproduction, as the case may be) except that (1) market should not exceed net realizable value (i.e., estimated selling price in the ordinary course of business, less reasonably predictable costs of completion and disposal) and (2) market should not be less than net realizable value reduced by an allowance for an approximately normal profit margin.	4	1.471–4(a)
10	Because of the many variations of circumstances encountered in inventory pricing, the statement relative to the meaning of the term "market" is intended as a guide rather than as a literal rule and should be realistically applied, with due regard to the form, content, and composition of the inventory.	28	—
	If a business is expected to lose money for a sustained period, the inventory should not be written down to offset a loss inherent in the subsequent operations.	—	—

Paragraph in App. A		Cross-reference to related paragraphs in	
		App. B	App. C
11	The most common practice is to apply the "lower of cost or market" rule separately to each item of the inventory; however, if there is only one end-product category, the inventory in its entirety may have the greatest significance.	16 & 29	1.471–4(c)
	Where more than one major product or operational category exists, the application of the rule to the total of the items included in such major categories may result in the most useful determination of income.	16 & 29	—
12	When no loss of income is expected to take place as a result of a reduction of cost prices of certain goods because others forming components of the same general categories of finished products have a market equally in excess of cost, such components need not be adjusted to market to the extent that they are in balanced quantities, provided the procedure is applied consistently from year to year.	31	—
13	To the extent stocks of particular materials or components are excessive in relation to others, the procedure of applying the "lower of cost or market" rule to the individual items constituting the excess should be followed.	—	—
14	When substantial and unusual losses result from the application of the "lower of cost or market" rule, it will frequently be desirable to disclose the amount of the loss in the income statement.	—	—
15	The basis of stating inventories must be consistently applied and should be disclosed in the financial statements; whenever a significant change is made therein, there should be disclosure of the nature of the change and, if material, the effect on income.	34	1.471–2(d)
16	It is generally recognized that income accrues only at the time of sale, and that gains may not be anticipated by reflecting assets at their current sales prices.	—	1.471–5 and 6

Paragraph in App. A		*Cross-reference to related paragraphs in App. B App. C*
16 (cont'd)	Inventories of gold and silver, when there is an effective government-controlled market at a fixed monetary value, are ordinarily reflected at selling prices, and a similar treatment is not uncommon for inventories representing agricultural, mineral, and other products, units of which are interchangeable and have an immediate marketability at quoted prices and for which appropriate costs may be difficult to obtain.	— —
	When inventories are stated at sales prices, they should be reduced by expenditures to be incurred in disposal, and the use of such basis should be fully disclosed.	— 1.471–4(b)
17	The recognition in a current period of losses arising from the decline in the utility of cost expenditures is equally applicable to similar losses which are expected to arise from firm, uncancelable, and unhedged commitments for the future purchase of inventory items.	— —

As is the case with other pronouncements by the AICPA Committee (and its successor organizations, the Accounting Principles Board ("APB") established in 1959, and the Financial Accounting Standards Board (FASB), which succeeded the APB in 1973) Chapter 4 of ARB 43 applies only to items material and significant in the relative circumstances. Items of little or no consequence may be dealt with as expediency may suggest.

Other literature relating to financial accounting for inventories is discussed in Chapter 15.

PRINCIPAL DIFFERENCES BETWEEN AICPA AND OTHER AUTHORITIES

The pronouncements by the International Accounting Standards Committee and by the Treasury Department include observations commenting on several subjects which are not covered in ARB 43. The additional paragraphs generally pertain to details of procedure rather than principles. In general the three statements are in basic agreement. Among the conflicting observations are a few which are deemed to be particularly significant.

International Accounting Standard 2

1. Paragraph 21 requires the disclosure of the fact that management has excluded or substantially excluded fixed production overhead from the valuation of inventories on the grounds that it does not directly relate to putting the inventories in their present location and condition. The Standard requires that manufactured inventories should include a systematic allocation of those production overhead costs that relate to putting the inventories in their present location and condition and that the allocation of fixed production overhead to the costs of conversion be based on the capacity of the facilities.

2. Paragraph 30 (one of a number of paragraphs dealing with the ascertainment of net realizable value) indicates that the net realizable value of the quantity of inventory held to satisfy firm sales contracts should be based on the contract price and if the sales contracts are for less than the inventory quantities held, net realizable value for the excess should be based on general market prices. However, the statement points out that firm sales contracts beyond inventory quantities held and firm purchase contracts are beyond the scope of the statement.

Federal Income Tax Regulations

1. Section 1.471–1 provides that the rules with respect to inventories, for federal income tax purposes, shall be applied to raw materials and supplies only to the extent that they have been acquired for sale or will physically become a part of the merchandise intended for sale (e.g., kegs, bottles, and cases), if title thereto will pass to the purchaser of the product to be sold therein.

2. Section 1.471–4(c) states that where the inventory is valued upon the basis of cost or market whichever is lower, the market value of each article on hand at the inventory date shall be compared with the cost of the article, and the lower of such values shall be taken as the inventory value of the article. There is no specific recognition of the alternative of comparing the cost with the value of the inventory as a whole or the aggregate of complementary inventory items.

3. There is no provision in the income tax regulations for a deduction based upon an anticipated loss to be incurred as a consequence of outstanding purchase commitments.

4. Section 472(b)(2) of the Internal Revenue Code stipulates that goods with respect to which LIFO is used shall be inventoried "at cost," and Section 1.472–2(b) of the regulations expands the requirement by stating that the inventory "shall be taken at cost regardless of market value."

Section 1.472–2(e) of the regulations provides that the taxpayer's use of market value in lieu of LIFO cost is not considered at variance with the requirement in the Internal Revenue Code that no method other than LIFO be used in ascertaining income, profit, or loss, in statements issued for credit purposes or in reporting to owners of the business. The amount of the write-down to market, however, will not be recognized as a deduction in computing taxable income.

HOW EXACT IS AN INVENTORY?

It must be recognized that with respect to an inventory of any magnitude there is always considerable probability of error in the determination of physical quantities. Errors in counting and the compilation of basic data are reflected in the final determination; but, if the inventory taking is performed with reasonable care, the effect of these errors is generally not material. Significant errors are usually detected in the normal accounting review and auditing procedures. Undetected minor errors can be expected to cause overstatements of the inventory as well as understatements, tending to offset one another.

In view of the probability of human error and the need for judgment in the handling of numerous details, it must be readily admitted that the amount assigned to any particular inventory is not beyond question. The absence of preciseness, however, should not be overemphasized. In the determination of business income for a stated period, judgment is exercised with respect to a large number of factors. The determination of depreciation is probably the outstanding example of a factor governed by rough approximations and the selection of a particular accounting procedure. Similarly, estimates are made of liabilities under product warranties and many other obligations arising out of current transactions.

A financial statement can do no more than present fairly the results of operations for the stated period. For any particular item, including the inventory, the determination will be made through the exercise of the best judgment possible, but it is not realistic to assume that every item has been precisely determined.

EFFECT UPON INCOME OF
ALTERNATIVE INVENTORY AMOUNTS

An admission that mechanical errors occur in the computation of an inventory and that the amount assigned to it will depend upon the exercise of judgment in selecting from equally acceptable accounting procedures does not imply that the computed net income fails to reflect fairly the results of the business operations.

Whether the use of a different inventory amount would have a material and significant effect on income depends upon (a) consistency between the opening and closing inventories for the period, (b) the relationship between the sales proceeds and the sum of the cost of goods sold plus expenses, and (c) the rate of inventory turnover.

Each of the authoritative pronouncements commented upon stresses consistency. Selected sentences provide a basis for comparison, but they are not the only statements emphasizing the importance of consistency.

Comparison of Statements on Consistency

American Institute	International Accounting Standards Committee	Federal Income Tax Regulations
While the basis of stating inventories does not affect the over-all gain or loss on the ultimate disposition of inventory items, any inconsistency in the selection or employment of a basis may improperly affect the periodic amounts of income or loss. [Par. 15.]	A change in an accounting policy related to inventories that has a material effect in the current period or may have a material effect in subsequent periods should be disclosed together with the reasons. The effect of the change should, if material, be disclosed and quantified. [Par. 34.]	In order clearly to reflect income, the inventory practice of a taxpayer should be consistent from year to year, and greater weight is to be given to consistency than to any particular method of inventorying or basis of valuation . . . [§ 1.471–2(b).]

The importance of consistency is obvious when one realizes that the net income for a stated period would be unchanged if the use of a particular inventory method, as compared with another, would merely increase both the opening and closing inventories by an identical amount.

Whether a company makes electrical appliances, cosmetics, food stuffs, or any other line of products or merely purchases merchandise for resale, the importance of consistency can be illustrated by the use of a hypothetical example in which it is assumed that the amount assigned to the inventory will be 10 per cent higher under inventory method B than it would be under method A.

	Assuming opening and closing inventory quantities are the same			
	Inventory method A		Inventory method B	
Sales......................................		$9,000		$9,000
Cost of goods sold:				
Opening inventory....................	$1,000		$1,100	
Incurred costs........................	6,000		6,000	
	7,000		7,100	
Closing inventory.....................	1,000	6,000	1,100	6,000
		3,000		3,000
Incurred expenses......................		2,000		2,000
Net income............................		$1,000		$1,000

Had the closing inventory actually contained 20 per cent more units than the opening inventory or been assigned an amount of $1,200 for any other reason, consistent application of the two hypothetical methods would result in the following comparison:

	Assuming closing inventory is larger than opening inventory			
	Inventory method A		Inventory method B	
Sales......................................		$9,000		$9,000
Cost of goods sold:				
Opening inventory....................	$1,000		$1,100	
Incurred costs........................	6,200		6,200	
	7,200		7,300	
Closing inventory.....................	1,200	6,000	1,320	5,980
		3,000		3,020
Incurred expenses......................		2,000		2,000
Net income............................		$1,000		$1,020

This illustrates that where an inventory method is applied consistently, the effect on net income as a consequence of the use of one method compared with another will be limited to the effect of the second method on only the net increase (or decrease) in the closing inventory. The inventory under method A increased $200 because of that amount of additional costs having been incurred during the period; therefore, the net income under method B is $20 more—10 per cent of $200.

If the opening and closing inventories are not determined by the consistent application of one or the other of the methods, the distortion in the computed net income is apparent. Either of the amounts of $1,000 or $1,020 could reflect fairly the results of the business operations, but under the assumed circumstances neither $1,120 nor $900 would meet requirements of the AICPA, The International Accounting Standards Committee, or the United States Treasury Department.

	Assuming a change in inventory method			
	From method A to method B		From method B to method A	
Sales..............................		$9,000		$9,000
Cost of goods sold:				
Opening inventory....................	$1,000		$1,100	
Incurred costs.......................	6,200		6,200	
	7,200		7,300	
Closing inventory....................	1,320	5,880	1,200	6,100
		3,120		2,900
Incurred expenses......................		2,000		2,000
Net income............................		$1,120		$ 900

The fact that the relationship between the sales proceeds and the sum of the cost of goods sold plus expenses has a bearing upon whether a different inventory amount would have a material and significant effect on income can also be illustrated by continuing the simplified example. Where the goods have been sold for $9,000, the use of inventory method B has the effect of increasing the computed net income only 2 per cent, that is, the net income is $1,020 rather than $1,000. In the case of a business selling goods acquired at a similar cost for only $8,100, the choice of inventory methods can increase net income 20 per cent, $120 compared with $100.

	Effect of profit margin			
	Inventory method A		Inventory method B	
Sales..............................	$9,000	$8,100	$9,000	$8,100
Cost of goods sold....................	6,000	6,000	5,980	5,980
	3,000	2,100	3,020	2,120
Incurred expenses......................	2,000	2,000	2,000	2,000
Net income............................	$1,000	$ 100	$1,020	$ 120

The greater the net income (the excess of sales proceeds over the sum of the cost of goods sold plus the expenses incurred), the less significant is the difference in the amounts which may be assigned to the inventory. This is true whether the difference results from mechanical errors or a management decision as to accounting procedures.

A simplified example is also helpful to illustrate that the rate of inventory turnover is a factor in determining whether a different inventory amount would have a material and significant effect on income. The computations of net income on page 17 assume an inventory turnover of approximately six times during the period. Had the inventory quantities been twice as large so that the rate of turnover was only three times, the choice of inventory method would be of greater significance. The fact that the choice of inventory method could affect the computed net income by 4 per cent does not preclude either of the amounts of $1,000 or $1,040 reflecting fairly the results of the business operations; however, the lower rate of inventory turnover has doubled the impact of the decision.

	Effect of inventory turnover			
	Inventory method A		Inventory method B	
Sales.................................		$9,000		$9,000
Cost of goods sold:				
Opening inventory....................	$2,000		$2,200	
Incurred costs.......................	6,400		6,400	
	8,400		8,600	
Closing inventory....................	2,400	6,000	2,640	5,960
		3,000		3,040
Incurred expenses.....................		2,000		2,000
Net income...........................		$1,000		$1,040

On the basis of the foregoing, it can be stated that among the factors having a bearing on how inventories enter into the determination of income and taxes are:

1. Exercise of sound business judgment in the maintenance of physical inventory quantities at the proper levels.
2. Analysis of all elements of "cost" and "expense" to determine the proper amount to be recognized as expenditures to be assigned to the goods on hand and charged against future revenue to be realized upon the ultimate sale of the goods.

3. Determination of the need to write down the inventory below cost because of a lower replacement price for certain items or in recognition of net realizable values.

4. Selection of alternative accounting concepts as to the flow of costs.

All these factors involve managerial decisions, and a detailed discussion of each is contained in subsequent chapters.

TWO

Relation of Inventory Management to Business Objectives

Every business carries some form of inventory. In terms of the retailer, a can of peas on a grocer's shelf is a form of finished goods inventory. In terms of the manufacturer, sheet steel in a stamping plant is a raw materials inventory. Both are examples of tangible items, requiring systems for planning and for control. Financial resources are employed to acquire and support these inventories. Ongoing expenditures are required to maintain inventories in stock.

Why do inventories exist? The primary reason for the existence of inventories is to permit an enterprise to meet the demands of the consumer, on a sufficiently timely basis to satisfy the needs of distribution and use. The competitive nature of the marketplace in which the seller operates dictates this need. Since a shopper would not be willing to wait a day or two for a can of peas from a given store (assuming that virtually the same product is available from convenient competitive sources), the grocer must have the product on hand when it is demanded, or face the consequences of a lost sale. In the same way, raw materials, purchased or manufactured parts and subassemblies must be available when required. Lack of these inventories causes production shutdowns, leading to shortages or stock-outs at subsequent levels of consumption, and ultimately to lost sales in the marketplace.

Inventories can be defined and classified in many different ways according to their function, importance, and type of company in which they exist. Generally, inventories in a manufacturing company can be divided into the following categories based on their state or condition: raw materials, work-in-process, finished goods, service parts, and factory supplies. These categories can be further subdivided or expanded into additional classifications, such as purchased parts, component parts, replacement parts, maintenance inventory, shop worn inventory, packaging and shipping material, miscellaneous operating supplies, etc. The exact definition of inventory in these categories varies from company to company. The category name is normally self-explanatory.

Modern production methods frequently make lot-type production necessary, from an economic standpoint as well as for ease of scheduling. Inventories resulting from this type of production program, and their associated expenses of maintenance, must be balanced against the economic advantages offered from lower machine setup costs, improved efficiencies, and lower administrative expenses. In some cases, the savings offered, resulting from increased procurement quantity (through freight rate breaks, quantity discounts, etc.), may well be greater than the expense of maintaining such higher quantities of inventories. In short, the test of effectiveness with which management controls inventories rests on its ability to plan for and maintain the most advantageous economic balance of many economic factors bearing on inventories; several of these are, by nature, opposing factors, and the most effective interaction of all of them is the goal of inventory control.

In industries where demand is not constant throughout the year, inventories are used as a means of leveling production and stabilizing the work force. Consider the case of a manufacturer of Christmas tree ornaments whose product is consumed only two or three months of each year. If the company were to produce only just prior to and during the period of consumption, it could be faced with numerous problems, including idle facilities, the need for a facility capable of producing for peak demand, and a highly transient labor force. Through intelligent utilization of inventories, such a business can stabilize its operations and work toward optimizing its investment in inventories.

SCOPE OF INVENTORY MANAGEMENT

It is not uncommon to hear a businessman say, "Inventories are a major problem in our company." This is more likely to be a statement of effect, rather than of cause. Often the real cause of the problem is not inventories per se, but the lack of effective inventory management.

The most important concept associated with inventory management is that effective control results only from the proper integration of and interaction among various systems and subsystems within a company. To attain its objectives, a business must meet the needs of the consumer. Normally the marketing or sales organization is made responsible for preparation of a short-range sales forecast. This forecasting "subsystem," in combination with the order entry system, triggers procurement and production subsystems, initiating activity aimed at meeting consumer needs. Changes in projected demand must also be communicated so that plans throughout the organization can be adjusted. This is a basic interaction among functional areas that must be handled effectively by any modern inventory management system.

By its nature, inventory management is the arbitrator between diametrically opposing forces. It is, therefore, important that the scope of inventory management be sufficiently comprehensive to consider all of these forces. While striving to meet corporate objectives, departments within a company may follow radically different policies. This may come about because the particular functions performed by a department tend to shape that department's motivation. Thus, the sales area may desire large amounts of stock in reserve to meet virtually any possible sales demand, whereas financial management may take the stand that minimum inventory levels are desirable so as to make available additional capital for other purposes. The resolution of such conflicts can be effected best by developing rules for desired levels of service. By determining an acceptable out-of-stock rate through weighing factors such as the cost of lost sales, demand variability, and replenishment cycle variability, an optimum balance can be reached. This balance can further be tempered by executive opinion. Such a system allows management to assume an active role in controlling a vital phase of operations.

Inventory decisions have impact in most areas of an organization. A decision to purchase a year's supply of all items would minimize the number of purchase orders placed, as well as associated paperwork expense, but would result in the commitment of substantial financial resources, and would normally exceed the storage facilities available. Conversely, purchasing one day's supply at a time would result in an excessive amount of paperwork and related administrative expense. Either decision would reveal failure on the part of management to understand the interrelationship and interaction of these functions operating within most business enterprises.

In the previous example, a physical interaction was discussed. There is also an economic interaction of functions in considering various expenses associated with inventory. Inventory carrying expenditures include a number of classes of items, e.g., the cost of capital, taxes, handling expenses in

INTEGRATED PLANNING AND CONTROL SYSTEM FOR A MANUFACTURING COMPANY

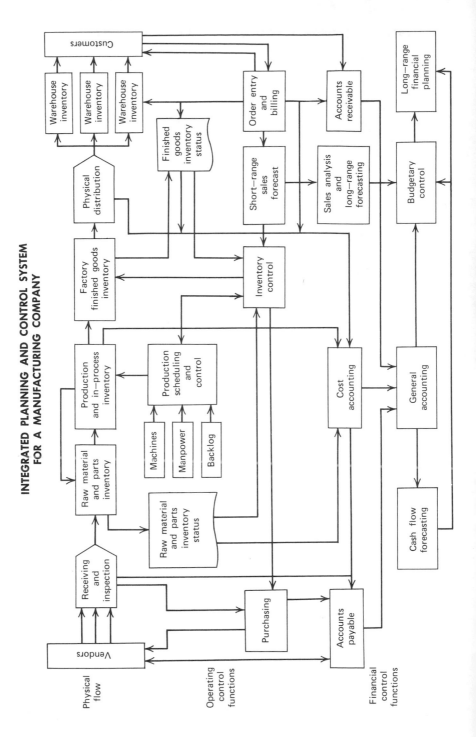

stores, and storage expenses. The expenses associated with procurement include purchasing and ordering expenses, transportation expenses, related materials and supplies expenses, and receiving expenses.

There is a continuing need to find a means of balancing physical, organizational, and economic factors related to inventories. The objective of any inventory management system is to arrive at the most effective compromise possible among these interrelated and interacting forces.

To illustrate this point, the figure on page 24 shows a hypothetical control network in a typical manufacturing company. The interaction of physical flow, operating controls and financial controls can be readily recognized. For example, the activities of "customers" (or the marketplace) are analyzed and translated into forecasts by the marketing function of the company. This forecast is introduced into the financial control system through the budgetary subsystem, and into the operating area by means of the inventory control system. The operation of this system activates the physical procurement and production system. As illustrated, numerous interactions of this nature occur perpetually.

The inventory management system is, thus, a modular entity composed of a number of subsystems. Each subsystem is designed to meet the needs of a specific inventory area; in turn, these subsystems are interrelated and interacting. The entire network comprising the system can be best understood if each subsystem is first isolated and examined as if it were an independent system.

The inventory management system shown below is a network of typical subsystems with common communications terminals. Each subsys-

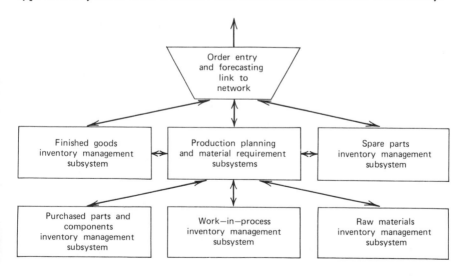

tem is linked to every other subsystem. The number of subsystems is determined by the areas of service required. The subsystems selected in the examples are for illustrative purposes only.

To examine the operation of the inventory management system, assume that an order is received and processed by the finished goods inventory management subsystem. If a manufacturing requirement is generated, it will be communicated to the production planning subsystem. This subsystem will determine when the item will be produced. If the decision modifies the finished goods inventory plan, it is communicated to the finished goods inventory management subsystem. The production planning subsystem then activates various other materials management subsystems as required to procure materials and manufacture the product. Through interaction of these subsystems, effective inventory management takes place.

By realizing that inventory control is a part of a hierarchy of systems within a company and, in turn, is composed of modular interacting subsystems, a satisfactory conceptualization of the operation and role of inventory management can be achieved.

The dependency of one subsystem on the others is illustrated by a situation experienced by a company that manufactured commercial cooking equipment. The company was unable to produce products in sufficient quantity because of continual outages of both manufactured and purchased parts. It was discovered that the inventory reorder points and reorder quantities had been developed using an "uneducated guess" method. As a result, purchased parts and components were not ordered with sufficient lead time and in sufficient quantity to keep pace with the increasing demands of the production scheduling and control system. Design and implementation of a new inventory management and purchasing system significantly increased the company's ability to schedule and produce greater volumes and ultimately to increase sales and profitability.

In another example of the interrelationships of various subsystems, the maintenance division of a large international airport was experiencing delays in completing routine terminal maintenance and repair work and also excessive worker idle time. Initially, the cause of these problems was thought to be an inadequate manpower scheduling and control system. Analysis revealed that the inventory control system used to manage replacement parts and maintenance supplies was not functioning properly. The inventory records were inaccurate, indicating out-of-stock conditions when inventory was on hand and vice versa. Purchasing lead times were poorly defined, which frequently resulted in stock-out situations. Design and implementation of an improved inventory control system incorporating improved controls to enhance record accuracy and scientifically based reordering guidelines improved worker utilization and reduced stock-outs without increasing inventory levels.

KEY COMPONENTS OF AN EFFECTIVE
MODERN INVENTORY MANAGEMENT SYSTEM

Inventory management systems can be very simple or extremely sophisticated. Effective systems—those that are responsive to the needs of management in terms of service, cost control, operating cost, and flexibility—are generally a blend of sophistication and simplicity that has been geared toward attaining practical, measurable objectives. This section briefly discusses key components of an inventory management system that must be considered in the most sophisticated as well as the most simple systems.

All systems of management and control achieve their objectives through the proper structuring of organization, the development, maintenance and enforcement of policies, and the implementation and utilization of sound and economical systems and procedures.

Organization

Effective inventory management can be achieved through numerous organizational arrangements, ranging from a centralized material management function that may encompass all materials activities from procurement and distribution and report to the Chief Executive Officer, to a single individual reporting to the plant manager. The most important considerations are that the responsibility for inventory management is clearly defined and accountability established, that the organization is tailored to the company's specific needs, and that it is staffed by competent personnel. The relationship of inventory management to other areas of the business is discussed in greater detail in a subsequent section of this chapter.

Policies

Effective inventory management can be achieved only when policies have been established and communicated and are properly understood and enforced. In regard to inventory management, policies should define the scope of inventory management responsibilities and related practices. Targets for inventory management should serve in setting managerial goals and in performance measurement. Some areas in which targets typically are established include inventory investment levels, inventory turn-over, levels of service to customer and/or dependent units, and spoilage and obsolescence experience.

Systems and Procedures

The following items comprise the key systems and procedural elements of an inventory management system.

Part numbering—Part numbers are a means of providing unique item (stock keeping unit—"SKU") identification for all inventory items on a controlled basis. Part numbers should serve as the uniform information key for manual and automated systems, including such applications as order entry, inventory and production control, and the engineering data base.

Specifications—These generally are maintained as files, which contain for each part number the relevant technical information required by the procurement and inventory management functions.

Inventory file—Generally, an inventory file (often referred to as a "Perpetual Inventory File") contains a record for each part number to be included in the file. Keyed to part number, each record normally contains indicative information such as description, unit of measure, stock location, receipts, issues, on-order quantity, requirements, and on-hand balance. Frequently, cycle counting procedures are used to enhance information accuracy.

Quantitative inventory management parameters—Included in this category are the factors used in determining:

Expected usage—statistical forecasts, history, estimates.

How much to order—economic order quantities, "min/max" approaches, time series offsets.

When to order—Reorder points, "minimums," time series planning.

Safety stock—statistical plan for service levels.

Approaches for the determination of these factors are covered in detail in Chapters 3 and 4.

Control reporting—Some of the most important reports associated with inventory management include:

Periodic budget reports comparing actual inventory levels to planned levels.

Key item or exception reports dealing with

Critical inventory status situations
Turnover performance
Service levels
Open order status

RELATIONSHIP OF INVENTORY MANAGEMENT TO OTHER AREAS OF THE BUSINESS

In the previous sections the relationships of inventory management to various broad functional areas (i.e., marketing, manufacturing, finance) were briefly discussed. Inventory management specifically affects the operations of numerous areas of a business. The purpose of this section is to discuss some of these relationships, and to highlight the departmental (or functional) goals involved in each. A complete understanding of the interaction of the various forces set in motion by such departmental objectives is a necessary prerequisite before the systems designer can establish the scope and approach that will best meet the needs of effective inventory management.

OBJECTIVES OF PRODUCT DESIGN AND ENGINEERING

There is a clear relationship between product design and inventory management. For example, if a product design change is contemplated, the lead time for its implementation should consider the inventory position of the item to be made obsolete. The "effectivity date" of an engineering change is thus of importance to the inventory management function. If an engineering change must be made immediately, the scrapping of existing inventories or the cost of modifying those inventories becomes part of the cost of the design change. Inventory policies may also have to be adjusted in the light of planned product design changes to minimize losses that might be incurred if disposal of large amounts of old models must take place after the introduction of a new design.

Engineering can play a significant role in improving the management and reducing the levels of inventories. A manufacturer of heavy equipment was experiencing a substantial inventory buildup while sales remained at approximately the same level. A detailed investigation revealed a tendency on the part of design engineers to design parts for new applications that differed only slightly from parts already existing. This practice resulted in an unnecessary proliferation of parts and thus an increase in inventory levels and eventually excessive obsolescence write-offs. The company undertook a program to improve its inventory management system and its engineering data base and engineering information system. A significant element in this program was an improved part numbering system that allowed engineers improved access to information regarding existing designs and related inventory status.

Concerted efforts to design products with standardized parts and components can result in a reduction in total inventories, since standardization makes it possible to draw production requirements from fewer inventoried items. In some areas, the application of value analysis techniques has led to simplifications in products or in component parts which have, in turn, contributed to standard component usage.

It should be noted that the ability of the engineering and product design function to respond to the need for, and contribute to the development of, standardized component parts inventories is to a great extent dependent on the accessibility of engineering information. The development of a responsive engineering data base computer system to provide design information on all existing parts and inventoried items will make the design engineer aware of all existing designs and allow use of these designs in new applications.

OBJECTIVES OF PURCHASING

Procurement is no longer principally national in scope. It is international, as are the new generation of problems and challenges associated with it. Components for a product may be purchased from a supplier in a foreign country almost as readily as from a supplier in a neighboring town. The purchasing and inventory management systems must be able to cope with the uncertainties in the constantly changing business environment.

Purchasing management is similar to manufacturing management in that the achievement of purchasing objectives also tends to increase inventory levels. In order to minimize the expense of the purchasing activity, a few large orders for materials and supplies are preferable to frequent orders of smaller amounts. Not only are clerical work load requirements and thus salaries in the purchasing department reduced by this policy, but substantial savings can be realized through quantity discounts.

The proficiency of the purchasing function influences, to a great degree, the total cost of a company's raw materials and purchased parts inventory. The major expenses incurred in the purchasing area are salaries and expenses for purchasing personnel and the related systems to support their activities. However, the purchasing agents' decisions can substantially add to or minimize the volume purchase discounts realized and the additional expenses incurred when stockouts occur. Stockouts can result in an additional expediting work load in the purchasing and manufacturing areas, paying premium prices for materials needed, high-cost transportation, and, at worst, production line shut-down.

The procurement procedures and policies of a company have substantial impact on inventory management. Proper follow-up and control of vendor delivery by the purchasing group contributes to better inventory management by reducing excessive variability of replenishment cycles. Efforts by this same group to reduce the length and variability of replenishment cycles through development of better communications facilities, and by developing alternative sources of supply, also contribute to better inventory management. A properly designed inventory management system also allows for optimum utilization of quantity and/or joint procurement discounts, perhaps utilizing a "blanket" purchase agreement supported by specific release schedules.

Under special conditions, the procurement function may have to initiate the purchase of materials—such as under conditions of impending shortages, availability of a special purchase discount, major price increases, or strikes. These actions are properly taken in conjunction with the inventory management function to insure that good communications exist, as well as to obtain desirable economic results.

The recent energy and materials shortages and the general uncertainty of the business climate have had a substantial impact on the purchasing function of most companies. Demands are placed on purchasing for greater flexibility and development of more reliable sources. Raw material and purchased part substitution knowledge has become an important capability of the successful buyer in today's economy.

OBJECTIVES OF PRODUCTION

Manufacturing management has as its principal objective the manufacture of specified products for the least cost. One way in which manufacturing can reduce its costs is to allow a substantial buildup in levels of inventory at all stages (raw materials, in-process, and finished goods).

A production department can ordinarily conduct its operations most efficiently, and at lowest cost, by scheduling lengthy production runs. Long production runs reduce the amount of idle machine time used for setups between runs. For each new production run, workers must be reoriented to the manufacturing procedures; fewer changes in production generally result in higher quality production as well as increased productivity. Set-ups and associated costs can be minimized by longer production runs. The utilization of labor, supervision, and physical facilities also can be increased through the elimination of idle time caused by raw material shortages. The job of production scheduling can be greatly facilitated if adequate supplies of raw materials can be assured. All of these factors tend to create pressure in the direction of maintaining substantial levels of inventories.

The costs to manufacturing of having to tolerate inventory levels that are not high enough for flexibility in scheduling can be calculated if appropriate standards are established by engineering. A major difficulty in cost determination is created in attempting to establish costs incurred by a material or in-process stockout that causes a manufacturing delay or shutdown. Such costs are substantial in situations where the labor force is assured a daily or weekly wage; in this case, the out-of-stock expenses are equal to the wages paid for such nonproductive labor.

The operations of the manufacturing area can, in a very real sense, be predicated on the prior plans developed in overall inventory planning. The planned labor requirements, and the plant and machine loading for each period, can be a direct result of the inventory plan. From these plans, various technical support areas, such as manufacturing engineering and quality control, can develop plans for utilization of their respective resources. The activities of production scheduling and of short-term facility loading—important parts of the manufacturing function—are thus dependent on the planned service levels and the existing inventory levels.

OBJECTIVES OF WAREHOUSING AND DISTRIBUTION

There is also interdependence between the inventory management system and an organization's system of distribution. The number of warehouses, their geographical interrelationship, and the level of service to be maintained at each location substantially affect inventory levels, particularly as related to reserves or safety stocks. Physical storage facilities can limit ordering quantities just as special storage requirements influence inventory policy. In cases of products being stocked at more than one location, the inventory management system must be designed to provide appropriate levels of "visibility" and to cope with multi-location distribution problems. Transportation time and cost also have a direct effect on inventory levels in some circumstances.

The expense of storing and warehousing inventories is usually proportional to inventory levels. The managements of warehouses and stockrooms, concerned with minimizing the expense of their respective operations, would like to see general inventory levels reduced.

Generally speaking, high inventory levels increase the risk of stocks becoming obsolete—a condition in which the value of inventory stocks deteriorates because of normal loss of usefulness in manufacturing, loss of saleability in the market, or by reason of physical deterioration. Because some items in inventory are more vulnerable to obsolescence than others, the assignment of an obsolescence charge should be done either individually, or according to fairly narrow categories of items.

Inventory handling can also be expensive. Handling includes all the physical activities requisite to stockroom and warehouse operations. The expense is usually measured in terms of wages paid for personnel involved in physical handling as well as in clerical and accounting functions. Computation of this expense may also require an analysis of the costs relating to automated material handling systems. To measure inventory handling expense, it is necessary to evaluate the amount of expenditure required at several inventory levels.

The most significant warehousing cost is that for the rental of, or investment in, storage space. It is usually possible to determine what level of inventory increase makes construction or leasing of additional warehouse space necessary, thereby incurring capital investment, or a rental charge. However, storage space charges tend to change only when fairly large amounts of inventory changes are involved, with the exception of certain types of public warehousing.

OBJECTIVES OF MARKETING

Marketing management is usually concerned that adequate inventories are maintained to fill customer orders and that they are at locations that make possible a level of service at least equivalent to that of competitors. Marketing management has good reasons for pursuing a policy of high inventories. Customer relations and marketing effectiveness usually suffer when finished goods are not available to meet customer demands. Outright loss of orders, and even of customers, may be the consequence. Also, substantial clerical and distribution expenses are usually incurred as a result of back orders, which affect the profitability of the sale.

The immediate costs of customer dissatisfaction are easily measured in business, where the customer must have immediate service and, failing to get it, goes to a competitor. The costs of that dissatisfaction are simply the profits that would have resulted from the unfilled order. The measure of an out-of-stock condition is complicated, however, when the customer becomes so dissatisfied that he never returns to the company with future orders. In this case, the long-range costs become all the profits foregone from that lost customer—a difficult calculation. Dissatisfaction cost is also hard to determine in cases in which the customer is willing to wait for the back order to be filled, but in which repeated impositions of this nature may eventually drive him to the competition.

The costs of processing and expediting back orders are also determinable to the extent that certain employees and systems would not have to be employed if back orders ceased to occur.

Thus, the communications link between marketing and the inventory management system is important in any business. Sales forecasting interrelationships with this system have been briefly discussed, as have the impacts of inventory management on levels of customer service. The inventory management-marketing link must also be used to communicate special needs, such as promotions and "one-time" sales of sizeable proportions. The inventory management system also provides marketing with sales management tools in the form of reports on items moving more slowly than forecasted, developing level of service information, disclosing back-order or lost-order trends, and highlighting items for possible elimination from the line. This communication link is also used in measuring the impact of marketing decisions on existing inventories and on the production plan.

OBJECTIVES OF LABOR RELATIONS

The task of labor relations is eased considerably when a company's employment level does not change. In most companies, however, the demand for finished products often fluctuates. In order to maintain a reasonably uniform level of skilled employees, most manufacturing concerns must build to inventory at some point in the production cycle. This stocked inventory creates a buffer that, among other things, is intended to prevent major fluctuations in product demand from directly affecting production rates and related manning levels.

The effect of avoiding fluctuations in production levels to maintain steady employment can be measured in terms of incremental inventory carrying costs, hourly payroll expenses, personnel expenses in the industrial relations and employment departments, and in actual outlays for severance pay, workmen's compensation, and—in severe cases—labor negotiations. In addition, unit labor costs, worker productivity, and product quality variations should be considered in determining inventory levels and related employment practices.

OBJECTIVES OF FINANCIAL MANAGEMENT

The financial management function is concerned with the creation of financial planning and control systems aimed at providing the greatest possible return on assets invested. One major element of any company's assets is usually represented by inventories. The return generated from that asset is a dual function, composed first of the amount of capital invested in inventories and its related turnover and, second, of the measure of profitability.

It may be said that financial management can serve its function best by acting to evaluate the relationships, quantify the amounts, and interrelate the objectives of all business functions—as they affect and are affected by inventories—so that a "best economic balance" is created. The creation of this balance is the purpose of inventory planning and control systems.

In a sense, the financial function has an obligation to act as an arbitrator between the forces set in motion by the various departmental objectives noted earlier. The correct response of financial management is to seek to develop systems that result in the best economic balance, rather than to exert pressure to force inventories to an arbitrarily low level. Financial management must recognize that, whereas a low inventory level will raise the return on the investment carried, this is true only if profit levels are considered to be unaffected no matter how low the inventory level is set. In fact, profitability of operations is materially affected by the respective expenses of acquiring versus carrying inventories and the related service levels provided.

Financial management is also affected by inventory management in planning for and obtaining funds to meet capital requirements. The sales forecast and the related production plan, considered together with inventory plans, can be stated in financial terms to measure their influence on working capital and cash requirements. Utilization of all these provides financial management with tools to measure performance and project capital needs. The inventory management system should also provide the financial manager with information for use if and when attractive opportunities for alternative uses of capital are available.

IMPACT OF DATA PROCESSING ON INVENTORY MANAGEMENT

Prior to the widespread commercial availability of data processing equipment, the existence of large numbers of inventoried items, and of numerous transactions, presented formidable obstacles to the application of effective inventory management concepts and techniques. The continuing sophistication of electronic data processing techniques and capabilities combined with lower cost per unit of computing power has made it possible to deal with these obstacles in a more effective manner. The speed, versatility and logical powers and cost of computers available today, coupled with effective systems design and availability of "packaged programs," provide the tools necessary for minimizing problems associated with managing a large number of inventory items and a substantial volume of transactions.

The use of data processing equipment not only makes possible the performance of highly integrated systems functions, which would be economically prohibitive to perform manually, but often permits reductions in existing clerical work forces through minimizing or eliminating manual records. Properly designed and controlled computer systems also can be expected to result in improved accuracy of inventory records.

In recent years the cost of buying or leasing computer systems and services has decreased to the point where all but the very smallest of firms generally can economically justify converting from manual to computerized inventory management systems. The tremendous expansion of capabilities in the mini-computer field, the development of effective software packages, and the diversity of services available through firms specializing in data processing support services provide many practical alternatives to effective automation of the inventory management function.

The inventory management function is closely related to the following activities: demand forecasting, inventory control, production planning and scheduling, and procurement and physical distribution. In each of these areas, considerable progress has been made in developing cost effective computer systems to improve management control.

One large manufacturer of farm and industrial equipment was able to substantially reduce its finished goods inventory and at the same time improve customer service by implementing an on-line order entry and finished goods inventory control system. The new system provides immediate, total visibility of equipment available for sale in the company's 24 distribution warehouses. With this new visibility, the inventory management function was able to reduce the inventory level of slower moving equipment at the outlying warehouses and respond immediately to customer inquiry on availability and anticipated delivery time for all types of equipment.

Use of data processing capabilities in conjunction with a properly designed inventory management system allows routine decision rules to be programmed, and subsequent decisions to be made by routinely applying these rules. Such a system insures prompt and complete review of items when they reach predetermined levels, calculation of order quantities based on given formulae, and, in some cases, direct placement of purchase orders by computer methods, all within a framework responsive to changing trends in demand rates, or in the lead time required to purchase or manufacture required items.

Systems normally are developed to provide management with "exception-type" reports that focus their attention on the unusual or abnormal conditions that require analysis and decision making. This technique can be applied to control situations involving items such as critical spare parts or to report when supplies fall below certain levels or when past-due order conditions exist.

Inventory management is predicated on forecasts of usage. One major capability computers provide is the ability to develop and easily adjust data such as demand forecasts and to determine the effect of these revisions on the other functional systems and operational requirements. The continuing trend toward integration of the various automated materials management systems improves communication between operating departments within the company. It also provides management the ability to more clearly see the interrelationships of alternative decisions in various areas of the company's operations.

Through the use of electronic data processing, management is able to evaluate potential policies—using simulation processes—and to insure that decisions are effectively implemented. The combination of the power of the computer with the integration of forecasting and inventory management techniques also makes possible the employment of the most refined management science techniques—using advanced mathematics and statistics—where and when they are required.

The basic management science techniques generally employed are not new. It is, rather, the ability to perform the required calculations at an acceptable speed that is provided by the computer.

THREE

Inventory Planning and Forecasting Techniques

The functions of forecasting and operational planning are two of the more important responsibilities of management. This is particularly true in connection with inventory management. Although they can be analyzed separately, the forecasting and operational planning functions are so closely interrelated that it is sometimes difficult to determine where one ends and the other one starts. In effect, every operational plan is based on a forecast of some type. Sometimes the forecast is a sophisticated analysis and prediction of future conditions; in other cases, the forecast is based on the intuitive judgment of the individuals preparing the plan, and is often not recognized as a forecast per se.

The term "forecast," in the context used here, refers to the prediction of future market demand, whereas operational planning may be defined as the means of attaining specific operating objectives established by management. Looking at planning and forecasting as two separate activities, forecasting would consider, among other factors, the external factors in the market over which the company has limited control. Operational planning, on the other hand, would consider those factors that the internal operations and decision processes of the company can control. There is, of course, a mix of planning and forecasting where the internal decisions of a company affect external factors, such as future market demand patterns. For example, the decision by a company to introduce a new product would be part of the internal planning function; however, this decision will influence future market demand for the new product, as well as for related and competitive products. The conclusion to be drawn is that many so-called external factors associated with forecasting can be influenced by internal planning decisions, especially over the longer term.

This chapter reviews the nature and types of planning, as related to inventory management. This is followed by a review of some of the fore-casting techniques that can be used to improve the effectiveness of an inventory management system and associated planning functions.

LONG-RANGE PLANNING RELATED TO INVENTORIES

Because inventories are classified as a current asset, the importance of long-range planning relative to inventories is frequently overlooked. How-ever, in light of the relatively large percentage of total company assets that inventory usually represents, it becomes apparent that long-range inventory planning should be an important aspect of any long-range corporate plan.

If the marketing patterns for a company are fairly stable, it may be appropriate to project long-term inventory requirements by expressing them as ratios to forecasted sales (or cost of goods sold). These ratios can be developed from historical relationships between inventories and sales; for example, inventory may equal two months' sales (or cost of goods sold). The accuracy of this method of projection can be improved by considering individual product lines, and then totalling the various product line inventory projections to determine the aggregate projected inventory.

In those situations when market conditions are more dynamic or when the business decisions associated with the long-range plan have a high dollar value, the use of more sophisticated methods should be considered. In this regard, the following factors should be considered in developing a long-range inventory plan.

Product Mix

As the product line expands, the need for additional inventory becomes apparent. As the number of models offered for sale increases, the sales volume per model may well decrease. This usually results in a higher total inventory, relative to sales results obtained. Therefore, if the product line is being expanded or consolidated, the impact on inventories should be considered.

Geographic Distribution of Sales

If sales increases are predicated on a broader geographic market coverage, it may be necessary to establish new regional warehouse inventories to maintain satisfactory levels of customer service. Also, the need for increased in-transit inventories should be considered.

Improvements of Customer Service

Marketing management often tends to place great emphasis on customer service, as a means of improving a company's competitive position. When this form of marketing strategy is incorporated into long-range plans, the impact on inventory should be considered, because a reduction in delivery lead times or stockouts usually can be generated through higher inventory levels.

Physical Distribution Systems

As a company modifies its physical distribution system, the net effect on inventories should be determined. For example, some companies have materially reduced inventory investment by centralizing inventories and utilizing air freight to respond to unusual demands or other special requirements. Other companies have consolidated warehousing locations, to take advantage of lower freight rates and to reduce fixed warehouse overhead costs.

Data Processing Systems

As noted in the preceding chapter, the increased use of data processing and related data communications has enabled many companies to reduce inventories, as a result of more timely reporting and improved control techniques. This does not mean that the anticipated installation of new data processing equipment necessarily justifies the projection of lower inventory levels; however, such a projection may be justified when not only have procedures been mechanized, but also an improved control system has been developed and when its expected effectiveness and turnover rates are compared, through simulation, to historical operating results.

Manufacturing Decisions

As a company becomes more vertically integrated from a manufacturing point of view, with a higher value-added per sales dollar, the aggregate inventory turn ratio will tend to decrease. Make-or-buy decisions that affect the degree of vertical integration will have an influence on inventories and should be considered in long-range plans.

Design and Engineering Decisions

Meaningful inventory savings can be realized through an engineering program designed to encourage the use of common parts and modular design of products. Through the use of modular design a large variety of end products can be assembled, using a relatively limited number of modular subassemblies. This provides marketing management with the advantages of a broad product line while retaining the advantages of mass production through the use of common modular subassemblies.

Marketing Channels of Distribution

Alternate channels of distribution can have a major impact on inventory. If a company decides to eliminate a step in the chain of distribution performed by another enterprise, it may be necessary to increase finished goods inventory. On the other hand, a company not using dealers or distributors may decide that the capital invested in distribution inventories can be more profitably applied in other areas, and thereby justify the establishment of "outside" channels of distribution, independent of the company.

These are some of the more important factors bearing on the long-range planning for inventory requirements of a company. In effect, they consider the basic structure of the company and the market it serves, the allocation of capital investment, and many of the marketing factors that will influence the company.

INTERMEDIATE-RANGE PLANNING RELATED TO INVENTORIES

In most cases, intermediate-range inventory plans are concerned with inventory adjustments to compensate for: seasonal variations, demand variations resulting from anticipated changes in the business climate, large contracts, introduction of new products, special promotions, etc. These plans usually cover a period of from six months to two years in the future. They differ from long-range plans in the sense that, within their time span, the market and company structure are fairly well defined. They contrast with short-range plans because they are not concerned with the type of day-to-day detail normally associated with short-range plans. In addition, the intermediate-range plan normally reflects *aggregate* inventory levels for categories such as raw material, work-in-process, and finished goods, whereas a short-range plan relates to *specific* part requirements.

When a company's manufacturing activity involves expensive capital equipment, it normally is necessary to schedule production so as to maintain a high equipment utilization rate. If production were geared substantially to variations in market demand, an increased investment in capital equipment would be required to provide adequate machine capacity during peak demand periods.

However, in companies where the value added during the manufacturing operation is relatively low, such as in many assembly plants, the cost of carrying seasonal inventories becomes excessive in comparison with the cost of varying the production rate. Thus, in general, companies with a high value added during manufacturing tend to vary inventories, whereas companies with a low value added tend to vary the production rate.

In a sense, the planned inventory becomes the buffer between variations in forecasted market demand and the manufacturing and purchasing plan, which, in turn, considers capacity restrictions, manning levels, and availability of material resources. In some cases, this balancing between the forecasted level of market demand and the manufacturing rate is fairly straightforward and tends to be handled on an intuitive basis in a quite effective manner. However, in some industries, especially those where the seasonal demand variations are large, a much more complex problem exists. Management must evaluate and determine how the marginal expenses associated with varying the production level interact with the marginal expenses of carrying seasonal inventory. This can be very difficult because the marginal expenses being considered are not readily found in the financial statement or in most cost accounting systems.

The intermediate inventory plan should be related both to operating plans and to financial budgets. A typical intermediate-range inventory plan is developed as a by-product of a formal operating schedule for the planning period. An example of a typical operating schedule and inventory plan to cope with fluctuating demand is shown on page 43.

In this particular case, assume that an analysis of marginal expenses, relative to changes in the production rate and the cost of carrying inventory, has indicated that the optimum strategy is to vary both the production rate and the inventory levels. Overall, this operating schedule reflects a "cascading" type of action, beginning with the sales forecast and ending with the finished goods, work-in-process, and raw material inventories needed to support it in each planning period. The final column in the table reflects the total inventory figure obtained by adding together finished

Operating Schedule and Inventory Plan
(millions of dollars)

| Month | Forecasted cost of sales | Planned production | Beginning inventory balances | | | |
			Finished goods	Work-in-process	Raw material	Total inventory
January	$ 2.0	$ 5.0	$ 2.0	$5.0	$4.5	$11.5
February	2.5	5.5	5.0	5.5	4.5	15.0
March	3.5	6.0	8.0	5.5	4.0	17.5
April	5.0	6.0	10.5	5.0	3.5	19.0
May	7.0	5.5	11.5	4.5	3.0	19.0
June	9.0	5.0	10.0	4.0	3.0	17.0
July	7.0	4.5	6.0	4.0	2.5	12.5
August	6.0	4.5	3.5	3.5	2.5	9.5
September	5.0	4.0	2.0	3.5	2.5	8.0
October	4.0	4.0	1.0	3.5	2.5	7.0
November	3.0	4.0	1.0	3.5	2.5	7.0
December	3.5	4.0	2.0	4.0	3.0	9.0
	$57.5	$58.0	—	—	—	—

goods, work-in-process, and raw material inventory values. This total inventory value then can be used in developing budgets and financial projections, especially for cash flow and working capital analysis.

SHORT-RANGE PLANNING RELATED TO INVENTORIES

The short-range inventory plan is a part of the inventory control system that responds to the day-to-day operating needs of the company. Although this type of plan may be summarized in terms of dollars, it must be primarily concerned with unit quantities of specific products, parts, and raw materials needed to meet customer orders and production plans.

When inventory requirements are associated with a fixed "build" schedule, as in the case of a job shop or a product with a relatively long manufacturing lead time, the inventory plan normally is dependent on the bill of material of the product to be built, and on the time sequencing of the manufacturing operations. There are several techniques available that can be used in this regard. In the case of discrete orders, such as in a job shop or in connection with certain types of government contracts, time phased Material Requirements Planning (MRP) may be appropriate (see Chapter 4). In addition, various network analysis systems such as

PERT, Critical Path, and Line-of-Balance can be used. By relating the timing of manufacturing operations to the volume of finished units to be produced, and to the bill of material relative to each model, an inventory plan can be developed. Such a plan would reflect when, and in what quantity, various materials would be required to meet the overall plan set forth in the network.

In contrast to a situation where future demands and requirements are fairly well defined, there are many inventory systems that must respond to random demand patterns. These random demand patterns usually can be broken down into a forecasted demand rate and a defined distribution of errors about that rate. When an inventory level is planned for a sales pattern that is random in nature, it is common to use a reorder point, or minimum balance type of control system. This type of system reacts by reordering when the physical or unassigned inventory balance drops below a predetermined inventory level referred to as the reorder point. The reorder point is determined basically by three factors: the lead time required to replenish the inventory, the projected demand rate during the lead time period, and the additional inventory, commonly referred to as "safety stock," which is required in the control of the number of stock-outs.

In addition to the decision establishing when to reorder, it is necessary to determine how much to order. This is frequently referred to as the economic order quantity; its establishment will be reviewed in detail in the next chapter, along with the method for establishing reorder points.

It should be pointed out that the reorder point, the economic order quantity, and the safety stock level are all dependent on the short-range demand forecast, and the error range associated with that forecast. This again points out the close relationship of inventory planning and sales forecasting.

FORECASTING RELATED TO INVENTORY MANAGEMENT

The planning phases of inventory management are all dependent upon some type of a forecast of future demand. In some cases the forecast will be more in the nature of an assumed demand level rather than a specific analysis of the various factors that may influence future demand patterns. For example, in one company the president may simply assume a five per cent annual growth in sales, for purposes of planning. In another company, the marketing research department may prepare a detailed forecast which is based upon such factors as population age composition, average family income, patterns of consumption, etc. This points out the wide variation in the degree to which quantitative standards are used in fore-casting methods.

Generally, forecasts can be broken down by time spans corresponding to the three types of planning, long-range, intermediate-range and short-range. The methodology required to develop each one of these forecasts varies, depending on the time span. The nature of the forecast itself and the techniques appropriate in each circumstance are also affected by its time span.

NATURE OF FORECASTS

The purposes served by a forecast may vary substantially from one oper-ating department to the next, depending on the kinds of plans and deci-sions that will employ the forecasted information. Often classified along functional lines, forecasting requirements in major areas could include:[1]

Marketing—reliable forecasts of market size and market characteristics; these forecasts can be used by the marketing department in its plans for advertising direct sales, pricing, and new product development.

Production and inventory control—forecasts of sales by individual product; the production and inventory control departments will use these forecasts to plan production schedules and inventories to meet sales demand at a reasonable cost.

Finance and accounting—forecasts of cash flows, interest rates, expenses, and revenues; these forecasts will be used for planning capital acquisitions, debt issues, treatment of accounts receivable, and other financial control functions.

Forecasts also are required in other functional areas of a business, and general forecasts of the regional or national economic environment may be useful to strategic decision efforts that take place at the very top man-agement level of an organization.

In spite of the wide diversity of purposes and end uses of forecasts, the general nature of forecasts can be defined by several elements that are common to all forecasts. These include: [2]

Time—all forecasts deal with the future, and time is directly involved.

Uncertainty—forecasting requires that information be gathered to support the forecast, and that judgments be made regarding adequacy of both the forecast and that information upon which it is based.

---

[1] Wheelwright, Steven C. and Makridakis, Spyros, *Forecasting Methods For Manage-ment,* 2nd Ed. (Wiley, New York, 1977), p. 2.
[2] Ibid., p. 3.

Reliance on history—forecasts usually are based upon information that is obtained from historical data or the experience of the forecaster.

These three elements are common to forecasts, regardless of the specific methods or techniques applied. They are present in the most complex and formal forecasts, as well as in the simplest and most informal forecasting efforts.

NATURE OF THE LONG-RANGE FORECAST

The long-range forecast, covering a period of two to ten years in the future, is normally expressed in fairly broad terms, such as dollar volume or over-all physical production quantities. When the forecast is expressed in dollars, the possible effects of price inflation should be considered. The forecast may be in terms of current dollars, or it could be expressed in terms of the anticipated inflated dollars of periods being projected. When a projected price inflation is included in a forecast, it should be so identified, and it should relate to historical price trends within the industry being considered. As a general rule, forecasts stated in current dollars or physical quantities are used for long-range plans that relate to the availability of *physical* facilities and organizational requirements. On the other hand, long-range forecasts for financial planning purposes should take into consideration the anticipated influence of price levels, related to the way in which loans will be repaid.

The preparation of a long-range forecast can be very complex in some cases because of limited knowledge regarding future market conditions such as overall economic activity, actual products to be sold, and the competitive market environment. On the other hand, the long-range forecast tends to be less detailed than the shorter-range forecast and, in most cases, the degree of accuracy required is not as great. A ten per cent error in a long-range forecast may well be acceptable from a general business strategy point of view, but unacceptable for short-range decision-making.

The long-range forecast is also characterized by the relatively substantial importance and length of time period of the business decisions which depend upon it. A company may well change its overall corporate objectives, based upon expectations revealed by the long-range forecast. Capital expenditures, product research programs, basic marketing strategies and organization planning are several examples of the types of major business decisions dependent on the long-range forecast.

INTERMEDIATE-RANGE FORECASTING

The intermediate-range forecast usually relates to a period of time from six months to two years in the future. In most companies it provides the basis for developing annual budgets, operating plans, cash flow projections and sales quotas. The intermediate-range forecast may also be used in developing marketing strategy, such as the timing of new product introductions, advertising campaigns, and sales promotion programs.

The format of the intermediate-range forecast normally differs from the long-range forecasts in the time period intervals being forecast. The long-range forecast is frequently expressed in annual demand periods, whereas the intermediate-range forecast is expressed in months or quarters. The intermediate-range forecast may also provide additional detail according to product characteristics and regional sales patterns. The Operating Schedule and Inventory Plan on page 43 shows how an intermediate-range forecast can be used in developing production plans and related inventory levels. A plan of this nature may be revised monthly or quarterly so as to reflect the latest forecast.

SHORT-RANGE FORECASTING

The short-range forecast, usually covering a time period of up to six months in the future, has received a great deal of attention recently because of a growing realization of the importance of integrating production, procurement and distribution logistics with market demand, the development of new statistical forecasting techniques and the availability of computers to perform large volumes of complex calculations, at high speed and relatively economically. The primary characteristics of the short-range forecast are the amount of detail required, the frequency of updating, and the timeliness of updating.

INVENTORY PLANNING AND FORECASTING

The primary functions of most short-range forecasting systems, relative to inventory management, are to adjust dynamically the reorder points for inventoried items, and to assign priorities for production planning purposes. To accomplish these functions, the short-range forecast must be expressed in units that are meaningful in the frame of reference of the inventory and production control system. Since these systems work in terms of physical quantities, usually by product or part number, the forecast should also be expressed in these units. The time interval of the forecast will usually be weeks or months, depending largely on the production-inventory planning cycle. In some cases, the forecast may be revised for every planning cycle; however, this is not always necessary. The frequency of revising a short-range forecast is dependent upon how sensitive the forecasting system is to new data, and on the degree of variability of such data. In cases where weekly demand is known to be highly erratic, limited weight would be given to the current week's demand, and a forecast revised on a weekly basis would not vary materially from the previous forecast. In such a case, the revision of the forecast would be delayed until sufficient data had been accumulated to make it meaningful to the forecasting system.

One form of a short-range forecast, which is not always recognized as such, is the reporting of order backlogs. The size and priority of items in the backlog serves, in effect, as a short-range forecast for the inventory-production control system. Although backlogs are often thought of only in a negative sense (i.e., as out-of-stock conditions), they can be an important factor in balancing a relatively unstable inflow of orders, thus obtaining the advantage of economies available by means of stability of operating volumes in the production area. A controlled backlog can be used to reduce the size of the finished goods inventory and, at the same time, to provide an acceptable level of customer service.

Short-range forecasts may also be a very valuable tool in sales analysis. The magnitude and sequence of deviations of actual results, when associated with short-range forecasts, may provide a means of identifying changing demand patterns before they are normally recognized. The short-range forecast may also be used in revising operating plans and budgets.

DEVELOPING A FORECASTING SYSTEM

In the development of a forecasting system, the initial step is to identify the various types of business decisions that are dependent upon or related to a forecast. When this analysis has been completed, the various forecast requirements should be grouped according to long-range, intermediate-range, and short-range forecasts, and listed accordingly. This listing should include the units in which the forecast should be expressed, the time span covered by the forecast, and the time unit to be used, such as year, quarter, month, or week.

Although different types of forecasts will be based on various forecasting techniques, there should be a consistent theoretical base for all the forecasts (in the sense that similar concepts and factors should be used) and there should be agreement between the forecasts; for example, the intermediate-range forecast for the second year should relate to the initial year of the long-range forecast.

The development and implementation of a forecasting system must recognize several important considerations. These include:

1. The proper determination of user department requirements for forecast information, and the specific identification of which variables should be forecasted.
2. The analysis of data availability, including the variability, accuracy, and timeliness of data on critical variables.
3. The selection of the best forecasting method for each item to be forecasted, based on accuracy requirements and cost trade-offs.
4. The development of an appropriate forecasting organization with regards to staff requirements and communication responsibilities.

Determination of User Requirements

The initial definition of user department requirements for forecast information would involve discussion and analysis of the major functional planning and decision processes noted earlier in this chapter. From this effort the forecaster should attempt to identify the specific variables that should be forecasted. In some cases, this may be more difficult than one would suspect. For example:

A heavy equipment manufacturer may produce only five or six basic models. However, major options such as power features as attachments may multiply the number of unique finished products to the level of several hundred. In such circumstances it would be a substantial task to develop a forecast for each final product. Generally, the approach adopted would be to forecast the demand for each of the basic models. Production of optional feature combinations above a predetermined level for each combination would be completed as firm customer orders are received.

As the forecaster defines those variables to be forecasted, he also should attempt to gain a general understanding of the behavior of costs that will result from forecast errors. The amount of effort that would be expended in reducing expected forecast error should be weighed against the expected reduction in operating costs due to the error improvement. This point will be elaborated on in our discussion of selecting the appropriate forecasting techniques.

Analysis of Data

Critical determinants of the ultimate capability and accuracy of a forecasting system will be the availability of accurate input data on a timely basis and the characteristics of the demand patterns represented by that data. Accuracy and timeliness theoretically can be improved through additional investment in resources for data collection and control. In practice, however, the forecaster may find it very difficult to satisfactorily justify to management a substantial investment in additional data collection and control efforts on the basis of expected improvements in forecasting capabilities. Therefore, all existing data resources should be thoroughly investigated.

One of the fundamental factors relative to demand forecasting is the recognition of the four basic components that make up demand, namely: trend, business cycle, seasonal, and irregular factors. Expressed as an equation, this relationship is as follows:

$$\text{Demand} = \text{trend} \times \text{cycle} \times \text{seasonal} \times \text{irregular}$$

In such an equation, trend can be expressed in units, whereas the other three components reflect percent variation from the trend. For example, the seasonal component associated with a product may increase sales by 20% for a specific month being forecast, and would therefore appear in the equation as 1.20. An alternative formulation that can be presented is:

$$\text{Demand} = \text{trend} + \text{cycle} + \text{seasonal} + \text{irregular}$$

In this formulation, the underlying assumption is that the basic components of demand are additive, rather than multiplicative, as assumed in the prior equation. In this latter equation, all components are expressed in units of demand. The chart on page 51 illustrates in graphic form the decomposition of a demand pattern into its four components. As shown in that chart, these components can be described as follows:

Trend: The trend component is defined as long-term patterns of growth, stability and decay. "Long-term" in this case should be defined in terms of the product life cycle of the item being forecast. Factors that typically influence trends are: size and age composition of the population, aggregate buying power of the markets being served (individuals, companies, or branches of government), social behavior as it relates to patterns of consumption, consumer acceptance of the product or service, physical and market distribution system, changes in the company or industry productive capacity, changes in unit costs (and related price), and availability of substitute products or services.

Business cycle: The cyclical component consists of wavelike movements

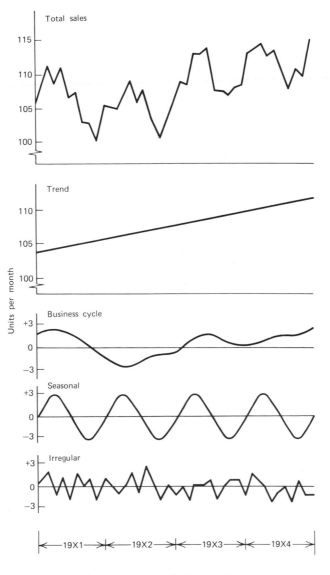

Components of Demand

reflecting changes in general business activity over a period of several years. Some of the factors which appear to influence general economic cycles are: capital expenditures, changes in business inventory, business profit margins, monetary policy, and fiscal policy as it relates to taxation and government expenditure. Cycles related to specific industries may be influenced by such factors as: mortgage rates, farm income, changes in import-export agreements, and prolonged industry-wide strikes.

Seasonal: The seasonal component reflects periodic variations having a duration of one year. The influence of seasonal factors varies greatly. In some industries it is the most important factor in predicting month-to-month changes in demand. The principal factors that are responsible for seasonality are: seasonal weather pattern which affects buying habits, holidays (particularly Christmas), annual promotions, and availability of supply, such as agricultural products.

Irregular: The irregular component reflects variations in demand which remain after discounting the trend, cycle, and seasonal components. The irregular component cannot be identified with specific events but arises as a result of errors in measoring demand and the random nature of the customers' decision to buy.

Selection of Forecasting Method

Given the definition of user department requirements for forecast information and a complete evaluation of data availability and demand characteristics, the forecaster should carefully select the appropriate forecasting method for each item or group of items to be forecasted. This selection requires detailed knowledge and understanding of the capabilities and limitations of all techniques considered. Later sections in this chapter discuss in more detail the types of techniques available to the forecaster, but the following list identifies the major characteristics that should be considered in selecting a forecasting method.[3]

1. The lead time or "time horizon" of the forecast
2. The pattern of the data (e.g., heavy seasonal, heavy cyclical)
3. The type of model inherent in the method (e.g., time series, causal)
4. The costs associated with using a given method
5. The accuracy of the method
6. The applicability of the method (e.g., the time required to prepare or update the forecast when such information is needed quickly).

The first three items on this list are discussed in later sections, and more complete explanations of these points are presented at that time.

The costs associated with using a given forecasting method or technique can be classified into three basic groups:

1. **Development costs**—the costs associated with identifying the proper form of the forecasting model or procedure, establishing the best values

[3] Ibid., p. 196.

of fixed parameters, and developing data collection and operating programs and procedures.

2. **Storage and maintenance costs**—the costs attributable to data storage, program storage and maintenance, and other record-keeping and custodial functions related to the method.

3. **Operating costs**—those costs incurred in the actual operation of the forecasting method or technique. Even in the age of the computer several forecasting techniques require significant amounts of time and resources. Other major operating costs may be incurred for data, forecasting staff, and outside expertise or opinions.

The expected accuracy of a forecasting method ordinarily is measured in terms of the method's capability to minimize overall forecast errors (deviations from actual occurrences) or to predict turning points (changes in direction of a series of occurrences). The accuracy characteristics of a given forecasting method are of critical importance in evaluating the above costs of the forecasting method relative to the value of the accuracy provided by that method. Generally speaking, the expected accuracy of a forecast may be improved by increasing the time and money invested in the development, maintenance, and operation of a forecasting system. The enhanced system might use more sophisticated methods or models to reduce expected error rates at the expense of higher forecasting costs.

From the standpoint of the user of the forecast, the cost of inaccuracy is of critical importance. It should be expected that as the accuracy of the forecast increases, the cost to the operating departments of forecast inaccuracy will decrease. For example, in production and inventory control, increased forecast accuracy would allow reduced safety stocks and thereby reduce associated carrying costs.

Given the identification of the above cost characteristics, it should be the joint responsibility of the forecaster and the operating manager to assess more sophisticated and more expensive forecasting techniques in terms of their potential savings as well as evaluating potential results from less sophisticated techniques. The chart on page 54 shows how cost and accuracy increase with sophistication of forecasting models, and charts this against a general curve describing the cost of forecasting errors. The appropriate forecasting technique would be one that falls in the region where the sum of the two costs is minimized.[4]

An interesting case where such evaluations are appropriate relates to the development of forecasting techniques within the framework of what is termed "ABC" inventory management, a concept discussed in detail in

[4] Chambers, John C., Mullick, Satinder K., and Smith, Donald D., "How to choose the right forecasting technique," *Harvard Business Review*, July/August 1971, p. 47.

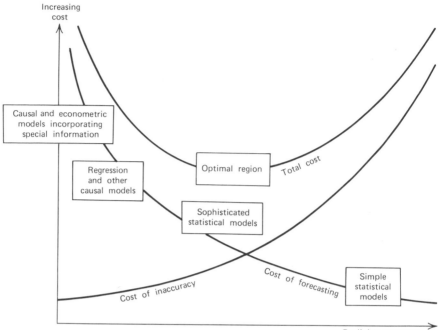

Chapter 4. In this framework high usage value and critical items are classified as "A" items, less critical or lower usage value items classified as "B" items, and routine inexpensive materials classified as "C" items. In this management scheme, the "A" items may warrant substantial investment in sophisticated forecasting models, due to the high cost of forecast inaccuracy. On the other hand, "B" and "C" items may require only simple forecasting applications.

The final item on the list of characteristics for consideration in choosing a forecasting method is the overall applicability of the method to the management environment in which it must work. By way of example, let us again consider the case of inventory control, where large numbers of items must be forecasted. Some of the requirements that a forecasting technique should satisfy in this environment include: [5]

1. It should not require maintenance of large histories of each item in the data bank, if this can be avoided.
2. Computations should take as little computer time as possible.
3. The technique should identify seasonal variations and take these into account when forecasting; also, preferably, it will compute the sta-

[5] Ibid., p. 64.

tistical significance of the seasonals, deleting them if they are not significant.

4. It should be able to fit a curve to the most recent data adequately and adapt to changes in trends and seasonals quickly.
5. It should be applicable to data with a variety of characteristics.
6. It also should be versatile enough so that when several hundred items or more are considered, it will do the best overall job, even though it may not do as good a job as other techniques for a particular item.

Development of a Forecasting Organization

Surveys of a variety of large business organizations have shown that, whereas many companies have established forecasting organizations and made substantial commitments to forecasting in terms of budgets and manpower, many believe that the full potential of these investments have not been realized.[6] Among the most frequent problems listed are:

1. Lack of effective communication between users and preparers
2. Lack of requisite skills on the part of both the users and preparers of forecast information, particularly in such endeavors as identifying forecasting opportunities and selecting appropriate methods for new applications
3. Disparity in user-preparer perceptions of the company's forecasting status and needs
4. Failure to plan a progressive set of actions to realize the company's full potential for forecasting.

The above points can be easily translated into positive statements of the major requirements to be considered in the development of a forecasting organization. They also serve to emphasize the importance of the organizational aspects of forecasting in business organizations.

FORECASTING METHODS AND TECHNIQUES

The method, or methods, that are most appropriate for a particular forecasting situation depend on the nature of the demand to be forecast, the value of the forecast, and the qualifications of personnel available to prepare the forecast. Whatever method is used, the one indispensable ingredient that must be present is sound business logic. The forecaster must always ask himself, "Does this forecast make sense and are the assumptions inherent in the forecast reasonable?"

---

[6] Wheelwright, Steven C. and Clark, Darral G., "Corporate forecasting: promise and reality," *Harvard Business Review*, November/December 1976, pp. 47–48.

Forecasting methods and techniques have proliferated in recent years. This has been largely the result of the growth of the complex business organization, with its expanding needs for information upon which to base assessments of uncertain future events, as well as the advent of the widespread business use of the computer, which has made manageable the heavy calculation burdens associated with many forecasting techniques. The following section presents a discussion of the four basic classes into which forecasting techniques may be grouped.[7] These include: (1) qualitative techniques, (2) practical subjective methods, (3) time series analysis, and (4) causal models. Within the discussion of each of these general classes, the major techniques represented in that class also will be noted.

It should be noted that, in practice, the forecaster will often use a combination of techniques to prepare a given forecast. These techniques may be used to generate estimates that are, in turn, used in other techniques to arrive at final forecast figures. Alternatively, the forecaster may develop forecasts for one item, using two or more separate techniques, and then arrive at the published forecast on a judgmental combination of those results.

Qualitative Techniques

Qualitative forecasting techniques are most useful in circumstances where data is relatively scarce. A prime example of such a circumstance would be the introductory stage of a new product. Qualitative techniques employ human judgment and opinion rating schemes to arrive at quantitative forecast figures. Included in this class of techniques would be:

1. **The Delphi method**—a procedure in which a number of experts are independently questioned, and an attempt is made to have the group arrive at a consensus through independent consideration of a sequence of questionnaires.

2. **Market research**—a systematic procedure for data collection and testing of hypotheses about the marketplace. This would include consumer surveys of various kinds.

3. **Panel consensus**—a group consensus forecast, based on communication between several experts. The executive opinion or sales force composite forecasts often are of this type.

4. **Visionary forecast**—a forecast that incorporates personal insights about the future and facts about alternative scenarios.

---

[7] Chambers, John C., Mullick, Satinder K., and Smith, Donald D., "How to choose the right forecasting technique," *Harvard Business Review*, July/August 1971, pp. 49–50.

5. Historical analogy—a forecast based on comparative analyses of historical growth of similar products.

Typical applications of qualitative forecasting methods are for new product sales and long-range forecasts of new and existing products. As an example, when considering the immediate growth potential of a new product, management may authorize a direct survey of potential customers' intentions to buy. This would provide near term input for decisions on initial financing, production capacity, and inventory levels. In formulating a long-term strategy for producing and distributing a product, however, immediate customer buying intentions are less important. A better technique for developing long-range forecasts in this case would be the Delphi method, where the panel members themselves may use such techniques as visionary forecasting or historical analogy.

SUBJECTIVE METHODS

Forecasts based on subjective methods can be extremely useful, particularly as a first step in establishing usage forecasts to be used in inventory management. Experience in design and implementation of inventory management systems has proven the practicality of this approach. The three most common forms of subjective methods are (1) executive opinion, (2) sales force composite, and (3) customer expectation.

The *executive opinion* forecast will reflect the intuitive judgment of a single executive or the composite judgment of several executives. The advantages of this type of method are that it usually involves limited effort, can be quickly prepared, and that communicating the forecast to management is readily accomplished. An executive opinion forecast is most frequently used in smaller companies where a specialized forecasting function is not justified, and in those situations where style changes are a predominating factor. Executive opinion forecasts are also used when the forecasted events are influenced by a great many variables which have a poorly defined cause-and-effect relationship with demand.

A *sales force composite* forecast involves totaling the individual forecasts of many salesmen and sales managers. The normal procedure is to have each level of sales management review and adjust the forecasts prepared by the next lower level. When this type of method is used, it is important to provide each salesman with historical sales data for his region, and also with his prior forecasts. This type of forecast can be useful in assisting the salesman in establishing his sales objectives, and in evaluating his past performance. In some cases, a sales force composite forecast can be justified on this basis alone, even if the forecast is not used for higher level planning and decision-making.

A *customer expectation* type of forecast is developed by asking customers how much they expect to order, over periods of time. It is frequently used in connection with very large customers such as chain stores and original equipment manufacturers, particularly when such customers account for a larger portion of total sales. Such large customers may also have developed long-term requirements, used as a basis for "blanket" purchase orders, with current release dates and quantities being furnished to the supplier. If these customers have done an adequate job of forecasting requirements, this type of a forecasting method can be meaningful. However, the weight given to a customer's forecast of requirements should be based on how accurately requirements have been projected in the past. In some cases, customers will forecast excessive requirements so as to insure an adequate vendor inventory of materials, thus minimizing vendor lead times, and the risk of vendor stock-out situations.

TIME SERIES ANALYSIS

A time series can be generally defined as the arrangement of measured data in chronological order. Time series analysis relates to evaluating and identifying patterns of stability and change, relative to a single variable over a period of time. The principle behind time series analysis, relative to forecasting, is that the level of demand follows identifiable patterns of change which can be projected into the future. For example, seasonal variations can be identified and expressed in quantitative terms, using time series analysis techniques.

Forecasting (relative to time series analysis) consists of identifying patterns—in terms of time—through the analysis of historical data, and then projecting these patterns into the future. The most common statistical techniques used in identifying and projecting these patterns are averages, moving averages, weighted averages, and trend fitting, using the method of least squares.

The use of averages is common to everyone in business. A straight arithmetic average (mean) can be used to identify a stable demand pattern; however, the forecaster is faced with several problems. First, he must determine the period to be covered by the average. Should it be three months, twelve months, etc.? Second, consideration must be given to the marketing factors which influenced historical demand data. The use of an average to forecast future demand implies the anticipated continuation of previous marketing conditions with regard to their effect on demand. The advantage of using an average is that it eliminates random fluctuations in demand which, in forecasting, are referred to as the irregular factor.

More sophisticated techniques involving averages, relate to moving and weighted averages. A moving average includes adding and dropping like demand periods, and then calculating a new average. The weighted average reflects assigning varying weights to different periods included in calculating the average. The theory behind a weighted average is that the more current months will reflect future demand more accurately, and therefore should exert a greater influence on the average than the demand data that is relatively old.

One type of a weighted average is termed "exponential smoothing." "Smoothing" refers to the common characteristic of all-averaging procedures whereby period-to-period fluctuations in demand are "smoothed" by using a moving or cumulative average. "Exponential" refers to the method of weighting historical demand data. In exponential smoothing, the weights assigned to historical demand data vary according to an exponential function. This results in reducing the weight, or influence, assigned to each demand period, according to the age of the data. The primary advantage of the exponential smoothing technique is the simplicity of the calculations to update the average, and its compatibility with computer capabilities. Although the calculations are relatively simple, the rationale behind the exponential smoothing equations is rather complex. This apparent simplicity sometimes results in inexperienced individuals using the technique, but not understanding the potential problems associated with its various aspects. For example, a demand which has a seasonal component must be adjusted for the seasonal factor before the exponential smoothing calculation is performed.

The trend or line fitting technique involves the statistical calculation of a line which minimizes the sum of the squares of the deviations. In the simplest case, the fitted line is linear. More sophisticated line fitting techniques result in a curved line which is represented by an equation. The forecast is based upon extrapolation of the fitted line. This type of technique is frequently used in conjunction with annual data to determine long-term trends which in turn relate to long-range forecasting.

A trend line can also be established directly by fitting a free-hand line to plotted data. Although this is a semi-subjective method, it can be useful because it can be done without any time-consuming statistical calculations, and does not require any special statistical know-how.

Causal Techniques

Causal models constitute the most sophisticated group of forecasting techniques. These techniques attempt to relate the behavior of the demand series being forecasted to the behavior of other factors that may affect the marketplace. Such factors could include economic forces such as housing starts, per capital income, employment, etc., or other factors such as competitors' actions, strikes, and advertising promotions.

Typically, causal models are the best tools for predicting turning points and developing long-range forecasts. However, data availability is the most common constraint on causal model development. If certain data elements are lacking, it may be necessary to make assumptions about certain relationships until such time as a more detailed model can be developed.

There are a wide variety of causal models in use today. Some of the most common model forms include:

1. **Regression model**—estimates a single equation that relates sales to other variables, and tests the validity of all relationships on a statistical basis.

2. **Econometric model**—describes some sector of sales activity, using a system of interdependent regression equations; equations may be solved simultaneously or in a predetermined sequence.

3. **Input/output model**—describes the flow or allocation of outputs and inputs in a system that could be the national economy, an industry, or a large company with a number of major departments or divisions.

In many cases, causal models are used to forecast sales by product class in a given company. One company, for example, has developed regression equations that forecast total sales in each of its thirteen major product classes. These forecasts cover a five-year period, and provide input for financial planning, marketing planning, and facilities planning. In addition, the forecast by product class becomes a constraint on the detailed forecasts by individual product, which are generated on a less scientific basis. This assists the inventory plan by product in recognizing expected changes in demand trends that may result from economic, advertising, sales contest, or other effects.

COMBINED APPROACH

So far, forecasting methods have been reviewed in terms of subjective and quantitative techniques. In actual business practice, forecasting systems are usually based upon a *mix* of subjective and quantitative techniques. In a particular forecasting system the trend and seasonal components may be projected using statistical techniques, whereas the cycle component and that part of the irregular component relating to abnormal factors may be based upon an executive opinion type of forecast.

In many cases a quantitative forecast is prepared by marketing research and then reviewed with a management committee. The use of graphs can be useful in this regard because they can convey to the committee the overall results of the statistical calculations without going into technical detail which may be confusing to individuals not trained in statistical techniques. The committee reviews the statistical forecast for reasonableness and then prepares adjustments to the forecast taking into consideration a specific list of abnormal factors which may influence demand, such as special promotions, strikes, abnormal pricing situations, etc. The final forecast is then prepared, taking into account the statistical forecast plus adjustments prepared by the management committee.

A follow-up to this type of system is the evaluation of the forecast errors. In this analysis a determination is made as to whether or not the adjustments of the management committee have reduced the magnitude of the forecast errors. This analysis is presented to the committee so that it can evaluate the prior adjustments and improve upon future adjustments. This is a type of a "gaming situation" where the players learn both from their correct and incorrect decisions, and modify their future actions accordingly.

FORECASTING ERRORS

One of the major problems relative to demand forecasting is a general lack of understanding by businessmen of the meaning of forecast errors. Unfortunately, perfect demand forecasting systems do not exist. It should be recognized that anticipation and analysis of forecast errors are integral parts of any forecasting system.

The term "error" is probably one reason for the confusion in this area. Normally, error implies a mistake; however, as it pertains to forecasting, it also refers to deviations between actual and forecasted results which arise from the irregular components of demand. In most forecasting systems, the magnitude of the irregular components establish the forecast error range. This error range is very important as it relates to planning because it identifies the degree of uncertainty to be associated with the forecast. For example, many economic forecasts of gross national product are stated in terms of a specific amount, plus or minus a certain level. This plus or minus portion of the forecast identifies the possible error range. In effect, it states how much reliance can be placed on the specific forecasted figure.

Forecasting error is particularly important as it relates to inventory management because it is one of the principal factors considered in setting up inventory safety stocks and related reorder points. Other factors being equal, the amount of safety stock required will vary proportionately to the forecast error.

The analysis of forecasting errors also can play an important role in the selection of the type of forecasting system to be used. In this regard, the selection of a forecasting system is largely dependent upon the magnitude of the errors it generates in comparison with alternative forecasting methods. The relative effectiveness of a forecasting system can be evaluated by comparing its error range with the error range resulting from the use of a so-called "naive" statistical forecasting model. A naive model could consist of any one of the following techniques: this year's sales will equal last year's sales, a twelve-month moving average, a simple exponential smoothing equation, a linear trend line based on the last five years' sales, etc. The naive model reflects a straightforward statistical forecast, disregarding intuitive judgment and complex statistical techniques found in more sophisticated systems.

The analysis of forecast errors can also be important in identifying and correcting deficiencies in a forecasting system. If errors can be associated with specific factors influencing demand, it may be possible to include these factors in the development of future forecasts.

FORECASTING AND THE COMPUTER

The widespread use of computers for business applications has had a profound impact on the development and application of scientific forecasting methods and techniques. Recent years have witnessed the proliferation of forecasting application software. These first received significant usage through computer time-sharing systems, and now are being installed in private systems, often as elements of larger planning and control systems.

In addition to the forecasting routines themselves, some time-sharing companies now offer access to input-output data banks that provide social, economic, and demographic information on a national, regional, and state-wide basis. When integrated with newer data management and analysis routines available on several of these systems, the forecaster achieves substantial power, indeed.

Looking into the future, the continuing decline in computer costs should make heavily statistical techniques such as Box-Jenkins more economically feasible, even for some inventory control applications. In addition, the entire concept of forecasting systems may become more complex and sophisticated, as computers allow the linkage of several different techniques in one large system, along with a systematic handling of qualitative information.

As forecasters gain experience in the use of computer-assisted forecasting methods, the use of man-machine systems will become commonplace. In such systems, nearly all statistical, causal, or other analyses are done on the computer, with man interacting frequently. Finally, consumer simulation models will be developed that predict consumer behavior and forecast human reactions, and relate these forecasts to pricing, advertising promotions, and other marketing strategies.

Chapter 4 discusses the various inventory management techniques that may be employed to control inventory levels and, in many cases, deal with the problem of forecast error. In the short run, inventory control techniques can be employed to react to high levels of forecast error. Ultimately, however, the manager has to choose between investing in higher inventory levels or paying for more accurate forecasts. Optimization of this solution requires clear understanding of both forecasting and inventory control techniques and their capabilities.

FOUR

Inventory Management Techniques

An effective inventory management system is dependent upon the development of efficient planning and control techniques and the proper implementation and administration of these techniques. In this chapter, various types of inventory management techniques will be described, along with typical operating environments in which they are frequently applied.

Prior to discussing specific techniques, a more precise definition of the respective functions of inventory *management* and inventory *control* seems appropriate.

Inventory management functions involve the development and administration of policies, systems, and procedures which will minimize total costs relative to inventory decisions and related functions such as customer service requirements, production scheduling, purchasing, traffic, etc. Viewed in that perspective, inventory management is broad in scope and affects a great number of activities in a company's organization. Because of these numerous interrelationships, inventory management stresses the need for integrated information flow and decision making, as it relates to inventory policies and overall systems.

The inventory control function, on the other hand, is frequently defined in a narrower sense than inventory management and pertains primarily to the administration of established policies, systems, and procedures. For example, inventory control activities might involve the maintenance of inventory records and reports, the initiation of material requisitions for purchased or manufactured items, and physical as well as accounting control over inventory transactions. Inventory control functions may also include special staff activities such as the development and evaluation of alternative inventory decision models, analysis of specific inventory problems, and the evaluation of existing inventory systems and procedures.

The various control techniques discussed in this chapter can be described as proven techniques which have been successfully applied in many typical business situations. Limited emphasis is placed here on certain sophisticated techniques which are normally based on complex statistical models. While these more complex techniques have been of value to a number of large companies, they are not necessarily applicable to, or economically feasible for, general inventory situations because they are frequently based upon specific assumptions and requirements which are associated with specialized operating conditions. It should also be pointed out that the use of sophisticated techniques per se does not necessarily result in an effective inventory management system. In many cases, the lack of accurate and timely data nullifies the advantages of using complex control techniques. There is also the potential problem that sophisticated control techniques may be misapplied because of a lack of understanding of their underlying rationale on the part of either management or the staff personnel directly concerned.

Finally, the benefits to be expected from the inventory control techniques described here can be said to include the major portion of those benefits available under much more sophisticated techniques which are usually also much more costly to apply.

When a company has decided to embark on an inventory management program, the first step taken should be a scoping study to establish the magnitude of such a program, the potential payback of the program, the probability of realizing the pay-back, and the resources which would be required. Some of the factors that should be considered in such a scoping study are:

1. The objectives of the company as they relate to inventories at the level of service to be provided to customers.
2. The qualifications of staff personnel who will design and coordinate the implementation of the system.
3. The capabilities of personnel who will be responsible for managing the system on a continuing basis.
4. The nature and size of inventories and their relationship to the other functions in the company, such as manufacturing, finance, marketing, etc.
5. The capability of present and future data processing equipment.
6. The potential savings that might be anticipated from improved control of inventories.
7. The current, or potential, availability of data that can be used in controlling inventories.

8. The present method for controlling inventories, and for making inventory decisions.
9. The degree of commitment by management personnel to the development of a more effective inventory management system and the results they anticipate from such a system.

A review of these factors should provide the framework for planning an inventory management program and should identify some of the techniques that will be incorporated into the program.

IDENTIFICATION OF INVENTORY LEVELS

Generally, the first step in recognizing inventory problems and improving management control of inventories is to identify inventory levels and associated costs and expenses, as these relate to the volume of business done. This usually starts with a review of the financial statements of a company. One of the most commonly used figures in this regard is the inventory turnover ratio, which is the annual cost of goods sold divided by the inventory amount. This ratio reflects approximately how many times the physical inventory is being "turned over" per year. The turnover ratio can be very useful; however, it is also frequently misunderstood by management when evaluating the effectiveness of the inventory management function of a company. A high inventory turnover ratio alone does not necessarily imply effective inventory management. This ratio should be evaluated, but along with many other statistics when appraising the effectiveness of the control of inventories (e.g., level of customer service, production set-up costs, purchase price variances as related to quantity discounts, and stability of the production labor force).

Inventory turnover ratios vary widely according to industry, and, within industry, according to the nature of manufacturing and distribution. A manufacturing company that assembles purchased components will require less inventory per sales dollar than a company in the same industry with comparable sales volume that is vertically integrated from a manufacturing point of view and, as a result, must carry additional work-in-process and raw material inventories. Therefore, the degree of vertical integration will affect a company's inventory turnover ratio. This also applies to the distribution system of a company. One company may distribute goods through independent wholesalers, whereas another company may rely upon its own regional warehouses and will naturally carry larger inventories.

In summary, inventory turnover ratios may be of value to management as a means of identifying possible inventory problems. For example, a decreasing trend of the inventory turnover ratio within a company, or a ratio that is lower than comparable industry averages, may indicate the need for further analysis. This analysis should indicate the factors which have caused ratio variations and the corrective action required.

Another consideration in the financial analysis of inventory has to do with the costing of inventory. If a company is on a LIFO accounting basis, any analysis relative to inventories should be based on the current cost of inventory rather than the LIFO book value. This is necessary so as to have consistent data because the cost of goods sold, other current assets, and current liabilities are stated in terms of current costs.

A typical organization may carry inventories of many types and in a number of different locations. Reaching conclusions regarding the effectiveness of inventory management or identifying specific inventory problems virtually always will require inventory analysis at more detailed levels than those presented on the balance sheet. One approach to analyzing inventories might be a breakdown of the balance sheet inventory amount by subsidiary, division, and/or plant. Depending on the size and organization of a company, a further breakdown may be made by profit or cost center, warehouse, sales region, and/or product line. In a manufacturing company, inventories also would be classified as raw material, work-in-process, finished goods, service parts, and factory supplies.

In addition to the classifications of inventory mentioned, there are many other detailed breakdowns that can be made, such as: commodity code (e.g., sheet steel, castings, forgings, etc.), slow-moving items, salvage stock, consignment stock, in-transit stock, etc. In cases such as obsolete and surplus stock, the inventory should be carried at a value that reflects its market, scrap, or rework value. The various types of breakdown described can assist a company in identifying current and potential inventory problems so that timely management action can be taken.

Another type of analysis is the recognition of inventories which are associated with specific decisions made by management. Inventories of this nature are usually associated with specific time periods and can be referred to as "programmed" inventories. Some examples are:

Seasonal inventory: The planned buildup of inventory to meet high seasonal demand while maintaining a reasonably stable production rate.

Strike-hedge inventory: Increased finished goods inventory, based upon a management decision, in anticipation of a potential internal strike, or increased raw material stock in anticipation of possible strikes against primary suppliers.

Price-hedge inventory: The stock piling of inventory because of known or anticipated price increases in materials.

Job order inventory: Increases in raw material and work-in-process inventories related to abnormally large special orders.

Proper recognition of programmed inventories can assist management in the planning and control of inventory levels and the projected needs for additional working capital.

In addition to the classifications of inventory mentioned, there are many other detailed breakdowns that can be made such as: commodity code (e.g., sheet steel, castings, forgings, etc.), slow-moving items (e.g., no activity in the last year), excessive stock (e.g., more than two years' projected usage), obsolete parts, perishable items, salvage stock, consignment stock, in-transit stock, etc. In cases such as obsolete and surplus stock, the inventory should be carried at a value that reflects its market, scrap, or rework value. The various types of breakdowns described can assist a company in identifying current and potential inventory problems so that timely management action can be taken.

The purpose of categorizing inventories is to provide management with a basis for the control of specific inventories through a continuing review of their relationship to the total inventory and of changes in specific levels from period to period. A knowledge of inventory costs also assists management in determining priorities in the development and implementation of improved inventory management techniques. There have been cases where companies directed a disproportionate amount of effort to the control of those portions of inventories which accounted for a relatively small percentage of the total. Recognition of the different types of inventory is also important in developing an integrated inventory management system. For example, different inventory control techniques are frequently required to control raw material, work-in-process, and finished goods inventories.

ABC APPROACH TO INVENTORY MANAGEMENT

One of the most widely recognized concepts of inventory management is referred to as ABC inventory control. The objective of ABC control is to vary the expense associated with maintaining appropriate control according to the potential savings associated with a proper level of such control. For example, an item having an inventory cost of $10,000, such as sheet steel, has a much greater potential for saving of expenses related to maintaining inventories than an item with a cost of $20. The ABC approach is a means of categorizing inventoried items into three classes, "A," "B," and "C," according to the potential amount to be controlled. When items have been classified, appropriate control techniques are developed for each class of inventory. "A" items justify the use of precise control techniques, where "C" items should be controlled by means of general control techniques.

The primary criteria for classifying inventoried items into "A," "B," and "C" categories is the annual dollar usage of each item. This is accomplished by multiplying the annual unit usage of each inventoried item by its unit cost and then listing all items in descending order according to annual dollar usage. This listing should also include a column to show the cumulative annual dollar usage by line item. Such a listing reflects the distribution of annual dollar usage. A typical distribution in a manufacturing operation shows that the top 15% of the line items, in terms of annual dollar usage, represent 80% of the total annual dollar usage. These items are normally classified as "A" items. The next 15% of the line items, in terms of annual dollar usage, reflect an additional 15% of the annual dollar usage and are designated as "B" items. The "C" items represent the remaining 70% of the items in inventory and account for only 5% of the total annual dollar usage. In some cases the ABC classifications will be developed independently for different types of inventory such as finished goods, raw material, and service parts.

In addition to annual dollar usage, several other factors need to be considered in developing criteria for classifying items into "A," "B," and "C" categories. In this regard, a "truth table" can be used to facilitate the classification process. A typical "truth table" is shown on page 70. The questions included in such a table, and the parameters associated with the questions, will vary according to the specific inventory being analyzed.

In this table six questions are asked regarding each inventoried item. A "yes" answer is indicated by a one in the appropriate column under the part number; a "no" answer is reflected by a zero. The column next to the question provides the key to the classification by indicating the inventory class associated with a "yes" answer to each question. When there is more than one "yes" answer per item, the highest classification is used. In a typical inventory, basic raw materials, such as sheet steel, bar stock, etc., and inventoried sub-assemblies are found in the "A" category. Small metal stampings with moderate usage are frequently "B" items; while "C" items are typically hardware items such as small nuts, bolts, and screws.

ABC inventory classification and related control techniques were developed originally for manual systems prior to the widespread use of automated inventory recordkeeping. "ABC control" placed emphasis on reducing recordkeeping requirements, redirecting clerical and review effort, and implementing stratified or varying inventory control techniques. These concepts also are generally applicable to automated systems. They can be used in structuring exception reports, determining safety stocks, cycling counting programs and in numerous other aspects of inventory management and control. Reference to this approach will appear throughout this chapter.

"Truth" Table for ABC Classification

Questions	Yes answer	Part numbers 1	2	3	4	5
1. Is Annual Usage More Than $10,000?	A	①	0	0	0	0
2. Is Annual Usage Between $1,000 and $10,000?	B	0	①	0	0	0
3. Is Annual Usage Less than $1,000?	C	0	0	①	①	①
4. Is the Unit Cost Over $100?	B	①	0	0	0	0
5. Does the Physical Nature of the Item Cause Special Storage Problems?	B	0	0	0	0	①
6. Would a Stock Out Result in Excessive Costs?	B	0	0	0	①	0
Classification		A	B	C	B	B

INVENTORY DATA REQUIREMENTS

The effectiveness of any inventory management system is dependent on the accuracy, timeliness, and scope of data available. Availability, quality, and timing of data ultimately determine the effectiveness of an inventory management system, the control techniques employed, and the structure of inventory control reports. The importance of reviewing inventory data requirements is emphasized by the fact that in some cases elaborate decision rules, complex reports, and sophisticated equations are developed to control inventory without properly considering the nature of the data that is available or the cost of generating new forms of data.

The first step that should be undertaken in developing an efficient inventory management system is an appraisal of current requirements for inventory, available data, and desired reporting procedures. This appraisal should include a precise determination of the type of inventories that the firm should maintain. For example, most manufacturing firms fabricate, assemble and distribute, or some combination thereof, products for customer consumption. The type of inventories that a firm can maintain includes raw materials, purchased components, work-in-process (fabricated piece parts and subassemblies), and finished goods. Depending on how the firm is structured, there may be several combinations of these three types of inventories and/or several levels of detail of a particular type. The point being emphasized here is that a firm attempting a project to improve its inventory management system should first thoroughly understand the type of business it is in and the type of inventories it is, or should be, maintaining and reporting on.

The next step in developing an inventory management system involves the collection and processing of the data required to provide an accurate recording of the status of the items that are in inventory and the precise location of the material in stock. An inability to determine exactly what is on hand, or where it is, has been a major cause of the failure of many inventory management systems. The status data collected on an inventoried item should include, at a minimum, the following: transfers to stock, transfers from stock, order quantity, control method, quantity on order and cost. Consequently, depending on the control methods used, each time an item is put into inventory, moved from location to location within the plant, has value added to it in terms of additional fabrication or assembly operations, or has been removed from stock and sold to a customer, the process should be documented and this data should be recorded in the inventory management system. An effective inventory management system requires that there always be tight control over the movement of all items contained in the inventory.

Because this information is a key component of an effective system of control, it is vital that a high degree of accuracy be maintained. "Cycle counting" is a technique that has been used to assure record accuracy, monitor physical control, and, in some applications, reduce or eliminate requirements for annual physical inventories. The concept of "cycle counting" is quite simple. A counting program, normally employing ABC classification, is developed. A typical program might call for all "A" items to be counted quarterly, "B" items twice a year, and "C" items once each year. Organizational responsibilities would be defined and a work force established. Procedures would be developed and implemented to make physical counts, reconcile "cut-off" periods, compare to records, and investigate and adjust for differences.

A next step in developing an inventory management system is the processing and analysis of historical and/or forecasted usage and cost data. This data is used by the system to develop the answers to the questions "When to order?" and "How much to order?" The answer to the question "When to order?" is generated by a system based on information concerning the status of inventoried items (quantity on hand, quantity on order, quantity reserved, and/or quantity in process), the lead time required to procure the item, and the historical and forecasted usage of the item during recent or forthcoming time frames. The answer to the question "How much to order?" is determined by the unit cost of the item, annual usage of the item, the expenses involved in creating and issuing an order for the item, and the expenses involved in carrying the item in inventory. In developing this type of information, a firm should assure itself of the accuracy and reliability of its purchasing system, its forecasting systems (which were discussed in the previous chapter), its manufacturing control system, and its cost accounting system.

The lead time element, mentioned in the previous paragraph, concerns the amount of time required to acquire additional stock when the need to replenish an item is recognized. Lead time can be defined as the elapsed time from the moment it is determined that an item needs to be reordered until the ordered items are physically available in inventory. There are two basic types of lead time, purchasing lead time and manufacturing lead time. The components generally associated with purchasing lead time include: the time interval between reviews of an item's status, the time required to generate and issue a requisition, the time required to initiate and send a purchase order, the vendor's delivery time (from the mailing of the purchase order to the physical receipt of the material), the time the material spends in receiving and incoming quality control, and the material handling time required to place the items in their appropriate storage location. The basis for establishing a manufacturing lead time is essentially the same as purchasing, with the exception that the components associated with the vendor delivery time and receiving time are usually replaced by the components associated with production time. Typically, lead times do not remain constant. They require updating as a result of selecting a new or different supplier, material shortages, changes in quoted delivery times, and variations in the shop work loads that result in production schedule changes. Lead time is one of the parameters of an inventory management system that must be closely monitored to assure that it is being constantly updated according to the changing environmental conditions.

In addition to the previously mentioned status, usage and cost information, most inventory management systems contain detailed descriptive and administrative data. Descriptive data generally includes a precise description of the item (exclusive of part number) and some dimensional and physical characteristics. The administrative data may include references to a higher and/or lower level assembly or commodity if it is a manufactured item, alternate vendors if it is a purchased item, and management control codes (ABC code, frequency of review, or seasonality considerations.) Some inventory management systems also contain data concerning the level of services provided on an item. Level of service, relative to inventory control, can be defined in a number of ways. Some examples are: percent of the item quantity ordered which was shipped within two working days after receipt of the order, percent of item quantity backordered versus the item quantity shipped, percent of items in the stockroom relative to the quantity of withdrawals for a period of time, or the number of production delays per period associated with a shortage of this item.

The exact nature and requirements of a data base for an inventory management system will vary greatly according to the circumstances. The important point to remember is that the effectiveness of the system is dependent upon the quality and reliability of the data base and the quality and reliability of the controls that monitor the data gathering and entry process.

MANUFACTURING CONTROL SYSTEMS

There are three basic forms of manufacturing firms: the job shop (builds discrete items in batches), the assembly or flow shop (builds discrete related items on a continuous basis), and a process shop (continuous production of a homogeneous product). In addition, the job shop can be broken down into two distinct subforms: a firm that manufactures items only to a precise customer order and a firm that manufactures items from stock. Within each of the basic forms, or subforms, of a manufacturing firm there will be a high degree of commonality of material flow within the operation. A modern manufacturing control system will recognize this similarity of flow within related firms and should provide techniques for identifying it, planning it, and controlling it.

A modern manufacturing control system should integrate the systems that are directly concerned with the manufacturing process. These sections include, among others: purchasing, manufacturing operations, manufacturing control (cost accounting, inventory control, and production planning), engineering, and general accounting. The objective of an integrated manufacturing control system is to provide information for management that will enable them to make decisions that will minimize their investment in inventory while maximizing the quality of the products produced and the level of customer service provided. Consequently, a system should be able to assist in planning production, reporting actual performance and measuring it to the plan, providing techniques for monitoring and controlling levels of inventory as compared to the level of customer service expected, and providing techniques for a complete accounting of all cost incurred and all deviations from the normal standards for the manufacturing process.

An integrated manufacturing control system provides for the functions of forecasting, capacity planning, order entry, material requirements planning and control, shop floor planning and control, and cost accounting. Forecasting and demand planning were discussed in the previous chapter. Order entry involves the processing of customers' orders and their entry into a system which assures that their completion, or delivery, will satisfy the goals set for the level of customer service. Capacity planning involves determination of what is necessary to produce the actual and forecasted demand on a short term basis. In addition, capacity planning should include what will be required over the long term in the form of capital equipment and personnel to produce anticipated demands several periods into the future. Material requirements planning and control is concerned with maintaining adequate levels of material so that all orders can be quickly accommodated while minimizing the investment in inventory. Shop floor planning and control concerns scheduling of the labor and equipment necessary to complete a job, the status and quantity of work in process, and the efficiency and utilization of the manufacturing asets. Cost accounting concerns the collection and analysis of direct manufacturing expenses and the application of related overhead expenses to produce accurate product costs. These costs are then used to evaluate inventory, price the product and assess engineering changes or modifications.

WAREHOUSING AND DISTRIBUTION CONTROL SYSTEMS

A typical distribution firm's inventory management system goes beyond the simple control of the inventories themselves. For example, an integrated distributor's order processing and inventory control system will contain modules for order entry, warehouse picking and packing, invoicing, purchasing and restocking, receiving, and file maintenance. In a typical automated system, a customer's order is received by mail or telephone, and entered into the computer. A picking/packing list is then produced. This list, which can be sorted in the order the material is stored in the warehouse, is then forwarded to the warehouse for picking, packing, labelling, and shipping. Exceptions to the picking process are noted on a copy, and the document is returned to the computer where these exceptions are entered. The completed order, as shipped, can then be priced and the invoice forwarded to the customer for prompt payment. Integrated distributor systems such as this are often combined with an accounts receivable system to assure proper retention of the necessary management data required to closely control accounts receivable.

An integrated distributor's system also considers the inventory restocking or replenishment process. Periodic reviews can be made of the material in stock as compared to order points, order quantities, or other statistical information upon which restocking decisions may be based. (Note: as compared to a manufacturing firm which will use an MRP system, an up-to-date distribution company will still use Order Point and other advanced statistical techniques, including transportation models combined with informed management judgment.) A computer can then print a suggested purchase order listing for review by inventory management personnel. Management adjustments can be made as they are deemed necessary. After these adjustments have been made, the computer can produce purchase orders in a variety of ways. For example, purchases for several commodities available from one vendor can be combined for the benefit of reducing freight and/or obtaining price break discounts. Also, common items stored in inventory can be coded to indicate that they can be purchased from several vendors. Thus if there is insufficient material being ordered from one vendor, alternate vendors can be selected until a vendor has sufficient quantities to justify the cost of placing an order. Finally, orders can be suspended so that certain vendors are handled only once a month, once a quarter, or some other time frame as determined by the user of the system.

The advantage of the use of an automated system in a distribution firm is its speed and ability to review large numbers of inventoried items in a short amount of time. This advantage can potentially provide for an increase in inventory turns per period, with a subsequent reduction in the amount of inventory in the warehouse and a corresponding decrease in the carrying and handling costs of this inventory. The economic evaluation of the use of a computer in a distribution firm is relatively easy to perform, as compared to evaluating a computer for accounting systems or other functions where there is not an easily identifiable potential cost reduction. For example, if, through the use of computerization, a distributor can reduce his on-hand inventory stock by $500,000, there may be a potential savings of $100,000 per year in carrying and handling costs. These savings can, in many cases, justify the serious consideration of an advanced warehousing and distribution control system.

Selection of Inventory Control Techniques

Inventory control techniques are tools that can be applied in both simple and sophisticated ways. In the final analysis, these techniques are used to answer two fundamental questions:

1. When to order?
2. How much to order?

Inventory management success results when techniques are tailored and combined to provide the blend of sophistication and simplicity required to effectively answer these questions.

Each organization is different and has unique inventory management needs. A few of the factors that must be considered in evaluating, selecting, and applying inventory control techniques include:

Nature of the business (manufacturer, distributor, etc.)
Nature of the product
Number of locations involved
Number of items to be inventoried
Degree of mechanization that is practical and economical
Forecast reliability
Customer service requirements

There is no single system that is necessarily "best," nor is there any experience that indicates that in practical application a certain type of system is "best" for a given industry. Choosing a single technique is not necessary: a blend of techniques may be desirable. The following sections describe a number of inventory control techniques that have been successfully applied and are in general use today.

MATERIAL REQUIREMENTS PLANNING

Material requirements planning (MRP) is a technique which a manufacturing firm can use to plan and schedule the material it needs to build items for inventory and/or open customer orders. MRP is based on how long it will take to procure and build items and what the anticipated demand for the items will be. MRP is concerned with when material is needed and the quantity of material required. MRP systems are predicated on the existence of two very basic information sources—accurate Bills of Material for all items produced by the manufacturing firm and an accurate master schedule of when all finished products are expected to be completed by manufacturing.

A Bill of Materials is a listing of all of the items used to manufacture a particular item. In some cases, the Bill of Material may be only one item long: a raw material used to produce a fabricated piece part. In other cases the Bill of Material may be 25,000 items in length, such as might be required in the aerospace industry to assemble a complete radar set. A Bill of Material should be looked upon as the recipe of the items necessary to produce an inventoried item (piece part, sub-assembly, or finished good) or an end product for shipment.

There are two basic forms of a Bill of Material: engineering bills and manufacturing bills. An engineering bill usually describes, in great detail, all of the components required to put a product together. An engineering bill will encompass many levels of assemblies, sub-assemblies, and piece parts, including such items as screws, nuts, bolts, and glue as may be required to produce the end product. On the other hand, a manufacturing bill is typically only one level deep. The manufacturing bill describes what is needed from inventory stocks by the manufacturing departments to complete production of a particular assembly or sub-assembly. Typically, a manufacturing bill does not include nuts, bolts, screws, glue, and other items that can generally be referred to as line stock or expense items. Additionally, if several sub-assemblies are built coincident with the operations required to build the completed product, then the manufacturing bill will contain all the items required to build these sub-assemblies as well as the end item. However, it usually will not reference the sub-assembly part number, if it exists. In summary, an engineering bill generally lists all of the items required to build a completed top level product, whereas a manufacturing bill lists only those items that are required to be issued from a store's inventory to build a product.

The master schedule required by an MRP system is a time phased listing of when all completed items are expected into finished goods inventory or promised for shipment to a customer. The master schedule assumes that accurate information is available on the amount of time required to perform each manufacturing operation necessary to produce the completed product. Typically, each item produced in a manufacturing firm will have a Routing, or Process, Sheet. This Routing Sheet indicates all the necessary manufacturing operations and the standard time required for each to produce a finished product. These Routing Sheets are then used by the MRP system to expand the master schedule into a detailed production schedule. The production schedule describes when piece parts and/or sub-assemblies will be needed to produce the finished goods by the time stated in the master schedule.

As has been mentioned, in order for an MRP system to function effectively, a manufacturing firm must first have reliable manufacturing Bills of Material and a Master Schedule. Once these two products have been developed, an MRP system, as well as other components of a manufacturing control system, can be developed and implemented. An MRP system starts with data concerning promised delivery dates for existing customer orders and/or estimated dates for forecasted customer orders. (These dates must be supplied by the manufacturing planner, because they are usually not automatically supplied by the system.) The orders, complete with the promised/estimated dates, are then input into the system. The system takes each order and explodes it into the individual components required ("gross requirements") for its completion. This explosion is accomplished by extending the manufacturing Bill of Material for the finished item times the quantity of the item desired. After the explosion is complete, the system reviews existing inventory status files to determine whether it has sufficient stocks on hand ("gross to net"). If sufficient stock is not available, manufacturing shop orders or purchase orders are released ("net requirements"), considering predetermined lead times and order quantities, to build the necessary components required for the completed product. Because of the Routing Sheets, precise information is known about the length of time it takes to acquire products and to fabricate and assemble products in the plant. Consequently, a production schedule can be developed showing when the components will be needed for the completed product to be available when shown on the master schedule. This production schedule can then be compared to the promised delivery dates provided the customer and can thus assist in determining what actions must be taken if it is necessary to speed up the process.

REORDER POINT SYSTEMS

As stated previously, the essence of an inventory management system can be defined in terms of two decisions, namely, (1) when to reorder and (2) how much to order. The first decision, when to reorder, is associated with reorder point systems which are responsible for initiating action to obtain additional material. The second decision, how much to order, is related to order quantity systems which will be discussed later in this chapter.

Reorder point systems can be divided into two basic categories: (1) those predicated on known material requirements and (2) systems which assume a degree of uncertainty in terms of future demand. A job shop type of operation schedules most materials for receipt based upon known orders in the production backlog, and is an example of the first type of system because material requirements are known with a high degree of reliability. Another example of such a system is a plant which operates according to a fixed production schedule.

The second type of system recognizes that material requirements are based upon forecasts with anticipated deviations between the forecasted and actual usage. It is assumed that these deviations or errors can be represented by known statistical distribution patterns, for example, the bell shaped (normal) distribution. Such a system is frequently referred to as a probability model because the reorder point is based in part upon the probability theory. In most cases, finished goods and service parts inventory control systems are based upon a degree of uncertainty regarding future demand.

Returning to the first category of reorder point systems, the decision to reorder is derived from an analysis of required shipping dates and production schedules. Frequently these production schedules are based upon network analysis which includes the use of such specialized techniques as Critical Path Method (CPM), Line of Balance, PERT, and Gantt charts. These techniques, in turn, utilize data such as lead times for purchased and manufactured items. The decision to reorder is based upon the materials requirements, as established in the bills of material, and the scheduling of these materials so as to meet established production and shipping dates. In most cases, materials will be scheduled into inventory prior to their immediate requirement in production. This is a form of safety stock and is used as a means of preventing production delays which might arise as a result of late receipt of purchased materials, or of production delays associated with manufactured component parts and sub-assemblies. The size of the safety stock to be carried will depend upon such factors as the potential loss from a production delay, the expense incident to carrying additional inventory for a specific period of time, and the probability of late delivery.

The second category of reorder point systems is based upon depicting the variation in stock level over a period of time. In this type of system, demand reflects a forecasted volume and an error range. The basic reorder point can be calculated as follows:

$$\text{Reorder point (ROP)} = L(D) + \text{safety stock}$$

where:
   L is the anticipated lead time in weeks.
   D is the forecasted demand in units per week.

When the stock level reaches the reorder point, an order is initiated for additional stock. The first portion of the equation regarding lead time multiplied by the forecasted demand is relatively easy to understand. If actual demand equals forecasted demand during the lead time period, and the delivery of materials is on time, the inventory level will reach the safety stock level at the same time as the replenishment order is received. The portion of the equation relative to safety stock is more complex and requires further explanation.

If both forecasted demand during the reordering cycle and the length of the lead time period were always known with certainty, safety stock would not be needed; however, both of these factors are normally variable and as a result represent averages rather than exact figures during a given reorder cycle. If no safety stock is carried, a stock-out condition could be anticipated fifty per cent of the time when stock is reordered. If stock were ordered twice a year, one stock-out per year would be anticipated; however, if stock were ordered weekly, twenty-six stock-outs per year would be expected. Using statistical techniques, safety stock quantities can be computed which will result in various predetermined levels of service. This relationship is expressed by the graph below. As the dollar investment in safety stock increases, the level of service improves. A review of a graph of this nature, based upon inventory simulation runs using a statistical inventory control model, can provide management with the type of information needed to balance inventory levels and levels of service.

**INVENTORY INVESTMENT AND
LEVEL OF SERVICE**

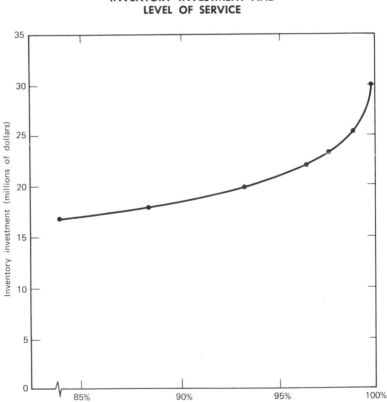

The level of service can be, and in many cases should be, varied by inventory category. For example, "C" items might have a higher level of service than "A" or "B" items because of the limited investment in safety stock required to improve the level of service. The level of service might also be varied according to the problems associated with a stock-out, as, for example, the risk of closing down an assembly line, or the profit contribution of a product line. A high-profit margin product would justify a higher level of service than a product with a very narrow profit margin.

Most computer-based inventory management systems rely on statistical calculations to determine safety stocks, while manual systems frequently depend upon decision tables, as illustrated at the bottom of the page. Such a decision table may indicate that an "A" item with a lead time of seven weeks should have a safety stock of three weeks' average usage, while a "C" item with the same lead time should have eight weeks' average usage as a safety stock.

So far in the discussion of reorder points, it has been assumed that they would be developed in an objective manner predicated upon the data in the inventory data base and a level of service as determined by a management policy decision. While in most cases this method is the most desirable, there are still many inventories which are controlled based upon reorder points which have been developed in a subjective manner. Although the subjective approach, which relies upon intuitive judgment, is normally a less time-consuming method of establishing reorder points, the resulting effectiveness of control over inventory is diminished. The subjective method of establishing reorder points can also make a company overly dependent upon the judgment of one individual. With very few exceptions, a comparison of reorder point systems based upon both subjective and objective approaches will indicate that the objective method results in a more effective control of inventory as compared with the subjective approach. Prior to discussing the subject of how much to order, several of the more popular techniques will be described relative to reorder points.

Routine Safety Stocks Expressed in Weeks of Average Demand

Inventory class	Lead time		
	4 weeks or less	5 to 13 weeks	13 or more weeks
A	2	3	4
B	3	4	5
C	6	8	10

VISUAL REVIEW

A highly subjective method of determining when to reorder is a visual review of stock in inventory. For example, in the old-time general store, the owner would inspect his inventory and determine what should be ordered. This technique still has limited application where the cost of the inventory is low and the cost of control needs to be minimized, for example, a small inventory of office supplies. Control is based upon the judgment of the individual ordering and a periodic review of the items being ordered.

TWO-BIN SYSTEM

The two-bin, or reserve stock system, is a method of control commonly used in connection with "C" type items. Under this type of control, it is not necessary to maintain a perpetual record of inventory status because the need to reorder is determined as a result of physically removing material from inventory. A two-bin system is set up by physically separating an amount of material equal to the reorder point. This reserve stock or second bin is not used until all the stock in the primary storage bin has been used. When the primary stock bin has been exhausted and it is necessary to issue stock from the second bin, a requisition is initiated to reorder stock. During the reorder cycle, the reserve stock in the second bin is used. When the reordered stock is received, a quantity of material equal to the reorder point is again placed in the second bin; the remaining material is placed in the primary storage bin. The physical separation of the second bin, or reserve stock, can be accomplished by using partitioned bins, by placing the reserve stock in a bag within the one bin or by maintaining reserve stock quantities in an entirely separate physical storage area.

The advantages of this form of control are minimum control expense and positive physical recognition of reorder points. The principal disadvantages are the limited information available regarding inventory status of items, lack of monthly usage data, and reliance on storeroom personnel to initiate requisitions when the reserve stock is first used.

MIN-MAX SYSTEM

The minimum-maximum (min-max) system is frequently used in connection with manual inventory control systems. The minimum quantity is established in the same way as any reorder point. The maximum is the minimum quantity plus the optimum order lot size. In practice, a requisi-tion is initiated when a withdrawal reduces the inventory below the mini-mum level; the order quantity is the maximum minus the inventory status after the withdrawal. If the final withdrawal reduces the stock level substan-tially below the minimum level, the order quantity will be larger than the calculated optimum order lot quantity.

The effectiveness of a min-max system is determined by the method and precision with which the minimum and maximum parameters are established. If these parameters are based upon arbitrary judgments with a limited factual basis, the system will be limited in its effectiveness. If the minimums are based on an objective rational basis, the system can be very effective.

REORDER POINT—EOQ SYSTEM

This system is normally based upon the use of equations and related deci-sion tables or charts to establish objectively the reorder point and the order quantity (EOQ). These equations quantitatively balance conflicting cost objectives, based on information in the data base, so as to determine the course of action which will minimize total costs. The method of estab-lishing the optimum order quantity will be reviewed in the next section of this chapter. When equations are used in establishing reorder points and order quantities, the set of equations used are referred to as a control model. The sophistication of the inventory control model is based upon the number of variables incorporated into the equations and the com-plexities of the statistical-mathematical techniques associated with the equations. In many cases, one of the principal problems associated with complex models, that of long mathematical calculations, can be resolved by developing tables and charts which reflect the result of the equations at various incremental levels. This approach has been successfully applied to the determination of reorder points as well as to that of order quantities.

A reorder point—EOQ system can be applied to all categories of inven-tory; however, the sophistication of the model used may be varied accord-ing to the inventory to be controlled. "A" items may justify a model which considers a large number of variables, while "C" items are controlled using a more simplified model.

RESERVATION SYSTEM

A reservation system is actually a modification of either the min-max system or the reorder point—EOQ system. Instead of simply reducing the inventory level as a result of physical disbursements, a reservation system recognizes requirements *prior to* disbursement and breaks down the stock status report in terms of available stock as well as physical stock. In effect, a reservation is made for known material requirements, such as orders received prior to physical disbursement. The available stock is normally defined as the physical stock on hand, minus open requirements, plus stock on order. The reorder point in a reservation system is based upon the available stock balance rather than the physical stock balance. The advantage of this type of system is that the need to reorder is recognized at an earlier point in time, thereby permitting action to be taken which may prevent a stock-out. Reservation systems are in common use throughout business, especially in regard to finished goods and to materials required for manufacturing operations with long production lead times.

In the case of fixed build schedules, reservations can be determined by multiplying the items comprising the bills of material by the production forecast. In some cases this explosion routine also recognizes reservations (requirements) in terms of time periods, or time "buckets." When this is done, the bills of material must include the lead times associated with each item on the bill of material. After requirements have been identified with time periods, they are netted against available stock to determine when additional orders should be placed. A time bucketing of material requirements normally requires a great deal of data manipulation and as a result is usually confined to computer-based inventory management systems.

In summary, there are a number of techniques which can be used to determine when to order. The particular technique that should be used will depend upon a number of factors which are related to the cost of the items and the expense of maintaining the controls.

ORDER QUANTITIES

Having determined the need to reorder material, a decision must be made as to how much material should be ordered. When this decision is based upon a quantitative analysis of related costs, the quantity to be ordered is frequently referred to as the economic order quantity, or EOQ. The term "economic order quantity" implies that a specific order quantity will result in the lowest total variable expenditures to a company in terms of the variables included in the quantitative analysis and of the assumptions inherent in the equation being used.

If there were no variations in demand or replenishment lead time, the problems of inventory control would be lessened considerably. The only major problems would then center about the determination of economic production, purchasing or delivery quantities so as to balance the expenses of carrying stock against the expenses resulting from the initiation and receipt of replenishment orders, and considerations relating to price discounts for quantity purchases.

One of the earliest developments in the use of mathematical techniques in the area of inventory control was the economic lot size or economic order quantity formula. Theoretically, the economic order quantity Q corresponds to the point at which the annual carrying and ordering expenses are equal.

The so-called classical inventory control formula is illustrated by use of hypothetical data on page 86. This formula takes into account the following factors:

C = Unit cost of the item.

S = Estimated annual usage of the item.

E = Expense of handling an order.

K = Expense of carrying the inventory, stated in terms of per cent of cost of goods on hand.

E_c = Annual expense of carrying the inventory.

E_o = Annual expense of ordering in the case of purchased items, and the expense of production order and set up in the case of manufactured items.

The development of the economic order quantity formula can be shown as follows:

$$TVE = E_c + E_o = KC\frac{Q}{2} + \frac{S}{Q}E$$

where TVE is the total variable expense associated with the inventory (the annual expense of carrying the inventory plus the annual expense of ordering), and $Q/2$ is the average level of inventory over the year.

The minimum TVE occurs where $E_c = E_o$, giving:

$$Q = \sqrt{\frac{2SE}{KC}}$$

where Q is the economic order quantity.

While the EOQ method is frequently used in business today, the procedures for establishing the parameters used in the equation are sometimes not fully understood. In the classic EOQ there are four variables that determine the order quantity, namely: (1) the forecasted annual demand for the item expressed in units, (2) the variable expenses associated with issuing and following up an order (whether for purchase or production) in terms of dollars per order, (3) the expense of carrying inventory

Illustration of Use of Classical Inventory Control Formula

	Valves (High-unit value, low-usage item)	Washers (Low-unit value, high-usage item)
Original practice:		
1. Unit cost..	$10.00	$0.10
2. Quantity on hand at inventory date................	250	8,000
3. Annual usage...................................	1,200	120,000
4. Average order quantity..........................	300	5,000
5. Expense of carrying inventory, in per cent...........	15%	15%
6. Annual expense of carrying average inventory $\left(\dfrac{\text{Item } 4}{2} \times \text{Item } 1 \times \text{Item } 5\right)$ ignoring safety cushion	$225.00	$37.50
7. Expense of handling an order.....................	$8.00	$8.00
8. Expense of handling year's orders $\left(\dfrac{\text{Item } 3}{\text{Item } 4} \times \text{Item } 7\right)$.	$32.00	$192.00
9. Total expense of carrying and ordering year's requirements....................................	$257.00	$229.50
Indicated practice:		
10. Economic order quantity* (approx.)................	115†	11,000
11. Number of orders per year (approx.)..............	10.5	11.0
12. Annual expense of carrying economic inventory $\left(\dfrac{\text{Item } 10}{2} \times \text{Item } 1 \times \text{Item } 5\right)$..................	$86.25‡	$82.50‡
13. Expense of handling year's orders (Item 11 × Item 7)..	$84.00‡	$88.00‡
14. Total expense of carrying and ordering year's requirements....................................	$170.25	$170.50
Annual Saving:		
Amount......................................	$86.75	$59.00
Per cent.....................................	34%	26%

* Formula—Economic order quantity is square root of twice annual usage times expense of handling an order, divided by unit cost times carrying expense percentage.

† The application of the formula is:

$$Q = \sqrt{\frac{2 \times 1,200 \times 8.00}{15\% \times 10.00}} = 115 \text{ (approx.)}$$

‡ Except for "rounding off" in connection with computation of square roots and number of orders to be placed, amounts on lines 12 and 13 would be equal.

for one year, expressed as a percentage, and (4) the variable cost of one unit. It should be noted that all expenditures considered in an EOQ calculation are variable or marginal costs, sometimes referred to as out-of-pocket costs.

In determining whether an expenditure is variable, it is necessary to determine how a specific item would be influenced by the decision to change the number of orders issued or the amount of material carried in inventory.

The variable costs of placing an order with an outside vendor include the following: the cost of preparing a material requisition and a purchase order, the time (and related costs) required to follow up a purchase order, the time and costs of receiving and inspecting, the time and costs required to place the material in the proper inventory location, and the time and costs associated with making payment to the vendor and maintaining related accounting records. The costs associated with a material purchase order may vary from as little as one dollar to over fifteen dollars per order. Normally, "C" items have a lower ordering cost than "A" items because less order follow-up is required. If detailed analysis indicates a significant variation in ordering costs between "A," "B," and "C" items, separate ordering costs should be used in developing order quantities. The application of computer programs in the purchasing and accounts payable areas has tended to decrease the marginal cost of issuing an order. In many cases this lower cost of ordering has not been properly recognized in the calculation of EOQ's; thus, an analysis of the current realism of order costs used in the control model should be undertaken.

The cost of ordering a manufactured item is determined in a similar manner to that used for purchased items. The primary factors to be considered are the cost of preparing a materials requisition and a production order, the costs to set up and tear down equipment used to produce the item, material handling costs associated with movement to and from the manufacturing operation, and inspection time. The cost of ordering a manufactured item is usually comparable to the cost of ordering a purchased item, with the exception of equipment set-up and tear-down costs. This component varies widely from item to item depending upon the manufacturing processes involved. If production of an item requires a number of operations, it is necessary to add together the individual set-up and tear-down costs associated with each operation. Normally the set-up and tear-down times associated with each operation are found on the route sheet for the item.

The forecasted demand figure is the one used in determining the reorder point; however, it is expressed in terms of annual demand. The variable unit cost of an item is normally available in the standard cost records of a company.

The fourth parameter, relating to the annual cost of carrying inventory, can be controversial and requires careful review. The cost of capital is usually the largest and often also the most controversial factor included in the carrying cost. The controversy is over whether to evaluate the capital tied up in inventory in terms of current interest rates on bank loans outstanding or as long-term commitments which would require a return on investment commensurate with other capital expenditures. In the short-term, the marginal cost of capital is based primarily on bank interest rates; however, an inventory management system results in establishing levels of inventory investment on a continuing basis. As such, the capital tied up in inventory should be viewed as a long-range investment, with a cost of capital commensurate with other capital investments. If a company has an objective of returning 10% after taxes on equity investment, the cost of capital before taxes would be approximately 20%.

In some companies the cost of capital relative to inventory investment is a weighted average, which takes into consideration the debt-equity structure of the company and the relative capital costs associated with each type of financing.

In addition to the cost of capital, the inventory carrying cost calculation should consider such factors as obsolescence, spoilage, insurance, property taxes, warehousing costs, and the cost of taking physical inventories. Frequently, indications of the relative importance of these costs can be found in the accounting records. At other times, special cost studies may have to be made. Again, it should be stressed that the costs considered in establishing inventory decisions are marginal costs. If a cost is included in the inventory carrying charge, it should actually be capable of being made to vary according to the volume of the inventory being carried.

In addition to the classic EOQ, there are a number of related equations which are refinements of the classic EOQ. They take into consideration additional variables and/or operating assumptions.

One of the primary reasons for modifying the classic equation relates to the assumption in the equation that the rate of demand is constant. While this assumption may be reasonably valid a majority of the time, there are cases where demand is periodic in nature, or intrinsically highly variable. For example, a job shop operation frequently has periodic demand requirements for some types of material. When this occurs, a modified approach is required in determining order quantity that takes such variability into account. Another situation relates to equations which reflect the impact of the interrelationship between the level of safety stock associated with the reorder point and the optimum order quantity. This is accomplished by including, as variables in the order quantity calculation, the variability in lead time demand and the desired level of service.

Another very important modification in the classic EOQ equation relates to quantity discounts which are frequently available when purchasing materials. The classical EOQ formula may indicate a purchase quantity of 115 units; however, a substantial price discount may be available when 150 units are ordered, and further discounts when 200 or 500 units are ordered. Under these circumstances it is necessary to compute the EOQ quantity at each of the quantity discount levels. In evaluating quantity discounts, material cost is considered separately because it varies according to the order size.

INVENTORY SYSTEM IMPLEMENTATION

The approaches and techniques that have been discussed are of value to a business enterprise only when they become operational—when they are implemented and functioning parts of the enterprise's business systems. Experience has demonstrated that successful implementation programs have had some common ingredients. The most important are:

A soundly conceived and well-documented system design. Whether the contemplated change involves simple modification of a form or a new automated system, adequate analysis followed by reducing the desired design change to written form have time and again demonstrated their value. A well-documented design generally consists of a statement of objectives, a narrative and flow chart of the system envisioned, and some description of the change from existing practices. This package serves as a vehicle for management review and user communication and establishes the objectives of subsequent implementation efforts.

An implementation plan specifying tasks, time frame, milestones and outputs, manpower requirements, and managerial responsibilities. Developing such a plan insures that management will have a realistic assessment of calendar time and resource requirements. The plan also serves as a "road map" and as the principal tool for monitoring progress against accomplishment.

Continuing meaningful management participation and commitment. Because of the potential broad gauge impact of an implementation program relating to an inventory control system, the most effective way to oversee such a project is through the formation of a Steering Committee comprised of the top management of key areas such as manufacturing, finance, marketing engineering, and data processing. This group generally provides guidance and formally monitors progress.

Effective communications with user groups and affected areas. By beginning implementation activities with an appropriate announcement and maintaining effective two way communications, a number of highly desirable results can be achieved. Among these are gaining employee acceptance and support, providing initial system orientation, and minimizing rumors and resultant anxiety.

Formation of a project task team. The day-to-day responsibility for carrying out a system implementation effort normally rests with a project team. For an inventory control system project, such a team might be composed of a systems analyst, an accountant, and representatives of involved user groups.

A well conceived, carefully organized, and closely directed implementation effort is the key to translating sound inventory control concepts and techniques into systems contributing to profitability.

SUMMARY

The intent of this chapter has been to explore the concept of inventory management in terms of practical techniques commonly used in business today. In addition to discussing the techniques, considerable stress has been placed upon the importance of developing an accurate data base relative to inventory decisions. The nature and importance of the parameters included in various inventory control equations have also been discussed. In conclusion, it should be stated that the benefits from modern inventory management control techniques are realized only when effective systems have been implemented by operating management. Techniques are not an end in themselves, but rather a means to an end—improved profitability.

FIVE

Concepts of "Cost" for Purposes of Business Management

In one way or another management concerns itself with every expenditure made, and it tries to obtain from each the maximum benefits for the business. Accounting aids in the accomplishment of this objective by presenting the financial data so as to provide a means of judging the wisdom of past decisions and predicting the consequences of adopting any particular course of future action.

The decisions made by management always involve risk. Sound (or lucky) decisions help the company economically. Unsound (or unlucky) decisions hurt. Sound decisions are made by informed managers. Of primary importance is the gathering of accurate information about events both past and present and realistic forecasts about the future.

THE ACCOUNTING FUNCTION

To understand the steps taken in the determination of income, it is necessary to have an appreciation of the bases underlying the classification of expenditures for purposes of accounting for, and maintaining control over, the capital utilized in the operations. In this context, "expenditures" include all transactions which result in the release of assets or the incurring of liabilities.

Controlling expenditures, with the basic and related objective of maximizing revenues, is a major factor in the success of every enterprise. At all times, the best efforts of management are directed at improving efficiency, which means getting the most for every dollar spent.

Much of the information required by business management is of a non-accounting nature, such as that provided by scientists, engineers, market researchers, and industrial psychologists; however, most business activities have an economic effect. The recording, classifying, analyzing, and summarizing into meaningful reports of the economic effects of these activities are all part of the accounting function.

The information provided by the accounting process must be accurate, timely, clear, and meaningful. Moreover, the information must be tailored toward the use to which it will be put and not considered as an end in itself.

MEANING OF "COST" AND "EXPENSE"

The attention given to definitions of the words "cost" and "expense" by various authoritative writers reveals the concern accountants have for their proper usage. Nevertheless, there is considerable confusion over just what the words should mean. Of particular interest is the fact that one is often used to define the other.

Set forth below are typical examples of definitions, taken from three sources:

Example A:

"Cost" is the amount, measured in money, of cash expended or other property transferred, capital stock issued, services performed or a liability incurred in consideration of goods or services received or to be received. Costs can be classified as unexpired or expired. . . . Expired costs are those which are not applicable to the production of future revenues and for that reason are treated as deductions from current revenues or are charged against retained earnings. Examples of such expired costs are costs of products or other assets sold or disposed of, and current expenses. . . . "Expense" in its broadest sense includes all expired costs which are deductible from revenues. In income statements, distinctions are often made between various types of expired costs by captions or titles including such terms as cost, expense, or loss, e.g., cost of goods or services sold, operating expenses, selling and administrative expenses, and loss on sale of property. These distinctions seem generally useful, and indicate that the narrower use of the term "expense" refers to such items as operating, selling, or administrative expenses, interest and taxes. . . .[1]

---

[1] Committee on Terminology, AICPA, "Cost, Expense, and Loss," *Accounting Terminology Bulletins*, No. 4 (July, 1957).

Example B:

Cost: 1. An expenditure or outlay of cash, other property, capital stock, or services, or the incurring of a liability therefor, identified with goods or services purchased or with any loss incurred, and measured in terms of the amount of cash paid or payable or the market value of other property, capital stock, or services given in exchange. . . . 2. Hence, the object of any such expenditure or outlay; e.g., direct labor in the expression "direct labor cost."

Expense: 1. Expired cost: any item or class of cost of (or loss from) carrying on an activity; a present or past expenditure defraying a present operating cost or representing an irrecoverable cost or loss; capital expenditure written down or off. . . . 2. A class term for expenditures recognized as operating costs of a current or past period.[2]

Example C:

The term "cost" . . . refer[s] to the amount invested in obtaining a product or a service that is expected to be useful later in a business concern, useful in obtaining sales revenue. The "investment" may be made directly by a cash payment or by a promise to pay, or by converting some kinds of assets into others. "Expense" on the other hand . . . refer[s] to expired costs, and particularly those that are charged to profit and loss for a period. . . . When the product is sold, its "cost" will be charged to profit and loss as "cost of goods sold"—an expense account. . . . The distinction is more appropriately applied to product costs than to administrative or distributive costs. The latter may be thought of as an investment in a valuable service, but it is the nature of the service to be used as fast as it is created, or as fast as the cost is recognized. Hence, as is customary, it may as well be called expense as soon as the cost of obtaining it is recorded.[3]

The word "cost" is the workhorse of accountants in discussing expenditures.

The *Accountants' Cost Handbook* lists twenty-two types of costs and states that the "word 'cost' is used in such a wide variety of ways that it is advisable to use it with an adjective or phrase which will convey the shade of meaning intended." [4] Included in this list are period costs, fixed and variable costs, controllable and noncontrollable costs, future costs, discretionary costs, and postponable costs.

Even among trained accountants, there is a tendency to consider all expenditures as "costs," when discussing the impact of the expenditures in the determination of income. In addition to the conventional term "cost of goods sold," a large variety of income charges are referred to as "costs." Even the charges which are customarily called "expenses" when incurred (such as general, selling, and administrative expenses) are often referred

[2] Kohler, *A Dictionary for Accountants* (5th ed., 1975), pp. 139, 201.
[3] Vance, *Theory and Technique of Cost Accounting* (rev. ed., 1958), p. 14.
[4] Dickey, *Accountants' Cost Handbook* (2d ed., 1960), p. 111.

to as "costs." It is not unusual to see discussions of administrative costs, distribution costs, legal costs, research and development costs, and finance costs.

The broad concept of "cost" as including all expenditures appears to be influenced by the fact that for almost every item of property owned by a business it is possible to establish an amount generally recognized as its cost. The cost of a trade receivable is the amount which would have been realized had the sale been made for cash rather than on credit. The cost of an insurance policy is the amount of the premium. The cost of a particular machine or automobile is its purchase price. When applied to these items, the cost concept is readily understandable. There is not the same degree of clarity when the word "cost" is applied to expenditures for such items as utility bills, the janitor's salary, a salesman's airline fare or hotel bill, and interest on a loan at the bank. When used in connection with statements of income, some limitation on the concept of cost appears desirable if the accounting function is to be fully performed.

Similarly, there is no particular benefit derived from applying the single word "expense" to all amounts deductible from revenues in determining the income resulting from the business activities of a particular period. This results in classifying as one group not only the amounts paid for gas and electricity, office maintenance, travel, and interest, but also the balance of a trade receivable which must be deducted from gross income because it is uncollectible, the portion of an insurance premium which is allocated to the period, and the provision for depreciation on machinery and automobiles.

Accountants could help themselves, and the results of their work would be better understood, if more specific and limited meanings were attached to the nouns "cost" and "expense." One group of terms which has been found to be useful is suggested on page 100 for the purpose of illustrating how expenditures may be classified to better appreciate the factors having a bearing on the determination of income.

MEANING OF "FIXED" AND "VARIABLE"

The effect of changes in the level of activity on the behavior of costs and expenses is most commonly reflected by a segregation based upon each item being either "fixed" or "variable." Simply stated, this procedure makes a distinction between fixed costs and expenses, which are not affected by changes in rate of activity, and variable cost and expenses, which increase with increases in activity and decrease with decreases in activity.

The segregation of business expenditures as being either "fixed" or "variable" reflects tendencies which actually exist; but the segregation is not as simple as the phrase "fixed-variable" implies. There are many qualifications and limitations which are essential to proper understanding. The significance to management of the fixed-variable segregation may be exaggerated.

The level of activity of the various phases of a business is under the control of management. For example, management determines the products and the quantity of each to be scheduled for production in a given period; it can order decreased or increased effort by the maintenance department; and it can direct a stepped up or reduced advertising campaign. This ability to set levels of activity does not, however, provide a direct means of controlling costs and expenses. It is as though activity levels had a power of direction in themselves. Although the activity levels are subject to control, once set they take over and determine to a considerable extent the course of future expenditures. Management must, therefore, understand the ways in which activity levels affect expenses.

The fixed-variable segregation may be a valid indication of the *tendencies* of the expenditures to behave in the way described, but they cannot necessarily be fitted neatly into one category or another—or even a third, middle-ground category of semifixed or semivariable.

It cannot be said that a large number of costs and expenses are so fixed as to be completely unaffected by the level of activity. This statement would imply that if there were no activity the cost would still be incurred. There would also be an implication that while other factors, such as inflation, might have some effect on the amount of the expenditure, the level of activity would have no effect. At the other extreme, few costs and expenses are so variable that they would cease if there were no activity. Changes in the amount of most variable costs and expenses are not directly proportional to changes in activity levels. Almost every item of cost or expense is both partially fixed and partially variable.

There are many costs and expenses which vary with volume, not in a uniform pattern but rather in stages. Costs and expenses of this type are constant for a certain range of volume. At a higher level of activity, additional costs are incurred, which remain constant for a certain range of volume. Some examples are factory supervision, service department expenses such as the typing pool or duplicating department, and the expense of having available for use such facilities as overhead material-handling equipment. Every usage of the fixed-variable segregation must take into consideration the semi-variable nature of most costs and expenses.

Another qualification in the fixed-variable segregation is the period of time involved. The shorter the period of time, the greater the number of items which tend to be fixed. The ability to carry on a particular business activity (such as the production of castings, or sales distribution in a certain territory) is not usually changed from month to month. On the other hand, management decisions as to the activity of the business can always result in changes in capacity over a longer period of time.

Additional machines are purchased, buildings are remodeled and additions are constructed, even entire new plants are built for the purpose of meeting increased needs. Conversely, excess capacity of long standing can result in leasing all or part of a facility to another user, sale of an unused plant or excess equipment, or other reductions in response to lesser requirements. For these reasons costs and expenses are actually fixed for relatively short time periods, and all tend to become variable over long periods of time.

At best the fixed-variable segregation only describes the effect of volume on expenditures. Not included are the effects of such items as changes in production technology, product mix, economy measures, such as deferring maintenance, or non-receiving expenditures such as year-end bonuses. There are numerous causes other than volume for changes in the amount of any class of expenditure.

These observations with respect to the fixed-variable segregation lead to the conclusion that it is a tool to be used with care and an understanding of the underlying patterns of the costs and expenses to be classified. Within the limitations inherent in the segregation, it is a useful device widely employed.

The National Association of Accountants has published the results of a study entitled "Separating and Using Costs as Fixed and Variable," in which it is stated that such separations "are widely performed and are put to an increasing number of uses helpful to management." [6] The report lists, in addition to flexible budgeting, the following applications found to be in use:

1. Management of utilization of facilities through a fixed cost rate.
2. Understanding of the company's profit structure.
3. Adjustment of operations to market conditions.
4. Determining relative profitability of products.
5. Marginal cost information to aid in sales and purchase price decisions or utilization capacity.
6. Development of planning as a major activity.
7. Evaluation of proposed capital outlays.

[6] National Association of Accountants, *Accounting Practice Report*, No. 10 (June, 1960).

8. Assistance in making other decisions among alternatives which will differ in cost effects.

It will be noted that these applications of the fixed-variable segregation practice principally represent special studies prepared for a particular management purpose. There is no inference that this segregation is the most informative for all purposes.

FACTORS IN CLASSIFYING EXPENDITURES

The selection of a basis for classifying expenditures depends, in part, upon the level of management for which the classification is being prepared. At the departmental level, certain expenses must be recognized as fixed, because the decision was made at a divisional level. Similarly, the divisional management may have no direct control over other items. From the standpoint of general management, all items could be considered controllable and should be viewed in an entirely different light. The rental payments for a fleet of trucks, for example, may have been decided upon only after extensive study by top management; however, at the departmental level the rental is fixed. Any analysis of costs and expenses must therefore be made with a realization of the authority possessed by the user to effect changes in the operations.

The amount of detail required is another consideration in classifying expenditures. In general, the lower the level of management, the greater the need for detail. A superintendent might need to know every item of expense incurred in his department. A plant manager needs reports in larger areas of responsibility, and there may be delegation of responsibility for the detailed control of expenditures. Top management will be concerned with the effect of such decisions as those involving capital asset changes, product selections, make-or-buy alternatives, and territory assignments. The reports, forecasts, and budgets designed as a basis for this class of broad decisions are normally in summary rather than in detailed form.

In some instances, the behavior pattern of certain costs and expenses will depend upon the accounting procedures adopted. Accounting procedures generally have no effect on when cash is paid or other assets are exchanged to obtained goods and services. The timing of payments is determined by the contract between the parties. Accounting procedures do, however, determine when and how a change in the assets owned should be recognized, and the time and manner in which assets are transformed into costs and expenses. Many areas in addition to inventories afford examples: depreciation provisions, instalment purchases under a contract which is ostensibly a lease, repairs which are so major as to be actual improvements to an asset, choice between the cash basis and accrual basis of accounting for liabilities, the designation of certain items as "period" charges because they are considered attributable to the current accounting period and should not be carried forward to be deducted from revenues of future periods.

The accounting procedures chosen govern the recognition of what has taken place, but they do not alter the facts. Accounting procedures themselves cannot affect the ultimate profitability of a company. What they can do is affect periodic income determinations. To the extent that accounting reports are relied upon, decisions are influenced by the procedures used in preparing them. Different procedures give different results and, presumably, could lead to different decisions. For example, providing for straight-line depreciation results in larger amounts of computed income for years of capital asset expansion than does double-declining-balance depreciation. The company is equally profitable, but the bookkeeping entries are different.

In the same way, the amount assigned to a particular inventory does not have any effect upon the quantity or condition of the goods on hand. If a company has 831 units of finished goods, 2,306 units of work in process at the sixth stage in the process, and 1,097 units of raw materials, no accounting procedure will change those facts.

The influence of accounting procedures on the behavior of expenses must be considered when analyzing expenditures for the purpose of making decisions during interim periods. It must also be considered when preparing expense classifications. Expenses which appear to fit a classification by their very nature may, on closer examination, prove to fit the classification only because of the accounting procedures used. Depreciation based on the passage of time may appear to be "fixed" with respect to activity levels. Where depreciation is computed on the basis of units produced, it would become "variable" with respect to activity levels.

RECOGNIZING ALTERNATIVE COURSES OF ACTION

The practicability of alternative courses of action and the effect of the alternatives on net income must also be understood in classifying expenditures. Over a long period there are alternatives to the making of all types of expenditures, and the nature of the alternatives has a bearing on the degree of control possessed by management.

Certain types of expenses may be readily reduced or eliminated; however, the result may be a loss of revenues or an increase in other substitute expenditures. In the case of a wholesale food distributor, the sales force may be reduced from ten to eight, but this action could result in a decrease in volume. In the case of a manufacturer, five production lines may be cut to four, but the per unit cost could increase because of the payment of overtime and shift premiums. A retailer can discontinue deliveries to outlying districts, but some customers may be lost.

Some expenses have ready substitutes, for example, owned automobiles can be substituted for leased cars, certain materials (such as stampings) can be manufactured or purchased, and sales can be made either from branch offices or through independent distributors.

Even more serious consequences may follow a decision to reduce or eliminate other types of costs or expenses, that is, those whose change would involve heavy penalties and those which are required for the company to be prepared to carry on a vital activity.

The penalties resulting from a decision to avoid certain future expenditures involve losses on sales of assets. Special-purpose industrial properties are frequently worth their investment only to the initial owner. Except for the effect of inflation or an increase in value of specific properties due to other economic forces, sales of such assets to stop the expenses involved in their ownership usually involve losses. It is seldom that a purchaser is found who can use the assets as profitably in the same location for the same purposes.

Some expenses are the result of contracts, such as interest on debentures. These expenses can often be stopped only by defaulting on the contract and incurring damages. Rent under a five-year lease on a building to be used as a gas station continues regardless of whether a new expressway takes all the traffic away from the road on which the facility is built. Without an escape clause, that rent could only be stopped by substituting a costly settlement.

Some expenses are necessary for a business to carry on vital activities. If the company does manufacturing, it must have a plant. Even if the plant were locked up tight during a prolonged strike, if owned, the real estate taxes and similar expenses would not stop; and, if leased, the rent would continue. Merely to retain the right to be recognized as a corporation may involve yearly franchise taxes. The alternative to expenses of this kind may require abandonment of a vital activity.

Within certain contexts it is convenient to consider some expenditures as being unchangeable. This is done with a reservation similar to the limitation placed on the fixed-variable segregation. This designation does no more than reflect generally that the amount of the expenditures will not fluctuate materially within certain ranges of activity levels and for certain periods of time. Thus, certain expenses are regarded as unchangeable under conditions of "business as usual." They are not in fact unchangeable, but any change may involve considerable operating difficulty and adverse economic consequences.

SUGGESTED CLASSIFICATIONS FOR EXPENDITURES

The foregoing discussion of concepts of "cost" for purposes of business management indicates the need for development of a meaningful classification of expenditures. The same classification may not be significant for multiple purposes, and the primary consideration in preparing any compilation of economic data is to present information which will be most useful to the reader.

Although a fixed-variable segregation will be the most practical in accomplishing a stated objective in many specific cases, it has its limitations. In considering the significance of the reported operating results for a particular period, there are instances when management will better understand the factors which have had an effect on net income if all expenditures are classified as prime costs, controllable expenses, recurring expenses, and continuing expenses. In the determination of income, if the entire amount expended for an asset consumed, lost, or disposed of is deductible from revenues of a particular period, it could be denominated a "prime cost" (such as cost of goods sold); but if only a portion of the cost of an asset is allocable to the period, the amount deductible would be classified into one of the three types of expenses, for example, a provision for depreciation.

Under this proposal the phrase "prime cost" is confined to expenditures resulting in the acquisition of assets—tangible or intangible, but in any event identifiable property which can be recognized as being owned. Prime costs include expenditures directly resulting in the addition of "form utility" or "place utility" to other property, in the sense that form and place utility are "goods" from an economic standpoint. The wages of productive labor and the transportation charges incurred in moving tangible goods to a desired location are therefore classified as *prime costs*.

The expenditures which do not represent prime costs are considered in a classification system under which *controllable expenses* are those incurred as a result of a current (or continuing) decision of management, *recurring expenses* are those necessary to keep the business operating even on a minimum basis, and *continuing expenses* are those which have resulted from decisions of management in a prior period.

Controllable expenses include such items as the maintenance of production equipment and gas and oil for delivery trucks. Expenses of this kind can be started or stopped by current decisions. Although management does not consciously decide every day whether to run certain equipment, the equipment runs as a result of a decision by management. This type of expense can be most readily changed, and the consequences which follow from the alternatives can be predicted and measured with reasonable accuracy. As a practical matter in day-to-day operations, assuming no major changes in internal or external conditions, the controllable expenses occupy the major portion of the attention of all levels of management.

Recurring expenses include such items as salaries of persons essential to operating the business, retainer fees, insurance, and franchise taxes and license fees required because of being organized for business. After a business activity has been started, recurring expenses require the least attention from management. They can be changed only with the greatest difficulty, if at all, and change may mean going out of business or into another activity.

Continuing expenses include such items as obligations under extended term contracts, pension plan expenses, salaries of persons not indispensable but hired on a permanent basis, depreciation with respect to long-lived assets, oil exploration, and expenditures incident to specific research, and other long-term special projects. The characteristic of continuing expenses is that they are largely determined by single decisions resulting in expenses which continue until other major decisions are made. Like recurring expenses, continuing expenses must be lived with for a considerable period; but they can generally be changed without the company going out of business or abandoning a major activity. Continuing expenses are in a middle ground between controllable and recurring expenses. They are subject to some control, but only with considerable difficulty. They require periodic review, but not daily attention.

The terms "controllable expense," "recurring expense," and "continuing expense" reflect the broad characteristics of expenses as to their origin and manageability. They are useful to characterize specific expenses for the use of management in its deliberations and decision making.

FACTORS IN DETERMINATIONS OF PRODUCT COSTS

In order for an enterprise to operate at a profit, it is necessary to recover through revenues all costs and expenses incurred. From this standpoint it is unimportant how the expenditures are classified. The objectives in classifying expenditures are primarily to reflect what has happened, to provide a basis for controlling both costs and expenses, and to indicate how the maximum benefits can be obtained from future expenditures. The manner in which these objectives are accomplished will depend upon the complexity of the organization, the attitude of the individuals who are compiling and using the economic data, and the availability of information.

There is no single basis for classifying expenditures which will be the most useful in all cases; and judgment is involved in applying any classification to a particular series of transactions. Consequently, with respect to a computation of the *cost* of a particular product or the *cost* of the entire production of a plant or enterprise during a stated period, no one amount can be said to be "correct" to the exclusion of all others. Cost determinations are made to be used for management purposes and are not an ultimate goal of the accounting function.

The elements represented in a computed cost for a specific product or for the production of a plant or enterprise are generally expenditures for raw materials, direct labor, and manufacturing (including extracting) overhead. No special definitions are needed for the material and direct labor cost elements, as the appropriate expenditures can usually be identified and are commonly referred to as "prime costs."

Expenditures which cannot be readily and specifically assigned to particular production are lumped into the category of overhead for disposition. It is then a question of which elements of overhead are to be included in cost.

The initial step is to ascertain which expenses will not be included because they do not aid in the productive activity. These expenses will not be included in overhead under any concept of cost. One obvious example is the expenses which must be incurred in connection with a closed plant.

There are several viewpoints as to the extent to which the expenses relating to production should be included in cost as a matter of principle. The alternatives with respect to the inclusion of overhead in production costs may, at a risk of oversimplification, be grouped as follows:

1. *Prime costing*, under which no overhead is included.
2. *Direct costing*, under which controllable expenses directly attributable to production are included but no fixed overhead is included.
3. *Analytical costing*,* under which overhead expenses attributable to production are included, except for the portion not taken into account because of the production facilities not being fully utilized.
4. *All-inclusive costing*,* under which the entire amount of overhead expense attributable to production is included.

---

* A related term, "full absorption costing," refers to the method of allocating overhead expenses attributable to production under the federal income tax regulations 1.471–11 (see Appendix C).

Circumstances may be such as to make it appropriate and useful to apply procedures falling into any of these four categories in preparing statements and reports for internal management purposes; however, management should understand what procedures have been followed. If the computed costs are utilized in determining selling prices, this is particularly important. The business will show a profit only if the revenues realized are adequate to cover the aggregate of all costs and expenses regardless of how individual expenditures are classified.

Prime costing is applied most frequently where the relative magnitude of the overhead expenses makes them of little importance. It has the advantage of simplicity.

Direct costing and analytical costing procedures are premised, in part, upon a recognition of the fact that, in addition to *controllable* expenses, the items of overhead include *recurring* expenses which are necessary to provide the capacity to carry on production activities, and *continuing* expenses resulting from decisions previously made to secure the production facilities which are available for use. It is fundamental that in order to be in a position to carry on production activities, a certain level of recurring and continuing expenses must be assumed. During any period, production may be all or only a part of the total possible with the available capacity. The question is, "how much of the expense required to provide that capacity to produce should be considered as part of the cost of the actual production?"

Under a direct costing procedure, none of the recurring and continuing expenses are included in the computations of cost. The reasoning is that the expenses were incurred as a consequence of decisions which had nothing to do with any particular units of production, they would have been incurred whether or not any specific units had been produced, and corresponding amounts of expense will be incurred in subsequent periods, regardless of the quantity of the current production. The practice of not including in overhead certain items considered to be period expenses is a partial application of the direct costing principle.

Under an analytical costing procedure, the recurring and continuing expenses are included in the computations of cost on the basis of a comparison between the actual rate of activity and a predetermined norm. For example, these expenses for a particular period might be included in cost to the extent they are allocable to the portion of the available capacity which was actually utilized. To the extent that the expenses are allocable to the unused portion of available capacity, they are considered to represent a loss. This is an economic loss attributable to the level of production set by management during the period and is not part of the cost of the units actually produced.

All-inclusive costing is most frequently applied in smaller enterprises where detailed analyses of the various expense accounts are not available. It may also be appropriate where a plant is consistently operated at a capacity rate or where the aggregate amount of overhead is relatively small. It shares with prime costing the advantage of simplicity. In the majority of instances there will be some elements of overhead attributable to events which are not customarily a part of plant operations, and the all-inclusive costing concept will not be literally applied where the amount of expense resulting from such events can be identified. Examples of events which could justify special recognition in determining the overhead expenses to be included in cost computations are shortages of materials; receipt of defective materials; labor slow-downs and strikes; and interruptions of production caused by a flood, fire, or other casualty. In a business which does not have a regular program for model or product changes, special recognition might also be given, even under an all-inclusive costing concept, to the effect upon expenses of disruptions caused by such factors as the introduction of a new product, the training of an expanded labor force, and the realignment of facilities incident to equipping a plant to manufacture a different product.

APPLYING OVERHEAD ON BASIS OF ACTIVITY

If the amount of overhead to be included in cost computations is based upon the level of activity during a particular period, the activity level at which all the expenses will be so included must first be established. Among the standards which may be used for this purpose are the following types of levels of activity:

1. Actual
2. Expected
3. Average
4. Practical capacity
5. Theoretical capacity

Depending upon the circumstances, the standard and actual levels of activity may be measured appropriately in terms of direct labor cost, direct labor hours, machine hours, units of product, or any other factor. Within the same plant or business many different measures may be used in connection with various departments or cost centers.

The first two procedures listed, based upon actual and expected levels of activity, are similar in intent and result. They are applicable to all-inclusive costing, and the thought behind each is to apply all proper overhead expenses of the current period to production costs. The only difference between them is the timing of the application of overhead during the accounting period. As regards the period as a whole, both procedures use actual production as a standard.

To illustrate the mechanics of each of the types of measures of activity and the significance of the different results obtained, an example will be used of an operating unit of The H Company for which the basic factors are as follows:

Summary of Data Used in Illustrating Application of Overhead

	Number of units produced	Rate of activity based upon a standard representing			
		Actual production	Average production	Practical capacity	Theoretical capacity
Standard number of units per year		*	3,200	4,000	4,500
Actual number of units produced and per cent of standard:					
1st year	3,000	100%	93.75%	75.0%	66.7%
2d year	4,500	100	140.63	112.5	100.0
3d year	2,400	100	75.00	60.0	53.3
4th year	2,700	100	84.37	67.5	60.0
5th year	3,400	100	106.25	85.0	75.5
Total	16,000				

* Although a standard may be used for interim statements based upon expected production for the period, the computations for the entire period will reflect only the actual production.

In this simplified example, the aggregate amount of overhead incurred during the five-year period is $360,000, or $22.50 per unit; but there are material variations from this simple average under all of the procedures illustrated.

Using actual activity as a basis for the application of overhead, the computations are made after the period in which the activity takes place. At the close of the period, the total production is determined and is divided into the total amount of overhead in order to establish the overhead rate per unit of production. The computation is as follows:

Application of Overhead Based on Actual Production

	Number of units produced	Overhead incurred	Overhead per unit
1st year	3,000	$ 70,000	$23.33
2d year	4,500	84,000	18.67
3d year	2,400	65,000	27.08
4th year	2,700	67,000	24.81
5th year	3,400	74,000	21.76
Total	16,000	$360,000	

This procedure applies all overhead expenses to cost in the period incurred. The shorter the period for which the computations are made, the greater the likelihood of fluctuations in the overhead per unit.

When the expected activity is used as a basis for the application of overhead, both the production and amount of overhead are estimated in advance for each accounting period. An overhead rate is calculated for use during the period. The expected activity method will apply all overhead expense to cost in the period incurred if the estimates are accurate. If the estimates are not accurate, there will either be an excess of expense over overhead applied (called "underabsorbed overhead") or an excess of overhead applied over expense (called "overabsorbed overhead"). These amounts are usually small, especially if the accounting period is short or the estimating good. Small excesses will be taken into account directly in computing net income, but larger differences can be applied to cost of sales and to inventory through the use of supplementary overhead rates after the close of the period.

From a theoretical viewpoint the use of an average level of activity may be justified if it is assumed the total production during the period the facility will be used in the business can be estimated with reasonable accuracy and either (a) the overhead amounts will be constant or (b) the total of the overhead amount for the entire period can also be estimated so that a constant overhead rate per unit can be applied. These are not conditions commonly found in practice. With respect to the operating unit represented by the current example, the total production of 16,000 units was probably not predictable, the overhead incurred was not constant at $72,000 per annum, and the aggregate amount of overhead for the five-year period could not have been calculated in advance. The argument advanced for the use of this type of average level of activity standard in applying overhead is that the expenses which recur or continue, period after period, have been knowingly assumed as a result of sound economic decisions by management. At the time of making the decision to acquire the production facility and assume the burden of these expenses, it was known (presumably) that the production would not be consistent because the facility would be used only to the extent that the company would be able to sell the product. It is further reasoned that idle time during slack periods was contemplated, and that idle time expenses are part of production costs during the periods when production is above average. Logic then leads to the conclusion that any amounts of underabsorbed or overabsorbed expenses at the end of any particular period should be carried forward to be offset in subsequent operating periods. Regardless of the logic of this approach to the application of overhead, practical considerations preclude its use. Business management is not clairvoyant, and few expenses are actually fixed in amount.

The use of a different average level of activity concept may, however, be meaningful with respect to a relatively short phase of a business cycle. Although annual production will fluctuate with sales, it may be practicable for The H Company to estimate that over a five-year period approximately 16,000 units will be produced and sold. It is known that the overhead expenses will not be constant, and it is generally impossible to estimate with a reasonable degree of accuracy what the total overhead amount will be for five years. The use of an average activity standard by the operating unit of The H Company under these conditions can be illustrated by the tabulation above. Where this type of use is made of the average activity standard, the amounts of overabsorbed or underabsorbed overhead are taken into account directly in computing net income for the period. These amounts will not necessarily offset one another and require analysis from

Application of Overhead Based on Average Production

	Percentage of units produced to standard	Incurred	Applied Amount	Applied Per unit	Over- (or under-) absorbed
1st year	93.75	$ 70,000	$ 65,625	$21.87	$ (4,375)
2d year	140.63	84,000	118,129	26.25	34,129
3d year	75.00	65,000	48,750	20.31	(16,250)
4th year	84.37	67,000	56,528	20.93	(10,472)
5th year	106.25	74,000	78,625	23.12	4,625
Total		$360,000	$367,657		$ 7,657

a management viewpoint. They reflect variations not only in volume but also in overhead expense. Had the overhead incurred been $72,000 each year, the per-unit amount applied would have been $22.50 in each case, and there would not have been a net overabsorbed amount of $7,657. Application of $26.25 of overhead per unit in the second year, for example, results from the fact that the overhead incurred was $84,000—an increase of 20 per cent over the previous year. An explanation for the increase should be obtained. Possibly it was partially the result of having to engage additional supervisory personnel because the production was increased from 3,000 to 4,500 units; however, it should be ascertained that the additional expense was needed. The 50 per cent increase in the number of units produced is gratifying, but inquiry should be made as to how this was achieved. There may have been inefficiencies in the operations during the first year which can be avoided in subsequent years.

The use of practical or theoretical capacity as a standard in determining the portion of incurred overhead to be included in cost involves establishing the number of units which will be considered as par for a given period of time, such as a month or a year.

Practical capacity allows for the estimated inevitable delays caused by necessary maintenance, unpredictable breakdowns, and the like. It reflects the manner in which management thought the facilities would be used during periods of normal demand at the time they were designed or acquired. Management decisions have a bearing on the capacity of a department or a plant. Management designates the number of days per week and the number of hours or shifts per day a plant is to be operated. Thus, the measurement of capacity is conditioned by regular anticipated usage, so that it is proper to speak of capacity based on a one-shift, five-day-a-week schedule. With enough sales orders to provide the demand, a plant could operate, year in and year out, at practical capacity. For limited periods, the production could exceed such capacity. In the absence of engineering studies, practical capacity may be established by reference to demonstrated capacity, that is, the actual production under normal operating conditions. In the present illustration, The H Company produced 4,500 units during the second year and 4,000 units might be accepted as practical capacity. In this type of situation, the amounts of overabsorbed and underabsorbed overhead are taken into account directly in computing net income for the period. Any overabsorbed overhead should be recognized as an indication that the computed costs reflect more than the expenses actually incurred during the period and that the operating conditions have been fortuitous. An explanation for the abnormally high production should be sought. Variations in the per-unit amount of

Application of Overhead Based on Practical Capacity

	Percentage of units produced to standard	Amount of overhead			
			Applied		Over- (or under-) absorbed
		Incurred	Amount	Per unit	
1st year	75.0	$ 70,000	$ 52,500	$17.50	$(17,500)
2d year	112.5	84,000	94,500	21.00	10,500
3d year	60.0	65,000	39,000	16.25	(26,000)
4th year	67.5	67,000	45,225	16.75	(21,775)
5th year	85.0	74,000	62,900	18.50	(11,100)
Total		$360,000	$294,125		$(65,875)

overhead applied reflect the trend of the total overhead expenses and should also be investigated.

Theoretical capacity would literally be that quantity which it is physically possible to produce with continuous uninterrupted production, assuming no shortages, no machine breakdowns, and no human errors. As thus conceived, it would be impossible to maintain production at theoretical capacity, since there are inevitable interruptions in all manufacturing operations over any extended period. For the purpose of determining what portion of the overhead expenses should be applied to cost, a modified version of theoretical capacity is adopted, that is, a rate of production determined by taking into account the possibility of extra shifts but with reasonable allowances for normal interruptions. If the theoretical capacity is one which is attainable even for relatively short periods, it can be useful in some cost determinations. Continuing the example, 4,500 units might be accepted as theoretical capacity for the operating unit of The H Company. As is the case when practical capacity is used as a standard, the amounts of underabsorbed overhead are taken into account directly in computing net income for the period. There will seldom, if ever, be any overabsorbed overhead, since that would indicate a level of activity in excess of theoretical capacity. Use of this type of standard does not generally develop data as meaningful as that produced by the other procedures discussed.

The amounts of overhead per unit which would be applied by The H Company under the various alternative procedures are summarized above to facilitate comparison. The effect upon income of utilizing the various procedures in assigning amounts to inventories is illustrated in Chapter 6.

Application of Overhead Based on Theoretical Capacity

	Percentage of units produced to standard	Amount of overhead			
			Applied		Over- (or under-) absorbed
		Incurred	Amount	Per unit	
1st year	66.7	$ 70,000	$ 46,690	$15.56	$(23,310)
2d year	100.0	84,000	84,000	18.67	—
3d year	53.3	65,000	34,645	14.43	(30,355)
4th year	60.0	67,000	40,200	14.88	(26,800)
5th year	75.5	74,000	55,870	16.43	(18,130)
Total		$360,000	$261,405		$(98,595)

Per-Unit Amounts Computed in Illustration of Methods of Overhead Application

	Rate of activity based upon a standard representing			
	Actual production	Average production	Practical capacity	Theoretical capacity
1st year	$23.33	$21.87	$17.50	$15.56
2d year	18.67	26.25	21.00	18.67
3d year	27.08	20.31	16.25	14.43
4th year	24.81	20.93	16.75	14.88
5th year	21.76	23.12	18.50	16.43
High	$27.08	$26.25	$21.00	$18.67
Low	18.67	20.31	16.25	14.43
Range	8.41	5.94	4.75	4.24

It is significant to observe at this point, however, that the widest range of amounts of overhead applied per unit results when actual production is used. From a management standpoint, this means that the use of such a method requires more extensive analysis to determine the reasons for fluctuations in computed costs.

SIX

Concepts of "Cost" for Purposes of Inventory Determinations

Discussions of inventories frequently proceed on the assumption that the cost for each item is a definitely known amount. This is true only in the simplest of costing problems. Any computed cost is the result of judgment exercised in making the numerous decisions required in analyzing detailed economic data and in selecting and applying the accounting procedures deemed most appropriate to the particular situation. The concepts of "cost" for purposes of inventory determinations are fundamentally special applications underlying the establishment of cost for all other phases of business management.

FACTORS INVOLVED IN DETERMINATION OF COST GENERALLY

Highlights of the discussion of concepts of "cost" for purposes of business management in Chapter 5 merit review and may be restated in general terms.

Analyzing and summarizing the economic effects of the activities of a business are part of the accounting function. In performing this function, expenditures should be classified in such a manner as will be the most helpful in securing the maximum benefits from similar future expenditures. No one classification will necessarily best serve all management purposes.

Cost determinations are made to be used and do not represent an ultimate goal.

There are no clearly established meanings for the nouns "cost" and "expense," and the significance of the adjectives "fixed" and "variable" may be exaggerated. Almost every item of cost or expense is both partially fixed and partially variable.

The fixed-variable segregation, within its inherent limitations, is a useful device and can be applied in making a variety of special-purpose studies. Any classification of expenditures should be made on a basis appropriate for the use to which it will be put. The classification and detail may have to be varied with the level of management to which the information is directed.

In order to reflect the origin and manageability of charges against income, a different type of classification is suggested: prime costs, controllable expenses, recurring expenses, and continuing expenses. This suggestion is made to emphasize that the word "cost" should not be applied by habit to every income charge. Most income charges can better be denominated as some type of "expense."

Accounting procedures will not alter the facts, but they can affect the time and manner of recognizing certain types of costs and expenses.

All costs and expenses must be recovered through revenues for a business to operate at a profit; but determinations of production costs are useful if the bases thereof are understood.

Expenses which do not aid in the productive activity are not part of overhead includable in cost computations. The extent of the inclusion of other expenses depends upon such factors as the complexity of the organization, the attitude of the individuals who are compiling and using the economic data, and the availability of information. Under an analytical costing procedure, there are several possible viewpoints as to what portion of the overhead expenses related to available facilities should be considered allocable to the actual production. Costs are computed to meet best the requirements of particular situations, and no one amount can be said to be "correct" to the exclusion of all others.

FACTORS INVOLVED IN DETERMINATIONS OF COST FOR INVENTORY PURPOSES

Assigning an amount to an inventory is but one of many determinations needed in the computation of the earnings of a business enterprise for a stated period. The acceptability of the amount so assigned is dependent upon recognized accounting procedures having been followed. Where there are alternatives, one of the principal tests of the appropriateness of the end result of the application of the procedure selected is the possible impact upon net income of applying alternative procedures.

The exact amount of the computed cost for an individual item is generally of little significance. Possible variations in such amounts seldom have a material effect on net income. The data developed in compiling the individual costs may be very important, however, from a management standpoint; and there will be a better understanding of both the income statement and the balance sheet if the aggregate inventory amount is based upon the individual costs.

There is no one prescribed procedure to be used in determinations of cost for inventory purposes. There is a wide range of procedures, and many combinations and variations, which result in a fair reflection of income if consistently applied from year to year.

From the authoritative pronouncements that are reproduced as appendices at the end of the book, the general statements concerning the elements of cost to be taken into account for inventory purposes are set forth in comparative form on the next two pages. It is particularly significant that the bulletin issued by the AICPA includes the statement that the *exclusion* of *all* overheads from inventory costs does not constitute an accepted accounting procedure, and then observes that the exercise of judgment in an individual situation involves a consideration of the adequacy of the procedures of the cost accounting system in use, the soundness of the principles thereof, and their consistent application. Whereas the bulletin of the AICPA (Appendix A) relative to inventory pricing was originally issued in 1947, its use as an authoritative source with respect to overhead allocation has continued to be recognized. Accounting research Study No. 13, "The Accounting Basis of Inventories," published by the AICPA in 1973, refers to the applicability of the above bulletin relative to the inclusion of overhead in inventory. Further, APB Statement No. 4, "Basic Concepts and Accounting Principles Underlying Financial Statements of Business Enterprises," published in 1970, indicates that the costs of manufacturing products should include elements of fixed overhead costs. The AICPA bulletin recognizes that there is no one standard for determining the portion of overhead to be included in cost for inventory purposes and that the extent of the inclusion depends on the accounting procedures and principles applied. The emphasis is again placed upon consistency.

The AICPA bulletin (Appendix A) contains only general statements with respect to the treatment of overhead expenditures. By contrast, International Accounting Standard 2 ("IAS 2"), which was issued in 1975 by the International Accounting Standards Committee, discusses the sub-

Comparison of Statements on Elements of Cost

AICPA Bulletin	International Accounting Standards Committee	Federal Income Tax Regulations
The definition of cost as applied to inventories is understood to mean acquisition and production cost,* and its determination involves many problems. Although principles for the determination of inventory costs may be easily stated, their application, particularly to such inventory items as work in process and finished goods, is difficult because of the variety of problems encountered in the allocation of costs and charges. For example, under some circumstances, items such as idle facility expense, excessive spoilage, double freight, and rehandling costs may be so abnormal as to require treatment as current period charges rather than as a portion of the inventory cost. Also, general and administrative expenses should be included as period charges, except for the portion of such expenses that may be clearly related to production and thus constitute a part of inventory costs (product charges). Selling expenses constitute no part of inventory costs. It should also be recognized that the exclusion of all overheads from inventory costs does not constitute an	(a) The historical cost of manufactured inventories should include a systematic allocation of those production overhead costs that relate to putting the inventories in their present location and condition. Allocation of fixed production overhead to the costs of conversion should be based on the capacity of the facilities. If fixed production overhead has been entirely or substantially excluded from the valuation of inventories on the grounds that it does not directly relate to putting the inventories in their present location and condition, that fact should be disclosed. (b) Overheads other than production overhead should be included as part of inventory cost only to the extent that they clearly relate to putting the inventories in their present location and condition. (c) Exceptional amounts of wasted materials, labour, or other expenses should not be included as part of inventory cost.	Cost means: (a) In the case of merchandise on hand at the beginning of the taxable year, the inventory price of such goods. (b) In the case of merchandise purchased since the beginning of the taxable year, the invoice price less trade or other discounts, except strictly cash discounts approximating a fair interest rate, which may be deducted or not at the option of the taxpayer, provided a consistent course is followed. To this net invoice price should be added transportation or other necessary charges incurred in acquiring possession of the goods. (c) In the case of merchandise produced by the taxpayer since the beginning of the taxable year, (1) the cost of raw materials and supplies entering into or consumed in connection with the product, (2) expenditures for direct labor, and (3) indirect production costs incident to and necessary for the production of the particular article, including in such indirect production costs an appropriate proportion of management expenses, but not including any cost of selling or return

Comparison of Statements on Elements of Cost—Continued

AICPA Bulletin	International Accounting Standards Committee	Federal Income Tax Regulations

accepted accounting procedure.

The exercise of judgment in an individual situation involves a consideration of the adequacy of the procedures of the cost accounting system in use, the soundness of the principles thereof, and their consistent application. [Par. 5.]

* In the case of goods which have been written down below cost at the close of a fiscal period, such reduced amount is to be considered the cost for subsequent accounting purposes.

on capital, whether by way of interest or profit. See § 1.471–11 for more specific rules regarding the treatment of indirect production costs.

(d) In any industry in which the usual rules for computation of cost of production are inapplicable, costs may be approximated upon such basis as may be reasonable and in conformity with established trade practices in the particular industry. Among such cases are: (1) Farmers and raisers of livestock (see § 1.471–6); (2) miners and manufacturers who by a single process or uniform series of processes derive a product of two or more kinds, sizes, or grades, the unit cost of which is substantially alike (see § 1.471–7); and (3) retail merchants who use what is known as the "retail method" in ascertaining approximate cost (see § 1.471–8). Notwithstanding the other rules of this section, cost shall not include an amount which is of a type for which a deduction would be disallowed under section 162(c), (f) or (g) and the regulations thereunder in the case of a business expense. [§ 1.471–3.]

ject in some detail. IAS 2 (Appendix B) indicates that there may be situations in which none of the overhead expenditures is considered part of inventory cost. Otherwise, it is in general accord with the AICPA bulletin.

TREATMENT OF OVERHEAD BY IAS 2

IAS 2 distinguishes between product and other overheads and discusses in detail the appropriateness of including or excluding the various overhead elements in inventory cost. Reference to the IAS 2 discussion of overhead should be helpful in interpreting the concise statements by the AICPA and appreciating the absence of rigid rules for the treatment of overhead in computations of cost for inventory purposes.

TREATMENT OF OVERHEAD
IN FEDERAL INCOME TAX REGULATIONS

The federal income tax regulations provide for the inclusion in cost, in the case of merchandise produced by the taxpayer, of "indirect production costs incident to and necessary for the production of the particular article, including in such indirect production costs an appropriate portion of management expenses, but not including any cost of selling or return on capital, whether by way of interest or profit." As adopted September 14, 1973, regulation section 1.471-11 provides specific rules for the inclusion of indirect production costs.

Indirect production costs are described as those costs, other than components of direct material or direct labor, that are incident to and necessary for production or manufacturing operations or processes. One of the more notable aspects of the regulations is that they distinguish between situations where the taxpayer uses "comparable" methods of accounting for tax and financial reporting purposes and those instances where the tax and financial reporting methods are not considered comparable. The chart on pp. 118–19 summarizes how various indirect production costs must be treated for federal income tax purposes, and their usual treatment for financial reporting purposes.

Where taxpayers use comparable methods of accounting for tax and financial reporting, the regulations separate indirect production costs into three classifications. (See Situation A on the chart on pp. 118–19). Costs in category 1 are required to be included in the computation of inventory cost, whereas costs in category 2 need not be included. There is no financial statement conformity requirement for either of these categories. Category 3 consists of costs that must be treated for tax purposes in accordance with the taxpayer's financial accounting treatment of such costs, provided it is not inconsistent with generally accepted accounting principles. Most notable among the items included in this category are taxes, depreciation, and current service pension costs.

When comparable methods of accounting for inventory are not used for tax and financial reporting (e.g., where the completed contract method is used for tax purposes and the percentage of completion method is used for financial reports), the regulations specifically reallocate category 3 costs between categories 1 and 2. (See Situation B on the chart on pp. 118–19).

USE OF SPECIFIC AND AVERAGE COSTS FOR INVENTORY PURPOSES

In addition to the question of what expenditures are to be taken into account in computing cost, consideration must be given to the procedure to be followed in attributing to the particular units on hand at an inventory date, the cost computed for or identified with quantities produced or acquired at different times. The attribution of costs has a direct bearing on the determination of income. The costs associated with specific units of goods as they are disposed of influence not only the amount of profit for the period in which the sales occur, but also the amount to be charged against the revenues of a subsequent period when the units included in the inventory are utilized.

In Chapter 13 there is a discussion of the procedure commonly referred to as the "retail method" of computing inventories, which has been developed to meet the practical problems inherent in any attempt to assign individual costs to the variety of merchandise normally included in the inventory of department stores. Chapter 8 discusses methods of allocating costs which are based upon concepts of a "flow of costs." In the determination of income it is not necessary that the flow of costs be related to the physical movement of goods.

The most obvious procedure for attributing costs to units received, sold, and on hand is by specific identification. Regardless of the costing method applied, each unit or batch of goods has a cost which presumably could be established for it. Where it is feasible to do so, the cost of specific units is sometimes used in the accounting records when reflecting the physical movement of goods. Specific identification is an accepted procedure, but it is time consuming even where feasible. Specific identification is used most often with respect to high-value, low-quantity items, especially for unique items and for items ordered for a particular job or customer.

Analysis of Indirect Production Costs

DESCRIPTION OF COST:	Situation A Taxpayers using comparable methods of accounting for inventory for tax and financial reporting purposes			Situation B Taxpayers not using comparable methods of accounting for inventory for tax and financial reporting purposes		Classification for Financial Reporting Purposes	
	Category 1 Required to be included in inventory cost	Category 2 Not required to be included in inventory cost	Category 3 Required to be treated same as financial statements	Category 1 Required to be included in inventory cost	Category 2 Not required to be included in inventory cost	Usually included in inventoriable costs	Not usually included in inventoriable costs
Repairs and maintenance	X			X		X	
Utilities	X			X		X	
Rent	X			X		X	
Indirect labor and production supervisory wages, including basic compensation, overtime pay, vacation and holiday pay, sick leave (other than payments pursuant to a wage continuation plan under section 105(d)), shift differential, payroll taxes and contributions to a supplemental unemployment benefit plan	X			X		X	
Officers' salaries related to business activities as a whole		X			X		X
Officers' salaries related to production			X		X	(4)	(4)
Pension contributions representing		X			X		

118

Other employee benefit costs, including workmen's compensation expenses, payments under wage continuation plans described in section 105(d), amounts includible in income of an employee under nonqualified pension, profit sharing and stock bonus plans, premiums on life and health insurance and miscellaneous employee benefits

Other employee benefit costs, etc. (see above)		X	X (1)(3)
Indirect materials and supplies	X		X
Tools and equipment not capitalized	X		X
Costs of quality control and inspection	X		X
Marketing, advertising and distribution expenses	X	X	
Interest	X	X	
Research and experimental expenses	X	X	X
Losses under section 165	X	X	X
Depreciation and depletion reported in financial statements		X	X (2)
Depreciation and depletion in excess of amount reported in financial statements	X	N/A	N/A

(1) Applies to employees incident to or necessary for production or manufacturing operations.

(2) Applies to assets incident to or necessary for production or manufacturing.

(3) Certain elements frequently included under other employee benefits are not usually included in inventoriable costs. Examples include recreational facilities for employees, expenses in support of recreation (such as an employee bowling league), etc.

(4) Officers' salaries related to production are included/excluded dependent upon nature and size of the business and/or specificity of identification of officers' duties with production effort.

119

Inventory Record with Specific Identification of Units

Date	Description	Unit cost	Receipts Quantity	Quantity consumed	Batch	Inventory Units	Cost	Amount
Jan. 12	Batch I	$300	247		I	247	$300	$ 74,100
Jan. 28	Batch II	370	316		I	247	300	$ 74,100
					II	316	370	116,920
								$191,020
Feb. 17	Batch III	280	147		I	247	300	$ 74,100
					II	316	370	116,920
					III	147	280	41,160
								$232,180
Feb. 23	Batch II			29	I	247	300	$ 74,100
	Batch III			76	II	287	370	106,190
					III	71	280	19,880
								$200,170
Mar. 13	Batch IV	320	73		I	247	300	$ 74,100
					II	287	370	106,190
					III	71	280	19,880
					IV	73	320	23,360
								$223,530
Mar. 18	Batch I			173	I	74	300	$ 22,200
	Batch IV			12	II	287	370	106,190
					III	71	280	19,880
					IV	61	320	19,520
								$167,790

Even if feasible, specific identification of costs may not be the most logical method from the viewpoint of portraying periodic income. When there is a large quantity of similar units having different costs, a business is not necessarily better or worse off, depending on which of the units were extracted from the available supply. Different profit amounts should result from real economic differences, not differences which have no bearing on the financial position of the company.

The most commonly used procedures for attributing costs to similar units involve the determination of averages. Averaging practices combine reasonable accuracy with practicality. The theoretical justification for the use of average costs is that when like units acquired at different times and at different costs are commingled so as to be equally available, the units become one entity. When units are removed, a certain portion of that entity has been severed, and a proportionate share of the cost attributed to the entity should be deducted from the total cost.

There are two commonly used basic methods of computing average costs and each involves weighted averages. A weighted average gives greater recognition to the unit cost of a greater quantity than to the unit cost of a lesser quantity. For example, the weighted average cost of 10 units at $0.87, 9 units at $1.20, 13 units at $0.73, and 7 units at $1.67 is $1.04, computed as follows:

Illustration of weighted average

Units		Unit cost		Amount				Average
10	×	$0.87	=	$ 8.70				
9	×	1.20	=	10.80				
13	×	0.73	=	9.49				
7	×	1.67	=	11.69				
39				$40.68	÷	39	=	$1.04

The two basic methods may be referred to as the moving-average method and the period-average method.

Under the moving-average method a new average cost is computed upon each addition to the commodity pool. The cost is the quotient of the sum of the cost of the units on hand before the receipt plus the cost of the units received, divided by the total number of units after receipt. For example, if the inventory consists of 316 units at an average cost of $1.10 each and 78 units having a cost of $1.00 each are received, the new average cost for the units on hand is $1.08, computed as follows:

Illustration of moving average

	Units		Unit cost		Amount				Average
Inventory	316				$347.60	÷	316	=	$1.10
Receipt	78	×	$1	=	78.00				
	394				$425.60	÷	394	=	1.08

The period-average method does not require the computation of a new average cost with each receipt, but only once each period, such as a month. Under this method, the new average cost is the quotient of the inventory on hand at the beginning of the period at the old average cost, plus the total cost for the units produced or otherwise acquired during the period, divided by the sum of the quantity on hand at the beginning of the period plus the quantities acquired during the period. For example, if the opening inventory consists of 1,063 units at an average cost of $2.18 each, and acquisitions during the period are 326 at $2.67, 712 at $2.14, and 186 at $2.32, the period-average for costing 1,430 units consumed is $2.25, and the same average cost will be assigned to the 857 units on hand at the beginning of the next period, tabulated as follows:

Illustration of period average

	Units	Unit cost			Amount				Average
Inventory	1,063				$2,317.34	÷	1,063	=	$2.18
Receipts	326	×	$2.67	=	870.42				
	712	×	2.14	=	1,523.68				
	186	×	2.32	=	431.52				
	2,287				5,142.96	÷	2,287	=	2.25
Consumed	1,430	×	2.25	=	3,217.50				
Inventory	857				$1,925.46	÷	857	=	2.25

The period-average method is obviously more practical than the moving-average method in process cost accounting or where there is a large volume of receipts and transfers out. The cost attributed to units consumed during a period is commonly computed after the close of the period, although in some instances time requirements make it necessary to use the average cost computed for the previous period and acceptable costs result.

As with other phases of the procedure for determining amounts to be assigned to inventories, consistency from year to year is of prime importance, whether the costs of particular units are specifically identified or one of the average cost techniques is used.

EFFECT UPON INCOME OF
COST DETERMINATION PROCEDURES

In considering the effect upon income of various cost determination procedures, it is helpful to appreciate the basic attributes of inventories.

Inventories have a physical attribute. They are tangible goods which can be counted or weighed or otherwise measured and tallied at any given point in time. The taking of a physical inventory involves the determination of the number of units of the various products which are on hand, and their stage of completion if the company does manufacturing. For many employees, this is all that "inventory time" means. This physical attribute is the basis for the discussion in Chapter 4 relative to inventory management techniques. The magnitude of the inventory in this physical sense has a bearing on the amount which will be assigned to it, but the amount assigned does not have any direct effect upon the magnitude of the inventory. Further, if adequate and meaningful data are available for purposes of management decisions, the amount assigned to the inventory will have no effect upon what the inventory is worth to the business.

Inventories also have a financial attribute in the sense that an amount is assigned to them for a variety of managerial purposes. Cost determinations involve the interpretation of voluminous economic data; and so long as the procedures followed result in a fair reflection of periodic income, it is desirable not to have to make additional computations just for inventory purposes.

The determination of inventory cost is essentially an income measurement problem, a means whereby there is a rational, orderly, systematic interpretation of the effect on the economic progress of the company of expenditures involved in acquiring goods or in maintaining and operating productive facilities. The problem is primarily connected with determining in what periods expenditures are to be charged off as expenses.

Expenditures made in any accounting period are either useful in producing revenue of a subsequent period or they are not. Expenditures that are not are to be charged off as expenses or losses in the present period. Expenditures that are useful in subsequent periods are to be carried forward to the period in which the goods or services acquired are used to obtain revenue. With regard to expenditures related to the production process, those expenditures which are useful in subsequent periods are deferred as part of the cost of units to be utilized in future periods.

Overhead is the element of cost with respect to which the most widely divergent results can be obtained under various recognized procedures. The principal types of alternatives are:

1. *Prime costing,* under which no overhead is included
2. *Direct costing,* under which controllable expenses directly attributable to production are included but no fixed overhead is included
3. *Analytical costing,* under which overhead expenses attributable to production are included, except for the portion not taken into account be-

cause of the production facilities not being fully utilized, as measured by a comparison with

    a) An average expected level of activity
    b) A practical capacity level of activity
    c) A theoretical capacity level of activity

4. *All-inclusive costing*, under which the entire amount of overhead expense attributable to production is included

Each of these procedures is discussed in Chapter 5, starting on page 102; however, it cannot be overemphasized that there are many variations and combinations possible in application of the general principles to specific circumstances. The design of a costing procedure appropriate for a given situation merits the attention of accountants with broad experience in that field. Care must be taken to assure that the maximum benefits will be derived from the available information and that any additional data required to accomplish the desired objectives will be compiled in the most meaningful and economical manner.

For purposes of external financial statements, the use of prime costing would not constitute an acceptable accounting procedure under the statement on inventory pricing by the AICPA. Furthermore, the AICPA Research Study dealing with inventories indicates that Maurice Moonitz, when Director of Accounting Research for the AICPA, stated in 1961 that nothing in the AICPA Bulletin can or should be used to support the use of direct costing in published financial statements. In practice, however, there is commonly a partial application of the direct costing principle through not including certain period expenses (e.g., depreciation, taxes, and other selected items which are relatively constant in amount from year to year) in the overhead considered as part of cost. If done consistently, the treatment of particular items as period expenses may have no material effect on net income, and such treatment is not considered to be a deviation from the inventory methods which are acceptable in recognized accounting practice, particularly for specific industries. The steel industry, for example, generally excludes depreciation from inventoriable overhead. A distortion of income could arise should a different procedure be used in assigning amounts to the beginning and ending inventories of an accounting period.

The regulations issued by the Internal Revenue Service in 1973 provide that all taxpayers engaged in manufacturing or production operations must use the full absorption method of inventory costing. These regulations specifically prohibit the use of the direct cost and the prime cost methods of valuing inventories for federal income tax purposes.

The regulations require an allocation method that "fairly apportions" indirect manufacturing and production costs among the various items produced, giving great weight to the method of allocation used for financial statement purposes in determining what is "fair." The manufacturing burden rate method and the standard cost method are, for the first time, specifically designated as acceptable. In using these methods, however, a pro rata portion of any under- or over-applied burden (favorable or unfavorable variances) must be reallocated to the goods in ending inventory unless the amount is not significant and is not reallocated for financial statement purposes. An exception to the reallocation rule is permitted where fixed indirect production costs are not absorbed due to the company's failure to produce at its practical capacity. These costs may be written off as a period expense.

To illustrate the effect upon periodic net income of the alternative cost procedures, the hypothetical computations made in Chapter 5 with respect to the operating unit of The H Company have been supplemented by adding the following assumed factors and making comparisons of the computed earnings:

Units sold and net realization:
  1st year—1,500 units⎫
  2d year—3,500 units⎪ at $200 per unit
  3d year—3,900 units⎬
  4th year—2,700 units⎭
  5th year—4,400 units   at $150 per unit

Direct production expenditures for:
  Material and labor.................... $ 90 per unit
  Controllable expenses................   10 per unit
     Total............................. $100 per unit

Expenses incurred—$20,000 annually

Taking these additional factors into account, the production costs and expenses and the number of units on hand at the end of the year are as given below. The amounts assigned to the inventories under the several alternative procedures for determining cost would be $90 per unit in the case of prime costing, $100 per unit in the case of direct costing, and $100 of direct production expenditures plus the current year's overhead applied per unit (assuming a first-in, first-out flow of costs) in the case of the other illustrations. The amounts resulting from all-inclusive costing reflect the overhead applied per unit as computed on the basis of actual production.

Income statements reflecting inventory determinations based upon prime costing and direct costing are very similar under the assumptions adopted for the purpose of the present illustrations.

Summary of Production Costs and Expenses and Statement of Inventory Quantities for The H Company

| | | Direct production expenditures | | Overhead incurred | Total production costs and expenses |
		Material and labor	Controllable expenses		
1st year		$ 270,000	$ 30,000	$ 70,000	$ 370,000
2d year		405,000	45,000	84,000	534,000
3d year		216,000	24,000	65,000	305,000
4th year		243,000	27,000	67,000	337,000
5th year		306,000	34,000	74,000	414,000
	Total	$1,440,000	$160,000	$360,000	$1,960,000

		In beginning inventory	Produced	Sold	In ending inventory
		Number of units			
1st year		—	3,000	1,500	1,500
2d year		1,500	4,500	3,500	2,500
3d year		2,500	2,400	3,900	1,000
4th year		1,000	2,700	2,700	1,000
5th year		1,000	3,400	4,400	—
	Total		16,000	16,000	

Amounts Assigned to Inventories of The H Company Under Alternative Procedures for Determining Cost

| | Prime costing | Direct costing | Analytical costing with rate of activity based upon a standard representing | | | All-inclusive costing |
			Average production	Practical capacity	Theoretical capacity	
1st year	$135,000	$150,000	$182,805	$176,250	$173,340	$184,995
2d year	225,000	250,000	315,625	302,500	296,675	296,675
3d year	90,000	100,000	120,310	116,250	114,430	127,080
4th year	90,000	100,000	120,930	116,750	114,880	124,810
5th year	—	—	—	—	—	—

Income Statements Based Upon Prime Costing

	1st year	2d year	3d year	4th year	5th year
Sales..................	$300,000	$700,000	$780,000	$540,000	$660,000
Cost of goods sold:					
Beginning inventory......	—	135,000	225,000	90,000	90,000
Cost of production......	270,000	405,000	216,000	243,000	306,000
Total.............	270,000	540,000	441,000	333,000	396,000
Ending inventory........	135,000	225,000	90,000	90,000	—
	135,000	315,000	351,000	243,000	396,000
Gross profit on sales.......	165,000	385,000	429,000	297,000	264,000
Expenses incurred.........	120,000	149,000	109,000	114,000	128,000
Pre-tax income	$ 45,000	$236,000	$320,000	$183,000	$136,000

Income Statements Based Upon Direct Costing

	1st year	2d year	3d year	4th year	5th year
Sales..................	$300,000	$700,000	$780,000	$540,000	$660,000
Cost of goods sold:					
Beginning inventory......	—	150,000	250,000	100,000	100,000
Cost of production.......	300,000	450,000	240,000	270,000	340,000
Total.............	300,000	600,000	490,000	370,000	440,000
Ending inventory........	150,000	250,000	100,000	100,000	—
	150,000	350,000	390,000	270,000	440,000
Gross profit on sales.......	150,000	350,000	390,000	270,000	220,000
Expenses incurred.........	90,000	104,000	85,000	87,000	94,000
Pre-tax income	$ 60,000	$246,000	$305,000	$183,000	$126,000

In the condensed income statements expenditures relating to the productive facilities which are not considered as costs for inventory purposes have been shown with other expenses incurred. In a complete operating statement, the nature of the various expenses would be identified.

If the overhead is applied to production on the basis of an average expected level of activity for the five-year period, there would be significant differences in the amounts of pre-tax income except in the case of the fourth year. The amount of overabsorbed or underabsorbed overhead would not necessarily be shown separately in published financial statements, but it would be a significant factor for management purposes.

**Income Statements with Overhead Applied on Basis
of Average Expected Level of Activity**

	1st year	2d year	3d year	4th year	5th year
Sales...............	$300,000	$700,000	$780,000	$540,000	$660,000
Cost of goods sold:					
Beginning inventory...	—	182,805	315,625	120,310	120,930
Cost of production....	365,625	568,129	288,750	326,528	418,625
Total...........	365,625	750,934	604,375	446,838	539,555
Ending inventory.....	182,805	315,625	120,310	120,930	—
	182,820	435,309	484,065	325,908	539,555
Gross profit on sales....	117,180	264,691	295,935	214,092	120,445
Overabsorbed (or under-absorbed) overhead..	(4,375)	34,129	(16,250)	(10,472)	4,625
Expenses incurred......	(20,000)	(20,000)	(20,000)	(20,000)	(20,000)
Pre-tax income	$ 92,805	$278,820	$259,685	$183,620	$105,070

Application of overhead by comparing the actual level of activity with practical capacity and the use of theoretical capacity would result in income determinations as illustrated on page 129. As previously stated, the use of theoretical capacity as a standard for comparison ordinarily eliminates the possibility of overabsorbed overhead, but it is not as generally acceptable as the use of practical capacity or an average expected level of activity.

The income statement would appear as on page 130 if the entire overhead is applied to production by an all-inclusive costing. Whether overhead is applied to production on the basis of the actual level of activity or the expected level of activity during the course of each period, with differences adjusted at the end of the period, the results would be the same.

The amounts of pre-tax income for the operating unit of The H Company, as computed in each of the illustrations, have been summarized for purposes of comparison.

On the basis of the foregoing, the following observations may be made:

1. The total income derived from a business activity during its entire period of operation will not be affected by the procedures followed in determining cost for inventory purposes.
2. All-inclusive costing results in larger amounts being assigned to the inventory and in more income during periods when the inventories are increasing in size.

Income Statements with Overhead Applied on Basis of Practical Capacity

	1st year	2d year	3d year	4th year	5th year
Sales..............	$300,000	$700,000	$780,000	$540,000	$660,000
Cost of goods sold:					
Beginning inventory...	—	176,250	302,500	116,250	116,750
Cost of production....	352,500	544,500	279,000	315,225	402,900
Total..........	352,500	720,750	581,500	431,475	519,650
Ending inventory.....	176,250	302,500	116,250	116,750	—
	176,250	418,250	465,250	314,725	519,650
Gross profit on sales....	123,750	281,750	314,750	225,275	140,350
Overabsorbed (or under- absorbed) overhead..	(17,500)	10,500	(26,000)	(21,775)	(11,100)
Expenses incurred......	(20,000)	(20,000)	(20,000)	(20,000)	(20,000)
Pre-tax income	$ 86,250	$272,250	$268,750	$183,500	$109,250

Income Statements with Overhead Applied on Basis of Theoretical Capacity

	1st year	2d year	3d year	4th year	5th year
Sales..............	$300,000	$700,000	$780,000	$540,000	$660,000
Cost of goods sold:					
Beginning inventory...	—	173,340	296,675	114,430	114,880
Cost of production....	346,690	534,000	274,645	310,200	395,870
Total..........	346,690	707,340	571,320	424,630	510,750
Ending inventory.....	173,340	296,675	114,430	114,880	—
	173,350	410,665	456,890	309,750	510,750
Gross profit on sales....	126,650	289,335	323,110	230,250	149,250
Underabsorbed overhead	(23,310)	—	(30,355)	(26,800)	(18,130)
Expenses incurred......	(20,000)	(20,000)	(20,000)	(20,000)	(20,000)
Pre-tax income	$ 83,340	$269,335	$272,755	$183,450	$111,120

3. The procedures followed in determining cost for inventory purposes have little effect on income when the beginning and ending inventories are the same size—as illustrated by the fourth year in the example.

4. Excluding the first and last year of a business activity, it cannot be predetermined which of the procedures will necessarily result in either the highest or the lowest amounts of income for any particular years.

Income Statements Based Upon All-inclusive Costing

	1st year	2d year	3d year	4th year	5th year
Sales..................	$300,000	$700,000	$780,000	$540,000	$660,000
Cost of goods sold:					
Beginning inventory......	—	184,995	296,675	127,080	124,810
Cost of production......	370,000	534,000	305,000	337,000	414,000
Total.............	370,000	718,995	601,675	464,080	538,810
Ending inventory........	184,995	296,675	127,080	124,810	—
	185,005	422,320	474,595	339,270	538,810
Gross profit on sales.......	114,995	277,680	305,405	200,730	121,190
Expenses incurred.........	20,000	20,000	20,000	20,000	20,000
Pre-tax income	$ 94,995	$257,680	$285,405	$180,730	$101,190

	Prime costing	Direct costing	Analytical costing using as standard level of activity			
			Average production	Practical capacity	Theoretical capacity	All-inclusive costing
1st year	$ 45,000	$ 60,000	$ 92,805	$ 86,250	$ 83,340	$ 94,995
2d year	236,000	246,000	278,820	272,250	269,335	257,680
3d year	320,000	305,000	259,685	268,750	272,755	285,405
4th year	183,000	183,000	183,620	183,500	183,450	180,730
5th year	136,000	126,000	105,070	109,250	111,120	101,190
Total	$920,000	$920,000	$920,000	$920,000	$920,000	$920,000

In the condensed income statement presentation the percentage of gross profit to sales is more consistent where direct costing or prime costing is used. This would not necessarily be true in the case of published financial statements because the effect of recurring and continuing expense could be disclosed in other ways.

PRACTICAL ASPECTS OF COSTING PROCEDURES

There is a tendency to think of the costing procedures, referred to by convenient names for purposes of discussion, as being absolute. In practice, it is doubtful that two applications of any of the types of procedures would be identical. There are innumerable variations and combinations of each of the general classes of procedures.

Although distortion of income as a consequence of inconsistent application of costing practices should be avoided, no procedure should be looked upon as completely unchangeable. Business management is, of necessity, dynamic; and if refinements of techniques are developed which provide a better way of accomplishing the objectives of the accounting function, they should be put into effect. Most of these refinements do not materially change net income or represent any inconsistency in the application of accounting principles.

If there is a change in the procedure for determining cost which has a material effect on income, the change and the amount involved should be disclosed in published financial statements, and it may be necessary to obtain advance permission from the Commissioner of Internal Revenue to make the new procedures operative in determining inventories for federal income tax purposes.

The federal income tax regulations provide that a change in the method of accounting includes a change in the treatment of a material item as well as a change in the over-all method of accounting for gross income or deductions. If a change in accounting method is to be made for federal income tax purposes, an application on Treasury Department Form 3115 should be filed with the Commissioner's office in Washington. The filing must be within 180 days after the beginning of the taxable year in which the desired change is to be made.

In his first year in office President Kennedy directed the Internal Revenue Service to give increasing attention to inventory reporting as an area of tax avoidance, and to step up emphasis on both the verification of the amounts reported as inventories and the examination of methods used in arriving at their reported valuation. In his Tax Message addressed to the Congress on April 20, 1961, the President referred to deviations from inventory methods which are acceptable in recognized accounting practice. The statements relating to inventories were:

It is increasingly apparent that the manipulation of inventories has become a frequent method of avoiding taxes. Current laws and regulations generally permit the use of inventory methods which are acceptable in recognized accounting practice. Deviations from these methods, which are not always easy to detect during examination of tax returns, can often lead to complete nonpayment of taxes until the inventories are liquidated; and, for some taxpayers, this represents permanent tax reduction. The understating of the valuation of inventories is the device most frequently used.

I have directed the Internal Revenue Service to give increasing attention to this area of tax avoidance, through a stepped-up emphasis on both the verification of the amounts reported as inventories and an examination of methods used in arriving at their reported valuation.[3]

The types of deviations which prompted this action were explained in a statement by the Secretary of the Treasury, Douglas Dillon, made before the Committee on Ways and Means of the House of Representatives on May 3, 1961.

After giving a simplified example of how the taxable income of a business would be understated $10,000 if an ending inventory was reported to be $50,000 rather than $60,000, Secretary Dillon observed:

> To the extent that an understatement of the ending inventory continues in future years, the taxpayer will not have paid tax on the full amount of his income. At the minimum, the result is deferral of the time of paying the tax. In some cases, as the result of losses, sale of the business, or death of the taxpayer, this income may escape taxation entirely.
>
> Understatement of the ending inventory may be accomplished by manipulation of the code provision permitting inventories to be valued at cost or market, whichever is lower. The use of very low market values, of course, reduces the amount of the ending inventory, thereby reducing taxable income. In addition, the amount of the ending inventory may be understated by not including therein a proper count of all inventory items.
>
> In order to assist in correcting abuses in the inventory area, taxpayers might be required to report in the tax return the cost of the closing inventory before any reductions to market. The taxpayer would then separately state the amount of any inventory valuation deduction. If market values are used for any items of inventory, the taxpayer would be required to explain on what basis the market value was determined and the relationship of recent purchases and sales to that market value. In addition, taxpayers might be required to state whether and by whom a physical count of the inventory was taken, whether such inventory was taken by management alone or by a certified public accountant, and the procedures followed to insure that all items of inventory were correctly counted.
>
> Legislation is not needed to carry out the recommendation of the President in this area, since the above reporting requirements can be effected by administrative action including changes in the data required to be included on tax returns.[4]

There is no question about there being a deviation from inventory methods acceptable in recognized accounting practice if the lower of cost or market rule is improperly applied or if the inventory is understated by not including therein a proper count of all inventory items. These areas of tax avoidance should be investigated by the Internal Revenue Service, and appropriate audit instructions are provided for the revenue agents.

The suggested procedure of requiring a statement in the tax return of

[3] President John F. Kennedy, *Address Before the Congress*—Tax Message, H.R. Doc. No. 140, 87th Cong. 2d Sess., p. 14 (1961).

[4] Secretary of the Treasury Douglas Dillon, *Statement Before the Committee on Ways and Means*, H.R. Doc. No. 140, 87th Cong. 2d Sess., p. 87 (1961).

the cost of the closing inventory before any reductions to market was found impractical. The procedures followed in ascertaining that the amount assigned to an inventory does not exceed market are not uniform, and in many cases the expense involved in compiling the data needed to state the amount of the inventory valuation deduction separately would be disproportionate to the benefits derived by the Internal Revenue Service. Similarly, the suggestion that taxpayers be required to state by whom a physical count of the inventory was taken and the procedure followed to insure that all items were correctly counted had to be considered from the standpoint of practicality.

On the federal income tax return, it is reasonable to provide space for a brief description of the "Method of inventory valuation"; to ask specifically whether there was any *substantial* change in the manner of determining quantities, costs, or valuations between the opening and closing inventory; and to require the attachment of an explanation of a substantial change in the procedures for making the determinations as to quantities, costs, or valuations. In order to reflect income properly, the inventory method should be consistent from year to year, and revenue agents should not propose that a taxpayer change his method of accounting where it has been consistently employed and taxable income is clearly reflected for the year under review. The consistency requirement should not, however, be applied in a manner which hampers the evolution of accounting techniques or the adoption of improvements in costing procedures designed to implement the method.

Following President Kennedy's 1961 tax message to Congress, the Internal Revenue Service commenced an intensive examination policy with respect to inventory practices that most likely resulted in abuses. In December 1971, regulations were proposed that permitted the use of the "full-absorption" method or a "modified full-absorption" method. In February 1973, the original proposed regulations were withdrawn and revised proposed regulations were substituted. The revised regulations deleted the optional modified full-absorption provision and made mandatory the use of the full-absorption method. The final regulations were adopted on September 14, 1973 and followed the February 1973 proposed regulations, except for minor modifications.

All taxpayers engaged in manufacturing or production operations must now use the full absorption method. A two-year period beginning September 19, 1973 was given for initial voluntary compliance. A voluntary election to change to the full absorption method must be designated on a Treasury Department Form 3115 filed within the first 180 days of the year of change. Inventory at the beginning of the year of change must be restated using the full absorption method. Assuming the restatement results in an increase in opening inventory, the additional income is reported as follows. For taxpayers voluntarily changing during the transitional period, the increase is taken into income ratably over a 10-year period, except for so-called "pre-1954" amounts that need not be reported as income under Internal Revenue Code Section 481. Taxpayers not changing voluntarily (or timely) must report all the additional income (except the pre-1954 amounts) in the year of change.

Without undertaking a detailed discussion of cost accounting procedures, some general observations and illustrations will be helpful as a guide to an understanding of any costing techniques. Specifically identified or acceptable allocated costs can usually be established for the material and direct labor represented in an inventory, but unless the concept of "prime costing" is appropriate, an allocation procedure for indirect manufacturing expenses is indispensable. This is true whether the basic concept being applied is "direct costing," "all-inclusive costing," or falls within the broad area of "analytical costing." It is also true that all allocation procedures are arbitrary to some degree, no matter how much *refinement* is incorporated in the mechanics of the computations.

The fundamental requirements of any cost accounting procedure are that it be practical in operation so as to provide timely information at a reasonable expense and that it be understood by and useful to those making management decisions. These requirements have logically led to the use of factors (commonly called "overhead rates" or "burden rates") which are applied to a base such as direct labor dollars, direct labor hours, or machine operating hours to establish the amount to be included in cost to represent indirect manufacturing expenses.

In a simple case, a burden factor may be applied to the total direct labor in the inventory. For example, if the material represented by the inventory is deemed to have a cost of $100,000 and the direct labor a cost of $50,000, with a 150% overhead rate the total cost of the inventory would be $225,000, including $75,000 (150% of $50,000) for indirect manufacturing expenses. In a more detailed cost accounting system, the various operations involved in manufacturing a particular part might be analyzed and several burden factors applied (some to the direct labor dollars, others to machining time, etc.) in order to establish a cost for that item. The various individual costs so established for the parts or subassemblies would then be applied to the quantities on hand to determine the aggregate cost for the inventory. Detailed computations provide information which can be useful in reaching many business decisions; however, the data needed to make such a procedure practical in operation, so as to provide timely information at a reasonable expense, are not readily available in every accounting system. Depending upon the availability of data, there is no limit to the number of factors which might appropriately be utilized in reflecting indirect manufacturing expenses in the cost of an inventory regardless of which of the basic costing concepts are adopted. Starting with the possibility of merely applying a single company-wide overhead rate to the total cost of all direct labor represented in the inventory, refinements are usually made by utilizing a separate rate for each plant, for each department, or for each operation within a department, and by applying the rate to machining time or other standards where appropriate rather than to direct labor dollars.

The second fundamental requirement of a cost accounting procedure (i.e., that it be understood by and useful to those making management decisions) relates primarily to the costing concept which is being applied.

Even under the all-inclusive costing concept, expenses which do not relate to the goods on hand at the inventory date should not be included in cost. For example, if overtime or extra-shift premiums are paid to produce seasonal goods and to meet a particular demand of the sales department, the premiums are fully chargeable against income. Earnings for the period of shipment would be overstated if any portion of the extra expense incurred were allocated to the inventory. Similarly, the expenses of the shipping department and any other department through which the goods in the inventory would not have passed (e.g., goods may pass through a paint or inspection department or other finishing process immediately prior to and only when ready for shipment) should not be included in indirect manufacturing expenses reflected in a burden rate.

In summarizing indirect manufacturing expenses for the purpose of setting burden rates, it is also necessary to ascertain the nature of the expenditures which are charged to the various accounts. In some cases, one digit in each expense account number may be used to indicate whether the control of the expense is considered the responsibility of the sales manager, the production manager, the purchasing agent, the controller, or other particular officer or supervisor. Where an account numbering system is so used to facilitate expense control, it should not be assumed that every account with the number indicating the production manager reflects an indirect *manufacturing* expense. The salary of the security guard in the lobby of the executive suite and sales office may be charged to Plant Protection, and the expense of the entire janitorial staff and yard crew may be charged to a maintenance account identified with the production manager even though a large number of employees may be required for the cleaning of non-manufacturing space. Inventory costs would be overstated if the entire maintenance expense were included in overhead.

There are many differences in philosophies reflected in the procedures followed in the costing of inventories. The following list of a few common types of indirect manufacturing expenses indicates some of the most frequently followed practices where other than the prime costing concept is adopted.

Items usually considered as being of a controllable nature, and part of cost:

Plant superintendent
Production foremen
Production scheduling
Quality control and inspection
Power, light, and water required for production
Machinery setups
Intra-plant trucking
Clean-up time
Factory janitorial services
Payroll taxes on direct labor and includable indirect labor

Items frequently considered as being of a continuing or recurring nature, and *not* part of cost:

General superintendent
Production planning
Engineering and product development expenses
Purchasing department
Receiving department
Stock room
Payroll department
Employee training
Job standards
Safety precautions
Property taxes
Inventory taking
Machinery relocating

Items commonly considered as resulting from errors, inefficiencies, and other events occurring during the year, and *not* part of cost:

Waiting time
Rework labor
Spoiled material
Union grievances

Among items meriting special discussion are pension and profit-sharing payments, and depreciation.

In the case of funded pension plans the charge to income may include a past-service element, which might be considered to be excludable from inventory cost because its relates to services rendered in prior years which services are unrelated to the production of goods in current inventories. The current-service portion of the charge for a funded plan is sometimes considered not to be part of cost for inventory purposes because, unless there is complete vesting of the benefits in the employees, there is no direct relationship to current production. Usually, however, all charges to income with respect to pensions of employees engaged in activities related to manufacturing are included in overhead for inventory costing purposes. As shown on the chart on pp. 118–19, the Internal Revenue Service takes the view that past-service pension costs are excludable from inventory costs, while the current service element follows the treatment used for financial reporting purposes.

It is not uncommon for production employees to participate in profit-sharing bonus distributions, and these payments are commonly considered to be part of cost for inventory purposes. Where it is concluded not to allocate a portion of these expenditures to the unsold goods on hand at the end of the accounting period, the factors taken into account may include a recognition of such facts as (1) the wages paid the production employees are comparable to the wages paid by other employers in the same locale who do not have a profit-sharing bonus plan, (2) the aggregate amount of the bonus fund is established by reference to *realized* income for the period and income is realized only from sales, not just by producing goods for inventory, and (3) the bonus is entirely discretionary and requires action annually by the Board of Directors or other officials and is recognized as being a distribution to the employee group of *realized* income, just as dividends are a distribution to the shareholder group.

Under the classification of expenses suggested in Chapter 5, depreciation would fall in the category of *continuing expenses*, i.e., it is an expense which results from previous management decisions made to secure the production facilities which are available for use. Although it can be reasoned that only *controllable expenses* should be recognized as a cost, the current provision for depreciation of machinery, factory buildings, and other production facilities is generally considered to be an element of manufacturing overhead. If a consistent practice of not including depreciation in cost has been followed, however, income can be considered to have been fairly reflected, where there would be no material differences in the computed income from year to year had depreciation been regularly included in the computation of overhead. This fact has been recognized for many years in the determination of income for federal income tax purposes. In 1953 the income tax regulations were amended to recognize the alternative acceptable accounting practices, and a revenue ruling (Rev. Rul. 141, 1953–2 CB 101) was issued to clarify the reasons for the amendment. Furthermore, in businesses which mature large stocks over long periods (e.g., whiskey, wine, and timber) it is usual not to include fixed overhead expense items in inventoriable cost in order to avoid carrying forward large and increasing amounts which may or may not be recovered in the ultimate selling price of the goods. The Internal Revenue Service treats depreciation as a category 3 cost, whose inclusion or exclusion from inventory cost is generally determined by its classification for financial reporting purposes.

Where depreciation is not included among the expenses considered in determining the amount to be assigned to an inventory, the rationale underlying the decision may be based upon a variety of factors. In some cases, the cost accounting system is designed primarily to develop statements which will be of maximum utility as a management tool in controlling the expenses of departments or other operating areas for which particular individuals have responsibilities. It can be reasoned that only *controllable expenses* should be included in such statements and that there should not be included depreciation and other *continuing expenses* which are the result of previous management decisions. Some *ad volorem* property taxes are subject to a similar conception of what items should be included in cost since these taxes result from prior capital expenditures for production facilities.

A decision not to recognize depreciation as an element of cost for inventory purposes may also be influenced by a realization that it is not feasible in most cases to make the analyses which would be necessary to ascertain a "theoretically sound" amount to be allocated to the inventory. Except where the depreciation provision is determined by some type of unit-of-production method the amount is computed basically to amortize the cost of the facility, on a time basis, over the period it will remain in a usable state. The depreciation provided in any year does not reflect the extent to which the facility was actually used, and it cannot be claimed that there is any precise matching of a proper amount of depreciation against revenue derived from utilization of the facility. Further, an analysis of the basis for the depreciation provision undertaken to ascertain a "theoretically sound" amount to be allocated to the inventory would involve the compilation of data by numerous cost centers and would have to reflect the processes through which each of the units on hand at the end of the year had physically passed. This type of analysis is incorporated in only the most detailed cost accounting systems. As stated at the outset of this discussion, however, the current provision for depreciation of machinery, factory buildings, and other production facilities is generally considered to be an element of manufacturing overhead and in that way included on a "broad-brush basis" in the cost for the inventory in most businesses.

Where the analytical costing concept is applied, a portion of the indirect manufacturing expenses which would be considered to be includable in cost were the production facilities being fully utilized is not taken into account during certain periods in recognition of unused capacity. In this context, facilities need not be operating at a *maximum* rate based upon a theoretical potential in order to be considered to be "fully utilized." The norm is generally a *practical capacity* rate. The most commonly used procedure for applying this concept is to establish burden rates by reference to what the aggregate expenses would be if the facility were operated at its practical capacity. There is no necessity to classify the expenses as between "fixed" and "variable" or analyze expenses into their *fixed* and *variable* elements. Historical data for prior periods may be used to establish budgets of what the expenditures would be for individual expense accounts or groups of related expenses, and modern budgeting techniques make possible the determination of appropriate overhead rates in a variety of ways.

The application of the analytical costing concept by reference to budgeted expenses at an operating level reflecting full utilization of a facility can be simply illustrated.

	Total expense when facility is fully utilized (based upon 1000x units)
Indirect manufacturing expenses:	
Item A (e.g., salary of plant superintendent) which is fixed in amount	$ 20,000
Item B (e.g., wages of production foremen) which amounts to $15,000.00 for each 100x units or fraction thereof	150,000
Item C (e.g., power) which is based on a flat charge of $5,000.00 plus $1.00 per x unit	6,000
Item D (e.g., payroll tax) which is based on $5.00 per x unit for each of the first 600 x units	3,000
Item E (e.g., trucking) which amounts to $2.00 per x unit	2,000
	$181,000
Overhead rate per x unit	$181

Analysis of costs at various operating rates:

	Units (upon which burden absorption is based) reflected in operating rate—					
	500x		**750x**		**1000x**	
	Expense allocable to —		Expense allocable to —		Expense allocable to —	
	Production	Unused capacity	Production	Unused capacity	Production	Unused capacity
Item A	$10,000	$ 10,000	$ 15,000	$ 5,000	$ 20,000	$ —
Item B	75,000	—	112,500	7,500	150,000	—
Item C	3,000	2,500	4,500	1,250	6,000	—
Item D	1,500	1,000	2,250	750	3,000	—
Item E	1,000	—	1,500	—	2,000	—
	$90,500	$ 13,500	$135,750	$ 14,500	$181,000	$ —
Total	$104,000		$150,250		$181,000	
Per x unit	$208		$200⅓		$181	

Expense per x unit allocable to production $90,500÷500=$181 $135,750÷750=$181 $181,000÷1,000=$181

Had the units that were reflected in the operating rate exceeded 1000x in any operating period, the use of an overhead rate of $181 per x unit would result in charging production with, "phantom dollars" to the extent the aggregate amount so charged exceeded the total of the actual expenditures. For example, if operations were at the rate of 1200x units, the total of the actual expenditures would be $211,600 (Item A, $20,000; Item B, $180,000; Item C, $6,200; Item D, $3,000; and Item E, $2,400), whereas 1200x units multiplied by $181 equals $217,200. The excess of $5,600 is commonly referred to as "over-absorbed burden," and where this factor is sufficiently material to distort the results of operations, an adjustment will be made to the tentatively computed inventory cost for an appropriate portion of such $5,600. *Theoretically*, an adjustment should always be made for overabsorbed overhead to avoid an overstatement of income for the period in which the inventory items are produced and an artificially high charge being made against the income for the period in which the items are sold.

In this simplified example, expense Items A and E illustrate the so-called *fixed* and *variable* expense, respectively. In the actual operations of a business, however, expense categories having these characteristics are seldom found. The other three items in the illustration are examples of how expenses can be affected by many factors. Item B illustrates an expense which increases by steps as the operating rate increases. For example, if a foreman can supervise 100x volume of work and he supervises only 80x volume, 20% of his salary can be considered allocable to unused capacity, and under the analytical costing concept only 80% of his salary would be allocated to production. Item C illustrates an expense which has both fixed and variable elements. Item D illustrates an expense which behaves differently from the others because the first dollars expended are not recoverable if the production facility is not fully utilized but carry a potential "bonus," in that the expense ceases (or it could have continued at a lesser rate) when a particular operating level is reached. In this case every $6y of wages upon which the payroll tax was considered to be payable means that $4y of additional productive wages could be incurred without the payment of any additional tax, i.e., 40% of each tax payment would be allocable to unused capacity if the facility were not fully utilized. At an operating rate of 750x, the expense allocable to unused capacity is 62.5% (250x/400x) of $1,200 (40% of $3,000), or $750.

The foregoing discussion of the practical aspects of costing procedures demonstrates that, in inventory determinations, no amount can be considered to be the *actual cost* or the *correct cost* because in every case there will be alternative amounts which are also acceptable. The word "cost" should preferably be used without an adjective. If a costing procedure meets the fundamental requirements of being practical in operation so as to provide timely information at a reasonable expense and of being understood by and useful to those making management decisions, the important factor is whether it has been consistently applied. Refinements of the costing procedure which make the accounting data more useful should be constantly encouraged, and unless there has been a substantial change in the costing concept adopted, these can be made without distorting income.

SEVEN

Lower of Cost or Market

A reference to inventories being stated at the lower of cost or market is so common that the significance of the phrase is not always fully appreciated. Further, it may not be recognized that this is an area where substantial disagreement among accountants exists. There are differences both on basic issues and on details.

The practice of stating inventories at the lower of cost or market does not necessarily reflect a fundamental accounting principle. As indicated by the following references to accounting literature and specific historical economic events, practical factors have prompted development of the rule as well as the general philosophy that, while potential losses should be provided for, no profit should be anticipated in preparing financial statements.

In the twentieth century, the word "valuation" is more commonly used in connection with inventories than with any other balance sheet item. This practice tends to obscure the fact that the amount assigned to a particular inventory is generally the cost considered to be applicable thereto with appropriate adjustments to reflect a lower market value.

EARLY REFERENCES TO VALUATION OF INVENTORIES

It is not claimed that the available information discloses the rule's real origin, but the material at hand indicates that it is a result of the mingling of two bloodlines: expediency and convenience. Medieval trading practices, banking and credit requirements, the aftermath of war, and inequitable taxation have profoundly influenced the development of this valuation rule. This mixed ancestry may partially account for the notion that taking an inventory is a process of evaluation.

As early as the beginning of the fifteenth century, goods in inventory were priced below their purchase cost. Dr. Baulduin Penndorf did considerable research work on bookkeeping practices (including a translation of Paciolo's writings) when he was professor of business administration and director of the College of Business Administration of Leipzig in the 1930's. This German scholar, writing of the manuscript records of an Italian businessman, Francesco di Marco, pointed out that certain stock bought for trade in 1406 at a cost of 60 florins, appeared still unsold in a later inventory at 50 florins. Beneath the item was this notation: "We have entered the 10 fl. in the debit of goods profit account as damage (loss) because we no longer value them (the goods) as above since they have fallen in price." It is doubtful that this change was made in the inventory merely for the satisfaction of producing an accurate profit calculation and a conservative statement of assets. It appears there may have been present some motive other than a high resolve to record the facts.[1]

This writer provides a clue to the reason for recognizing declines in inventory values when he points out [2] that the tax burden in Italian cities early in the fifteenth century was very heavy. The taxes were calculated on the amount of a citizen's land, investments, and business capital less certain deductions. Since the amounts of lands and investments could be determined by tax officials with considerable exactness, "endeavors to pay the lowest possible amount of taxes could only be made with reference to business capital." Penndorf does not give the details of the methods used in stating business capital at a minimum.

In 1494, Paciolo published the first printed text on bookkeeping. In discussing what would now be called an opening entry, he advised the merchant who desired to begin keeping systematic accounts to prepare a statement (*bilancio*) "of whatever he has in this world, personal property or real estate." Precious stones should be included "according to current prices"; for silver articles he mentions, "give each thing its customary price." The reader is left in doubt as to what prices are meant. Until systematic business records came into use, *valuing* the inventory was no doubt the usual practice and a proper base for the inventory rules which Paciolo mentions.

One of Paciolo's followers, Don Angelo Pietra, a monk of Genoa, offered

[1] Littleton, "A Genealogy for 'Cost or Market,'" 16 *Accounting Rev.* 161 (June, 1941).

[2] Penndorf, "The Relation of Taxation to the History of the Balance Sheet," 5 *Accounting Rev.* 247 (Sept., 1930).

the advice that a value should be given to things harvested and things manufactured, but this value should be lower than current prices "so that the proceeds will not fall below this value in case of sale." His book published in 1586 showed a thorough knowledge of mercantile accounting adapted to the requirements of monasteries and is chiefly remarkable for the completeness of the stocktaking which he introduces. Pietra, incidentally, was cellarer of his monastery and took charge of its business affairs.

In France, under an ordinance promulgated by Louis XIV in 1673, merchants and bankers were required to keep a journal of their transactions for reference in case of dispute. They were also to have the book authenticated by the signature of a public official. Furthermore, as one author points out, they were required to make a statement (*inventaire*) of all their fixed and movable properties and their debts receivable and payable every two years.[3] The French law at this point used words that are almost identical with those used by Paciolo in writing about the opening entry. That early writer's instructions about opening entries were thus reflected in European law regarding periodic financial reports.

Jacques Savary, the principal author of the ordinance of 1673, published a book in 1675 entitled *Le Parfait Mégociant (The Complete Tradesman)*. In this book he explained the statute and described current business practices. Among other things, he made some observations on the treatment of merchandise for inventory purposes. The reader is vaguely advised to take care not to estimate merchandise at more than it is worth. If the merchandise is newly purchased, he goes on to say, "and if one judges that it has not decreased in price at the factory . . . it should be put in at the current price." If the merchandise has begun to deteriorate or go out of style, he says to "reduce the price considerably." In 1712, he suggested that merchandise which could be replaced at 5 per cent less should be reduced to the replacement price.[4]

It appears that questions of business solvency prompted the inventory practices fostered by the French law. The ordinance of 1673 served as the basis for a part of the Napoleonic Code of 1807. In the section dealing with books of account, four items dealt with bookkeeping rules, such as authentication, making an inventory of all property, and the like, and six items dealt with the use of the records in case of litigation. French legal commentators have explained the relation of these rules to bankruptcy. A merchant's records would contribute a factual basis for a fair settlement

---

[3] Howard, "Public Rules for Private Accounting in France, 1673 and 1807," 7 *Accounting Rev.* 92 (June, 1932).

[4] Littleton, *Accounting Evolution to 1900* (1933), p. 152.

with the creditors. If a merchant did not keep authenticated records, his bankruptcy was fraudulent under several conditions, namely, if the merchant kept no records, if he concealed records, or if the records did not correctly show his financial position. Legal regulations affecting inventories in France seem to be related to frauds suffered by creditors at the hands of a bankrupt.

In 1797, John Harries Wickes, of Egham, England, published his *Bookkeeping Reformed* which suggested inventory valuation "at prime cost."

At about the same time, a Bristol accountant, Edward Thomas Jones, subscribed to the prime cost rule in his *English System of Bookkeeping*. This book, incidentally, was introduced to the English public with great promotional fanfare and thus proved to be a great financial success for Jones. The full title of the work is indicative of the claims made by the author for his new system: "Jones English System of Bookkeeping by Single or Double Entry, in which it is impossible for an error of the most trifling amount to be passed unnoticed. Calculated effectually to prevent the evils attendant on the methods so long established and adopted to every species of trade. Secured to the Inventor by the King's Letters Patent, Bristol, 1796." Launched as a death-blow to the Italian method (Paciolo *et al.*), the book met with considerable ridicule and derision in England. His fame, however, spread abroad. The book undoubtedly was the first English work on accounting to achieve international renown, and even at the turn of the twentieth century, it was possibly the most widely known book on the subject of accounting in the English language.

James Morrison, a Glasgow accountant, in his *Elements of Book-keeping by Single and Double Entry* (1813), suggested estimating inventory "at prime cost, or at the current prices." This statement is, of course, ambiguous. It may mean that the inventory should be valued either at prime cost or at current prices, or at the lower of cost or market. In any event, Morrison's book marks one of the earliest disagreements with the straightforward prime cost rule.

In 1819 another English writer, Clerk Morrison, endorsed the market-price view in his *Introduction to Bookkeeping and Business*, in which he stated that it was fallacious to value at cost if the present price of an article is less than cost. He suggested that "the gain is in reality obtained as soon as the prices rise, or the loss suffered as soon as they fall."

Seventeen years later, in 1836, an English publication, entitled *New Check Journal upon the Principle of Double Entry*, written by George Jackson, strongly advocated valuation at cost. He insisted that at inventory time price increases or price decreases should not be taken into account since the gain or the loss is not realized or "has not actually yet been suffered."

Thus in the first half of the nineteenth century, British writers were noting the conflict between the balance sheet viewpoint as expressed by Clerk Morrison and the profit and loss viewpoint expressed by George Jackson.

In 1857 a conference was called for the purpose of drafting a uniform commercial code for the German independent states. This draft, which specified valuation at the lower of cost or market, was not approved in that form. In 1861 the statute was made to read that goods and materials should be shown at the "value which ought to be ascribed at the date as of which the inventory and balance sheet are being drawn up."

A wave of promotion and stock speculation in Germany, which began in 1870, came to an abrupt and disastrous climax in 1873. The resulting depression prompted a legislative investigation. It was found that promoters and their attorneys, who were supported by a German court decision in 1873, had interpreted a phrase of the law of 1861 as permitting the use of probable sales price in stating balance sheet assets. This enabled them to publish very attractive balance sheets and to sell vast quantities of stock on the surpluses shown. A new corporation law was developed in 1884 which approved the rule of cost or market. Section 261 of the German Commercial Code of 1897 provided: "Securities and merchandise that have an exchange or market quotation may not be valued higher than at the price at which they were carried at the date of the balance sheet. Or if such price exceeds the price at which they were acquired or produced, then at the last mentioned price."

In 1885, C. R. Trevor, addressing the Manchester Accountants Students' Society, endorsed the cost or market rule. His paper is of slight significance except for the discussion which followed its delivery. One member of the Society commented that it was so thoroughly orthodox from beginning to end that it was very difficult to find any fault with the views expressed. This remark leaves little room for doubt that the cost or market rule had been generally accepted for a considerable period of time.

RECOGNITION OF COST OR MARKET IN THE UNITED STATES

The concept of valuing inventory at lower than its cost was alluded to in an opinion of the Supreme Court of Massachusetts in 1871. The court decided that loss in value of inventory due to a fire should be deducted in computing the profits of the business. In his opinion, the judge said: "The profit and loss of trade in merchandise is not confined to that which results from sales. Depreciation or advance in value of the stock unsold must also be taken into account. Depreciation may come from fluctuation of prices in the market, from deterioration in quality, or diminution in quantity, occasioned by the numerous causes incident to the business." [5] Although this statement suggests that market should be used even where cost is the lower figure, the facts before the court involved a lower market figure. The reference by the court to a situation involving a lower cost is of doubtful significance.

In 1897, two American authors, Broaker and Chapman,[6] insisted that it was "a sound principle to carry the stock at its actual cost, and let the profits or losses be determined upon final sale or disposition." These authors qualify this instruction somewhat, but it is interesting to note their insistence upon the profit and loss viewpoint. Incidentally, Frank Broaker and Richard Chapman became rather famous in accounting circles through their prodigious efforts pressing for public accounting legislation in New York State. In 1896 the legislature passed the first law in the United States creating the professional designation Certified Public Accountant, and Broaker and Chapman received certificates Nos. 1 and 2.

At the St. Louis World's Fair in 1904, a Congress of Accountants was held under the auspices of the Federation of Societies of Public Accountants. Arthur Lowes Dickinson, then senior partner of an American public accounting firm and an outstanding Cambridge-educated accounting authority well acquainted with British and American practices, presented a paper in which he stated, "The general rule for valuation of stocks on hand, namely, 'cost or market, whichever is the lower,' has been evolved and is adopted by the most conservative commercial institutions." [7] The significance of this is threefold. First, Dickinson was an undoubted authority; second, he refers to the rule as a "general rule"; and third, by inference, he justifies the rule by the doctrine of conservatism.

In 1909, W. R. MacKenzie endorsed the rule's consistent application when he affirmed that once adopted, the cost or market rule "should be strictly adhered to, as one year at cost and another at market, regardless of market being lower, will never produce any degree of dependability. Like depreciation, it is only the regular pursuit of the principle adopted that will give satisfactory comparative results." [8]

5 *Meserve v. Andrews*, 106 Mass. 419, 422 (1871).

6 Broaker and Chapman, *The American Accountants Manual* (1897), p. 60.

7 Dickinson, *Congress of Accountants Official Record 1904 World's Fair, St. Louis*, under the auspices of the Federation of Societies of Public Accountants in the United States of America, p. 182.

8 MacKenzie, "The Verification and Treatment of Inventories in Audits and Examinations of Manufacturing and Trading Concerns," 9 *J. Accountancy* 115 (Dec., 1909).

In 1910, Leo Greendlinger, an Austrian-born accounting writer who later became a director, treasurer, and secretary of the Alexander Hamilton Institute in New York, attacked the cost or market rule when he stated:

> It is wrong in principle to value it (inventory) at market price as it interferes with the correct showing of the profit and loss account. If we take the inventory for any reason, not for the purpose of rendering a correct profit and loss account for any given period, we are at liberty to use either form, cost or market value, but when we take inventory for the purpose of ascertaining the cost of sales, for the purpose of showing a correct profit and loss account, we must figure it at cost price only.[9]

This statement seems to mark the beginning of modern expressions of accounting thought which question the soundness of the cost or market rule because of the effect upon income determinations.

From an income tax viewpoint, 1917 marked a most important year in the history of the cost or market rule. The British Board of Inland Revenue, based upon recommendations of a committee of accountants, affirmed the general correctness of using cost or market. In this same year, the United States Treasury Department took similar action. United States taxpayers were given an option to adopt the basis of either (1) cost or (2) cost or market, whichever is lower, for their 1920 inventories. The basis adopted for that year or for any subsequent year when inventories are first a factor in the determination of income must be used consistently, and can be changed only after permission is secured from the Commissioner of Internal Revenue.

During the period commencing with the 1929 stock market crash and concomitant depression, there was a marked change from the former balance sheet viewpoint toward financial accounting. At least equal attention has since been given to the income statement.

A letter dated September 22, 1932, was written to the Committee on Stock List of the New York Stock Exchange by the American Institute of Accountants' Special Committee on Co-operation with Stock Exchanges, officially emphasizing that "the income account is usually far more important than the balance sheet" and referring to the cost or market rule as the principal exception to the primary accounting objective of securing "a proper charge or credit to the income account for the year."[10]

George D. Bailey [11] pointed out, in 1940, that the theory of the lower

---

[9] Greendlinger, *Accountancy Problems with Solutions*, Vol. I (1910), pp. 192, 193.

[10] Quoted in May, *Twenty-five Years of Accounting Responsibility, 1911–1936* (1936), p. 112.

[11] Bailey, "Some Thoughts on the Theory of Inventory Pricing," *Experiences with Extensions of Auditing Procedure and Papers on Other Accounting Subjects Presented at the Fifty-third Annual Meeting, American Institute of Accountants* (1940), p. 60.

of cost or market need not be discarded in favor of a cost theory for income determination if the former results in provision for *anticipated loss*, rather than being used as an artificial rule applied regardless of the probability of loss.

Theoretical discussions of the cost or market rule were interrupted around 1942 by the exigencies of accounting in wartime, and since then the questions have been of lesser immediate concern because of the effects of the inflationary trend.

From this brief history of the cost or market rule, it is interesting to observe the relationship of some of the dates in its development to wars, panics, and taxes. The German depression of 1873 was accompanied by legal approval of the cost or market rule. The year 1917, when the cost or market rule was approved by the British Board of Inland Revenue and the United States Treasury Department, was a year of war and high taxes. The year 1932, which may be identified as the beginning of a period when the arbitrary application of the rule was questioned because of a new emphasis upon the income statement, represented a low point in the depression which had started in the fall of 1929. In recent years, instances where market values for inventory items are below their costs have been found with increasing frequency.

CONCEPTS OF "MARKET" IN INVENTORY DETERMINATIONS

Just as there is no single concept of "cost" that will be the most meaningful in all situations, there is no universally acceptable basis for determining "market." The International Accounting Standards Committee in Statement No. 2 (IAS 2) makes no reference to the term "market" but uses the term "net realizable value." Other commonly used definitions of "market" are "replacement price" and "net realizable value less normal profit."

IAS 2 defines "net realizable" value as being "the estimated selling price in the normal course of business less costs of completion and less costs necessarily to be incurred in order to make the sale." This determination requires giving recognition to all available information, including changes in selling prices subsequent to the inventory date. Consideration is also given to the prospects for disposing of the inventory, giving due regard to the quantity and condition of the goods on hand.

"Replacement price," or "replacement cost," represents the amount for which, in the ordinary course of business, the inventory items could have been acquired or produced either at the inventory date or during the last operating period. For this purpose, recognition is given to the volume in which the company usually purchases the various inventory items and the normal sources of supply.

"Net realizable value less normal profit" represents the amount remaining after allowing for the profit which the business can be expected to realize from the sale of the items included in its inventory.

The bulletin of the AICPA (paragraph 9 of Appendix A) states that the term "market" is to be interpreted as indicating utility on the inventory date and may be thought of in terms of the equivalent expenditure which would have to be made in the ordinary course at that date to procure corresponding utility. The AICPA position is that the cost for an inventory will generally be compared with current replacement cost (by purchase or reproduction), but replacement cost should not be used if it exceeds net realizable value (the estimated selling price in the ordinary course of business less reasonably predictable costs of completion and expenses of disposal) or is less than the latter reduced by an approximately normal profit margin.

IAS 2 states that a decline in the price of materials and other supplies held for incorporation in the production of goods does not necessarily require a writedown to net realizable value. Only if the eventual selling price of the finished product is expected to be less than its historical cost should a writedown of materials inventory be effected. In such cases, the best available measure of the material's net realizable value may be its current replacement cost.

Where the lower of cost or market basis has been adopted for federal income tax purposes, the regulations provide (section 1.471–4 of Appendix C) that under ordinary circumstances and for normal goods in an inventory, cost is to be compared generally with replacement price. Goods on hand or in process of manufacture for delivery on firm sales contracts or contracts not legally subject to cancellation by either party, at fixed prices entered into before the date of the inventory for which the taxpayer is protected against actual loss, must be inventoried at cost, regardless of market value.

An interpretation of this and related provisions in the regulations was the subject of litigation in the case of *D. Loveman & Son Export Corporation*. The decision by the Tax Court (34 T.C. 776) was filed August 5, 1960; the decision in favor of the government was affirmed by the Court of Appeals for the Sixth Circuit on December 16, 1961, without any detailed discussion; and on April 23, 1962, the Supreme Court denied a petition to review the decision.

In the *D. Loveman & Son Export Corporation* case, a warehouser had purchased steel from a premium mill, because during a period of steel shortage the major producing mills sold their production to other customers. The inventory of steel on hand was valued at the posted prices of the major producing mills which were lower than the taxpayer's cost. Where the steel was ultimately sold at a price in excess of the price paid to the premium mill, it was held that the posted prices of the major steel producers did not represent "market." The following paragraphs are quoted from the opinion of the Tax Court:

> The parties are in basic disagreement as to what petitioners' "market" was during the years involved herein. Petitioners argue that the "combination of unusual circumstances" which "temporarily prevented (them) from buying their steel requirements from their usual sources did not effect any change in (their) market for inventory valuation purposes, nor require them to change their customary method of inventory valuation." In support of this contention, they point out that the major mills produced "close to 100 per cent" of all the carbon steel plate rolled in the United States, and that the determination of market value by reference to the published prices of those mills was not only "consistent with petitioners' prior practice, but * * * customary in the steel warehouse business."
>
> Respondent, on the other hand, maintains that the term "particular merchandise," as used in the above-quoted regulation, refers only to the steel which was available to the petitioners during the taxable years in question and, therefore, that petitioners' market did not include steel produced by the major mills. The record, viewed in the light of applicable precedent, compellingly supports respondent's position on this issue.

This case also considers the appropriate treatment of "freight-in" expenditures. It was held that the transportation expense had to be added to the cost of the steel in order to reflect income clearly. The inventory volume had not been at all constant, so the decision is not applicable to a situation involving an established accounting practice of consistently considering "freight-in" as a current expense where there are only normal fluctuations in the annual inventories.

The income tax regulations (section 1.471–4(b)) specifically recognize situations in which net realizable value may be the appropriate amount to be assigned to an inventory item. Replacement cost of work in process and finished goods (or articles bought for resale) would not constitute market if it exceeds what could be realized upon sale in the ordinary course of business. For example, paper stock may have a definite market value, but if it is converted into a printed book which no one wants to buy, its market value has become nil. Replacement cost valuations for income tax purposes must be supported by actual sales within a reasonable period, generally thirty days, before and after the inventory date. The practicality and necessity of the thirty-day rule is subject to serious question.

The federal income tax regulations also provide in section 1.471–2(c) that, whether cost or the lower of cost or market basis of stating inventories is used, the amount assigned to goods which are "unsalable at normal prices or unusable in the normal way because of damage, imperfections, shop wear, changes of style, odd or broken lots, or other similar causes, including second-hand goods taken in exchange" should not exceed net realizable value. Further, it is stated that if the inventory items unusable in the normal way "consist of raw materials or partly finished goods held for use or consumption, they shall be valued upon a reasonable basis, taking into consideration the usability and the condition of the goods, but in no case shall such value be less than the scrap value." Under the regulations these adjustments, made under a procedure for stating inventories at cost as well as under a lower of cost or market election, represent redeterminations of the cost allocable to the units on hand rather than writedowns to market. When a shipment of merchandise is received or a production order is completed, it is normally expected that some units will be unsalable at normal prices or unusable in the normal way. It cannot be predicted precisely which or how many units will reach this status so for convenience all units may be considered tentatively as though they have the same cost. After the major portion of the shipment has been disposed of in the normal manner, hindsight is applied to adjust the cost allocated to the remaining units. The correct cost for these units is net realizable value, and the excessive amount tentatively allocated is an addition to the cost of the units sold. Similarly, if secondhand goods taken in an exchange cannot be sold for an amount equal to the credit allowed on the trade-in transaction, there is no writedown to market when the cost of the secondhand goods is reduced to net realizable value. The cost revision represents an adjustment of the originally computed profit on the prior sale.

In 1975 the Tax Court considered the proper handling of excess inventory *quantities*, that is, inventory quantities in excess of the amount that could reasonably expected to be sold during the normal business cycle. The case is *Thor Power Tool Company* (64 T.C. 154). The decision was filed May 6, 1975 and affirmed by the Court of Appeals for the Seventh Circuit, and the U.S. Supreme Court.

The taxpayer in the *Thor Power Tool Company* case was a manufacturer of hand held power tools, replacement parts, and accessories. It had three manufacturing plants for tools: Aurora, Illinois; LaGrange, Illinois; and Los Angeles, California. A fourth plant in Cincinnati, Ohio manufactured rubber products. From time to time the company would discontinue production of a particular tool and retain an inventory of replacement parts, the only market for which was former purchaser of the discontinued tool.

In 1964 new management concluded that existing inventory quantities were excessive. Prior management had reflected inventory at cost, including portions of the inventory that new management viewed to be in excess of anticipated market demand. A physical inventory was taken at all factories and branches, after which a writedown was deemed necessary. Two procedures were employed: first, based on forecasted demand for 1965 and later years, (a) items not in excess of 12 months' anticipated demand were not written down; (b) items in excess of 12 months' anticipated demand, but not in excess of 18 months' anticipated demand, were written down 50%; (c) items in excess of 18 months' anticipated demand, but not in excess of 24 months' anticipated demand, were written down 75%; and, (d) items in excess of 24 months' anticipated demand were completely written off. Second, for spare parts and accessories stocked for tools no longer manufactured, the cost was amortized over 10 years.

The 1964 ending inventory contained items that, in the opinion of Thor management, were unsalable in the normal course of business because they were in excess of reasonably foreseeable demand. Thor produced expert witnesses whose testimony convinced the Court that the procedures followed in making the writedowns resulted in an inventory at lower of cost or market in accordance with generally accepted accounting principles.

In making the writedown, Thor kept no detailed records of prices, dates, quantities, or other relevant details. Thor made no effort to determine the purchase or reproduction cost of each item that it determined to be in excess at December 31, 1964. Thor made no effort to determine the market value of each item on hand at the inventory date. There was no segregation or earmarking of specific units, and no distinction was apparent between specific units so as to distinguish those carried at full value from those written down or written off.

In upholding the Commissioner's disallowance of Thor's inventory adjustment for 1964, the Court cited four reasons:

1. Although Thor amply demonstrated that the writedown was made in accordance with generally accepted accounting principles and within the term "best accounting practice," Thor failed to show that the method "clearly reflects taxable income."
2. The procedures used by Thor to identify and value excess inventory failed to clearly reflect income because they were "speculative."
3. Thor did not compare the replacement value of each item with its cost to determine which was lower.
4. If the IRS were to approve a concept permitting a writedown of inventory based on an otherwise unsupported opinion of the taxpayer as to its ultimate salability, "it would, within some unknown limits, permit the taxpayer to determine how much income tax it wanted to pay for a given year."

The result of *Thor Power Tool Company* is a different inventory value for accounting and tax purposes, both using lower of cost or market.

The Supreme Court of the United States sustained the government's position in the Thor Power Tool Company case in January, 1979, reasoning that there are two tests to which an inventory method must conform in tax accounting. Thor Power satisfied the first test—it conformed to generally accepted accounting principles. But it did not meet the paramount test—it failed, "in the opinion of the [IRS]", to clearly reflect taxable income.

Although Thor's write-down of approximately $1,000,000 under the inventory "aging formula" was held to be unacceptable for federal income tax purposes it should be noted that the IRS did allow Thor to deduct approximately $3,000,000 in inventory write-downs in 1964 for obsolete parts, damaged or defective tools, demonstration or sales samples, parts stocked for unsuccessful products, and similar items.

It should also be noted that the Internal Revenue Service has reported that the income tax regulations relative to cost or market are under review and may be revised.

Application of the various concepts of "market" can be illustrated by assuming situations involving an inventory item as to which the profit factors would normally be as follows:

	Amount	%
Sales value.............................	$3.00	100
Expense incurred in disposing of inventory	.30	10
Net realizable value........................	2.70	90
Cost of inventory item......................	2.10	70
Gross profit..............................	$ .60	20

The amounts assigned to the ·item for inventory purposes under each of six different assumed conditions, in accordance with the AICPA bulletin, the statement by the International Accounting Standards Committee and the United States income tax regulations, are shown on page 155.

In the first of these assumed situations, there would be justification for assigning to the inventory an amount less than cost if the explanation for the 10 per cent smaller selling price was that the goods on hand were damaged or otherwise not in their normal condition. On the same basis, an amount less than $1.95 might be justified for the inventory in the second situation.

A smaller amount than has been stated as being in accordance with the AICPA bulletin would be assigned to the inventory under the sixth situation if the normal profit of 60¢ had been deducted from the net realizable value of $2.43 rather than the 54¢ determined by applying the same *rate*

Application of Different Lower-of-Cost-or-Market Rules Under Varying Circumstances

| | Replacement price exceeds cost, but | | Cost exceeds replacement price and | | | |
| | | | | Net realizable value declines | | |
	Normal profit will not be obtained (1)	Cost exceeds net realizable value (2)	Sales value is unchanged (3)	In proportion to decline in cost (4)	More than cost (5)	Less than cost (6)
Cost..........	$2.10	$2.10	$2.10	$2.10	$2.10	$2.10
Replacement price.........	2.20	2.20	1.89	1.89	1.89	1.68
Net realizable value.........	2.40	1.95	2.70	2.43	2.16	2.43
Net realizable value less normal profit (7/9 of net realizable value).....	1.86⅔	1.51⅔	2.10	1.89	1.68	1.89
Amount assigned to inventory in accordance with:						
AICPA.........	2.10	1.95	2.10	1.89	1.89	1.89
International Accounting Standards Committee........	2.10	1.95	2.10	2.10	2.10	2.10
Income tax regulations.........	2.10	1.95	1.89	1.89	1.89	1.68

Assumed situations with respect to inventory item:
(1) Sales value is down 10 per cent, i.e., $2.70.
(2) Sales value is down 25 per cent, i.e., $2.25.
(3) Replacement price is 10 per cent below cost and net realizable value is unchanged.
(4) Replacement price is 10 per cent below cost and net realizable value is down 10 per cent.
(5) Replacement price is 10 per cent below cost and net realizable value is down 20 per cent.
(6) Replacement price is 20 per cent below cost and net realizable value is down 10 per cent.

155

of profit. Whether the amount or rate of profit should be used for this purpose must be determined by the circumstances of each individual case. The controlling consideration is which procedure will make the financial statements more useful to the reader.

The objective of the AICPA bulletin is to assign to the goods in the inventory an amount reflecting their usefulness. The reasons for the recommended procedure are stated as follows:

> . . . As a general guide, utility is indicated primarily by the current cost of replacement of the goods as they would be obtained by purchase or reproduction. In applying the rule, however, judgment must always be exercised and no loss should be recognized unless the evidence indicates clearly that a loss has been sustained. There are therefore exceptions to such a standard. Replacement or reproduction prices would not be appropriate as a measure of utility when the estimated sales value, reduced by the costs of completion and disposal, is lower, in which case the realizable value so determined more appropriately measures utility. Furthermore, where the evidence indicates that cost will be recovered with an approximately normal profit upon sale in the ordinary course of business, no loss should be recognized even though replacement or reproduction costs are lower. [Par. 9, Appendix A.]

Hence, the AICPA bulletin supports the replacement cost interpretation of market on the grounds that a decline in replacement price below cost indicates that the usefulness of the inventory as having a revenue-producing potential declined and that this loss should be charged against revenues of the period in which it occurs. Fundamentally, this interpretation assumes that a decrease in purchase or reproduction cost will be followed by a decrease in selling price.

The International Accounting Standards Committee recommends the use of net realizable value, and its statement does not refer to the term market; however, the use of replacement cost as mentioned previously as a measure of net realizable value is also recognized as appropriate in some situations.

APPLICATION OF LOWER OF COST OR MARKET RULE

The AICPA publication provides that the lower of cost or market rule may be applied to aggregate values of inventories, to different categories, or to individual items. The reasons for the alternative bases of comparison are summarized below:

1. If there is only one end-product category, the utility of the total stock— the inventory in its entirety—may have the greatest significance.

2. When no loss of income is expected to take place as a result of reduced replacement prices for certain goods because others forming components of the same general categories of finished products have a market equally in excess of cost, such components need not be adjusted to market to the extent that they are in balanced quantities.

3. To the extent that the stocks of particular materials or components are excessive in relation to others, the procedure of applying the lower of cost or market to the individual items constituting the excess should be followed. This would also apply in cases in which the items enter into the production of unrelated products or products having a material variation in the rate of turnover.

Unless an effective method of classifying categories is practicable, the cost or market rule should be applied to each item in the inventory. This is the basis for comparison contemplated by section 1.471–4(c) of the federal income tax regulations.

Under IAS 2, the lower of cost or net realizable value rule may be applied to groups of similar items or to individual items. There is no provision in IAS 2 for applying the rule to the aggregate values of inventories as in ARB 43.

Obviously, the amount assigned to the inventory in its entirety may differ substantially, depending upon the procedure followed in making comparisons between cost and market. The most appropriate procedure will depend upon the character and composition of the inventory, and the selection should be that which most clearly reflects periodic income. Whatever procedure is adopted should be applied consistently from year to year.

INVENTORY WRITEDOWNS AND THE INCOME STATEMENT

The evaluation of inventories is significant from the standpoint of both the balance sheet and the income statement. In the former, the inventory evaluation influences the current asset total, the grand total of all the assets, the ratio between current assets and current liabilities, and the retained earnings figure. In the latter, the inventory evaluation may materially influence the cost of goods sold and the net profit.

Aware of this problem, the Securities and Exchange Commission in late 1976 issued Accounting Series Release 190, which requires companies meeting certain reporting criteria (based on size) to disclose in the notes to the annual financial statements filed with the Commission replacement cost data as it relates to inventories. The Commission stated, in releasing this pronouncement, that under current economic conditions, disclosure of data relating to the impact of changes in the prices of specific goods was of significance to investors in understanding the current operations of any company. Information required to be disclosed includes the current replacement cost of inventories. If the current replacement cost exceeds the related net realizable value, that fact must be stated.

From an accounting standpoint, the cost or market rule was originally justified on the basis of balance sheet conservatism. In general, it is wise to anticipate no profits and to provide for all possible losses. As the historical review has demonstrated, the cost or market rule was developed during the long period when bankers and other creditors were primarily concerned with the balance sheet and when relatively little consideration was given to the income statement. By those who thought in terms of realizable value, inventory was considered in relation to possible cash proceeds from selling that inventory. Inventories were valued under the same general theory as receivables by reasoning that all assets ultimately will be converted into cash and should not be stated at an amount greater than their cash equivalent.

Since the 1930s, the income statement has become more generally recognized as a significant measure of debt-paying ability and investment desirability. As a consequence, bankers, other creditors, business management, and stockholders are becoming increasingly concerned with the reported earnings—not only with the income statement for a single period, but with the trend of earnings over a series of years.

There is an inconsistency in absorbing against current profits an unrealized loss on unsold merchandise, while ignoring an unrealized potential increase in gross profit which may result from a rising market. This inconsistency is justified on the grounds of conservatism; however, unless there is adequate disclosure, the cost or market rule may not be as conservative as it appears to be. This is particularly true when giving consideration to the income statements for a series of periods. If, at the close of one period, the market value of the inventory is less than its cost, the reduction of the inventory valuation to market undoubtedly produces a conservative balance sheet valuation and a conservative computation of income in the statements for that period. Nevertheless, the amount of earnings reported by periods may be altered materially by the shifting of income from one period to another.

For the purpose of illustration, it is assumed that at the beginning of January merchandise was purchased at a cost of $100,000; that half of the goods were sold in January for $75,000; that the remaining half were sold in February for $73,000; and that the inventory at the end of January, which cost $50,000, had a market value of $40,000. The following statement shows the computation of gross profit for the two months, both under the cost or market rule and with the inventory valued at cost.

	With inventory valued at	
	Cost or market	Cost
January:		
Sales..	$75,000	$75,000
Cost of goods sold ($100,000 of purchases minus the inventory).	60,000	50,000
Gross profit......................................	$15,000	$25,000
February:		
Sales..	$73,000	$73,000
Cost of goods sold (consisting of the opening inventory).......	40,000	50,000
Gross profit......................................	$33,000	$23,000

The $40,000 balance sheet valuation for the inventory at the end of January and the statement of $15,000 of gross profit for the month may be accepted as conservative. Some explanation is required, however, for showing $33,000 of gross profit for February even though the selling prices had to be reduced so that $2,000 less was actually realized from the second half of the merchandise. The reader of the income statements must be made to realize that the increase in February profit was caused by the $10,000 writedown of the inventory at the end of January.

In the illustration, it was assumed that the anticipated market decline did not fully materialize in February. The next statement assumes that the sales proceeds decreased $10,000—an amount equal to the decrease in inventory valuation—during the second month:

	With inventory valued at	
	Cost or market	Cost
January:		
Sales....................	$75,000	$75,000
Cost of goods sold........	60,000	50,000
Gross profit............	$15,000	$25,000
February:		
Sales....................	$65,000	$65,000
Cost of goods sold........	40,000	50,000
Gross profit............	$25,000	$15,000

The figures in the "Cost" column reflect what actually happened. The company made less profit in February than in January because of the decrease in selling prices. The "Cost or Market" column tells a very strange story. The company made more profit in February than in January, despite the decrease in selling prices. Where there has been an inventory writedown from cost to market, the gross profit margin may bear no relation to the volume of sales.

The cost or market inventory-pricing basis is founded on the assumption that a decrease in market purchase costs will be followed by a decrease in selling prices before the disposal of the inventory. In the long run there is a tendency for cost and selling prices to move together, but a lower market value at the close of one fiscal period need not always mean a loss of profit in the following period. Selling prices are not always adjusted downward to accord with a decline in current buying cost. Furthermore, not all declines in market value are permanent. A counter market movement often restores the price prior to the sale of the inventory. It should also be noted that the loss which is feared is not always a loss of cost, but rather a loss of potential profit. Hence, there is a trend toward the opinion that it is not necessary or desirable to reduce the inventory valuation to market if there is no probability that sales prices will also decrease.

From the standpoint of measurement of net income, consideration must be given to the procedures associated with the assignment or "matching" of costs against related revenues. The emphasis should not be one of inventory "valuation," but of cost assignment, the aim being to carry forward the amount of unabsorbed costs (residue) properly chargeable against future sales. As stressed by George O. May,

. . . The primary objective in accounting for those items which are subject to inventory accounting is to assure a proper charge against revenue in the determination of periodic income in accordance with the concept of income by which the accounting is governed. This involves (a) a proper matching of costs against the revenues that are attributed to the period and (b) the elimination of such part, if any, of the remaining costs as is found to be in excess of the useful costs properly chargeable against future periods.[12]

Thus, an inventory writedown because of a price level decline is predicated on loss of utility.

When a diminution in the revenue-producing potential of an inventory is recognized, it may be desirable in detailed income statements prepared for management purposes to disclose any material amount of loss as a charge separately identified from the consumed costs described as "cost of goods

[12] May, "Inventory Pricing and Contingency Reserves: Comment on New Accounting Research Bulletins," 84 J. Accountancy 366 (Nov., 1947).

sold." Such disclosure allows comparisons to be made between operating results of different periods without the abnormal loss arising from the ownership of inventory when the market value declined. In shareholders' reports and other published financial statements, this type of loss is seldom specifically identified because it is not generally material in amount, and, further, the treatment of the loss as a separate item may be interpreted as implying that management should not be held accountable for the fact that there are goods held in the inventory with respect to which the market value has declined below cost.

Application of the lower of cost or market rule in financial statements translated from one currency to another involves special considerations which are set forth in Paragraph 14 of Statement of Financial Accounting Standards No. 8 [13] and a subsequent interpretation of that statement.[14]

[13] "Accounting for the Translation of Foreign Currency Translations and Foreign Currency Financial Statements," issued by the Financial Accounting Standards Board in October 1975.

[14] FASB Interpretation No. 17 (February 1977)—"Applying the Lower of Cost or Market Rule in Translated Financial Statements."

EIGHT

Flow of Costs vs. Flow of Goods

Mrs. Smith is asked to serve coffee at her church for a group of visiting ministers. There is a pound can of coffee on her pantry shelf imprinted "20¢ off regular price," and the rubber stamped cost of $3.20 is still legible. Her kitchen canister is almost empty and Mrs. Smith stops at her favorite supermarket on the way to the church. Another pound can of the same brand is purchased for $3.35. When she arrives at the church, Mrs. Smith uses the $3.20 coffee for the ministers, leaving the $3.35 can in the car to take home for her family's use, and later in the day she starts wondering whether she did the right thing. The vacuum pack assured the freshness of the coffee served the ministers and many complimentary remarks had been made during the social hour, but would it have been a more generous act to have used the pound for which $3.35 had been paid?

The discussion at the Smith family dinner table that evening started with considering whether the contribution to the church had been $3.20, $3.35 or $3.40. Mrs. Smith made a plea for the $3.40 figure (after all, the fact of a 20¢ saving was printed in large letters and she should get credit for an advantageous purchase), but her husband pointed out that their family accounts and those of business generally reflect only the actual amounts expended. In concluding that the contribution was $3.35 rather than $3.20 the Smiths were basically applying a concept of the flow of costs independent of the flow of goods.

Under normal circumstances, financial statements reflecting the results of the operation of a business enterprise during a particular period are prepared on a going-concern basis. Consistent with this concept of continuing operations, there will always be goods on hand available for sale.

The goods owned at the end of an accounting period will seldom be exactly comparable to the goods in the opening inventory, but the purpose of the inventory will be the same: to make possible uninterrupted realization of income through sales.

ALTERNATIVES TO USE OF SPECIFIC COSTS

The appropriateness of using average costs rather than specifically identified costs has been discussed in Chapter 6, beginning on page 120. The averaging process is in one sense a concept of a flow of costs; but it can also be viewed as merely a compilation of the actual cost for a group of similar items under circumstances where the amount paid for each item has no significance. The entire group of items is considered as a single entity; and when particular items are separated, they are treated as merely a proportionate part of the whole.

The retail method discussed in Chapter 13 is another example of a procedure not dependent upon identifying the actual cost of particular items. This inventory method, like the others, was developed to summarize in a significant manner the voluminous transactions of an enterprise. The assumptions upon which the retail method is based are sound, and the determinations of amounts to be assigned to inventories permit a fair reflection of the results of business operations.

Other inventory methods not dependent upon the actual cost for the specific items on hand have been developed for use in particular industries. Products of agriculture and mining are sometimes inventoried at sales prices less expenditures to be incurred in marketing.[1] A dealer in securities may inventory unsold securities at market value.[2] Livestock raisers may use the unit-livestock-price method, which provides for the valuation of the different classes of animals in the inventory at a standard unit price for each animal within a class.[3] These inventory methods are of special-purpose design, and there may be other procedures appropriate for particular circumstances; but there are two important inventory procedures based upon assumptions as to the flow of costs which will be considered in some detail: *first-in, first-out* and *last-in, first-out*.

Computations of income which attempt to reflect the actual flow of goods are not necessarily the most meaningful to business management, investors, or creditors. Each of these groups is normally more concerned with what the future earnings of the business enterprise will be than with the amount which could be realized from the inventory if it were liquidated completely and the activity discontinued.

[1] Paragraph 16, Appendix A; and section 1.471–6(d), Appendix C.
[2] Section 1.471–5, Appendix C.
[3] Section 1.471–6(e), Appendix C.

FIRST-IN, FIRST-OUT (FIFO) INVENTORY METHOD

Under the first-in, first-out (FIFO) inventory method, cost is computed on the assumption that goods sold or consumed are those which have been longest on hand and that those remaining in stock represent the latest purchases or production.

The federal income tax regulations (section 1.471–2(d) of Appendix C) imply that the FIFO method should be used only where the goods in the inventory have been so intermingled that they cannot be identified with specific invoices. On the other hand, it is recognized by the American Institute of Certified Public Accountants (paragraph 6 of Appendix A) that if the materials purchased in various lots are identical and interchangeable, the use of identified cost for the various lots may not produce the most useful financial statements. Regardless of the restrictions implied in the wording of the federal income tax regulations, there is no actual conflict between the procedures used for financial statement and federal income tax purposes. Both the Internal Revenue Code and the income tax regulations provide that inventories are to be taken on such basis as will conform as nearly as may be to the best accounting practice in the trade or business and most clearly reflect the income.

In practice, some form of FIFO method is used in the majority of inventory computations. The principle can be applied to individual items, such as particular parts, or to the entire production of a plant or department (particularly in the application of overhead). A FIFO assumption was made for the purpose of the illustration in Chapter 6.

LAST-IN, FIRST-OUT (LIFO) INVENTORY METHOD

The second of the important inventory procedures is the last-in, first-out (LIFO) method. Under LIFO it is assumed that the stocks sold or consumed in any period are those most recently acquired or made. As a consequence of this assumption, the stocks to be carried forward as the inventory are considered as if they were those earliest acquired or made.

The result of the LIFO method is to charge current revenues with amounts approximating current replacement costs. To the goods owned at the end of any period are assigned costs applicable to items purchased or made in earlier periods.

The number of companies switching to the LIFO method of inventory costing has been very significant. A report by AICPA in 1977[5] suggested that LIFO usage more than doubled between 1973 and 1976. Presently, approximately 20% of the annual reports contained in the National Automated Accounting Research System report the use of LIFO. The change

[5] AICPA: Accounting Trends and Techniques, 31st Edition. AICPA; New York: 1977.

to LIFO has been attributed to the high rates of inflation being experienced in the United States and management's desire to match more closely current costs with current revenues, thereby minimizing the impact of inventory inflation on profits and income taxes.

It is more obvious with respect to LIFO than FIFO—although true under both inventory methods—that the concepts are as to the flow of costs independent of the flow of goods. A company roasting, grinding, and selling coffee, or one dealing in meats or produce, will not physically have in its closing inventory the same units that were on hand at the beginning of the year. Similarly, it must be emphasized that the dollar amount assigned to an inventory has no effect upon its actual value to the company. The revenue-producing potential of the property owned is not changed by the inventory method adopted.

The federal income tax regulations (section 1.472–1(b) of Appendix C) recognize that the LIFO flow of cost concept can be extended to transactions involving goods which cannot be physically identified, and may not even be in existence. In the case of a business which regularly and consistently matches purchases with sales in a manner similar to hedging on a futures market, contracts not legally subject to cancellation by either party, entered into at fixed prices on or before the date of an inventory, may be included in purchases or sales, as the case may be, in determining the cost of goods sold. The only requirements are that the practice be regularly and consistently adhered to and that it results in income being clearly reflected.

Many types of business risks can be shifted to others by the purchase of insurance, but no general insurance is available specifically against price fluctuations. A large part of the risk of price declines and advances can be shifted to others, however, for goods traded on organized commodity exchanges. These exchanges make hedging possible, and some businesses strive similarly to avoid the risk of price changes by matching purchases with sales and entering into firm contracts for future delivery whenever a purchase or sale is made. The objective is to permit the manufacturer or processor to concentrate on performing his own conversion function efficiently and to minimize the extent to which income is affected by fluctuations in the market value of the material involved.

The development of the LIFO principle, its acceptance for financial statement and federal income tax purposes, and the procedures followed in its application under varying circumstances are discussed in subsequent chapters. The fact that LIFO is fundamentally a principle for determining income is evidenced by the name "last-in, first-out." The phrase itself connotes a flow of costs. It is easier to compute a cost for the items in an inventory than to compute a cost for each sales transaction; consequently, the inventory approach is adopted to accomplish as simply as possible the desired objective of properly stating income under this flow of cost concept.

RECOGNITION OF LIFO IN
INTERIM FINANCIAL STATEMENTS

Except for paragraph 14b of APB Opinion No. 28, authoritative accounting literature does not presently prescribe the appropriate treatment of the income effect of interim LIFO increments or decrements, that is, whether such effect should be based upon a separate interim calculation or upon a pro rata (based on estimated sales, cost of sales, or expired portion of the year) recognition of the estimated annual effect.

In 1978 the Research Foundation of the Financial Executives Institute published the results of a survey which showed the bases on which 79 respondents (who maintain internal accounting records on a FIFO or average cost basis and make "off-line" LIFO conversions) indicated they would account at interim for an annual LIFO adjustment (i.e., the increase in the LIFO reserve) in a year of steadily rising unit costs. The bases presented and responses were as follows:

1. Allocate equally to each interim period		28%
2. Allocate to interim periods based on:		
(a) Estimated annual sales		10
(b) Estimated annual cost of goods sold		10
		48
3. Allocate to interim periods on the basis of a computation for each period similar to that performed on an annual basis		52
		100%

The Accounting Standards Division of the AICPA has requested the Financial Accounting Standards Board to give prompt consideration to this matter in view of the recent popularity of the LIFO method and the increased emphasis being given to reporting results of operations for interim periods. The Financial Accounting Standards Board issued on May 25, 1978 a discussion memorandum which analyzes the LIFO and other issues related to "Interim Financial Accounting and Reporting."

For financial statement purposes LIFO can be applied to any accounting period—a month, a quarter, or a full year. For federal income tax purposes, however, it is applied to the period for which the tax is computed, which is normally a full year. Most companies prepare, in addition to their annual financial statements, detailed or summarized financial statements for monthly or quarterly periods within the year. Where inventory quantities remain constant throughout the year, the application of LIFO is relatively simple. Since such a condition is rare, an accounting system must be sufficiently flexible to recognize adequately the impact of LIFO on operating results. When LIFO is used, an estimate of the year-end LIFO inventory must be made as of the end of each period for which financial statements are to be prepared. If such estimate indicates that the year-end LIFO inventory will be equal to or greater than the beginning of the year LIFO inventory, differences between the beginning of the year LIFO inventory and the LIFO inventory at the end of the interim period might be treated as follows:

> **Decreases**—Cost of sales would be charged with the cost of goods purchased plus an estimated amount to cover the cost to be incurred in making good the temporary decrease in inventory.

> **Increases**—The charge to cost of sales might be based on any of the approaches listed above, pricing the increase as of the end of the interim period on a basis which takes into consideration the basis on which the year-end increment will be priced, i.e., first-purchase, last-purchase, or average-purchase costs.

If the year-end LIFO inventory is expected to be less than the beginning of the year LIFO inventory, how should the LIFO cost of the goods liquidated be treated? A substantial difference between LIFO cost and replacement cost will result in an abnormally low (or high) cost of sales for the period in which the liquidation occurs, thus results in a distortion of operating results for the period. Generally, the low cost related to liquidation is reflected in cost of sales for the period in which the liquidation occurs with, if material, separate disclosure.

ILLUSTRATION OF LIFO FOR QUARTERLY FINANCIAL STATEMENTS

Compilation of the information required to prepare quarterly income statements under the LIFO method may be illustrated by the case of a company using a commodity measured in tons, such as steel scrap. Quarterly acquisitions are as follows:

	Tons	Cost Total	Cost Per ton
First quarter	28,000	$ 952,000	$34.00
Second quarter	25,000	937,500	37.50
To date	53,000	1,889,500	35.65
Third quarter	37,000	1,480,000	40.00
To date	90,000	3,369,500	37.44
Fourth quarter	28,000	1,232,000	44.00
To date	118,000	$4,601,500	39.00

Quarterly inventories and activity during each quarter are as follows:

Summary of Quarterly Inventories

Inventory quantities (tons):

	Opening inventory	Acquired	Consumed	Closing inventory
First quarter	21,000	28,000	28,500	20,500
Second quarter	20,500	25,000	34,500	11,000
Third quarter	11,000	37,000	30,000	18,000
Fourth quarter	18,000	28,000	21,000	25,000

Inventory amounts:

		Cost	
	Tons	Per ton	Total
Opening inventory			
Initial layer	15,000	$24.00	$360,000
First increment	1,000	40.00	40,000
Second increment	5,000	28.00	140,000
	21,000		540,000
March 31			
Initial layer	15,000	24.00	360,000
First increment	1,000	40.00	40,000
Second increment	4,500	28.00	126,000
	20,500		526,000
June 30			
Initial layer	11,000	24.00	264,000
September 30			
Initial layer	15,000	24.00	360,000
First increment	1,000	40.00	40,000
Second increment	2,000	28.00	56,000
	18,000		456,000
December 31			
Opening inventory	21,000		540,000
Current increment	4,000	34.00	136,000
	25,000		676,000

The current increment in the December 31 inventory has been priced at the average per ton acquisition cost for the first quarter as shown in the summary of quarterly acquisitions. If the average cost for the year ($39.00) were used, there would be a $20,000 increase in the carrying value of the December 31 inventory.

Assuming that the liquidations in the first three quarters were considered temporary, cost of sales for such periods has been charged with the anticipated replacement cost of the temporarily depleted LIFO layers, as required by Opinion No. 28 of the Accounting Principles Board. Unless this were done, the charge to cost of sales for periods in which the temporary liquidations occurred would be artificially low and the charges in the replacement periods would be artificially high. The contra credits and charges to the cost of sales adjustments shown below should be to accounts payable rather than to inventory since the costs in question relate to products sold and the accounting treatment specified in paragraph 14b of Opinion No. 28 relates to "costs associated with revenue."

Charges to cost of sales for each quarter, recognizing the temporary nature of the LIFO liquidations:

Quarter	Opening inventory	Cost of acquisitions	Closing inventory	Charged to Cost of Sales		
				Unadjusted	Adjustment *	Adjusted
First	$540,000	$ 952,000	$(526,000)	$ 966,000	$ 4,750	$ 970,750
Second	526,000	937,500	(264,000)	1,199,500	119,250	1,318,750
Third	264,000	1,480,000	(456,000)	1,288,000	(76,000)	1,212,000
Fourth	456,000	1,232,000	(676,000)	1,012,000	(48,000)	964,000
		$4,601,500		$4,465,500	$ —	$4,465,500

Determined as follows:

Quarter	Tons liquidated (replaced)	LIFO cost		Anticipated replacement cost		Deferred credit
		per ton	total	per ton	total	(charge)
First	500	$28	$ 14,000	$37.50	$ 18,750	$ 4,750
Second	4,500	28	126,000			
	1,000	40	40,000	40.00	380,000	119,250
	4,000	24	96,000			
Cumulative adjustment **					1,250	
To date	10,000		276,000	40.00	400,000	124,000
Third	(4,000)	24	(96,000)			
	(1,000)	40	(40,000)	40.00	(280,000)	(76,000)
	(2,000)	28	(56,000)			
Cumulative adjustment **					12,000	
To date	3,000		84,000	44.00	132,000	48,000
Fourth	(3,000)		(84,000)	44.00	(132,000)	(48,000)
	—		$ —		$ —	$ —

* To adjust to latest estimated total replacement cost.

The reasonableness of the adjusted costs and the need for the adjustments in preparing quarterly financial statements are evident from the following comparison:

	Per ton cost of acquisitions		Per ton cost of tonnage consumed	
	Quarter	Year-to-date	Unadjusted	Adjusted
First quarter	$34.00	$34.00	$33.89	$34.06
Second quarter	37.50	35.65	34.77	38.22
Third quarter	40.00	37.44	42.93	40.40
Fourth quarter	44.00	39.00	48.19	45.90

ANALYZING LIFO INVENTORIES FOR BALANCE SHEET PURPOSES

An indication of the extent to which an inventory is composed of raw materials, work in process, and finished goods may be significant to readers of financial statements. In certain cases other or more detailed breakdowns may be considered desirable. This information is important to the extent that it permits the reader to ascertain whether the inventory is reasonably balanced. For example, a larger portion of the inventory being in the form of finished goods at the end of the year than at the beginning of the year may indicate the consumers' demand for the product is diminishing. Under other circumstances the accumulation of a finished goods inventory may reflect management decisions made in anticipation of difficulties incident to renewal of an agreement with a labor union.

Where inventories are determined under a LIFO method and pools are established on a natural business unit or other broad basis, no amounts can be specifically identified with the various types of goods within a pool. In some instances, however, significant information will be provided if the total LIFO cost is allocated to whatever classifications of goods are deemed appropriate by reference to the relative current values for each classification. Alternatively, this allocation might be made by considering the relative amounts of base-year costs for the various types of goods in the inventory. The amount assigned to the inventory as a whole will reflect a last-in, first-out flow of costs, but the flow of goods will govern the allocation of the total to the items owned on the balance sheet date.

NINE

Development of LIFO

The significance of the income statement and the necessity for matching costs with revenue is generally acknowledged by bankers, management, and others interested in financial statements. It is not always appreciated, however, that in periods of rapid price change a part of the increase in earnings during the upward cycle is attributable to the rise in prices of raw materials, labor, and overhead items. Among the factors upon which businessmen base selling prices are the anticipated costs which will be incurred in replacing the units sold.

During an inflationary period, the goods on hand at the beginning of the year will generally be sold at a higher price than contemplated at the time they were acquired. This increase in sales proceeds will be reflected in the income for the year; but, if the inventory is maintained at the same level in terms of physical quantities, the additional dollars received from the sales transactions will have been expended to a substantial extent in acquiring the replacement units.

Dollars of earnings needed to maintain the inventory so that the business operations may continue are not available for plant expansion, the payment of dividends, or any of the other purposes to which funds derived from sales at a profit are applied.

LIFO has been developed as a modification of other accepted inventory cost theories to give a more meaningful income statement.

171

DEVELOPMENT OF LIFO BY THE PETROLEUM INDUSTRY

In August, 1934, the chairman of the Committee on Uniform Methods of Oil Accounting of the American Petroleum Institute notified the board of directors of that Institute that, after several years' study, his committee had voted unanimously the previous May to recommend for approval the determination of inventories of petroleum companies on a LIFO basis. This recommendation was considered and approved by the board of directors of the Petroleum Institute on November 12, 1934.

The basic LIFO principles for petroleum inventories approved in 1934 and an illustration of its application are reproduced below. The reader will note, however, that the unit prices have lost all significance in light of the demand-supply picture of the current day.

Basic Principles of

"LAST IN, FIRST OUT"

Uniform Method of Valuing Petroleum Inventories [1]

Recommended by the Committee on Uniform Methods of Oil Accounting and approved by the Board of Directors of the American Petroleum Institute, Dallas, Texas, November 12, 1934.

Current Costs Against Current Sales: Current costs of crude oil and products should be charged against current sales as long as inventory quantities remain approximately unchanged, or sales are about equivalent to new acquisitions (production and purchases).

Crude Oil: In the costing of crude oil stock (inventory), current production and current purchases should be the first applied to current cost of sales and current operations. Wherever practicable, the various grades of crude oil handled by the company may be classified or grouped into a minimum number of "Grades." "Grades" of crude oil mean a major grouping of crude oils such as used in reporting to the Bureau of Mines. This method should be applied to stocks in the field, storage, transit, at refineries, and all other points, as far as it is practicable for the company to do so.

Products: In the costing of product inventories, current purchases and current production should be the first applied to current cost of sales and current operations. This method should be applied to stocks at refineries, bulk terminals, in transit, and at all other points, as far as it is practicable for the company to do so.

The various kinds or brands of oil products handled by the company may be classified or grouped into a minimum number of "Products." The term "Products" means a combination of a number of individual brands or kinds of finished or unfinished oils. Examples of "Products" are: Kerosene (Refined Oil), Gasoline

---

[1] Quoted by permission of the American Petroleum Institute.

(Naphthas), Lubricating Oils, Motor Oils, Gas Oils, Fuel Oils, Waxes, Asphalts, Coke, etc. No definite recommendation is made as to the number of products each company should carry as a separate item on the inventory. However, it is suggested that it be the smallest number feasible to obtain full advantage of the equalizing effect of the "Last In, First Out" inventory plan.

Valuation: In starting the "Last In, First Out" inventory plan, the prices should be set at a conservative or reasonable figure. In the future, inventory prices should not be reduced to market prices, when lower than the regular inventory value. Where the market value of the inventory is less than that carried in the Balance Sheet, such condition should be shown in parenthesis or as a footnote in such manner that the approximate difference can be ascertained, either in dollars or percentage.

Transportation: In ascertaining the inventory value, all transportation should be taken at full tariff or market rates. Obviously, where a company has had a Reserve for the Elimination of Inter-Company Profits in Inventory, such reserve will remain practically constant under this method of valuing inventory, so long as the quantity of inventory on hand remains about the same.

COMMENTS ON EXAMPLE

1. To illustrate the principles of the inventory plan, an example has been prepared showing the various effects, month by month, on the inventory at the beginning and end of each month, as well as the cost of sales.

Assuming the accounting period is the fiscal year of the company, the calculations are made at the end of each month on a "year to date basis."

2. *January:* Since 200 units were acquired (produced or purchased), and only 150 units disposed of, obviously, under the "Last In, First Out" plan the 150 units would take a cost of 9c, or the average of the units produced or purchased. Accordingly, the 150 units on hand January 31st would be inventoried as follows:

100 at 10c

50 at 9c

3. *Two Months Ended February 28th (Line 3):* For the year to date, 400 units have been produced or purchased at an average price of 8.5c each. Since there have been only 325 units disposed of, being all acquired in the current year, the price is 8.5c each. Therefore, the original 100 units are still on hand at 10c each, plus 75 units of this year's acquisition at 8.5c each. The single month of February (Line 2) is simply the difference between Lines 1 and 3.

4. *Three Months Ended March 31st (Line 5):* At the end of the first quarter of the accounting period, 575 units have been acquired at an average price of 8.043c each. However, 600 units have been disposed of. Since more units have been disposed of than acquired, it becomes necessary to charge cost of sales with 25 units at 10c each, being the average price at the beginning of the year. As set forth in the preceding paragraph, the month of March (Line 4) is the difference between Lines 3 and 5.

5. From the above, it will be seen that so long as the quantity on hand is not in excess of the opening inventory, the closing inventory price will be the same as the opening inventory price.

At the end of any month, if the quantity on hand exceeds the opening inventory, such excess will be priced at the average production or purchase cost.

Example of the "Last In, First out"

Uniform Method of Valuing Petroleum Inventories
(When applied on a year-to-date basis)

Approved by the American Petroleum Institute, Nov. 12, 1934

1936.	Opening Inventory	Production or Purchases	Cost of Sales	Closing Inventory
1. January	100 @ 10c	200 @ 9c	150 @ 9c	100 @ 10c 50 @ 9c
2. February	100 @ 10c 50 @ 9c	200 @ 8c	175 @ 8.07c	100 @ 10c 75 @ 8.5c
3. 2 Months	100 @ 10c 75 @ 8.5c	400 @ 8.5c	325 @ 8.5c	100 @ 10c 75 @ 8.5c
4. March	100 @ 10c 75 @ 8.5c	175 @ 7c	275 @ 7.681c	75 @ 10c
5. 3 Months		575 @ 8.043c	575 @ 8.043c } Avg. 25 @ 10c } 8.125c	75 @ 10c
6. April	75 @ 10c	225 @ 7.5c	175 @ 7.086c	
7. 4 months	100 @ 10c 25 @ 7.890c	800 @ 7.890c	775 @ 7.890c	100 @ 10c 25 @ 7.890c
8. May	100 @ 10c 25 @ 7.890c	220 @ 9c	240 @ 8.904c	100 @ 10c 5 @ 8.130c
9. 5 Months	100 @ 10c 5 @ 8.130c	1,020 @ 8.130c	1,015 @ 8.130c	100 @ 10c 5 @ 8.130c
10. June	100 @ 10c 5 @ 8.130c	215 @ 10.5c	230 @ 10.426c	

11. 6 Months	90 @ 10c	1,235 @ 8.543c	1,235 @ 8.543c 10 @ 10c } Avg. 8.554c	90 @ 10c
12. July		205 @ 11.5c	225 @ 11.369c	
13. 7 Months	70 @ 10c	1,440 @ 8.964c	1,440 @ 8.964c 30 @ 10c } Avg. 8.985c	70 @ 10c
14. August		210 @ 12.5c	200 @ 12.625c	
15. 8 Months	80 @ 10c	1,650 @ 9.414c	1,650 @ 9.414c 20 @ 10c } Avg. 9.412c	80 @ 10c
16. September		230 @ 13.5c	215 @ 13.744c	
17. 9 Months	95 @ 10c	1,880 @ 9.914c	1,880 @ 9.914c 5 @ 10c } Avg. 9.914c	95 @ 10c
18. October		235 @ 13c	230 @ 13.065c	
19. 10 Months	100 @ 10c	2,115 @ 10.257c	2,115 @ 10.257c	100 @ 10c
20. November		240 @ 12.5c	235 @ 12.545c	
21. 11 Months	100 @ 10c 5 @ 10.485c	2,355 @ 10.485c	2,350 @ 10.485c	100 @ 10c 5 @ 10.485c
22. December		250 @ 11.5c	240 @ 11.533c	
23. 12 Months	100 @ 10c 5 @ 10.485c	2,605 @ 10.583c	2,590 @ 10.583c	100 @ 10c 15 @ 10.583e } Avg. 10.076c

1937 (New Opening Inventory)
January 115 @ 10.076c

PARTICIPATION BY ACCOUNTING PROFESSION
IN THE DEVELOPMENT OF LIFO

The Special Committee on Inventories of the American Institute of Accountants (now the American Institute of Certified Public Accountants) collaborated with the American Petroleum Institute's committee and in May, 1936, submitted a report to the Council of the American Institute in which the activity was discussed in detail. The conclusion of the Special Committee, as stated in its report, was:

> The "last-in, first-out" method for the valuation of oil company inventories, as recommended by the American Petroleum Institute, constitutes an acceptable accounting principle for those companies, which, finding it adaptable to their needs and views as correctly reflecting their income, apply it consistently from year to year; it is important, however, that full and clear disclosure, in their published financial statements, be made by the companies adopting it, both as to the fact of its adoption and the manner of its application, including information as to the period adopted for the unit of time within which the goods "last-in" are deemed to be the "first-out," that is, whether the fiscal year or a shorter or longer period.
>
> Since the method as outlined by the committee of the American Petroleum Institute requires that the valuation to be placed upon the inventory be "conservative or reasonable," without, however, providing for a uniform standard or common basis in the determination of such valuations, it must be understood by readers of the financial statements of companies adopting the method that the inventory valuation of one such company is not to be regarded as comparable with that of another, except only in so far as the current replacement valuation, required to be disclosed when less than the valuations arrived at under the method, afford such a comparison.
>
> The foregoing conclusion of our committee, however, does not preclude our viewing other methods as being either equally acceptable or preferable in the case of other companies where different conditions may prevail.

Briefly, this conception of LIFO is that current costs of crude oil and products should be charged against current sales. Where an increase in the inventory quantity occurs during the year, the increase is to be reflected at the average cost of purchases or production for the year. Where a decrease in inventory quantity occurs, the entire inventory is to be stated at the same unit price as was used at the beginning of the year.[2]

---

[2] For a more detailed description of oil inventory practices, see *Outline of Petroleum-Industry Accounting* (1954 ed.), pp. 133–43, published by the Financial and Accounting Committee, American Petroleum Institute; see also Irving and Draper, *Accounting Practices in the Petroleum Industry* (1958).

The January, 1938, issue of *The Journal of Accountancy* contains the text of a report to the Council of the American Institute by another special committee on inventories. The first paragraph of the report reads:

> In connection with the appointment of this committee, the president, at the beginning of the current fiscal year, expressed the desire that the committee, having previously concerned itself with the discussion of methods of valuation of oil inventories, now turn its attention to inventory problems in other industries. The current activities of the committee in this respect have not followed the form or scope of its deliberations with the representatives of the American Petroleum Institute, in the prior years; it has, however, during the year participated in discussions on the subject of the "last-in, first-out" method, through the attendance of its chairman at informal conferences held by unofficial groups representative of the non-ferrous metals and leather industries interested, not only in the adoption of the method under discussion for corporate reporting purposes, but also in efforts to have the Internal Revenue Bureau approve such method for the computation of taxable income. There is, however, nothing for final reporting by the committee in this connection at the present time.

Another example of the activity of representatives of the accounting profession in furthering the development of a practical procedure for applying LIFO in particular industries is found in a report by the Institute's Committee on Cooperation with Controllers' Congress of the National Retail Dry Goods Association (now the National Retail Merchants Association) published in the February, 1942, issue of *The Journal of Accountancy*. In this report the Committee analyzes the advantages claimed for the use of the LIFO method by retailers, and the report concludes with the following summary:

> The LIFO inventory basis, being one of three inventory bases in general use, is an acceptable basis for the purpose of preparing financial statements for management, security holders, and creditors, provided it is adequately disclosed and consistently applied and provided a representative price index is prepared and maintained currently which is sufficiently departmentalized to embrace the inventories of the stores.
> For federal income-tax purposes the LIFO basis is specifically allowed under section 22(d) of the Internal Revenue Code. The Treasury Department should not object to its use by retailers by the application of a price index, although considerable discussion may be necessary. . . .

A practical method of applying LIFO by retailers has been accepted for federal income tax purposes since the decision of the Tax Court in the *Hutzler Bros. Co.* case in 1947.[3]

The acceptance by the American Institute of Certified Public Accoun-

---

[3] *Hutzler Bros. Co. v. Commissioner*, 8 T.C. 14 (1947).

tants of the LIFO inventory method is officially reported in paragraph 6 of Appendix A.

STATUTORY AUTHORIZATION OF LIFO
FOR FEDERAL INCOME TAX PURPOSES

At the insistence of taxpayers, the Congress of the United States in the Revenue Act of 1938 authorized the use of LIFO, but only for specified raw materials used by tanners, and the producers and processors of certain non-ferrous metals. The designation of these particular businesses appears to have been the result of their use of the base stock method for financial statement purposes and the fact that representatives of those industries had been unsuccessful in efforts to develop with the Bureau of Internal Revenue a satisfactory procedure for recognizing sales commitments for future delivery as being in the nature of hedges against fluctuations in the market value of inventories.

Representatives of the tanning and non-ferrous metals industries had asserted for several years prior to 1938 that they needed special consideration from the standpoint of determining income for federal tax purposes. The base stock inventory method some were using for financial statement purposes was disapproved by the Treasury Department. Processors of certain materials were able to protect themselves against price fluctuations by transactions on well-established commodity futures markets—particularly cotton and wheat—but the same opportunities for hedging were not available to these other processors. The Bureau of Internal Revenue had been unable to establish an administrative procedure for recognizing the economics of their position. There were a number of industries in the same position as the tanners and producers and processors of non-ferrous metals, and equitable treatment could not be accorded taxpayers by merely adding to the list of industries for which LIFO would be available.

In 1939 Congress expanded the provisions for the elective use of LIFO and removed the restrictions in the 1938 Act. Under the Revenue Act of 1939, any taxpayer could elect the LIFO method for any of the goods in his inventory. The general LIFO provision has been continued in the Internal Revenue Code without material change.[4]

After the outbreak of World War II, shortages developed in some commodities and manufactured products, which had the effect of depleting inventories in many industries. Under the general LIFO procedures, depletions having a LIFO cost below current replacement cost directly affect

[4] The section in the current statute is set forth in section 1.472, Appendix C.

income and produce high profits subject to normal tax, surtax, and during the war years, excess profits tax. It was foreseen that when conditions again became normal, the replacement of these depletions would have to be inventoried at the prevailing costs in the year of replacement. This would have the effect of subjecting to extremely high tax rates the difference between LIFO costs (at 1939, 1940, or 1941 prices, depending on the year a taxpayer adopted (LIFO) and the costs prevailing when replacements became available.

To meet this situation, Congress amended the Internal Revenue Code in the Revenue Act of 1942 by adding a provision commonly referred to as the "Involuntary Liquidation and Replacement Section." Under this section a taxpayer having a liquidation due to wartime conditions in any goods subject to LIFO pricing had the privilege at that time of electing to replace such liquidation at a future date. It is significant that the statutory definition of an "involuntary liquidation" emphasizes the taxpayer's *inability to replace* the goods because of war conditions.

The election to replace had the effect of carrying back to the year of liquidation the difference between the LIFO cost for the goods involuntarily liquidated and the cost of the replacement. If the cost of replacement exceeded the cost of the quantities liquidated, the taxpayer was entitled to a tax refund (without interest) for the year of liquidation. If the cost of replacement was less than the cost of the quantities liquidated, the taxpayer was assessed an additional tax for the year of liquidation. In either case, taxes for years other than the year of liquidation might also require adjustments, due to the carryback and carryover provisions for losses and unused excess profits credits.

The summary of the 1947 inventory of A Packing Company, on pages 182–83, reflects a replacement that year of involuntary inventory liquidations which occurred in each of the three previous years. Although the replacement quantities are inventoried at the original LIFO cost, the purchases taken into account in computing the cost of sales for 1947 will be reduced by the amount of $134,250, representing the aggregate excess replacement cost. A recomputation of taxable income for the prior years will be made with increases in cost of sales of $12,750 for 1944, $65,000 for 1945, and $56,500 for 1946.

The 1942 Act provided that an involuntary liquidation had to occur before the termination of World War II as proclaimed by the President, and the replacement had to occur within three years after that date. Congress later specified that the liquidation had to take place before January 1, 1948, and the replacement had to occur before January 1, 1953. Although the law required the taxpayer to show that the liquidation was involuntary, which meant that it was due to a condition arising out of the war, no special proof was required of taxpayers in some of the cases because the conditions causing the material shortage were a matter of common knowledge.

Replacements in years after an involuntary liquidation are considered as replacements of the most recent liquidations whether or not involuntary. Thus in the case of a taxpayer with a liquidation in 1942 which he elected to replace and also a liquidation in 1943 for which he made no election, a replacement in 1944 was deemed to apply first to the 1943 liquidation (includable in inventory at current 1944 costs) and then to the 1942 liquidation (includable in inventory at the cost of the goods liquidated in that year).

Material shortages similar to those in World War II were again experienced in 1950 when hostilities began in Korea. Congress provided relief by giving taxpayers the same elections as in World War II with respect to involuntary liquidations occurring between June 30, 1950, and December 31, 1954. Replacements of liquidations during this period were required to be made by January 1, 1956.

As a consequence of the general rule concerning the order in which replacements were applied to liquidations, a taxpayer could have replaced a liquidation incurred after June 30, 1950, without having replaced World War II liquidations for which no relief would be afforded unless a replacement could be made by the end of 1952. To avoid hardship in such a situation, Congress provided that the liquidations after June 30, 1950, should be deemed to have occurred before World War II liquidations for the purpose of the replacement section. Generally replacements were applied to the most recent liquidations, but the statutory amendment [5] providing that involuntary liquidations during 1950 and 1951 should be treated as having occurred prior to unreplaced 1941–1947 liquidations gave effect to the extended replacement period.

No substantive changes in the general provisions governing the use of LIFO were made at the time of enactment of the Internal Revenue Code of 1954. There was added, however, a new provision [6] which may have an effect upon corporations using LIFO or contemplating adoption of the method. As a general rule a corporation does not realize taxable income on the distribution of its property with respect to its stock, but this section provides for the recognition of taxable income when inventory which has been costed on the LIFO method is distributed. The amount of income, which is treated as if arising from the sale of inventory assets, is equal to the amount by which the aggregate cost at which the LIFO

[5] Rev. Act of 1951, § 306.
[6] Int. Rev. Code of 1954, § 311 (b).

inventory is carried, is below the amount which would be assigned to the inventory at the time of distribution, if LIFO had not been used.

This section is not applicable to a distribution of property pursuant to a plan for complete liquidation of a subsidiary corporation. In the case of other corporations contemplating complete liquidation, consideration should be given to making a sale of substantially all the inventory to one person in a single transaction. If the inventory is disposed of in this manner and the other conditions are met,[7] no gain or loss is recognized to the corporation from the disposition of its property.

SHORTCOMINGS IN LIFO PROVISIONS OF INTERNAL REVENUE CODE

From the business viewpoint, two major deficiencies exist in the LIFO method as it has developed for federal income tax purposes. For tax purposes, no writedown to market is permitted when market is lower than LIFO cost, while for accounting purposes it is recognized that inventories should be priced at market when lower than cost, irrespective of the method employed in determining cost. Further, there is no current procedure for a replacement of temporary liquidations being priced at the cost of the goods temporarily liquidated.

One of the prnicipal reasons why a larger number of businesses did not adopt LIFO was the fear of declines in prices below the costs prevailing on the basic LIFO date. From time to time proposals have been submitted to amend the Internal Revenue Code to provide for a deduction, in computing taxable income, equal to the amount by which the LIFO inventory cost exceeds the market value of the goods on hand.

For several years after the Internal Revenue Code permitted the use of LIFO regardless of industry, interpretations by Treasury Department representatives were so restrictive that many companies were led to believe the method could not be applied in their case. Narrow limitations upon acceptable LIFO groups rendered the method impracticable except for such industries as oil, steel, and meat packing, where the character of the inventories does not vary substantially from year to year. A somewhat broader view as to groupings was adopted by the Treasury Department in 1944 with the issuance of Treasury Decision 5407; but the *Hutzler Bros Co.* case (8 T.C. 14), which approved the application of LIFO to taxpayers using the retail inventory method, was not decided until 1947, and the Tax Court decision approving the use of the dollar-value principle was more than a year later.

[7] Int. Rev. Code of 1954, § 337.

	LIFO inventory			Non-LIFO inventory at lower of cost or market
	Green weight	Unit cost	Amount	
Group I:				
1940 base....................	600,000 lbs.	$0.10	$ 60,000	
Increments—1941.............	300,000	.11	33,000	
1942.............	350,000	.15	52,500	
1943.............	100,000	.25	25,000	
1947.............	150,000	.40	60,000	
	1,500,000			
Group II:				
1940 base....................	150,000	.08	12,000	
Increments—1941.............	30,000	.10	3,000	
1942.............	320,000	.15	48,000	
	500,000			
Group III:				
1940 base....................	100,000	.04	4,000	
Increments—1942.............	50,000	.07	3,500	
1947.............	100,000	.18	18,000	
	250,000			
Group IV:				
1940 base....................	300,000	.02	6,000	
Increments—1941.............	25,000	.05	1,250	
1943.............	50,000	.05	2,500	
1945.............	25,000	.06	1,500	
	400,000			
Processing expense.............				$ 75,000
Other pork sausage, and canned meats......................				200,000
Cattle and beef................				175,000
Supplies......................				350,000
Ice plant.....................				10,000
Power plant...................				15,000
			$330,250	825,000
Total inventory.........				$1,155,250

Inventories at December 31, 1947, Inventory Cost of Cost of Replacing Liquidated in Prior Years

			Excess replacement cost			
Quantity replaced	Replacement cost	LIFO inventory cost	1944 liqui-dation	1945 liqui-dation	1946 liqui-dation	Total

Replacements in 1947 of inventories involuntarily liquidated in prior years

Quantity replaced	Replacement cost	LIFO inventory cost	1944 liquidation	1945 liquidation	1946 liquidation	Total
100,000 lbs.	$ 40,000	$11,000			$29,000	$ 29,000
350,000	140,000	52,500		$60,000	27,500	87,500
100,000	40,000	25,000	$10,000	5,000		15,000
25,000	4,500	1,750	2,750			2,750
			$12,750	$65,000	$56,500	

Reduction in purchases for purpose of cost of sales computation, attributable to inventorying at original LIFO cost the quantities involuntarily liquidated in prior years and replaced in 1947 $134,250

It was, therefore, not until almost ten years after the LIFO provision was included in the law that even the broad principles of procedure were established. The general trend of prices in this country at that time was quite uncertain. Not until 1950 was there a renewed interest in LIFO occasioned by further price increases and the national preparedness program, indicating the probability of another extended period of inflation. Companies not adopting LIFO until 1950 because of the critical position taken by the Treasury Department during the preceding decade have not enjoyed advantages comparable to those derived by taxpayers who applied LIFO as of an earlier date and have a lower basic inventory cost.

It is also significant that it was not until January, 1961—after more than another ten years had elapsed—that any explanation of the dollar-value method of pricing LIFO inventories was added to the regulations.[8]

The practical justification for a statutory amendment to permit a write-down to market where lower than the LIFO cost is that such a provision would tend to equalize the position of all taxpayers.

The theoretical justification for an amendment to permit a writedown to market is based upon the fact that in the view of most businessmen, economists, and accountants, no inventory carried on financial statements at an amount in excess of market is realistic. Over fifty years ago it was recognized that for tax purposes inventories need not be stated at costs which are in excess of current market value, and this change in earlier procedures was effected by an amendment to the income tax regulations.

Consistent with the accounting practice of providing for measurable expected future losses, the amount of accumulated earnings to the date of a financial statement will be overstated if market declines are not taken into account.

The Sixteenth Amendment to the Constitution says simply, "The Congress shall have power to lay and collect taxes on incomes, from whatever source derived, without apportionment among the several States, and without regard to any census or enumeration." Congress has had to provide for all the details as to how incomes are to be taxed. As developed over the years, the underlying principle of the Internal Revenue Code is to tax the income for each accounting period irrespective of the happenings of prior or subsequent years. It can be argued that if events occur during any particular year (including a decline in the market value of inventories) which have an effect on the measurement of the accumulated amount of the earnings retained in the business, such events should be recognized as part of the basis for computing taxes on income.

Although the most fundamental of the justifications for the LIFO

8 Section 1.472–8, Appendix C.

method is that income for any particular period is more clearly reflected thereby, as presently provided for in the Internal Revenue Code, this is true only for completed transactions. The increase in the amount of accumulated earnings between two dates, with appropriate recognition of distributions to shareholders and other special factors, can be a measure of the income during the elapsed period; and if a decline in value of an inventory occurs during any year, that event should also be recognized to reflect properly the accumulated earnings for the business.

ARGUMENTS FOR PERMITTING THE REPLACEMENT OF TEMPORARY LIQUIDATIONS

The factors which prompted enactment of the temporary provisions of the Internal Revenue Code permitting a retroactive adjustment of income after the replacement of LIFO inventory quantities involuntarily liquidated as a result of war conditions or economic causes attributable to the national preparedness program are equally significant in demonstrating the need for a relief provision applicable to liquidations of inventory quantities attributable to other causes.

For example, if the inventory quantities at the end of a particular year should be reduced below the quantities as of the beginning of the year because of labor difficulties in the taxpayer's plant or the plant of one or more suppliers of its materials, the entire excess of the proceeds of sale over the LIFO inventory cost would be included in income. Such cost might represent the price paid for that type of goods many years before. Even if the quantities are replaced in the following year, under the present provisions of the Internal Revenue Code, no correction could be made of the income for the year of liquidation. The inventory replacement would be treated as any other increment and would be carried at the cost incurred in making the replacement. This type of "involuntary liquidation" should be recognized in the Internal Revenue Code to make the LIFO provisions complete.

In cases where the inventory quantities are diminished as a consequence of a fire, it might be possible to apply the involuntary conversion provision of the Internal Revenue Code if the inventory is fully covered by insurance. This section [9] provides that if property is converted into cash as a consequence of fire, theft, and the like, and then into similar property, no gain is to be recognized for federal income tax purposes, and the replacement property is deemed to have the same cost as that destroyed. But if

[9] Int. Rev. Code of 1954, § 1033.

the insurance proceeds do not cover the entire cost of replacing the inventory, the involuntary conversion provision would not provide a satisfactory solution to the problem.

The possible causes of an inventory liquidation as a result of accident are innumerable. Conceivably, it could be the result of delays in shipping, a flood, or even inclement weather; consequently, it is not possible to prepare a completely satisfactory definition of an involuntary liquidation which might be replaced and restored to the inventory at the original LIFO cost. Because of the basic need for protection against such liquidations, it had once been suggested that the statute be amended to permit taxpayers to file an election to consider any decrease in LIFO inventory quantities as being subject to replacement within a reasonable period, such as five years. The decision of the taxpayer would, of course, be made at the time of filing the income tax return for the year of liquidation or shortly thereafter. It should not be possible for the company to await the actual incurrence of the replacement cost before deciding whether or not income should be adjusted retroactively.

An automatic right of election to effect replacement of liquidations of LIFO inventory quantities would largely remove the disturbing economic conditions in some markets when the principal members of an industry are attempting at the same time to make abnormal purchases to build up inventory quantities which were temporarily diminished. In certain industries prices have risen merely because concerns using LIFO were making purchases to avoid closing inventory quantities being below those at the beginning of the year. The statute should be amended to eliminate the cause of purchases made to avoid the tax consequences of a liquidation in the LIFO inventory quantities rather than because of existing market conditions.

The making of abnormal purchases is but one of the ways of increasing LIFO inventory quantities at the end of any particular year. Businesses using the LIFO method have also, on occasion, deferred making shipments. Wherever normal shipments are being deferred because of tax considerations, management is not exercising normal business judgment. The impact of taxes upon the company's profitability can be greater than was intended by the lawmakers.

In considering statutory amendments involving a recomputation of tax on a previous year's income, a procedure might be incorporated whereby the net decrease or increase in previous years' taxes could be deducted from or added to the tax computed on the income for the year of replacement. From an administrative standpoint this might be preferable to a specific refund of, or assessment of a deficiency in, tax for a prior year. Another suggested procedure would provide that the income for the year of involuntarily liquidation be reduced initially in the return by the difference between the inventory cost and the current replacement cost of the liquidated items. The difference between such current cost and the replacement cost as determined in the year of actual replacement could be adjusted in such year. If replacement is not made, the interim adjustment could be reversed in the last year in which a replacement would have been recognized.

INTERPRETATIONS OF THE INTERNAL REVENUE CODE BY LITIGATION AND REGULATIONS

A review of the legislative history of LIFO does not disclose the many differences that arose between taxpayers and the Commissioner of Internal Revenue in practice. After the enactment of the Revenue Act of 1939, the general opinion seemed to be that LIFO was applicable to industries with relatively few basic commodities that could be accounted for readily in terms of units of quantity, for example, oil, rubber, textiles, leather, chemicals, lead, copper, and other metal industries. The application of LIFO to commodities that could be accounted for in terms of barrels, yards, gallons, or tons was accepted by the Treasury Department. Members of other industries carrying inventories composed of heterogeneous goods, such as retail department stores and wholesale and retail grocery stores, used the LIFO method but were challenged by the Treasury on the grounds that separate LIFO computations had to be made for each item. Some of these companies submitted to the Commissioner's interpretation by either applying LIFO to individual items or going back to the lower-of-cost-or-market method. Others took up the challenge and subsequently received favorable decisions from the Tax Court.

The Commissioner of Internal Revenue acquiesced in vital decisions rendered by the Tax Court and amended his regulations, so that since 1949 taxpayers have been officially permitted to use any method of LIFO computation established to the Commissioner's satisfaction as being reasonably adaptable to the purpose and intent of the statute. The first amendment dealt with taxpayers which had, as a matter of past practice, determined inventories under the retail method of accounting. As explained in Chapter 14, the application of LIFO to the retail method is accomplished by reducing the retail sales value of an inventory at the close of the year to the price level existing at the beginning of the year when LIFO was first adopted. This conversion from current sales prices to the level when LIFO was first adopted is done by means of an index especially developed for this purpose by the Bureau of Labor Statistics.

The second major amendment to the regulations was made after the decision of the Tax Court in the *Basse* case.[10] That case dealt with the application of LIFO to the inventories of a wholesale grocer. As in the case of department stores, it is not practicable for wholesale grocers to compare quantities of inventories by items at the beginning and end of each year. This wholesaler utilized a procedure referred to as the "dollar-value method" which in essence compares the investment in inventory by groups at the beginning of the year when LIFO was adopted with the investment at the end of the year stated in terms of dollars at the same price level.

The dollar-value method is similar to the procedure followed by department stores in that in both cases there is no comparison of quantities of individual items, and the relative inventory quantities are determined only by aggregate dollar amounts allocated to the inventories. The application of the department store procedure is generally limited to stores using the retail method of inventory valuation, and it is to be noted that the price index is computed by reference to sales value rather than cost levels.

The dollar-value method can be applied by any business, including retail stores which compute the cost or lower-of-cost-or-market for their merchandise directly rather than by the retail method. Under the dollar-value method, the extent of change in cost levels is generally determined by a dual extension of the quantities in the closing inventories. The quantities on hand at the end of the year may be priced first at the costs prevailing at the beginning of the year when LIFO was adopted and again at the costs prevailing at the end of the current year. The ratio of the total dollars produced in the first computation to the total dollars produced in the second computation reflects the rise or decline in prices for the period since the beginning of the year in which LIFO was first adopted. Manufacturers and others unable as a practical matter to make dual pricings have developed indexes of price changes of materials, labor, and overhead during each year reflecting their particular circumstances.

Some of the early LIFO applications grouped items of inventory on the basis of being raw material, goods in process, or finished stock. It soon became apparent that a substantial part of the inflationary profit in inventories, which Congress recognized need not be subjected to tax, was being included in the taxable income stream where there were no material changes in the total inventories. Violent fluctuations in quantities occurred from year to year between the categories of raw materials, goods in process, and finished stock.

In 1944, the regulations were amended so as to permit the application

---

[10] *Edgar A. Basse v. Commissioner*, 10 T.C. 328 (1948).

of LIFO to raw materials and the raw-material content of in-process and finished stock. In the example illustrating this procedure, labor and overhead are priced at current rather than LIFO cost.[11] Application of the LIFO principle to only a portion of the costs attributable to the goods included in the inventory was not a completely logical procedure, and efforts were continued to have the Treasury Department approve the techniques essential to applying dollar-value methods to inventories generally.

The amendment to the regulations in 1949 provided merely that if a taxpayer uses consistently the so-called dollar-value method of pricing inventories, or any other method of computation established to the satisfaction of the Commissioner as reasonably adaptable to the "purpose and intent" of the LIFO provisions of the Internal Revenue Code, and if an appropriate election is made, the inventory shall be determined by the use of the "appropriate adaptation.[12]

Internal Revenue Service representatives started as early as 1954 working on a revenue ruling or amendment to the regulations to describe the procedures to be followed in applying the dollar-value principle. Such an amendment to the regulations was finally published as T.D. 6539 on January 20, 1961.[13]

The major change in the amended regulations is the addition of a specific section (Section 1.472–8 of Appendix C) pertaining to the dollar-value method. The position of the Treasury Department and the questions encountered in the application of the regulations are discussed in Chapter 12.

PRACTICAL IMPETUS FOR USE OF LIFO

The artificiality of paper profits resulting from assigning a larger amount to a closing inventory merely because market prices have increased—when from the standpoint of physical attributes the opening and closing inventories are comparable—has particular practical significance when tax rates are high. Only the income remaining after paying taxes can be used to replace inventories, expand the plant, pay dividends, and so forth. The higher the taxes, the lower the rate of earnings, and the greater the proportion of the year's earnings needed to maintain inventories during a period of rising prices.

Assuming no additional capital is invested for this purpose, the portion

[11] Section 1.472–1(c), Appendix C.
[12] Section 1.472–1(1), Appendix C.
[13] See McAnly, "The Current Status of LIFO," 105 *J. Accountancy* 5, 55 (May, 1958), and Barker, "Dollar-Value LIFO and the Klein Chocolate Case," 112 *J. Accountancy* 3, 41 (Sept., 1961).

of the net earnings of a business needed to maintain the inventory required for continuing operations during a period of rising costs can be expressed as a formula. If—

I = Cost of the inventory at the beginning of the year

t = Turnover rate for the inventory investment

r = Rate of earnings stated as the percentage which the net income after tax is of the total cost of goods sold for the year

then the product of the three factors Itr equals the net earnings. If i represents the percentage of increase during the year in the replacement cost for the inventory and e represents the fraction of the year's earnings needed to maintain the same physical volume of inventory, then

$$iI = eItr, \qquad \text{and } e = \frac{i}{tr}$$

In most situations, the percentage of increase during the year in the replacement cost for the inventory i and the other factors t and r can be computed with reasonable accuracy. After these three factors are established, the computation of the fraction of the year's earnings needed to maintain the same physical volume of inventory e is automatic.

Use of the formula developed above can be illustrated by an example.

Given:

The cost of goods sold for the year is six times the inventory $(t = 6)$.

The net income after tax is 5 per cent of the cost of goods sold $(r = 5\%)$.

The replacement cost for the inventory has increased 2 per cent during the year $(i = 2\%)$.

Computation:

$$e = \frac{i}{tr} = \frac{0.02}{6 \times 0.05} = \frac{1}{15} = 6\tfrac{2}{3}\%$$

Under these circumstances $6\tfrac{2}{3}$ per cent of the net earnings for the year is needed to maintain the same physical volume of inventory.

The results produced by this formula are illustrated on page 191.

Use of the table can be demonstrated by a situation in which there is an increase in inventory cost of 5 per cent, the rate of net earnings to cost of sales is 3 per cent, and the inventory is turned over 4 times each year. Approximately 41.7 per cent of the earnings is needed to maintain the same physical volume of inventory.

Income tax rates are significant in this analysis of the consequences of increases in inventory replacement cost because of their effect on the amount of net earnings. Every increase in income tax rate causes a reduction in the rate of earnings and results in a larger portion of the net earnings being required to maintain the inventory during a period of rising costs.

Costing an inventory by reference to the LIFO assumption as to the flow of costs will not alter the amount required to maintain, or the intrinsic

Portion of Earnings Needed to Maintain Inventory

Increase in cost of inventory	% of net earnings to cost of sales	Approximate % of net earnings needed to maintain inventory, if annual turnover is					
		2 times	3 times	4 times	6 times	10 times	12 times
1%	3	16.7	11.1	8.3	5.6	3.3	2.8
	5	10.0	6.7	5.0	3.3	2.0	1.7
	10	5.0	3.3	2.5	1.7	1.0	0.8
	15	3.3	2.2	1.7	1.1	0.7	0.6
	20	2.5	1.7	1.3	0.8	0.5	0.4
2%	3	33.3	22.2	16.7	11.1	6.7	5.6
	5	20.0	13.3	10.0	6.7	4.0	3.3
	10	10.0	6.7	5.0	3.3	2.0	1.7
	15	6.7	4.4	3.3	2.2	1.3	1.1
	20	5.0	3.3	2.5	1.7	1.0	0.8
5%	3	83.3	55.5	41.7	27.8	16.7	13.9
	5	50.0	33.3	25.0	16.7	10.0	8.3
	10	25.0	16.7	12.5	8.3	5.0	4.2
	15	16.7	11.1	8.3	5.6	3.3	2.8
	20	12.5	8.3	6.3	4.2	2.5	2.1

Effect of Increases in Income Tax Rates on Net Earnings

If income tax rates are increased		Net earnings (income after tax) will be reduced
From	To	
13¾%	25%	13.04%
25%	38%	17.33%
38%	52%	22.58%
52%	80%	58.33%

value of, the inventory, but its use will tend to prevent "paper profits" from being included in income from operations as the result of cost increases. Also, any reduction in the amount of income taxes payable by a business will result in more dollars being available to maintain the inventory and for other needs of the enterprise.

COMPARISON OF EFFECT OF LIFO AND FIFO

The effects upon income of using either LIFO or FIFO in the costing of inventories are generally compared on page 193. The Internal Revenue Code requires (Section 1.472 of Appendix C), as a condition to electing and continuing to use LIFO, that no other procedure be used in inventorying the goods covered by the LIFO election to ascertain the income, profit, or loss for the purpose of an annual report or statement to shareholders or other owners of the business or for credit purposes. The regulations (Section 1.472–2(e) of Appendix C) state that the use of market value in lieu of cost, or the issuance of reports or credit statements covering a period of operations less than the whole of a taxable year, is not considered at variance with the statutory requirement.

The generalizations as to the effects upon income of using LIFO are illustrated on pages 194–96.

FINANCIAL STATEMENT DISCLOSURES WITH RESPECT TO LIFO INVENTORIES

On January 23, 1975 the Internal Revenue Service released Revenue Procedure 75–10 [14] Revenue Ruling 75–49 [15] and Revenue Ruling 75–50 [16] all relating to disclosures concerning LIFO inventories. Accounting Series Release No. 169 (ASR 169), "Financial Disclosure Problems Relating to the Adoption of the LIFO Inventory Method," seems primarily intended to ensure awareness of the IRS pronouncements and their importance. ASR 169 consists of a letter dated January 20, 1975 from the chief accountant of the Securities Exchange Commission to an assistant commissioner of the Internal Revenue Service setting forth the former's "understanding of the solutions agreed upon to prevent possible conflicts between financial disclosure principles and Revenue Ruling 74–586" and the latter's acknowledgment dated January 23, 1975. Revenue Ruling

[14] IRB 1975–7, 16.
[15] IRB 1975–7, 11.
[16] IRB 1975–7, 11.

Generalizations as to Effect upon Income of Alternative Inventory Methods

	Effect upon income with flow of costs assumed to be	
	First-in, first-out	Last-in, first-out
If the closing inventory volume is equal to or greater than that of the opening inventory, and		
Costs increase	—	Increase in cost of replacing opening inventory is charged against income.
Costs decrease but not below LIFO cost	Excess cost for opening inventory is charged against income.	—
Costs decrease below LIFO cost	Excess cost for opening inventory is charged against income.	Reserve is provided to reduce LIFO cost to market value.
If the closing inventory volume is less than that of the opening inventory, and		
Costs increase	—	Increase in cost of replacing opening inventory is charged against income; and excess of current cost over LIFO cost for liquidated quantity is credited to income.
Costs decrease but not below LIFO cost	Excess cost for opening inventory is charged against income.	Excess of current cost over LIFO cost for liquidated quantity is credited to income.
Costs decrease below LIFO cost	Excess cost for opening inventory is charged against income.	Excess of LIFO cost over current cost for liquidated quantity is charged against income; and reserve is provided to reduce LIFO cost to market value.

Illustrations of Effect of LIFO upon Income

| | | First-in, first-out | | Last-in, first-out | | Effect of LIFO upon income |
	Quantity (barrels)	Per barrel	Amount	Per barrel	Amount	I—Increase D—Decrease
Assuming both inventory volume and costs increase:						
Opening inventory......	300	$12.00	$ 3,600	$ 9.60	$ 2,880	
Purchases.............	1,500	14.00	21,000	14.00	21,000	
Total............	1,800		24,600		23,880	
Closing inventory:						
Opening volume.....	300	14.00	4,200	9.60	2,880	
Increase...........	200	14.00	2,800	14.00	2,880	
Total............	500		7,000		5,680	
Cost of sales..........	1,300		$17,600		$18,200	
Difference—300 bbl. at $2.00.........						D $(600)
Assuming inventory volume increases and costs decrease but not below LIFO cost:						
Opening inventory......	300	$12.00	$ 3,600	$ 9.60	$ 2,880	
Purchases.............	1,500	11.00	16,500	11.00	16,500	
Total..............	1,800		20,100		19,380	
Closing inventory:						
Opening volume.......	300	11.00	3,300	9.60	2,800	
Increase..............	200	11.00	2,200	11.00	2,200	
Total..............	500		5,500		5,080	
Cost of sales............	1,300		$14,600		$14,300	
Difference—300 bbl. at $1.00..........						I $300
Assuming inventory volume increases and costs decrease below LIFO cost:						
Opening inventory......	300	$12.00	$ 3,600	$ 9.60	$ 2,880	
Purchases.............	1,500	9.00	13,500	9.00	13,500	
Total.............	1,800		$17,100		$16,380	

Closing inventory:					
Opening volume.....	300	$ 9.00	$ 2,700	$ 9.60	$ 2,880
Increase............	200	9.00	1,800	9.00	1,800
Total.............	500		4,500		4,680
Market reserve....			—		(180)
Net.............			4,500		4,500
Cost of sales..........	1,300		$12,600		$11,800

Difference—		
300 bbl. at $3.00..	I $	900
Market reserve....	D	(180)
Net.............	I	720

Assuming inventory volume decreases and costs increase:

Opening inventory.......	500	$12.00	$ 6,000	$ 9.60	$ 4,800
Purchases............	1,500	14.00	21,000	14.00	21,000
Total.............	2,000		27,000		25,800
Closing inventory.......	300	14.00	4,200	9.60	2,880
Cost of sales..........	1,700		$22,800		$22,920

Difference—		
500 bbl. at $2.00..	D	$(1,000)
200 bbl. at $4.40..	I	880
Net.............	D $	(120)

Assuming inventory volume decreases and costs decrease but not below LIFO cost:

Opening inventory......	500	$12.00	$ 6,000	$ 9.60	$ 4,800
Purchases............	1,500	11.00	16,500	11.00	16,500
Total.............	2,000		22,500		21,300
Closing inventory.......	300	11.00	3,300	9.60	2,880
Cost of sales..........	1,700		$19,200		$18,420

Difference—		
500 bbl. at $1.00..	I	$500
200 bbl. at $1.40..	I	280
Total............	I	$780

Assuming inventory volume decreases and costs decrease below LIFO cost:

Opening inventory......	500	$12.00	$ 6,000	$ 9.60	$ 4,800
Purchases............	1,500	9.00	13,500	9.00	13,500
Total.............	2,000		$19,500		$18,300

| | Quantity (barrels) | Cost of sales with flow of costs assumed to be | | | | Effect of LIFO upon income |
| | | First-in, first-out | | Last-in, first-out | | I—Increase D—Decrease |
		Per barrel	Amount	Per barrel	Amount	
Closing inventory.......	300	$9.00	$ 2,700	$9.60	$ 2,880	
Market reserve......			—		(180)	
Net...............			2,700		2,700	
Cost of sales..........	1,700		$16,800		$15,600	
Difference—						
500 bbl. at $3.00...						I $ 1,500
200 bbl. at $0.60...						D (120)
Market reserve......						D (180)
Net...............						I $ 1,200

74–586 [17] was issued in December 1974 and took a very hard line as to what disclosures are permitted before a taxpayer is considered to have violated the conformity requirements of Internal Revenue Code Section 472(c) and to be subject to termination of his LIFO election. Although the chief accountant's letter reproduced in ASR 169 uses language that in many cases is very similar to language found in the pronouncements of the Internal Revenue Service, and although the acknowledgment from the assistant commissioner says "Your letter is consistent with my understanding and the position of the Internal Revenue Service . . . ," the specific wording of the pronouncements should not be considered to be in any way modified by ASR 169.

A company that changes to the LIFO method of inventory costing from some other method is required by Accounting Principles Board Opinion No. 20 (APB 20) [18] to disclose the effect of the change on the results of operations of the period. Revenue Procedure 73–37 [19] issued by the IRS in December 1973, permits such "one-time" disclosure of the effect on net income without violation of the LIFO book/tax conformity requirements of Code Section 472(c).

Under either Revenue Procedure, for all years subsequent to the year of adoption, any disclosure made or required to be made should be limited

[17] 1974–2 C.B. 156.
[18] See Chapter 15 for a discussion of changes in accounting method and LIFO problems.
[19] 1973–2 C.B. 501.

to "the excess of replacement or current cost over stated LIFO value"; any disclosure of the effect on reported income and earnings per share of using LIFO versus another method should be avoided since such action could jeopardize the continued use of the LIFO method. If LIFO is first adopted for the year ended December 31, 19X3, disclosure in the 19X3 financial statements of the change and the effect thereof on the results of operations for the year 19X3 is required by APB 20 and is permitted by Revenue Procedures 73–37 and 75–10. In reporting on 19X4, when financial statements for only 19X3 and 19X4 are presented, disclosures relating to the change are not mandatory in the annual report to shareholders, because the financial statements for 19X3 and 19X4 are on a consistent basis, and the auditor need not refer to the change in his report in a situation where the FIFO to LIFO change occurs in the earliest year both presented and reported on.[19] Although Revenue Procedure 73–37 states that the effect of the change on results of operations can only be disclosed in the year of change, the effect (repeated for the year of change *only*) must also be disclosed in subsequent years whenever the change has created an inconsistency among the years being presented; for example, if a change is made in 19X3 and a registration statement is filed in 19X5 that includes income statements for 19X2, 19X3, and 19X4, the effect of the change made in 19X3 needs to be disclosed, with appropriate qualification as to consistency in the auditor's report, because the year 19X2 is not consistent with the years 19X3 and 19X4. Because "Rule 3–07 of Regulation S-X requires that a disclosure made in the year of change be repeated at any the financial statements for that year are subsequently reported" (quoted from Sec. 2 of Revenue Procedure 75–10) and "the LIFO election will not be terminated for federal income tax purposes solely because a taxpayer is subject to and complies with the disclosure requirements of . . . Rule 3–07" (quoted from Section 3.01 of Revenue Procedure 75–10), no problem should arise in complying with Rule 3–07 requirements in filings with the Commission.

The example of a footnote disclosing a change to LIFO as set forth in Section 3.03 of Revenue Procedure 75–10 as "acceptable" to the Internal Revenue Service is not considered satisfactory to many accountants. The example predicates the adoption of LIFO on "an overstatement of profits if use of the first-in first-out method were continued." Profits are not *misstated* when one generally accepted accounting principle or method is used rather than another. If LIFO is a preferable accounting method during periods of heavy inflation, it is because LIFO matches the most

---

[19] This is the conclusion reached in the Auditing Interpretation published in the January 1975 *Journal of Accountancy* on the "Impact on the Auditor's Report of FIFO to LIFO Change in the Earliest Year Reported On."

recent inventory acquisition costs against current sales. Whereas LIFO may very well result in lower income, this does not mean income is *overstated* if FIFO is used. Rather, the adoption of LIFO reflects management's conclusion that income calculated using LIFO is a clearer indication of the true economic situation *of the specific company* and that LIFO is therefore *preferable*.

The impact of inflation on different companies can vary considerably and there would normally be no compelling reason to adopt LIFO unless the effect on the matching process could reasonably be expected to have a significant effect on the determination of net income. On the other hand, the mere fact that net income would be less if LIFO were adopted does not necessarily mean that the adoption of LIFO would be preferable *for a specific company*. There are other factors besides the effect on net income that a company should consider before switching to LIFO—that is, tax effects, likelihood of maintenance of current inventory quantities and current cost levels, extra clerical work necessary to make the LIFO calculations, and loan indenture covenants.

A footnote disclosing a change to LIFO should be carefully worded. Justification for the change should be related to the specific company and should not be worded so broadly as to sound like justification for *every* company to make the change.

Section 3.02 of Revenue Procedure 75–10 should allow the permitted disclosures to be repeated when annual earnings are included in "news releases, reports to creditors, president's letter section of the annual financial statements, oral and written statements at stockholders meetings, and security analysts meetings, etc."

The SEC chief accountant's letter reproduced in ASR 169 says that "the Service would not terminate a LIFO election if *the same language* used in the financial statements footnote to disclose the effect of the change to LIFO is repeated in management's analysis of operations" (emphasis supplied). Although Revenue Procedure 75–10 does not use that same terminology, disclosures about changes to the LIFO method made outside the annual financial statements must be no more extensive than those required by APB 20, APB 28, FAS 3, ASR 159, SEC Release 11079, and Rule 3–07 of Regulation S-X (and permitted by the Internal Revenue Service pronouncements) *in* the financial statements relative to the year of change.

SEC Release 11079 requires that annual reports to shareholders include a summary of operations for the last five fiscal years, with a management analysis thereof, and Rule 3–07 of Regulation S-X requires that a disclosure made relative to the year of change be repeated at any time the financial statements for that year are subsequently reported. APB 20 requires that historical financial summaries presented in annual reports should be prepared on the same basis as that prescribed for financial statements; therefore, under generally accepted accounting principles, in any annual report to shareholders, whether by SEC or nonSEC reporting companies, reference to a change to LIFO and the effect thereof (repeated relative to the year of change *only*) in a note to such summaries needs to be made as long as a financial summary includes years prior to the year of change to LIFO. Section 3.05 of Revenue Procedure 75–10 is worded in terms of allowing the disclosures required by Release 11079 and Rule 3–07 for SEC reporting companies presenting 5-year summaries. Naturally, any disclosures presented would have to be "strictly limited to the effect *on* the year of change" (emphasis supplied), as specified in Section 3.05.

It seems only reasonable that the disclosure requirements in APB 20 that are equivalent to the disclosure requirements in Section 3.05 should be allowed (a) for SEC reporting companies to the extent the summaries in their annual reports to shareholders include in excess of five years and (b) for nonSEC reporting companies presenting any number of prior periods in the form of a financial summary. However, a degree of uncertainty remains as to exactly how much latitude exists before a violation of the book/tax conformity rules occurs.

FAS 3, Reporting Accounting Changes in Interim Financial Statements, says that when a publicly traded company makes an accounting change during the fiscal fourth quarter and does not report the data specified by APB 28, Interim Financial Reporting, in a separate fourth quarter report or in its annual report to shareholders (but apart from its financial statements), the disclosures required by APB 28 or FAS 3 shall be made in a note to the annual financial statements.

A footnote to paragraph 14 of FAS 3 warns of the limitations imposed by the IRS on disclosures about changes to the LIFO method. When Revenue Ruling 74–586 was issued in December 1974, it seemed to effectively limit the required disclosures about changes to the LIFO method to the footnotes, whereupon companies would have been forced to make *all* required fourth quarter disclosures as part of the annual financial statements only.

Whereas Revenue Ruling 74–586 could have been interpreted to prohibit publication of certain disclosures about changes to the LIFO method anywhere other than the footnotes to the financial statements, Revenue Procedure 75–10 appears as now allowing the disclosures required by APB 8 and FAS 3 to be made in the year of change in a separate fourth quarter report or in the annual report to shareholders apart from the financial statements.

Rule 5–02.6(b) of Regulation S-X calls for the disclosure of "the excess of replacement or current cost over stated LIFO value . . . if material," parenthetically or in a note to the financial statements. In an interpretation of Rule 5–02.6(b), the SEC stated in ASR 141 that "any inventory method may be used (such as FIFO or average cost) which derives a figure approximating current cost." In times of inflation, FIFO or average cost may not necessarily approximate current cost. In this regard the Internal Revenue Service has issued Revenue Ruling No. 73–66,[20] dated February 5, 1973, which states that such disclosure does not violate the financial statement reporting requirement of Section 472(c) of the Internal Revenue Code, but the Ruling refers only to the FIFO method of determining current cost. Revenue Ruling 75–50 [21] I.R.B. 1975–7, 11 now makes it explicit that FIFO is not the only acceptable method of determining "replacement or current cost."

In view of the fact that Regulation S-X, Revenue Ruling 73–66, and Revenue Ruling 75–50 are all worded in terms of disclosing "the excess" of current cost over LIFO, it may be wise to follow the technique recommended in those documents if additional disclosure is considered desirable by management in the annual report to shareholders (whether or not the company reports to the SEC) or when compliance disclosure is made as required by SEC regulations in a filing with the Commission. As a matter of logic, the Internal Revenue Service should agree that disclosing current cost of LIFO inventories at the balance sheet date is similar to disclosing market value of marketable securities, but that showing the excess of current cost over LIFO (especially if this is done for more than one year as illustrated in Revenue Ruling 73–66) tends (a) to imply that the disclosure is not intended for balance sheet purposes only and (b) to encourage readers to calculate a different net income figure, an undertaking for which they probably do not possess adequate information and which the IRS presumably wishes to discourage.

It should be noted that compliance with Rule 5–02 of Regulation S-X requires disclosure of the excess of replacement or current cost over LIFO for all balance sheets presented in a filing with the SEC. For this reason, and to minimize the differences between SEC filings and the annual report, it would be desirable for the financial statements in reports to shareholders to include the same disclosure. If replacement or current cost is computed using the FIFO or average method, provision should be made, to the extent considered necessary, for all anticipated losses, such as obsolescence, slow-moving quantities, and costs in excess of net realizable value, which

[20] 1973–1 C.B. 218.
[21] IRB 1975–7, 11.

would have been required to have been made had the company actually been using the FIFO or average method at the current balance sheet date.

LIFO Liquidations

In cases where old LIFO pools (or layers) carried at low acquisition costs of prior years are liquidated, the current net income will, of course, be increased. In these situations the prime principle underlying the LIFO method of inventory will be negated, because there will not be a matching of current costs with current revenue to the extent of inclusion of the lower prior years' LIFO costs in cost of sales for the current year. Where the effect of such liquidation on the current year is material, disclosure thereof should be made.

Disclosure of material amounts resulting from LIFO liquidations is in accordance with APB 30, "Reporting the Results of Operations," which requires disclosure of the nature and financial effects of each material event or transaction that is unusual in nature or occurs infrequently. Guide 1 from ASR 159, which has been made applicable to annual reports to shareholders by SEC Release 11079, requires presentation of a 5-year summary of operations and disclosure of material changes from period to period in the amounts of the items of revenue and expenses, including explanations ("textual analysis") of the changes. Such disclosures are considered by the SEC to be "necessary to enable investors to compare periodic results of operations and to assess the source and *probability of recurrence* of earnings" (emphasis supplied). Management's analysis of the summary of operations "should include a discussion of material facts . . . which . . . may make historical operations or earnings as reported in the summary of operations *not indicative of current or future operations or earnings*" (emphasis supplied).

In September 1977 the IRS issued Revenue Procedure 77–33 which permits disclosure of the effect of a LIFO liquidation on cost of goods sold as well as the effect on net income. It also permits these disclosures to be made in various media for reporting earnings in addition to financial statements. Language similar to the following is acceptable disclosure:

During 19___, inventory quantities were reduced. This resulted in a liquidation of LIFO inventory quantities carried at lower costs prevailing in prior years as compared with the cost of 19___ purchases, the effect of which decreased cost of goods sold by approximately $XXX and increased net income by approximately $XXX or $X per share.

Revenue Procedure 77–33 requires that the effect of a LIFO liquidation be computed on the same basis as that used in valuing LIFO increments. If a taxpayer computes LIFO increments by reference to earliest acquisition costs, the income effect must be determined by reference to earliest acquisition costs.

In situations where the specific period and reason for the LIFO decrement can be identified, it is appropriate to compute the income effect by reference to costs of the particular period. For example, a decrement might occur in the third quarter of the year because of a strike or other unforeseen event, with no possibility of restoring the decrement before year end. In such case, computation of the income effect using third-quarter inventory costs would be appropriate even though the company uses first-quarter costs to value LIFO increments.

Although the IRS has the authority to terminate a LIFO election in the case of a conformity violation, it is not required to do so. It does not appear that use of a method other than that prescribed by Revenue Procedure 77–33 to determine the effect of a LIFO liquidation poses a serious threat of termination of a LIFO election. Use of another method should, however, be approached cautiously with the knowledge that its use may have to be defended.

THE FUTURE OF REQUIRED BOOK–TAX CONFORMITY

The restrictive attitude of the Service in its interpretation of the statutory requirement (such as in Revenue Ruling 74–586 and numerous subsequent rulings, both published and private) that the books must conform if the LIFO method is to be used for tax purposes has created uncertainties and undue concern among LIFO users. To eliminate this problem the American Bar Association has recommended legislation that would repeal the book–tax conformity requirement. The AICPA's Federal Tax Division has suggested that either remedial legislation, if required, or administrative action should limit the conformity requirement to the primary financial statements, thus allowing non-LIFO disclosure in notes to the financial statements and elsewhere.

The foregoing discussion has been directed principally to tax considerations. Reference should be made to Chapter 15 for discussion of financial accounting and reporting in conformity with GAAP.

It is hoped that most of the uncertainties and concerns with the LIFO conformity problem have been put to rest by the proposed regulations, reproduced in Appendix D, which the IRS has issued and which were published in the *Federal Register* on July 20, 1979. These proposed rules can be followed in financial reports pending the adoption of final regulations. Any final regulations which are less favorable would be effective only after their issuance.

TEN

Timing of LIFO Election, The Significance of Volume, and Special Factors

"Brawny" Brown, who had been a star athlete during his college days and was voted by his fraternity as the one "most likely to succeed," was tramping through the North woods with his guide. "Silent Joe" had been highly recommended as a guide who knew the steep climbs of the trails and the density of the underbrush and also the dangers of rocks, rapids, and waterfalls in the streams. From time to time, Brown looked toward the stream and wondered when the portable canoe would be used to continue their journey. The trail was rough in many spots, and the going had not been easy.

In front of the campfire that night, Brown raised the question as to *when* it would be advantageous to change from the trail to the stream. In some respects "Silent Joe" was in the same position as a business adviser who is asked whether a business should elect to use LIFO or continue with FIFO or some other inventory method. Many factors must be considered and judgment must be exercised.[1]

[1] For a report on a study directed specifically to an appraisal of the force of the income tax factor, see Butters, *Effects of Taxation: Inventory Accounting and Policies* (1949).

Adoption of the LIFO inventory method does not guarantee that the effects upon income and taxes will be beneficial. LIFO will be helpful only if its adoption—with respect to all or part of the inventory—is timed in a judicious manner. If this is not done, not only can the potential benefits of the method be dissipated but, due to those shortcomings in the provisions of the Internal Revenue Code discussed in the preceding chapter, detrimental income tax consequences may result.

Before deciding to use LIFO, management must make realistic appraisals of future trends in the following areas:

Price levels, specifically production or purchase costs for the company's products

Inventory quantities, particularly with respect to volume increases or possible uncontrollable liquidations of significant items

Technological changes, including new products, materials, and production processes

Only after a company has considered possible future trends in each of these areas with respect to the major components of its inventory investment can it make informed decisions as to whether LIFO should be adopted at all and, if so, when the election should be made, with respect to which products, and what pooling methods should be used.

This chapter discusses various factors to be considered in timing the election of LIFO. The considerations relate to the potential tax savings from the adoption of LIFO in certain circumstances. However, it should be noted that recent developments in accounting have imposed restrictions on the timing and extent of the LIFO election for entities that purport to present financial statements in accordance with generally accepted accounting principles. Moreover, because of the book tax conformity requirement imposed by the Code on LIFO inventory accounting, the effect is to curb the flexibility of adopting LIFO for tax purposes. Companies adopting LIFO must satisfy the requirements of Accounting Principles Board Opinion No. 20—Accounting Changes. Under that opinion, a company must justify a change to an alternative generally accepted accounting principle on the basis that it is preferable. In an interpretation of APB Opinion No. 20, The Financial Accounting Standards Board concluded that preferability with respect to the adoption of a new method of accounting for inventory should be determined on the basis of whether the new method constitutes an improvement in financial reporting and not on the basis of tax effect alone. If a change to LIFO is to be justified as a change to a preferable method, it is questionable whether such change could be limited to applying LIFO only to specific products or classes of product.

Accordingly, some of the points discussed in this chapter covering partial or piece-meal adoption of LIFO, while appropriate from a tax point of view, will not be practical for those companies presenting financial statements in accordance with generally accepted accounting principles. See Chapter 15 for further discussion of these matters.

PRICE LEVEL CONSIDERATIONS

Where the quantity of goods in an inventory remains constant or increases during a period of rising costs, LIFO will result in charging larger amounts against current income rather than reflecting the full effect of higher costs in inventory as paper profits. For example, assume that at the beginning of a particular year Company A has 500 units in its inventory at a current cost of $1 per unit, or a total inventory investment of $500. During the next ten years the per-unit cost increases at the rate of 10¢ per year, so that at the end of the decade the then current replacement cost for each unit is $2.

If Company A has used FIFO, its inventory investment in 500 comparable units at the end of the period will be $1,000. Included in its reported (and taxable) income will have been an amount of $500 reinvested in maintaining a constant volume of inventory. On the other hand, had Company A adopted LIFO at the beginning of the period, its reported income would have been $500 less, and its income taxes would have been reduced $250. At the end of the period its inventory investment would remain at the base-year cost of $500, and $250 more cash would have been available for use in the business.

Consider next what the effect would be had LIFO been adopted in the eighth year, at which time the FIFO cost per unit was $1.70. At the end of the tenth year the reduction in reported earnings, as opposed to remaining on FIFO during the entire period, would have been 30¢ per unit, or $150 before income tax and approximately $75 after tax. Delaying the LIFO election until the price spiral has reached an advanced stage diminishes the extent to which the reporting of unrealized inventory appreciation could be avoided. Nevertheless, it may be that adopting LIFO is still a favorable move.

The danger, however, lies in the possibility of subsequent cost decreases. Assume that in the eleventh year the current (FIFO) cost drops to $1.60 per unit. Since Company A adopted LIFO with a base cost of $1.00 per unit, the election continues to be advantageous despite the price decline. Had LIFO not been adopted until the eighth year, however, the LIFO cost of $1.70 would be greater than the $1.60 current FIFO cost.

Although permissable for financial reporting purposes, for federal income tax purposes, no writedowns from LIFO cost to market (replacement cost) are recognized. Moreover, a company may not switch from LIFO to another inventory method without the consent of the Commissioner of Internal Revenue. For tax purposes, a company may have to carry its inventory at a LIFO cost in excess of market value, and report a greater amount of income than if LIFO had not been adopted at all.

It is obvious that LIFO yields the greatest benefits, in terms of reduced taxes, if adopted at or near the bottom of a price spiral. If LIFO is elected after a period of rising prices has elapsed, it may still prove beneficial, but the predicted trend of future costs must be carefully considered.

Since LIFO first became a permissible inventory method for federal income tax purposes (1938), a dramatic rise in the general price level has taken place in the United States. Most economists agree that the trend of rising prices will continue in the foreseeable future, although disagreement exists on the projected magnitude of the increase.

It is not the general price level, however, which determines whether a particular company should elect LIFO. The future cost prospects for its specific products are an essential consideration. After appropriate study, management may conclude that during the next three to five years the cost of its principal products will rise, although there may be temporary or isolated decreases in certain areas. In this case, the company might consider placing its entire inventory on LIFO in a single dollar-value pool as described in Chapter 12. Under this method, minor price decreases for certain products will tend to average out, and the pool as a whole should show satisfactory cost stability.

If, on the other hand, it is foreseen that for one or more significant products, the immediate outlook is for decreased costs, such products may be omitted from the immediate LIFO election. LIFO may be elected for tax purposes for only part of the goods in the inventory. If at some future date it appears the cost of other products is likely to rise, an additional election can be made.

VOLUME CONSIDERATIONS

While the expected trend of future costs is the keystone to deliberations involving the adopting of LIFO, physical volume of the inventories must also receive consideration.

To the extent possible, LIFO will generally be adopted at a time when inventory quantities are at or near normal levels. This is to guard against a twofold danger:

1. If the election is made when quantities are low, increments during years of inflated prices may have to be carried in the LIFO inventory at high costs indefinitely.
2. If the election is made at a time when inventory quantities are in excess of normal requirements, subsequent quantity reductions during periods of high prices can result in charging relatively low LIFO costs against inflated income and, should higher income tax rates be applicable to the year of inventory liquidation, more of the cash resources of the company may be required to discharge the tax liability.

In some cases, the inventory volume is an important consideration in selecting a fiscal year-end for seasonal businesses. The larger the volume at the end of the year, the greater the impact of price-level changes and of the difference in results from using FIFO or LIFO.

Assume that Company X normally carries 40,000 tons of material A in inventory. During 19X3 the price falls to a low point of $3 per ton, and an election is made to place material A on LIFO, although the quantity in inventory at the end of 19X3 is only 10,000 tons. During succeeding years inventory quantities are built up to normal levels, but at higher prices. At the end of 19X5 the situation is as follows:

Additions to LIFO Inventory at Increasing Costs Followed by Decline in Market Value

	Tons	Unit cost	LIFO cost
19X3 base	10,000	$3	$ 30,000
19X4 increment	25,000	5	125,000
19X5 increment	5,000	6	30,000
Total inventory	40,000		$185,000
Average LIFO cost—$4.625			

Although LIFO was originally elected when the price for material A was low, subsequent quantity increments have raised the average LIFO cost to the relatively high level of $4.625 per ton. Company X may be in a vulnerable position in view of the volatile price structure for the material. If in 19X6 the cost should fall to $4 while the inventory quantity is held at 40,000 tons, the replacement (FIFO) cost of the inventory ($160,000) will be lower than the LIFO cost ($185,000). Under these circumstances, Company X would be required to carry its inventory at an amount in excess of market value for federal income tax purposes; however, if the year-end inventory quantity could be reduced to 20,000 tons, the average

LIFO cost would be equal to the market value, and the $25,000 excess cost could be charged against income as part of the cost of sales. If a writedown to market is required for financial reporting purposes, the writedown would not be a violation of the conformity requirement of the Internal Revenue Code (see Rev. Proc. 77–50).

The observation concerning vulnerability is inapplicable where the price trend is predominately upward rather than cyclical. Under such circumstances, the LIFO election can advantageously be made as soon as an upward price trend is discernible with reasonable assurance, whether inventory quantities are at or below normal level. This is particularly pertinent for an expanding business operation where inventory quantities may be expected to show normal increases from year to year. Assume LIFO has been adopted by Company Y with inventory increments as follows over three succeeding years:

Additions to LIFO Inventory at Increasing Costs Where Market Value Continues Upward

	Tons	Unit cost	LIFO cost
19X3 base	10,000	$2	$ 20,000
19X4 increment	5,000	3	15,000
19X5 increment	20,000	4	80,000
19X6 increment	10,000	5	50,000
Total inventory	45,000		$165,000

Had Company Y waited until 19X5 to elect LIFO, its inventory at the end of 19X6 would have been $10,000 higher. To generalize, it may be concluded that when dealing with a material subject to cyclical cost variations,

Effect of Delaying LIFO Election Where Market Value Continues Upward

	Tons	Unit cost	LIFO cost
19X4 base	15,000	$3	$ 45,000
19X5 increment	20,000	4	80,000
19X6 increment	10,000	5	50,000
Total inventory	45,000		$175,000

the correlation of normal inventory quantities with a bottoming-out of the price cycle presents the optimum point at which to make the LIFO election; and if prices are expected to show a steady rise, the earlier the election, irrespective of volume, the lower will be the LIFO inventory cost.

If the LIFO election is made at a time when inventory quantities are in excess of normal requirements, a subsequent reduction in quantity can have the effect of offsetting base-year LIFO costs against inflated sales income. Assuming no increase in tax rates, an election by Company Z would still be beneficial, as in the following example:

Partial Liquidation of LIFO Inventory
Where Market Value Continues Upward

	Tons	Unit cost	LIFO cost
19X4 base	30,000	$3	$ 90,000
19X5—No change	—		—
19X6 liquidation	(10,000)		(30,000)
Total inventory	20,000	3	$ 60,000

Company Z is better off having elected LIFO, despite the subsequent liquidation, since the inventory cost on a FIFO basis at the end of 19X6 would be $100,000 that is, 20,000 tons at $5 per ton.

As discussed on page 185, the Internal Revenue Code at present contains no relief provisions applicable to a current involuntary liquidation of a LIFO inventory quantity. Thus, the consequences of volume reductions must be considered. This does not mean, however, that a potential involuntary liquidation is necessarily a reason for not adopting LIFO. From an income tax viewpoint, the disadvantage of an involuntary liquidation is merely that previously deferred income becomes taxable. Even if the LIFO base is completely liquidated, the company is no worse off than if it had not elected LIFO in the first place, *assuming* no increase in the effective tax rate. If the amounts of paper profits in the inventory and the taxable income are sufficiently small so that the former would be taxed at 20 per cent, a LIFO election would normally not be advisable. A subsequent liquidation of the inventory could result in the income deferred as a consequence of the LIFO election being subjected to tax at up to 46 per cent even if there is no change in the federal income tax law.

The projection of anticipated inventory volume is at least as significant in selecting from the pooling methods discussed in Chapters 11 and 12 as is deciding upon the adoption of LIFO in the first instance. Some businesses use separate LIFO pools for their inventories of raw materials, work in process, and finished goods; but this method is not normally recommended if significant relative differences in the volume of goods in each of the three groups from year to year or gradual changes over an extended period are expected. If, for example, the bulk of the inventory investment would be concentrated in finished goods one year and raw materials the next, the result during a period of rising prices would be the liquidation of the finished goods LIFO base and the accumulation of a high-cost layer in the raw materials pool. Under such circumstances it would be advantageous to employ a single pool for the entire inventory of a natural business unit. Similarly, where at any year end the quantity of one or more significant material components of a company's inventory might be temporarily cut back below normal level, a broad pooling arrangement would be preferable. See Chapter 15 for further discussion of GAAP considerations.

The volume of the inventory is also significant in selecting an accounting period. To illustrate, the following assumptions have been made as to acquisition costs for a material regularly stocked at October 31 in a volume equivalent to 140 per cent of the quantity owned at the calendar year end.

The costs charged against income for the units consumed on the basis of accounting periods ending on either October 31 or December 31 are tabulated on page 212. If the accounting period is changed during 19X5 from the calendar year to a fiscal period ending October 31, costs would be absorbed in a different manner.

The following examples of the effect of the accounting period used upon the manner in which costs are allocated to units consumed are summarized in comparative form on page 214.

A reserve to provide for the excess cost of replacing the 40 units temporarily liquidated at December 31, 19X6, would under these circumstances be provided where the accounting period was a fiscal year ending October 31. For accounting purposes, the cost of the units consumed during the months of November and December, 19X6, including the excess cost of replacing the 40 units, would be recognized as being $4,800 in all three situations.

From the illustrations, it can be concluded that during a period of rising prices, the increase in costs will be absorbed sooner, and the amount of income will be less, if the accounting period ends when the inventory volume is at its maximum. Also, if the replacement cost for an inventory item is less than the LIFO cost, changing the accounting period to one ending when the inventory volume is at a minimum will have the effect of a partial liquidation, and a portion of the excess cost will be charged against income.

Hypothetical Inventory of Seasonal Goods

| | Acqui-sition cost per unit | Quantities | | LIFO inventory cost if accounting periods end on | | | | | |
| | | | | Oct. 31 | | | Dec. 31 | | |
		Ac-quired	Con-sumed	Units	Per unit	LIFO cost	Units	Per unit	LIFO cost
19X3:									
Closing inventory.				100	$10	$1,000	100	$10	$1,000
19X4:									
Jan.–Oct........	$10	700	660	140	10	1,400	140	10	1,400
Nov.–Dec.......	15	200	240	100	10	1,000	100	10	1,000
19X5:									
Jan.–Oct........	15	700	660	140	10	1,400	100	10	1,000
							40	15	600
							140		1,600
Nov.–Dec.......	20	200	240	100	10	1,000	100	10	1,000
19X6:									
Jan.–Oct........	20	700	660	140	10	1,400	100	10	1,000
							40	20	800
							140		1,800
Nov.–Dec.......	20	200	240	100	10	1,000	100	10	1,000

The volume of the inventory and recurring seasonal fluctuations are factors in selecting an accounting period. This is particularly true in the case of canners of fruits and vegetables, meat packers, and manufacturers of products purchased to an appreciable extent for Christmas and graduation gifts, for example, toys, watches, fountain pens, and small electrical appliances.

The practical significance of the accounting period can be dramatically illustrated by assuming an energetic businessman sells ice cream bars by the swimming pool during the summer and wool mittens by the toboggan slide during the winter. The ice-cream bar business presents no inventory problem because whatever has been expended to acquire the merchandise will be deducted from sales proceeds in determining profit. In computing income on a calendar basis, however, an inventory will be required of the wool mittens. Assume the normal practice is to purchase one gross (144 pairs) during October as the season's stock, and there are 100 pairs

Costs for Units Consumed During Alternative Accounting Periods

| | Cost of acquisitions | | | LIFO inventory cost and cost of units consumed if accounting periods end on | | | |
| | | | | October 31 | | December 31 | |
	Per unit	Units	Total cost	Inven-tory	Costs absorbed	Inven-tory	Costs absorbed
19X3:							
Closing inventory..				$1,000		$1,000	
19X4:							
Jan.–Oct.........	$10	700	$ 7,000	1,400	$ 6,600		
Nov.–Dec........	15	200	3,000			1,000	$10,000
19X5:							
Jan.–Oct.........	15	700	10,500	1,400	13,500		
Nov.–Dec........	20	200	4,000			1,000	14,500
19X6:							
Jan.–Oct.........	20	700	14,000	1,400	18,000		
Nov.–Dec........	20	200	4,000			1,000	18,000
			$42,500				
Total costs absorbed for completed accounting periods					38,100		$42,500
Costs absorbed during interim period, Nov.–Dec. 19X6:					4,400		
					$42,500		

on hand at both the beginning and end of the year. The quantity sold is equal to the quantity purchased, and under the LIFO inventory method the same dollar amount assigned to the 100 pairs in the opening inventory will be assigned to the 100 pairs in the closing inventory. The amount expended during October to maintain the inventory and continue the business will be deducted from the sales proceeds for the closing months of the prior season and the beginning of the current season, even though in fact 100 pairs were sold before the purchase and only 44 pairs afterward. LIFO is a theory of a "flow of cost" and is not dependent upon the physical movement of goods.

If the hypothetical vendor of mittens had 110 pairs on hand at the end of the year, the closing inventory cost would be the amount assigned to the 100 pairs in the opening inventory plus an amount considered as the cost of 10 of the pairs purchased during the year. If at the end of the year following the 110-pair inventory there are only 95 pairs on hand,

Costs for Units Consumed if Accounting Period Is Changed During 19X5

	Cost of acquisitions			LIFO inventory cost and cost of units consumed if accounting period is changed	
	Per unit	Units	Total cost	Inventory	Costs absorbed
19X3:					
Closing inventory.....				$1,000	
19X4:					
Jan.–Oct............	$10	700	$ 7,000		
Nov.–Dec...........	15	200	3,000	1,000	$10,000
19X5:					
Jan.–Oct............	15	700	10,500	1,600	9,900
Nov.–Dec............	20	200	4,000		
19X6:					
Jan.-Oct............	20	700	14,000	1,600	18,000
Nov.–Dec............	20	200	4,000		
			$42,500		
Total costs absorbed for completed accounting periods					37,900
Costs absorbed during interim period, Nov.–Dec. 19X6					4,600
					$42,500

the closing inventory cost would be such portion of the amount assigned to the original 100 pairs as is applicable to 95 of them. The cost of sales for the year would be the sum of (a) the total purchases made during the year, (b) the cost established in the preceding year for the 10 pairs considered to have been purchased in that year and on hand at the year end, and (c) such portion of the amount assigned to the original 100 pairs as is deemed applicable to 5 pairs.

A computation of the income of the hypothetical mitten vendor for a fiscal year ended September 30 or October 31 could show results substantially different from those for the calendar year. There would be no inventory at all on September 30. On October 31 the entire season's stock of 144 pairs would be on hand, so that the investment in unsold goods would be greater than on December 31, and there could be a larger amount of inventory profit to be eliminated from income by the LIFO method.

The possibility of income being distorted by unrealized inventory profits

Different Allocations of Costs Resulting from Election of Accounting Period

		Cost of units consumed if accounting period				
		Ends on October 31		Ends on December 31		Is changed
	Units consumed	Per unit	Costs absorbed	Per unit	Costs absorbed	Per unit	Costs absorbed
19X4:							
Jan.–Oct.	660	$10	$ 6,600	$10	$ 6,600	$10	$ 6,600
Nov.–Dec.	200	15	3,000	15	3,000	15	3,000
	40	15	600	10	400	10	400
			10,200		10,000		10,000
19X5:							
Jan.–Oct.	660	15	9,900	15	9,900	15	9,900
			20,100		19,900		19,900
Nov.–Dec.	200	20	4,000	20	4,000	20	4,000
	40	20	800	15	600	20	800
			24,900		24,500		24,700
19X6:							
Jan.–Oct.	660	20	13,200	20	13,200	20	13,200
			38,100		37,700		37,900
Nov.–Dec.	200	20	4,000	20	4,000	20	4,000
	40	10*	400	20	800	15*	600
			$42,500		$42,500		$42,500

* LIFO cost for units temporarily liquidated.

necessarily increases with the size of the inventory, but few businesses have inventory fluctuations to the extent of the hypothetical vendor.

SIGNIFICANCE OF FORESEEABLE TECHNOLOGICAL CHANGES

In the case of a retail or other commercial trading operation "cost" is usually a single amount—the purchase price. For a manufacturer there are various elements of cost: the cost of raw material used and conversion costs (labor and overhead). In LIFO as well as in FIFO determinations, each element should be considered separately.

Because business is constantly striving to be more efficient, it is not uncommon to encounter situations in which the material cost per unit shows an upward trend, but the conversion cost element either remains constant or decreases. This conversion cost trend may result from automation, decreased labor hours per unit produced, increased volume, or numerous other factors. The conversion cost per unit can decrease even though there have been increases in labor rates and in the individual items of overhead expense. If LIFO is applied to the aggregate of the cost elements as a unit, the cost reductions made possible by increased production efficiency would be offset against the increases attributable to the materials. This can be seen in an example which reflects what can happen through an interplay of cost factors. The material cost element per unit has increased from $5.00 to $6.00, whereas conversion costs have decreased from $6.00 to $4.62. If the aggregate of the material and conversion costs is treated as a single amount, the LIFO cost will continue to be $11.00 per unit, 38¢ in excess of replacement cost. If, however, LIFO is applied only to the material cost, the inventory will be carried at $9.62 per unit, i.e., a LIFO cost of $5.00 for the material content plus a FIFO cost of $4.62 for labor and overhead.

First year:
Material cost......................	$ 5.00
Labor cost—2 hr. at $2..............	4.00
Overhead cost—50% of labor.......	2.00
	$11.00

Second year:
Material cost......................	$ 6.00
Labor cost—1.5 hr. at $2.20..........	3.30
Overhead cost—40% of labor.......	1.32
	$10.62

The material-content pooling method combines in one LIFO pool both the cost of raw materials on hand and the material cost element of work in process and finished goods. Conversion costs may be inventoried on a FIFO basis.[2] Material cost increases are charged off to current earnings, while the benefits of technological improvements in production efficiency are reflected in lower per unit inventory amounts for conversion costs. Where conversion costs are relatively small, this procedure is satisfactory because it minimizes the liquidation problem caused by shifts in volume

[2] See Chapter 15 for a discussion of possible problems under GAAP.

in the raw materials, work in process, and finished goods components of the inventory from year to year.

Where the details of cost elements can be established from the accounting records, the benefits of lower per-unit conversion costs resulting from increased efficiency may be maintained by inventorying conversion costs on the basis of direct labor hours. Labor is purchased in a manufacturing business in terms of hours, just as steel is purchased in terms of tons, and the inventory analysis may disclose that at the beginning of a period there was on hand the product of 1,500 direct labor hours and at the end of the period the inventory represents the fruits of 1,800 direct labor hours. The number of hours will, in many situations, be a better measure of the "form utility" element of the goods on hand than the number of units of particular articles.

In contemplating an election to use LIFO, consideration should be given to possible effects of future changes in production methods and product lines. These changes may result in the substitution of new types of raw materials for materials presently used, the purchase of materials presently manufactured or vice versa, or even distinct changes in the type of finished product.

For example, a member of the woolen industry which adopted LIFO 35 years ago would have faced the problem of integrating into its inventory computations certain synthetic fibers substituted for natural wool previously used. A business originally engaged in the manufacture of railroad locomotives or equipment may now be subcontracting for the automobile or aircraft industry. An appliance manufacturer which 20 years ago used principally metal parts may now be using plastic components. A pharmaceutical producer which formerly purchased fine bulk chemicals may begin manufacturing them. Industry is constantly substituting new products, materials, and production methods for the outmoded and obsolete. With the passage of time almost any business may expect some changes of this nature. In every case the question is whether the substitution of new materials or products will cause a liquidation of the LIFO base for a superseded inventory item. The GAAP and IRS implications arising from new items are discussed in more detail in Chapter 15.

In the case of the woolen company, if the natural fibers no longer in use had been carried in separate, specifically identified quantity pools, a liquidation of those pools would have occurred, with a consequent recognition of inventory profits deferred by LIFO. If on the other hand the company had carried all fibers in a single generic pool under the dollar-value method, the new synthetic fibers could be included in that pool without recognizing any significant loss of LIFO base. To facilitate the integration of new products and materials into existing pools, careful consideration should be given at the time of making the LIFO election to the description of the inventory goods—a general description by basic function may be preferable to specific names. A single dollar-value pool for the entire inventory investment of a natural business unit or a few pools grouped by broad product classifications, presently offers the best means of avoiding substantial liquidations upon the substitution of new materials for old in the inventory.

In the case of a company which switches to manufacturing a material or group of materials previously purchased, the problem of recognition of previously deferred income arises if the company has been using a material-content pool, with conversion costs included in separate pools or inventoried on a FIFO basis. Here the effect is partial liquidation of the material pool. At best only the raw-material element of the product's cost could now be included in the original material pool, whereas the LIFO principle would previously have been applied to the entire purchase cost. The conversion cost element would be treated as a current increment in another pool, or would be part of the FIFO inventory.

If the change in operating practice from purchasing to producing could have been foreseen and the expectation was for rising prices, the LIFO election could have been so phased as not to cover this particular item. Alternatively, it might be feasible for the company to organize the new production facility as a separate operating subsidiary which would then sell the finished item to the parent company. The parent would continue to treat the product as a purchased material, and no change in its inventory pooling would be necessary.

All potential consequences of LIFO under changed future conditions cannot be foreseen, but management must weigh carefully the various possibilities in making the original LIFO election. Decisions that appear to yield the best tax result may raise problems from the standpoint of generally accepted accounting principles.

ILLUSTRATION OF ALTERNATIVES IN TIMING A LIFO ELECTION

The observations concerning the timing and extent of a LIFO election may be illustrated by a hypothetical case. The Panacea Corporation, a manufacturer of cosmetics, is considering the adoption of LIFO in 19X9. Panacea's finished product line is in a constant state of flux, with new items and packaging being introduced continuously, and faded products dropped as soon as practicable. Essentially, however, its products are compounded from groups of the same basic materials termed, with a confessed lack of grace, the "musk," "wax," "lavender," and "gum" groups. As of the end of 19X8, Panacea's inventory on a FIFO basis is as follows:

Raw materials:	
Musk—50,000 lb. at $3.00.............	$ 150,000
Wax—160,000 lb. at $5.25............	840,000
Lavender—80,000 lb. at $6.00.........	480,000
Gum—30,000 lb. at $3.00.............	90,000
Others—...........................	60,000
	1,620,000
Packaging materials....................	3,000,000
Work in process........................	300,000
Finished goods........................	4,500,000
	$9,420,000

An analysis of the cost elements of a typical Panacea product discloses the following:

Raw materials......................	25%
Packaging materials................	60
Conversion costs...................	15
	100%

Packaging materials constitute the largest product cost element, but this category of inventory is composed of a multitude of individual items which are constantly being added to, dropped, or otherwise changed. Although no single individual item dominates this inventory category, the prices which the company must pay for its packaging materials have been constantly increasing in recent years, and there is every expectation that they will continue to rise in the foreseeable future.

With respect to the various groups of raw materials, the outlook is as follows:

Musk—This group has a volatile price history. Current average price of $3.00 per pound is expected to rise sharply to between $4.50 and $5.25 within the year. These prices, however, are believed to result from unusual shortages at the present time. It is expected that within a few years the price will fall below $3.00. Two years ago it was $1.88.

Wax—Price has shown a slow but steady increase in recent years. It was $4.50 a pound five years ago, and it is believed that the price will continue to rise at a similar rate in future years.

Lavender—Price has been fairly stable in recent years averaging $6.00 per pound, with only minor variations. This trend is expected to continue.

Gum—It is expected that the price of this material will increase within the next few years; however, the company is presently investigating a substitute material which can be obtained at a lower cost.

Labor costs per man-hour are expected to remain stable within the immediate future, although a moderate increase in future years is foreseen. Gradual but constant increases in the cost of overhead items such as payroll benefits, maintenance, depreciation, and taxes are also foreseen. In total, however, conversion costs per unit of product will probably decline slightly or at least hold steady over the next several years, due to production efficiencies and increased volume.

Based on this analysis of cost and other trends, unless the management of The Panacea Corporation wishes to adopt LIFO with a natural business unit pool so that in the future less attention will need to be given to the inventory position for the various materials, maximum tax benefit would result from adopting LIFO at the present time for only a portion of the inventory investment. As previously mentioned, adoption of LIFO for only selected products or classes of product could be construed as not meeting the preferability criteria imposed by APB Opinion No. 20. Because the future outlook for conversion costs does not indicate substantial increases on a per-unit basis and significant direct labor hour statistics are unavailable, these costs could be continued on FIFO. Material-content pools (raw materials plus the material-cost element of work in process and finished goods) could be established advantageously for only two broad groupings of materials: packaging materials and waxes.

All packaging materials should be grouped within a single pool, and the dollar-value principle of measurement applied. The dollar-value method is essential in this situation so that cost increases can be eliminated from the amount assigned to future inventories without distortions caused by changes and liquidations of individual items. Applying LIFO by comparing quantities of individual packages would be impractical.

Because of the upward price trend for waxes, a LIFO pool should also be established for this group of materials.

There would be no present advantage in electing LIFO for lavender. If the price trend should turn upward, an election can be made to include this material at some future date. Gum should also be omitted from the initial LIFO election, since a new, lower-priced material may be substituted for this item in the near future. Because of its volatile price tendencies, musk is the type of material which should be on LIFO, but only if the election is made when the price has touched bottom and materials are on hand in at least normal quantities. Because the present price of musk is expected to dip sharply within a few years, the election of LIFO for this item should be deferred.

If the election is to use a single pool for the entire inventory in recognition of the fact that the business of The Panacea Corporation constitutes one natural business unit, the pool will consist of all items—raw materials, packaging materials, work in process, and finished goods.

TRANSFERS OF LIFO INVENTORIES IN NONTAXABLE EXCHANGES

In general any sale or exchange of an asset can give rise to a taxable gain under the provisions of the Internal Revenue Code. The statute provides, however, that no gain (or loss) shall be recognized as a consequence of certain types of exchanges. Although such exchanges are currently nontaxable, it is more accurate to think of merely a deferment of recognition of the gain or loss. The previously established federal income tax basis for the asset is usually not changed when its ownership is transferred from one person to another in a nontaxable exchange; however, unless the transaction is considered as a "pooling of interests" for financial accounting purposes the inventories may have to be restated.

One question encountered in a nontaxable exchange involving a LIFO inventory concerned the necessity for making a new election in order to continue using that method for federal income tax purposes.[2] A corporation was organized in 1946 and acquired the assets of three proprietorships in exchange for shares of its capital stock. The proprietorships had used LIFO. For income tax purposes the cost of the inventory to the corporation was the same as the cost in the hands of the prior owners, and the corporation continued the LIFO basis in its first tax return. It did not, however, file an election as required by the Internal Revenue Code and regulations.[3] The Internal Revenue Service was upheld by the Tax Court in its contention that Textile Apron Company could not use LIFO. The closing inventories for the corporation were determined on a FIFO basis, and the inventory profits deferred by the proprietorships were included in taxable income.

[2] *Textile Apron Co. v. Commissioner*, 21 T.C. 147 (1953).
[3] Sections 1.472 and 1.472-2, Appendix C.

Many companies which acquired LIFO inventories in nontaxable exchanges made appropriate elections and had to decide whether a new average cost for the entire opening inventory should be computed or the cost previously established for each LIFO inventory layer should be carried over. The common practice approved by representatives of the Internal Revenue Service was for the transferee of the inventory to continue the same layer stratification for the inventory whether the LIFO inventory was acquired in a statutory merger, a consolidation, or other type of nontaxable transaction. This conclusion is justified by considering each inventory layer as a separate item of property, which is consistent with the fact that each layer is computed to represent a definite quantity of inventory with a specifically identified cost.

Since 1954 the Internal Revenue Code has provided that continuation of a predecessor's inventory method is required after certain types of nontaxable exchange, that is, a distribution by a subsidiary corporation of all its assets in exchange for the stock held by the parent company where the cost of the stock is not to be assigned to the assets, and a corporate acquisition of assets in exchange for voting stock, whether or not the exchange is incidental to a statutory merger or consolidation, or a reorganization involving only a change in identity, form, or place of organization. The continuation of the inventory method is not mandatory in cases of nontaxable exchanges representing transfers of assets to controlled corporations, so the current statutory provision would not have eliminated the necessity for an affirmative election by Textile Apron Company.

The wording of the Internal Revenue Code is as follows:

In any case in which inventories are received by the acquiring corporation, such inventories shall be taken by such corporation (in determining its income) on the same basis on which such inventories were taken by the distributor or transferor corporation, unless different methods were used by several distributor or transferor corporations or by a distributor or transferor corporation and the acquiring corporation. If different methods were used, the acquiring corporation shall use the method or combination of methods of taking inventory adopted pursuant to regulations prescribed by the Secretary or his delegate. [Int. Rev. Code of 1954, § 381 (c) (5).]

Although this provision has been part of the Internal Revenue Code since 1954, the regulations referred to were not even proposed until December 29, 1960. The final regulations were not adopted until January 14, 1975.

Under the regulations, the inventory basis depends upon whether the operation of an acquired business is continued as a separate business. If so, the general rule is that the same inventory method is required. This does not preclude an election to use LIFO where FIFO has been previously used, however, because the Code specifically permits adoption of LIFO commencing with any taxable year.

If the acquired business is combined with another, the regulations require that the "principal" inventory method in use prior to the nontaxable exchange be followed in resolving any variations. "The fair market value of the particular types of goods of each group of component trades or businesses with respect to which one method of taking inventories common to all was employed shall be compared," say the regulations, "with the fair or market value of comparable types of goods of other groups of component trades or businesses with respect to which another method of taking inventories common to all was employed. . . . The method of taking inventories of the group of component trades or businesses having the largest fair market value of such inventories shall be the principal method of taking inventories."

The regulations provide that the determination of the principal inventory method applies not only to the overall inventory method, such as FIFO v. LIFO, but also to such sub-methods as cost v. cost or market (whichever is lower), methods of pooling, dollar value v. specific goods, and methods of determining LIFO layers. The regulations specify that the principal inventory method must be used unless either (a) the principal method does not clearly reflect income or (b) the use of the principal method would be inconsistent with the provisions of a closing agreement previously reached with the Internal Revenue Service.

If the acquiring corporation does not wish to use the principal inventory method, or if the principal method does not clearly reflect income or violates a closing agreement, an application must be filed with the Commissioner of Internal Revenue, Attention: T:I:C, Washington, D.C. 20224 not later than 90 days after transfer. If the application is filed because the acquiring corporation seeks to use a method other than the principal method, the Commissioner may impose conditions or adjustments in granting permission. If the application is filed because the principal method does not clearly reflect income or violates the terms of a closing agreement, the Commissioner makes a unilateral determination of the proper inventory method to be used by the acquiring corporation.

LIFO CONSIDERATIONS IN ACCOUNTING FOR BUSINESS COMBINATIONS

The Internal Revenue Code and the related regulations require that the LIFO method of determining the cost of inventories must be used in the preparation of financial statements, including consolidated financial statements of a parent company, when the LIFO method is used for federal income tax purposes. In a business combination accounted for by the purchase method, APB Opinion No. 16 ("APB 16") requires that the inventories of an acquired company be recorded at their fair values at the date of acquisition. The apparent dilemma of how a LIFO tax basis in inventories may be preserved in this situation if the combination is effected by a tax-free exchange has been resolved by Revenue Procedure No. 72–29, which clearly applies where (1) a tax-free merger is booked as a purchase or (2) a taxable acquisition is recorded as a pooling and, based upon private letter rulings, also applies where a taxable acquisition is accounted for as a purchase but the rules used for allocating costs for tax purposes and for assigning costs under APB 16 result in different LIFO valuations for book and tax purposes. In a situation not covered explicitly by Revenue Procedure 72–29, it would be prudent to request a ruling from the IRS.

Revenue Procedure No. 72–29 states that the LIFO method may continue to be used for tax purposes provided that any resulting differences between (a) taxable income for federal income tax purposes and net income for financial statement purposes and (b) LIFO inventories reflected in the balance sheets for federal income tax purposes and financial statement purposes be disclosed both in the financial statements and the federal income tax return of the acquiring corporation. In this situation, Section 472(c) of the Internal Revenue Code still requires the use of the LIFO method for financial statement purposes after the combination. The disclosure in the financial statements and in the federal income tax return may be in the form of a footnote or a separate schedule, but must explain the amount of and the reason for the variance in the LIFO inventories. Such disclosure is required in all taxable years in which the differences occur or exist regardless of the year of acquisition and regardless of the materiality of the differences.

For financial accounting purposes, the LIFO inventories are treated as a current year's purchase since the transaction is treated as a purchase. In such a transaction neither the LIFO costs nor the LIFO layers will be the same for federal income tax and financial accounting purposes with respect to the acquired inventories in the hands of the acquiring corporation.

Rule 5–02(6b) of Regulation S-X as amended calls for the disclosure of the excess of replacement or current cost over stated LIFO value, if material, parenthetically or in a note to the financial statements. In this regard Revenue Ruling No. 73–66 and Revnue Ruling No. 75–50 state that such disclosure does not violate the financial statement reporting requirement of Section 472(c) of the Internal Revenue Code. The disclosure requirement of Regulation S-X is for balance sheet purposes only and does not represent disclosure of the income effect of using an inventory method for financial reporting purposes different from that used for tax purposes.

Impact of tax effects on amounts assigned to LIFO inventories APB 16 states that the amount assigned to identifiable assets should recognize that the fair value of an asset to an acquirer is less than its market or appraisal value if all or a portion of the market or appraisal value is not deductible for income taxes. The impact of tax effects on amounts assigned to individual assets depends on numerous factors, including imminence or delay of realization of the asset value and the possible timing of tax consequences. (See paragraph 89 of APB 16).

The basic principle of LIFO is that current income is better determined during inflation by deducting from the sales of the accounting period the cost of the most recent merchandise used in making the sales. Accordingly, taxpayers on the LIFO method should avoid liquidation of existing LIFO pools, where historical costs are below the current cost of replacing the merchandise. It can be assumed, therefore, that some portion or all of the existing LIFO inventories of a company will remain on the balance sheet indefinitely and not enter cost of sales for either financial statement purposes or income tax purposes. As the probability of material liquidations of existing LIFO pools decreases so does the appropriateness of recognizing the tax effects on amounts assigned to LIFO inventories in a business combination. Therefore when it is expected that a liquidation of the purchased LIFO inventory quantities is unlikely, a reduction in the fair value assigned to the LIFO inventories by reason of imminence of taxes on the lower tax basis is *not* required. However, if the acquiring company intends to liquidate all or a portion of the purchased LIFO inventories, the fair value assigned inventories should be reduced by the present value of the estimated future tax effects of differences between the tax base and the amount otherwise appropriate to assign to the asset according to the estimated future period of liquidation.

ACCOUNTING FOR PURCHASED LIFO INVENTORIES

The following example illustrates our understanding of how LIFO inventories which are acquired in a tax-free exchange accounted for as a purchase would be recognized in the financial statements and federal income tax return of the acquiring company in the most complex situation

—where the separate LIFO pools of each company are appropriately combined or are combinable for tax purposes because the inventory items are similar. Less complex and more frequently encountered situations would occur when either the acquired company is not liquidated into the acquiring company, or the LIFO inventories are dissimilar products and are not combined, or for some other valid reason separate LIFO pools are maintained after the business combination.

Assumptions:

1. Both Company P and Company S use the LIFO inventory cost method.
2. Company P acquires Company S in a tax-free exchange accounted for as a purchase: hence for federal income tax purposes the historical LIFO cost basis of the inventory of Company S survives the acquisition. Company S is immediately liquidated into Company P and its entire operations are combined with Company P.
3. Inventory of both Company P and Company S is similar Product A to be accounted for in a single pool.
4. The LIFO inventory cost method continues to be used in:
   a. Financial statements of Company P which include the accounts of Company S after the acquisition and liquidation.
   b. Tax return of Company P which includes the accounts of Company S after the acquisition and liquidation.
5. Company S:
   a. Basic facts regarding inventory cost and selling price of Product A—

Selling price to customers	$15
Less:	
Cost of disposal	(1)
Selling profit (covers advertising expense)	(4)
Selling price less cost of disposal and selling profit	10
Manufacturing profit	(1)
Current cost to manufacture	$ 9

   b. Units of Product A on hand at acquisition date of Company S by Company P   10
6. Company P:
   a. Current cost to manufacture one unit of Product A both at acquisition date and subsequent to acquisition date of Company S $ 8
   b. Units of Product A on hand in Company P at acquisition date of Company S   80
   c. Fair value to be assigned to the units of Product A inventory of Company S in consolidated financial statements at acquisition date in accordance with APB 16:
      Selling price, less cost of disposal and selling profit (as above) $10

A summary of the Product A inventory by LIFO layers held by Company P and Company S prior to Company S liquidation together with the combined Product A inventory by LIFO layer held by Company P after Company S liquidation is shown below.

The summary illustrates the underlying records after the immediate liquidation of the assets of Company S into Company P. If Company S is not liquidated but survives for some time, consolidating entries will have to be maintained to account for the differences between historical LIFO inventory costs maintained on the books of Company S and fair value of such inventories reflected in the consolidated financial statements of Company P.

| | Product A LIFO Inventory | | | |
| | Financial Statements | | Income Tax Return | |
	Units	Amount	Units	Amount
Company P				
Base 1941	60	$360	60	$360
Layer 1967	20	160	20	160
Total	80	520	80	520
Company S				
Base 1966	6	42	6	42
Layer 1969	2	18	2	18
Layer 1971	2	18	2	18
Total	10	78	10	78
Company P (after liquidation of Company S)				
Base 1941	60	360	60	360
Layer 1966	–	–(1)	6	42(2)
Layer 1967	20	160	20	160
Layer 1969	–	–(1)	2	18(2)
Layer 1971	10	100(1)	2	18(2)
Total	90	$620	90	$598

Notes:

(1) At date of acquisition the LIFO inventories of Company S are reflected in Company P financial statements as one layer at a fair value of $10 per unit (see assumption 6c). Company P intends to continue production of Product A and considers liquidation of the purchased LIFO inventory quantities unlikely; hence, a reduction in the fair value of the new LIFO book base by reason of the imminence of taxes on the lower tax basis is not required.

(2) For federal income tax purposes the acquired LIFO inventories are carried over at the same tax basis and with the same LIFO layers.

SUBSEQUENT INVENTORIES TRANSACTIONS

When inventory quantities increase (net of decreases) and are not reduced in periods subsequent to the business combination below the combined level at date of combination, the higher inventory cost maintained for financial statement purposes will, with the possible exception noted in the following paragraph, represent a constant difference over the historical LIFO costs maintained in the federal income tax returns. In these circumstances, the use of the LIFO method for financial statements and tax returns will produce the same cost of sales to be charged against income for periods subsequent to the business combination. However, when inventory quantities on hand at the end of the accounting period are reduced below those on hand at the date of the business combination, the inventory cost to be charged against income in the financial statements for quantities sold will be greater than the cost charged against income for tax purposes.

The acquisition of a company in a tax-free exchange accounted for as a purchase will normally result in the establishment of a new basis, for book purposes, of most assets, including fixed assets. This basis will normally exceed that reflected in the tax return which continues to reflect historical asset costs. To the extent that the higher fixed asset costs, resulting from the establishment of the new book basis of these assets, are amortized to costs of production, the carrying values of LIFO inventory layers added for book purposes will exceed those added for tax purposes. Absent a liquidation of the acquired company, such a refinement would have to be undertaken by consolidating entries maintained from period to period. A tax-free acquisition of a company accounted for as a purchase normally involves substantial record keeping in order to account for the book/tax differences. The further refinement explained above, while theoretically correct, is often not undertaken when the effect is immaterial in the determination of book income because it adds further complexity to such record keeping.

LIFO INVENTORIES IN A *TAXABLE TRANSACTION* ACCOUNTED FOR AS A POOLING OF INTERESTS

The foregoing discussion of LIFO inventories in business combinations accounted for by the purchase method should be referred to in connection with this section.

Under certain circumstances a business combination accounted for by the pooling of interests method for book purposes may result in the establishment of a different basis for assets and liabilities of one or more of the combining companies for income tax purposes. Such business combinations are referred to as "taxable poolings."

When, among other things, a company (issuing company) exchanges its voting common stock for all of the voting common stock of another company (combining company), the transaction may be required to be treated as a pooling of interests under APB 16. Under APB 16, voluntary disposition of acquired shares by shareholders of the combining company does not preclude pooling treatment (see Interpretation No. 34 of APB 16 as to certain *required* dispositions.) However, if the shareholders of the combining company in a pooling of interests dispose on their own accord of a significant amount of stock received under circumstances which violate the continuity of ownership requirements in the tax law, the transaction may not qualify as a "reorganization" as described in Section 368 of the Internal Revenue Code and as the result it would become a "taxable pooling."

As long as the combining company continues its separate corporate existence, the book and tax accounting for its LIFO inventories will be the same whether layers are added or liquidations are experienced. Generally, there is no step-up in the tax basis of the assets of the acquired company unless it is liquidated into the issuing company within two years. When the combining company in a pooling is liquidated in a transaction that for tax purposes provides for a new tax basis in the acquired assets, the values assigned the inventories for tax purposes will usually exceed the historical LIFO cost which will continue to be used for financial statement purposes. In fact, upon liquidation all of the assets of the combining company, not just the inventories, are assigned fair values for tax purposes only. The combined corporation, while not required to, may elect to continue to use the LIFO method for valuing these inventories for tax purposes with the LIFO cost established at this higher basis.

Revenue Procedure No. 72–29, including the disclosure requirements, discussed previously in this chapter also applies to LIFO inventories in a taxable pooling. Hence, for financial statement purposes any LIFO inventories of the combining company are carried over at the same historical LIFO basis and with the same LIFO layers of such combining company. For federal income tax purposes, however, the LIFO inventories are treated as a current year's purchase since the transaction is not a tax-free reorganization.

INVENTORY PROBLEMS IN CONSOLIDATED TAX RETURNS [4]

Property transfers between members of an affiliated group have resulted in some differences in method of computing inventory costs for financial-statement and tax purposes. Where consolidated federal income tax returns are filed, the income is first determined for each of the corporate entities, and, except for various types of intercompany transactions, the consolidated income merely represents the combination of the amounts of net income as computed for the several members of the affiliated group. For the purpose of consolidated financial statements, however, the inventory may be determined as though one LIFO computation was made for the inventories of all the companies. This practice has the effect of offsetting increments in a LIFO group for one company against liquidations in the corresponding group of other companies. The computation of LIFO inventories on this basis is consistent with the theory of consolidated accounts, but raises problems as to the amount of intercompany profit in the inventory and the recognition to be given federal income taxes paid on the intercompany profit.

Under the commonly followed practice of making separate LIFO computations for each member of an affiliated group, individual companies may have inventory increments at a current intercompany transfer price for the year. In eliminating intercompany profit in the inventory, the comparison is made with an amount determined by reference to the LIFO computation for the supplying company. If it happens to have a liquidation for the year in the same LIFO pool, the cost will be that applicable to a prior year's increment or to the basic LIFO inventory rather than the cost incurred in the current year. This measurement of intercompany profit should be acceptable for federal income tax purposes where consolidated returns are to be filed.

Quoted on the following pages are the principal paragraphs specifically referring to inventories in the consolidated federal income tax regulations applicable to years beginning after December 31, 1965.

---

[4] See Chapter 15 for a discussion of intercompany profit eliminations in GAAP financial statements.

§ 1.1502–18   Inventory adjustment

(a) *Definition of intercompany profit amount.* For purposes of this section, the term "intercompany profit amount" for a taxable year means an amount equal to the profits of a corporation (other than those profits which such corporation has elected not to defer pursuant to § 1.1502–13(c)(3) or which have been taken into account pursuant to § 1.1502–13(f)(1)(viii)) arising in transactions with other members of the group with respect to goods which are, at the close of such corporation's taxable year, included in the inventories of any member of the group. See § 1.1502–13(c)(2) with respect to the determination of profits. See the last sentence of § 1.1502–13(f)(1)(i) for rules for determining which goods are considered to be disposed of outside the group and therefore not included in inventories of members.

(b) *Addition of initial inventory amount to taxable income.* If a corporation—

(1) Is a member of a group filing a consolidated return for the taxable year,

(2) Was a member of such group for its immediately preceding taxable year, and

(3) Filed a separate return for such preceding year,

then the intercompany profit amount of such corporation for such separate return year (hereinafter referred to as the "initial inventory amount") shall be added to the income of such corporation for the consolidated return year (or years) in which the goods to which the initial inventory amount is attributable are disposed of outside the group or such corporation becomes a nonmember. Such amount shall be treated as gain from the sale or exchange of property which is neither a capital asset nor property described in section 1231.

(c) *Recovery of initial inventory amount—*(1) *Unrecovered inventory amount.* The term "unrecovered inventory amount" for any consolidated return year means the lesser of—

(i) The intercompany profit amount for such year, or

(ii) The initial inventory amount.

However, if a corporation ceases to be a member of the group during a consolidated return year, its unrecovered inventory amount for such year shall be considered to be zero.

(2) *Recovery during consolidated return year.* (i) To the extent that the unrecovered inventory amount of a corporation for a consolidated return year is less than such amount for its immediately preceding year, such decrease shall be treated for such year by such corporation as a loss from the sale or exchange of property which is neither a capital asset nor property described in section 1231.

(ii) To the extent that the unrecovered inventory amount for a consolidated return year exceeds such amount for the preceding year, such increase shall be treated as gain from the sale or exchange of property which is neither a capital asset nor property described in section 1231.

(3) *Recovery during first separate return year.* For the first separate return year of a member following a consolidated return year, the unrecovered inventory amount for such consolidated return year (minus any part of the initial inventory amount which has not been added to income pursuant to paragraph (b) of this section) shall be treated as a loss from the sale or exchange of property which is neither a capital asset nor property described in section 1231.

(d) *Examples.* The provisions of paragraphs (a), (b), and (c) of this section may be illustrated by the following examples:

Example (1). Corporations P, S, and T report income on the basis of a calendar year. Such corporations file separate returns for 1965. P manufactures widgets which it sells to both S and T, who act as distributors. The inventories of S and T at the close of 1965 are comprised of widgets which they purchased from P and with respect to which P derived profits of $5,000 and $8,000, respectively. P, S, and T file a consolidated return for 1966. During 1966, P sells widgets to S and T with respect to which it derives profits of $7,000 and $10,000, respectively. The inventories of S and T as of December 31, 1966, are comprised of widgets on which P derived net profits of $4,000 and $8,000, respectively. P's initial inventory amount is $13,000, P's intercompany profit amount for 1965 (such $13,000 amount is the profits of P with respect to goods sold to S and T and included in their inventories at the close of 1965). Assuming that S and T identify their goods on a first-in, first-out basis, the entire opening inventory amount of $13,000 is added to P's income for 1966 as gain from the sale or exchange of property which is neither a capital asset nor property described in section 1231, since the goods to which the initial inventory amount is attributable were disposed of in 1966 outside the group. However, since P's unrecovered inventory amount for 1966, $12,000 (the intercompany profit amount for the year, which is less than the initial inventory amount), is less than the unrecovered inventory amount for 1965, $13,000, this decrease of $1,000 is treated by P for 1966 as a loss from the sale or exchange of property which is neither a capital asset nor property described in section 1231.

Example (2). Assume the same facts as in example (1) and that at the close of 1967, a consolidated return year, the inventories of S and T are comprised of widgets on which P derived profits of $5,000 and $3,000, respectively. Since P's unrecovered inventory amount for 1967, $8,000, is less than $12,000, the unrecovered inventory amount for 1966, this decrease of $4,000 is treated by P for 1967 as a loss from the sale or exchange of property which is neither a capital asset nor property described in section 1231.

Example (3). Assume the same facts as in examples (1) and (2) and that in 1968, a consolidated return year, P's intercompany profit amount is $11,000. P will report $3,000 (the excess of $11,000, P's unrecovered inventory amount for 1968, over $8,000, P's unrecovered inventory amount for 1967) for 1968 as a gain from the sale or exchange of property which is neither a capital asset nor property described in section 1231.

Example (4). Assume the same facts as in examples (1), (2), and (3) and that in 1969 P, S, and T file separate returns. P will report $11,000 (its unrecovered inventory amount for 1968, $11,000, minus the portion of the initial inventory amount which has not been added to income during 1966, 1967, and 1968, zero) as a loss from the sale or exchange of property which is neither a capital asset nor property described in section 1231.

Example (5). Corporations P and S file a consolidated return for the first time for the calendar year 1966. P manufactures machines and sells them to S, which sells them to users throughout the country. At the close of 1965, S had on hand 20 machines which it purchased from P and with respect to which P derived profits of $3,500. During 1966, P sells 6 machines to S on which it derives profits of $1,300, and S sells 5 machines which it had on hand at the beginning of the year (S specifically identifies the machines which it sells) and on which P had derived profits of $900. P's initial inventory amount is $3,500, of which $900 is added to P's income in 1966 as gain from the sale or exchange of property which is neither a capital asset nor property described in section 1231, since such $900 amount is attributable to goods disposed of in 1966 outside the group, which goods were included in S's inventory at the close of 1965. If P and S continue to file consolidated returns, the remaining $2,600 of the initial inventory amount will be added to P's income as the machines on which such profits were derived are disposed of outside the group.

Example (6). Assume that in example (5) S had elected to inventory its goods under section 472 (relating to last-in, first-out inventories). None of P's initial inventory amount of $3,500 would be added to P's income in 1966, since none of the goods to which such amount is attributable would be considered to be disposed of during such year under the last-in, first-out method of identifying inventories.

(e) *Section 381 transfer.* If a member of the group is a transferor or distributor of assets to another member of the group within the meaning of section 381(a), then the acquiring corporation shall be treated as succeeding to the initial inventory amount of the transferor or distributor corporation to the extent that as of the date of distribution or transfer such amount has not yet been added to income. Such amount shall then be added to the acquiring corporation's income under the provisions of paragraph (b) of this section. For purposes of applying paragraph (c) of this section—

(1) The initial inventory amount of the transferor or distributor corporation shall be added to such amount of the acquiring corporation as of the close of the acquiring corporation's taxable year in which the date of distribution or transfer occurs, and

(2) The unrecovered inventory amount of the transferor or distributor corporation for its taxable year preceding the taxable year of the group in which the date of distribution or transfer occurs shall be added to such amount of the acquiring corporation.

(f) *Transitional rules*—(1) *In general.* If—

(i) A group filed a consolidated return for the taxable year immediately preceding the first taxable year to which this section applies,

(ii) Any member of such group made an opening adjustment to its inventory pursuant to paragraph (b) of § 1.1502–39A, and

(iii) Paragraph (c) of § 1.1502–39A has not been applicable for any taxable year subsequent to the taxable year for which such adjustment was made, then subparagraphs (2) and (3) of this paragraph shall apply.

(2) *Closing adjustment to inventory.* (i) For the first consolidated return year to which this section applies, the increase in inventory prescribed in paragraph (c) of § 1.1502–39A shall be made as if such year were a separate return year.

(ii) For the first separate return year of a member to which this section applies, the adjustment to inventory (whether an increase or a decrease) prescribed in paragraph (c) of § 1.1502–39A, minus any adjustment already made pursuant to subdivision (i) of this subparagraph, shall be made to the inventory of such member.

(3) *Addition and recovery of initial inventory amount.* Each selling member shall treat as an initial inventory amount its share of the net amount by which the inventories of all members are increased pursuant to subparagraph (2) (i)

of this paragraph for the first taxable year to which this section applies. A member's share shall be such net amount multiplied by a fraction, the numerator of which is its initial inventory amount (computed under paragraph (b) as if such taxable year were its first consolidated return year), and the denominator of which is the sum of such initial inventory amounts of all members. Such initial inventory amount shall be added to the income of such selling member and shall be recovered at the time and in the manner prescribed in paragraphs (b) and (c) of this section.

(4) *Example.* The provisions of this paragraph may be illustrated by the following example:

Example. (i) Corporations P, S, and T file consolidated returns for calendar 1966, having filed consolidated returns continuously since 1962. P is a wholesale distributor of groceries selling to chains of supermarkets, including those owned by S and T. The opening inventories of S and T for 1962 were reduced by $40,000 and $80,000, respectively, pursuant to paragraph (b) of § 1.1502–39A. At the close of 1965, S and T have on hand in their inventories goods on which P derived profits of $80,000 and $90,000, respectively. The inventories of S and T at the close of 1966 include goods which they purchased from P during the year on which P derived profits of $85,000 and $105,000, respectively.

(ii) The opening inventories of S and T for 1966, the first year to which this section applies, are increased by $40,000 and $80,000, respectively, pursuant to the provisions of subparagraph (2)(i) of this paragraph. P will take into account (as provided in paragraphs (b) and (c) of this section) an initial inventory amount of $120,000 as of the beginning of 1966, the net amount by which the inventories of S and T were increased in such year. Since the increases in the inventories of S and T are the maximum allowable under paragraph (c) of § 1.1502–39A (i.e., the amount by which such inventories were originally decreased), no further adjustments will be made pursuant to subparagraph (2)(ii) of this paragraph to such inventories in the event that separate returns are subsequently filed.

(5) *Election not to eliminate.* If a group filed a consolidated return for the taxable year immediately preceding the first taxable year to which this section applies, and for such preceding year the members of the group did not eliminate gain or loss on intercompany inventory transactions pursuant to the adoption under § 1.1502–31A(b)(1) of a consistent accounting practice taking into account such gain or loss, then for purposes of this section each member shall be treated as if it had filed a separate return for such immediately preceding year.

Section 1.1502–13(c)(2), to which reference is made with respect to the determination of profits, reads: "In determining the amount of deferred gain or loss, the cost of property, services, or any other expenditure shall include both direct costs and indirect costs which are properly includible in the cost of goods sold or cost of the services or other expenditures. See §1.471–3 for costs properly includible in cost of goods sold." The last sentence of Section 1.1502–13(f)(1)(i), to which reference is made for rules to determine which goods are considered to have been disposed of outside the group, provides that the determination is to be made by reference to the "method of inventory identification (e.g., first-in, first-out, last-in, first-out or specific identification)" of the member of the affiliated group which made the transfer outside the group.

Section 1.1502–13 of the consolidated federal income tax regulations applicable to years beginning after December 31, 1965, contains the general provisions relating to the treatment of intercompany transactions. Under this section the gain from intercompany sales of inventory items, unless an election is made by the affiliated group not to defer recognition of such gains, is taken into account by the selling member as of the date the goods are disposed of outside the group.

Under the regulations, applicable to years beginning after December 31, 1965, as and when gain is realized by a disposition outside the group or when income is subjected to tax because of a company's terminating its affiliation, the income is attributed to the corporation which made the intercompany sale rather than to the corporation which made the sale to the unrelated party or which owned the goods at the time the affiliation is terminated. Identifying the corporation to which income is attributed is particularly significant in determining the accumulated earnings and profits of the various corporations or where the income of one of the corporations is the basis for measuring a special tax-computation factor, such as the income of a Western Hemisphere trade corporation.

Adding the intercompany profit in the opening inventory for the first consolidated return year (i.e., the "initial inventory amount") to income as the goods are disposed of outside the affiliated group is duplication because the same income was included in the return for the year in which the sale was made, when separate returns were filed by each corporation rather than a consolidated return. A deduction will ultimately be allowed, however, to offset this duplication, and as long as the amount of intercompany profit in subsequent inventories is at least as large as the initial amount, the realized income for the affiliated group will be appropriately stated on a consolidated basis. This can be illustrated by a simplified example based upon the following assumptions:

Corporation P produces goods for sale only to its subsidiary, Corporation S

Corporation S sells only the goods purchased from Corporation P

Corporation S determines its inventories on a first-in, first-out basis

Corporation S had in its inventory at the end of each of the years 1970–1973 and 1975–1976 all of the goods produced by and purchased from Corporation P during the year

	Sales	Costs	Expenses	Pre-tax income
Corporation P—				
1970	$ 300,000	$ 200,000	$ 10,000	$ 90,000
1971	360,000	240,000	10,000	110,000
1972	300,000	200,000	10,000	90,000
1973	240,000	160,000	10,000	70,000
1974	300,000	200,000	10,000	90,000
1975	270,000	180,000	10,000	80,000
1976	330,000	220,000	10,000	100,000
1977	300,000	200,000	10,000	90,000
Total 1971–77	$2,100,000	$1,400,000	$ 70,000	$630,000
Corporation S—				
1970	$ —	$ —	$ —	$ —
1971	350,000	300,000	20,000	30,000
1972	420,000	360,000	20,000	40,000
1973	350,000	300,000	20,000	30,000
1974	630,000	540,000	20,000	70,000
1975	—	—	20,000	(20,000)
1976	315,000	270,000	20,000	25,000
1977	735,000	630,000	20,000	85,000
Total 1971–77	$2,800,000	$2,400,000	$140,000	$260,000

Corporation S had no inventory at the end of either of the years 1974 or 1977

Consolidated income tax returns are filed for years subsequent to 1970.

From this example, it can be observed that (a) the aggregate amount of consolidated income for the period 1971–77 equals the sum of the income of the corporations separately computed (i.e., the addition of the inter-company profit in the opening inventory for the first consolidated return year has been offset by deductions allowed as inventory adjustments) and (b) the realized income for the affiliated group has been appropriately stated on a consolidated basis in each year in which the amount of inter-company profit in the inventory is at least as large as the initial amount. The goods sold by Corporation S in 1971 for $350,000 cost Corporation P $200,000 to produce in 1970, and after deducting the expenses incurred by both corporations in 1971 aggregating $30,000, the pre-tax consolidated income is $120,000. The goods sold by Corporation S in 1972 for $420,000 cost Corporation P $240,000 to produce in 1971, and after deducting the $30,000 of 1972 expenses, the net consolidated income is $150,000. The

	Inter-company profit in year-end inventory	Unrecovered inventory amount	Adjustments for consolidated return		
			Net change in deferred gain	Initial inventory adjustment	Net increase or (decrease)
1970	$100,000	$100,000*			
1971	120,000	100,000	$(120,000)	$ 100,000*	$(20,000)
1972	100,000	100,000	20,000	—	20,000
1973	80,000	80,000	20,000	(20,000)	—
1974	—	—	80,000	(80,000)	—
1975	90,000	90,000	(90,000)	90,000	—
1976	110,000	100,000	(20,000)	10,000	(10,000)
1977	—	—	110,000	(100,000)	10,000

* Initial inventory amount

	Corporation P			Corporation S	Consolidated Pre-tax income
	Per books	Adjustments	Adjusted		
1970	$ 90,000			$ —	**
1971	110,000	$(20,000)	$ 90,000	30,000	$120,000
1972	90,000	20,000	110,000	40,000	150,000
1973	70,000	—	70,000	30,000	100,000
1974	90,000	—	90,000	70,000	160,000
1975	80,000	—	80,000	(20,000)	60,000
1976	100,000	(10,000)	90,000	25,000	115,000
1977	90,000	10,000	100,000	85,000	185,000
Total 1971–77	$630,000	—	$630,000	$260,000	$890,000

** Returns not filed on consolidated basis

net consolidated income for 1976 of $115,000 includes a $10,000 gain required to be recognized under Section 1.1502–18(c)(2)(ii) of the regulations. The total net consolidated income for the seven year period of $890,000 can be accounted for by the factors of sales by Corporation S ($2,800,000), costs of production incurred by Corporation P ($1,600,000 including $200,000 for the 1970 production), expenses of both corporations ($210,000), and the elimination of the $100,000 of intercompany profit in the January 1, 1971 inventory of Corporation S which was recognized in the 1970 separate return filed by Corporation P.

INVENTORY DETERMINATIONS FOR STATE TAX PURPOSES

For purposes of computing taxable income, the general policy of the states is to accept inventories as reported in federal returns. Therefore, where LIFO is used for federal tax purposes, generally its use is also accepted for state tax purposes.

More than 75% of the states and the District of Columbia impose corporate taxes on income or measured by income. Only a few of these states have specific statutes, rulings, or regulations pertaining to LIFO. Some states have incorporated the federal inventory and accounting procedures in their law and regulations by reference. Other states have their own inventory and accounting provisions which are sufficiently broad to encompass the use of LIFO, or have no specific provisions but do not take exception to LIFO. Particularly in the case of these states, it would be advisable to make specific inquiries as to local practice at the time LIFO is being adopted. In general, however, state tax authorities are primarily concerned with the allocation and apportionment of income to their respective states rather than the computation of total income or inventory determinations.

Notice and permission requirements for the use of LIFO vary among the several states, but generally follow a pattern based upon the type of provision under which the use of LIFO is authorized. States with specific provisions relating to LIFO generally require a copy of the federal election form or a similar statement. Some states which do not have specific LIFO provisions but have provisions pertaining to inventory and accounting methods treat the adoption of LIFO as a change in accounting method for which permission must be obtained from the tax authorities. Where the states have merely incorporated the federal provisions by reference, usually no notice or permission is required.

In many cases costing of inventories on a LIFO basis for federal purposes is a prerequisite to reporting on that basis in the state return. In others, if the LIFO basis is used for federal purposes, it is a mandatory basis in the state return, and in still other cases the LIFO basis is allowed for state purposes even though such method is not used in reporting income to the federal government.

The principal factors in state practices relating to LIFO adoption, readoption, termination, etc. are summarized in Appendix E.

USE OF LIFO FOR FOREIGN INCOME TAX PURPOSES

LIFO is not recognized for use in the United Kingdom, either for financial statement or income tax purposes. The tax laws of a few foreign countries permit the use of LIFO, and one enumeration includes Canada, Nationalist China, Italy, Japan, and The Netherlands in this group.[5]

The acceptability of LIFO for Canadian income tax purposes is questionable. The leading case dealing with the use of LIFO in Canada involved Anaconda American Brass Limited.[6] The case was first heard in the Exchequer Court of Canada, and a decision favorable to the taxpayer was issued on June 7, 1952. This decision was upheld on November 1, 1954, by the Supreme Court of Canada; but on further appeal to the Privy Council in London, in one of the last cases taken before that body from Canada, the decision was reversed. The Privy Council decision issued on December 13, 1955, held that LIFO was not acceptable for Canadian tax purposes.

Although the present Canadian Income Tax Act differs to some extent from the Income War Tax Act applicable to the years considered in the *Anaconda* decision, there has been no litigation under the current act and the reasoning of their Lordships is probably still applicable.

---

[5] MacNeill, "Accounting for Inflation Abroad," 112 *J. Accountancy* 2, 67 (Aug., 1961), where it is also observed that the base stock method is widely used in Sweden, recommended by professional accountants in Japan (although not permitted there for tax purposes), and permitted in modified form in France and Italy.

[6] *Minister of National Revenue v. Anaconda Brass, Ltd.*, 1 All E.R. 20 (P.C.), (1956).

ELEVEN

Use of LIFO for Federal Tax Purposes

This chapter and Chapter 12 review in detail tax rules relating to LIFO adoption and subsequent usage. Certain of the recommendations, particularly with respect to partial adoption of LIFO, may not be appropriate to a company which presents its financial statements in conformity with generally accepted accounting principles. Reference should be made to Chapter 15 for additional discussion of financial accounting considerations.

OUTLINE OF INVENTORY PROVISIONS OF INTERNAL REVENUE CODE

The provisions of the Internal Revenue Code relating to amounts assigned to inventories can be outlined as follows:

Appendix C:

§ 1.471. The general rule is inventories are to be taken:
   A. Whenever necessary in order clearly to determine income.
   B. On such basis as is prescribed—
      1. As conforming as nearly as may be to the best accounting practice in the trade or business, and
      2. As most clearly reflecting income.

§ 1.472. Whether or not the method is prescribed under the general rule, LIFO may be used in inventorying goods provided:
   A. An application specifying the goods has been filed at such time and in such manner as prescribed by regulations.

B. Taxpayer establishes no procedure other than LIFO has been used in inventorying the goods to ascertain the income, profit, or loss of the first LIFO taxable year for purposes of a report or statement to shareholders or other owners, or for credit purposes.

C. In determining income for the year preceding the first LIFO year, the closing inventory of the goods is at cost.

D. Taxpayer shall—

1. Treat the goods remaining on hand as being: *First,* those included in the opening inventory of the year (in the order of acquisition) to the extent thereof; and *second,* those acquired in the year;

2. Inventory the goods at cost; and

3. Treat the goods included in the opening inventory of the first LIFO year as having been acquired at the same time and determine their cost by the average cost method.

E. The change to, and the use of, the method is in accordance with such regulations as may be prescribed in order that income may be clearly reflected.

F. The change to, and the use of, a *different* method for a subsequent inventory shall be in accordance with such regulations as may be prescribed in order that income may be clearly reflected, where—

1. A change to the different method is authorized by the Secretary of the Treasury or his delegate; or

2. The Secretary of the Treasury or his delegate:

   a) Determines that the taxpayer has used for a year subsequent to the first LIFO year some other procedure in inventorying the goods to ascertain the income, profit, or loss of such subsequent year for the purpose of a report or statement to shareholders or other owners, or for credit purposes; and

   b) Requires a change to a different method beginning with such subsequent year or any taxable year thereafter.

The statutory provisions are not complex, but do not state how to determine amounts to be assigned to inventories.

REQUIREMENTS OF ELECTION TO USE LIFO
FOR FEDERAL INCOME TAX PURPOSES

Reproduced on page 243 is Treasury Department Form 970. This form is technically an application for adoption and use of LIFO, and its principal features are stipulations by the taxpayer as to:

1. The specific goods to be inventoried under LIFO.
2. The goods for which LIFO will not be used.
3. Whether any of the LIFO goods on hand at the beginning of the year were taken into the closing inventory of the preceding taxable year at values other than cost.
4. The inventory method used in ascertaining income, profit, or loss for the purpose of credit statements, or reports to shareholders or other owners, covering the first LIFO year.
5. Method selected to determine the cost of goods in a closing inventory in excess of the quantity in the opening inventory.
6. An agreement "to such adjustments incident to the change to or from the LIFO method, or to the use of such method, in the inventories of prior taxable years or otherwise, as the District Director of Internal Revenue upon the examination of the taxpayer's returns for the years involved may deem necessary in order to clearly reflect income."

The instructions printed on the reverse side of the application form are as follows:

1. Attach this form, in duplicate, to your income tax return for the year as of the close of which the LIFO inventory method is first to be used.
2. State the taxable year as of the close of which the LIFO method is first to be used, and specify in detail the goods to which it is to be applied. Attach an analysis of all inventories as of the beginning and as of the end of the taxable year for which the LIFO method is proposed first to be used, and also as of the beginning of the preceding taxable year. Also, include the ending inventory as reported on the return for the preceding year. Prepare this analysis in detail in accordance with sections 1.472-2 and 1.472-3 of the regulations.
3. The taxpayer may not change to the LIFO method unless he agrees to and makes such adjustments incident to the change to or from such method, or incident to the use of such method, in the inventories of prior taxable years or otherwise, as Internal Revenue may deem necessary to clearly reflect income for the years involved.
4. The LIFO inventory method, once adopted, is irrevocable and must be used in all subsequent years unless the Commissioner requires or permits a change to another method.

5. Any taxpayer may elect to determine the cost of his LIFO inventories under the so-called "dollar-value" LIFO method, provided that method is used consistently and clearly reflects income in accordance with section 1.472–8 of the regulations.

   Section 1.472–8(b) of the regulations sets forth the principles for establishing the dollar-value LIFO pools of manufacturers and processors. Subject to the provisions of that section, they may use natural business unit pools, multiple pools, or raw materials content pools.

   Section 1.472–8(c) of the regulations sets forth the principles for establishing dollar-value LIFO pools for wholesalers, retailers, jobbers, and distributors.

   Section 1.472–8(e) of the regulations sets forth the methods of computation of the LIFO value of a dollar-value pool. If the "double-extension" method as described in section 1.472–8(e)(2) of the regulations is not used for computing the value of the dollar-value pool, a statement describing the method used must be furnished in sufficient detail to facilitate the determination as to whether the method used meets the standards set forth in section 1.472–8(e)(1) of the regulations.

6. If the taxpayer is a corporation, the application must be signed by either the president, vice-president, treasurer, assistant treasurer or chief accounting officer, or by any corporate officer (such as tax officer) authorized to sign.

7. Identifying number.—Individuals enter their social security number; all others enter their employer identification number.

The formal application to use LIFO for federal tax purposes is made with the *completed* income tax return and not when an extension of time for filing is requested. It is important that the return be timely filed, because a LIFO election with a delinquent return may not be effective. Since the LIFO election need not be made until after the end of the year for which the method is first used and since it is not unsual to secure as long as a six-month extension of time for filing the "completed" return, a taxpayer can actually have the benefit of 20½ months of hindsight as regards the initial price rise to be eliminated from inventories by LIFO.

Instruction C on Form 970 calls for an analysis of all inventories at the beginning and end of the first LIFO year and also at the beginning of the preceding taxable year. This request is generally complied with by furnishing summaries of each of the three inventories in whatever detail is readily available. In the case of a manufacturer, however, the regulations state the analysis shall show in detail the manner in which costs are computed for raw materials, goods in process, and finished goods, segregating the products (whether in process or finished goods) into natural groups on the basis of (1) similarity in factory processes through which they pass, (2) similarity of raw materials used, or (3) similarity in style, shape, or

Form **970**
(Rev. April 1977)
Department of the Treasury
Internal Revenue Service

Application to Use LIFO Inventory Method

▶ Attach to your tax return.

Name _____ **Identifying number** *(See instruction B)*

Address *(Number, street, city, State and ZIP code)*

The taxpayer named above hereby applies to adopt and use the LIFO inventory method provided by section 472. This method is to be applied for the first time as of the close of the taxable year ending ...., to the following specified goods *(see instruction C; use additional sheets if necessary):*

The taxpayer agrees to make any adjustments incident to the change to or from the LIFO method, or incident to its use, in the inventories of prior taxable years or otherwise, as the District Director of Internal Revenue upon the examination of the taxpayer's return deems necessary to clearly reflect income for the years involved. See also 3(a) and 3(b) below.

1. Nature of business

2. (a) Inventory method used up to this time

   (b) Will inventory be taken at actual cost regardless of market value? If "No," attach explanation. . . . . ☐ **Yes** ☐ **No**

3. (a) Was the closing inventory of the specified goods at the end of the immediately preceding taxable year valued at cost, as required by section 472(d)? If "No," attach explanation. . . . . ☐ **Yes** ☐ **No**

   (b) Were the adjustments resulting from the change to LIFO taken into income of the prior year by filing an amended return? . ☐ **Yes** ☐ **No**
   See Rev. Proc. 76–6, 1976–1, C.B. 545. If "No," attach explanation.

4. (a) List goods subject to inventory but which are not to be inventoried under the LIFO method

   (b) Were the goods of the specified type included in opening inventory considered as having been acquired at the same time and at a unit cost equal to the actual cost of the aggregate divided by the number of units on hand? If "No," attach explanation. . . . . ☐ **Yes** ☐ **No**

5. (a) Did you issue credit statements, or reports to shareholders, partners, other proprietors, or beneficiaries, covering the first taxable year to which this application refers? . . . . ☐ **Yes** ☐ **No**

   (b) If "Yes," state to whom, and on what dates

   (c) Show the inventory method used in determining income, profit, or loss in those statements

6. Method used to determine the cost of the goods in the closing inventory in excess of those in the opening inventory. *(See section 1.472–2, of the regulations.)*
   ☐ Most recent purchases ☐ Earliest acquisitions during the year ☐ Average cost of purchases during the year ☐ Other—Attach explanation

7. Method used in valuing LIFO inventories
   ☐ Unit method   ☐ Dollar-value method

8. (a) If pools are used, list and describe contents of each pool

   (b) Describe briefly the cost system used

   (c) Method used in computing LIFO value of dollar-value pools
   ☐ Double extension method   ☐ Other method *(If other, describe and justify—see last paragraph of instruction F.)*

9. Did you change your method of valuing inventories with the permission of the Commissioner for this taxable year? If "Yes," attach a copy of the National Office's "grant letter" to this Form 970. . . . . ☐ **Yes** ☐ **No**

10. Were you ever on LIFO before? If "Yes," please attach information and explanation indicating which taxable years and the reason LIFO was discontinued . . . . ☐ **Yes** ☐ **No**

Under penalties of perjury, I declare that I have examined this application, including any accompanying schedules and statements, and to the best of my knowledge and belief it is true, correct, and complete.

_____ Date   _____ Signature of taxpayer

_____ Date   _____ Signature of officer   _____ Title

use of finished products. Details of the manner in which costs are computed could presumably be supplied by attaching a copy of the cost accounting manual or manuals or a concise description of the procedures followed in establishing costs. In practice, however, it is customary to give only a limited description of the manner of costing.

The analysis should show each of the categories of inventories for which LIFO is elected and also each of those for which LIFO is not elected. The sum of all categories should agree with the total inventory shown in the tax return of the previous year. Where there was a writedown from cost to market at the close of the preceding year, the writedown must be added back as required by the Code and regulations.

The goods to which LIFO is being applied included in the opening inventory of the first LIFO year are to be stated at the average of their cost, and the total cost for those goods is to be used as the closing inventory in determining income for the preceding year. ". . . The actual cost of the aggregate," according to section 1.472–2(c) of Appendix C, "shall be determined pursuant to the inventory method employed by the taxpayer under the regulations applicable to the prior taxable year with the exception that restoration shall be made with respect to any writedown to market values resulting from the pricing of former inventories."

The Commissioner cannot deny the use of LIFO to any taxpayer. The manner in which it is used and the extent to which it is used (if elected for only part of the inventory by the taxpayer) are, however, subject to the Commissioner's approval. Thus the Commissioner may require LIFO to be used for other goods if in his opinion it is necessary to clearly reflect income. As an example, a taxpayer having two raw material commodities that can be used interchangeably in the process of manufacture could elect LIFO for but one. In such a situation it might be held that income can be clearly reflected only if neither or both of the commodities are on LIFO.

The general rule is that only goods which are the property of the taxpayer should be included in inventory. It is also a general rule that the LIFO method of pricing must be applied to all the goods, wherever located, which fall into the LIFO group and are the property of the taxpayer. Although this will usually be sound, situations may arise where it is undesirable or impractical and logic may justify separate pools by locations, or using LIFO for some locations and FIFO for others. For example, a retailer using LIFO for its principal operating units in New York acquired a department store in a city 500 miles away. Operations of this store were continued without interruption and for valid management reasons it was determined that LIFO should not be applied to the additional inventories. Similarly, where a manufacturer acquired a plant producing a somewhat comparable but distinct product line, and continued to operate the newly acquired business as an independent unit, continuing the use of LIFO for one plant and FIFO for the other was justified although both were in the same metropolitan area.

When, in the examination of the return for the first LIFO year, a conflict arises between the Commissioner's representatives and the taxpayer as to categories of inventories or method of application, it has been the practice of the Internal Revenue Service to permit taxpayers to return to FIFO or other prior method. This usually arises where the LIFO categories or details of application acceptable to the Service are not satisfactory to the taxpayer.

Determination of "Cost" for Opening Inventory

The regulations require, as a condition precedent to the adoption of LIFO, that the closing inventory for the preceding year be stated at cost and that any income effect of a restatement of the closing inventory be reflected in the taxable income of the preceding year. For years, many taxpayers have distinguished between so-called "market write-downs" of the type described in regulation 1.471–4 and so-called "cost adjustments for subnormal goods" of the type described in regulation 1.471–2(c). It was generally believed that 1.471–4 write-downs must be restored to income, whereas goods described in regulation 1.471–2(c) could be omitted from the LIFO election. With the proliferation of LIFO elections in the early 1970s, many taxpayers took a "wait-and-see" attitude with regard to the income of the preceding year, hoping the Internal Revenue Service would provide definitive rules differentiating between market write-downs and subnormal goods.

In early 1976, the Internal Revenue Service issued a series of procedures and announcements to force compliance with the requirement to file an amended return for the year prior to the adoption of LIFO. The effort culminated on July 2, 1976 with the issuance of Revenue Ruling 76–282 [1] and Revenue Procedure 76–28. [2]

Revenue Ruling 76–282 does not define or clarify the term "market write-downs." It simply provides that when the LIFO method is elected (or extended) for a class of goods, the election goes to the nature of the goods and not to their condition, salability, or other characteristics. The LIFO election must therefore include all the goods within the class, including those that are unsalable at normal prices or unusable in the normal way [subnormal goods that may have been covered by a cost adjustment under regulation 1.471–2(c)]. The ruling goes on to say that the restoration required as a condition for a LIFO election (Section 472(d)) en-

[1] 1976–2 C.B. 137.
[2] 1976–2 C.B. 645.

compasses these cost adjustments of subnormal goods, as well as the pure market write-downs of regulation 1.471–4.

Revenue Procedure 76–28 holds that so-called excess stock and percentage write-downs applied to a class or type of goods fall within the contemplated write-down restoration rules of Section 472(d) In essence, all write-downs, whether they are characterized as cost adjustments, market, or excess quantity write-downs for accounting purposes, are treated alike for purposes of perfecting a LIFO election. They must be restored.

As to write-downs under regulation 1.471–2(c), the effective date of the new rules was for taxable years that began on or after September 24, 1976. Taxpayers who had elected (or extended) LIFO for years prior to the effective date were not required to file amended returns to reflect the restoration to income of the write-downs if the written-down goods were disposed of prior to the effective date and *if such goods were appropriate write-downs under regulation 1.471–2(c)*. If, on the other hand, a taxpayer had such goods on hand on or after the effective date, it was necessary to value such goods at actual cost at the end of the preceding taxable year to the extent that restoration had not been made previously.

For example, assume a calendar year taxpayer who elected LIFO in 1974 and either excluded subnormal or excess inventories from the LIFO election or included them at the written-down value. If the written-down items at December 31, 1973 (and such items written-down in subsequent LIFO years) had been disposed of by December 31, 1976, no further action was required. If some of the goods were still on hand at December 31, 1976, write-downs attributable to such goods must be restored to 1976 income to restate the goods to actual cost if the taxpayer wished to perfect its original LIFO election.

As to write-downs under regulation 1.471–4, amended returns must have been filed not later than August 12, 1976 in accordance with the provisions of Revenue Procedure 76–6, as revised, with respect to those goods whose carrying value was determined under Section 1.471–4 of the regulations, that is, pure market write-downs of normal goods.

The pronouncements of July 2, 1976 do not deal with the possible conformity question arising from write-downs of inventory to market or replacement cost and inventory reserves for excess stock or subnormal goods for financial statement purposes. The Internal Revenue Service has said [3] that differences in inventory valuation arising from such write-downs will not jeopardize a taxpayer's LIFO election—if the write-downs are required for financial statements under generally accepted accounting principles.

---

[3] Revenue Ruling 77–50.

The existence of reserves for market declines, excess stock, and other obsolescence factors on financial statements should not be considered a violation of the conformity requirements of Sections 472(c) and (e). These reserves should come within the market value exception to conformity provided in regulations 1.472–2(e).

ALTERNATIVE METHODS FOR COSTING INVENTORY INCREMENTS

Form 970 requires that the taxpayer select a method for determining the cost of increases in inventories, and a method should be selected even where there are no increases in the first year for any of the goods subject to LIFO. Any proper method which in the opinion of the Commissioner clearly reflects income is acceptable; but whatever method is adopted, it must be consistently followed in all subsequent years. A change in the method can be made only with the approval of the Commissioner.

The rules in the regulations for costing increases in inventory quantities are more specific for taxpayers engaged in the purchase and sale of merchandise (such as a retail grocer or druggist) or in the initial production and sale of goods (such as a miner selling his ore output without smelting or refining) than for those engaged in manufacturing or processing. In the case of the former group it is provided that costs of additions to inventories shall be determined as follows:

1. By reference to the actual cost of the goods most recently purchased or produced

2. By reference to the actual cost of the goods purchased or produced during the taxable year in the order of acquisition

3. By application of an average unit cost equal to the aggregate cost of all of the goods purchased or produced throughout the taxable year divided by the total number of units so purchased or produced, the goods reflected in such inventory increase being considered as having been acquired all at the same time

4. By any other proper method which, in the opinion of the Commissioner, clearly reflects income.[4]

In the case of taxpayers engaged in manufacturing, fabricating, processing, or otherwise producing merchandise, it is provided that costs shall be determined for raw materials by one of the methods described above. For finished goods and for goods in process, regardless of the stage to which

4 Section 1.472–2(d) (1) (i), Appendix C.

manufacturing, fabricating, or processing may have advanced, costs may be determined "pursuant to any proper method which, in the opinion of the Commissioner clearly reflects income."

The opening inventory for the year of adoption is the basic LIFO "layer." At the close of the year the quantity of goods on hand is compared with the quantity at the beginning. If there is no increase, the average cost of the basic layer is applied to the quantity at the end of the year to obtain the inventory cost. If there is an increase in quantity, such increase is treated as having been acquired during the taxable year and must be reflected at costs for the year as determined under the various methods available.

Many companies that elect to price quantity increments by reference to the actual cost of goods most recently acquired, or by reference to the actual cost of goods acquired during the taxable year in the order of acquisition, determine an average cost of acquisition for each month during which acquisitions are made, the aggregate of which equals or exceeds the increase in inventory, and then treat the quantity acquired and average cost as a single "layer" for inventory purposes.

Assume purchases and average costs as follows:

	Quantities	Average cost	Amount
January............	5,000	$0.80	$ 4,000
February..........	7,500	.90	6,750
March.............	9,500	.90	8,550
April..............	4,000	.80	3,200
May...............	6,000	.90	5,400
June..............	9,000	1.00	9,000
July...............	4,500	1.00	4,500
August............	5,500	.90	4,950
September.........	6,000	1.00	6,000
October...........	6,500	1.10	7,150
November.........	7,000	1.00	7,000
December..........	7,500	1.20	9,000
	78,000	.9679	$75,500

Assume an increase of 21,000 units during the first LIFO year.

I. Acquisitions stated at cost of most recent purchases or production. Months necessary to include all of increase:

	Quantities	Average cost	Amount
December.........	7,500	$1.20	$ 9,000
November........	7,000	1.00	7,000
October..........	6,500	1.10	7,150
	21,000	1.10238	$23,150

The inventory cost for the increment would be $23,150.00, that is, 21,000 times $1.10238.

Another taxpayer electing to use most recent costs might contend that his closing inventory consisted of the basic layer plus three layers representing the additions for the taxable year, which three layers would be as follows:

	Quantities	Average cost	Amount
December..........	7,500	$1.20	$ 9,000
November.........	7,000	1.00	7,000
October..........	6,500	1.10	7,150
	21,000		$23,150

Theoretically, it would be proper to price additions by individual items instead of averaging costs for even a period of a month or more. In practice, however, one average cost is frequently used (i.e., $1.10238) in preference to even separately computed monthly averages although the example in the regulations supports the use of monthly averages.

II. Acquisitions stated at cost of earliest purchases or production. Months necessary to include all of increase:

	Quantities	Average cost	Amount
January...........	5,000	$0.80	$ 4,000
February..........	7,500	.90	6,750
March.............	9,500	.90	8,550
	22,000	.8773	$19,300

The inventory cost for the increment would be $18,423.30, that is, 21,000 times $0.8773, if one average cost is used.

III. Average unit cost of all acquisitions during the taxable year.

Increase in inventory	Average cost	Amount
21,000	$0.9679	$20,325.90

Of the three methods, the second is frequently advantageous from a practical standpoint, not only because it results in a lower inventory cost in case of a rising market, but also because it permits a determination early in the year of the cost at which any increment will be carried. Under the first and third alternatives this determination cannot be made until the end of the year, and this may delay the closing of the accounts.

Decreases in quantities during a taxable year are taken from the most recent acquisitions. Using the figures in the preceding illustration, if the basic layer were 100,000 units at 80 cents (that is the opening inventory when LIFO was adopted) and the quantity increase for the year of adoption was 21,000 units, and assuming at the end of the second year an inventory of 110,000 units, the closing inventory under the various methods would be as follows:

I. Acquisitions stated at cost of most recent purchases or production. Basis of costing layers by months:

	Quantities	Cost	Amount
Basic layer..............	100,000	$0.80	$80,000
First-year additions:			
December.............	7,500	1.20	9,000
November............	2,500	1.00	2,500
	110,000		$91,500

Basis of costing which treats additions for year as one layer:

	Quantities	Cost	Amount
Basic layer..............	100,000	$0.80	$80,000
First-year increment.......	10,000	1.10238	11,024
	110,000		$91,024

II. Acquisitions stated at cost of earliest purchases or production. Basis of costing layers by months:

	Quantities	Cost	Amount
Basic layer..............	100,000	$0.80	$80,000
First-year additions:			
January..............	5,000	.80	4,000
February.............	5,000	.90	4,500
	110,000		$88,500

Basis of costing which treats additions for year as one layer:

	Quantities	Cost	Amount
Basic layer.............	100,000	$0.80	$80,000
First-year increment.......	10,000	.8773	8,773
	110,000		$88,773

III. Average unit cost of all acquisitions during the taxable year.

	Quantities	Cost	Amount
Basic layer.............	100,000	$0.80	$80,000
First-year increment.......	10,000	.9679	9,679
	110,000		$89,679

Care should be used in selecting a method of costing inventory incre-ments, and separate methods may be followed for each of the LIFO pools. In a business having consistently higher prices or costs in a particular month or months in the year than in others, the months in which costs are high should generally be avoided. A discussion of the use of the alter-native procedures for costing increments where the dollar-value principle of measuring inventory quantities is applied commences on page 273.

DISCONTINUING THE USE OF LIFO

Having made the election to adopt LIFO, a taxpayer must continue its use unless prior approval to change to another method is obtained from the Commissioner. The Commissioner, however, may determine that the taxpayer has used for any taxable year subsequent to the year of adoption a method other than LIFO in ascertaining income, profit, or loss for credit purposes or for the purpose of reports to shareholders, partners or other proprietors, or to beneficiaries, and he may require the taxpayer to change to a different method for such subsequent taxable year or any taxable year thereafter.

If LIFO becomes disadvantageous from a practical income tax stand-point, a change to another inventory method for accounting purposes (assuming it is justified as preferable under GAAP) will not necessarily cause the Commissioner to insist on a change for tax purposes. Under the terms of the Code the use of a method other than LIFO gives the Secretary of the Treasury (or his delegate) the *right* to require a change to a non-LIFO method beginning with the year in which the taxpayer used an inconsistent method *or* in any taxable year thereafter. Reading the statute literally, the Internal Revenue Service appears to have unlim-ited discretion in picking the year when the right to use LIFO must be forfeited because of the treatment of inventories in financial statements. If this discretion were exercised in an arbitrary manner, with unreasonable hardship resulting to the taxpayer, it is doubtful the courts would sustain the action. There has been no litigation on this point.

Although a change *to* the LIFO method does not require the prior approval of the Commissioner of Internal Revenue, a change *from* LIFO to another method can be made only with prior approval. An application to change from LIFO must be filed within 180 days after the beginning of the taxable year in which the change is to be made on Treasury Department Form 3115. A discussion of changes in accounting methods begins on page 131. Permission to change will not be granted unless the taxpayer and the Commissioner agree to the terms and conditions under which the change will be effected.

Where companies have obtained permission to discontinue the use of LIFO, generally, the only terms imposed by the Commissioner have been (1) that the LIFO cost of the closing inventory for the preceding year will be used as the opening inventory for the year of change and (2) that the company will again apply for permission to make a change in its method of accounting for inventories should a further change be desired, and it cannot reelect LIFO in a subsequent year by merely filing Treasury Department Form 970 with its tax return.

Accepting, as a condition to the discontinuance of the use of LIFO, that the LIFO cost of the closing inventory for the preceding year will be used as the opening inventory for the year of change has the effect of including in the taxable income for the year in which the change is made the entire difference between the LIFO cost and the amount at which the opening inventory would have been stated under the newly adopted method. Where the recognition of a substantial amount of income had been deferred as a consequence of using LIFO, many companies which might otherwise change to another method for valid business reasons may be reluctant to make the change because of the immediacy of the abnormal income tax payment. (For financial reporting purposes APB 20 specifically requires that a change from the LIFO method to another method be effected by restating the financial statements of all prior periods presented.)

To alleviate this situation, Revenue Procedure 72–24 (1972–1 C.B. 749) provides that, for years beginning after December 31, 1968, taxpayers who have used LIFO for 2 or more years will be permitted to spread the effect of the change over twice the number of years LIFO had been used, to a maximum of 10 years. In extraordinary situations, Revenue Procedure 71–16 (1971–1 C.B. 682) allows taxpayers to request that a positive adjustment resulting from the discontinuance of LIFO be spread ratably over a period of as much as 20 years. The "twice the years" spread is automatically granted along with permission to discontinue LIFO. The granting of a longer period is at the discretion of the Commissioner of Internal Revenue. Revenue Procedure 71–16 states that the dollar amount of the adjustment is one of the elements that will be considered in granting a longer adjustment period. The request for permission to defer recognition of the income over the longer period should be made at the same time as the Form 3115 is filed, by a statement attached to the form.

SELECTING LIFO GROUPS OR POOLS

Any taxpayer owning inventories may use LIFO for federal income tax purposes, and the regulations recognize that the LIFO method is not dependent upon the character of the business in which the taxpayer is engaged, or upon the identity or want of identity through commingling of any of the goods on hand. The most important decision to be made in any specific case, however, is how the inventory is to be analyzed into LIFO "groups" or "pools" for the purpose of comparing the relative quantity of goods on hand at the end of each year.

The principal general provisions of the regulations referring to LIFO "pools"—which is the more frequently used of the two terms—may be summarized as follows:

Appendix C
§ 1.472–

Where a taxpayer is engaged in more than one trade or business, the Commissioner may require that if LIFO is used for goods in one business it shall also be applied to similar goods in the other, where uniform treatment is essential to a clear reflection of income.   2(i)

LIFO may be applied to types of materials, depending upon the character, quality, or price, and each type of material in the opening inventory must be compared with a similar type in the closing inventory.   1(d)

In the *cotton textile industry* there may be different raw materials depending upon marked differences in length of staple or in color or grade of the cotton. But where different staple lengths or grades are being used from time to time in the same mill to produce the same class of goods, the differences would not necessarily require classifications of raw materials.   1(e)

In the *pork packing industry* a live hog is considered as being composed of various raw materials, different cuts of a hog varying markedly in price and use. Generally a hog is processed into approximately 10 primal cuts and several miscellaneous articles; however, due to similarity in price and use, these may be grouped into fewer classifications, each group being classified as one raw material.[5]   1(f)

[5] Pork cuts are commonly classified in four LIFO pools: (1) hams, loins, bellies, butts, and picnics; (2) spareribs, regular trimmings, and squares; (3) fat backs, plates, lard, and jowls; and (4) tails, hearts, livers, snouts, skins, bones, and hocks.

Appendix C
§ 1.472–

A *manufacturer or processor* may elect to apply LIFO to one or more types of materials and include the material in goods in process and in finished goods—commonly referred to as a material-content pool.   1(c)

    A material-content pool may be limited to that phase in the manfacturing process where a product recognized generally as salable is produced. For example, in the textile industry one phase of the process is the production of yarn. In the case of copper and brass processors, the material-content pool may be limited to the material identified with the production of bars, plates, sheets, etc., although these may be further processed into other products.   1(i)

    When the finished product contains two or more different materials, as in the case of cotton and rayon mixtures, each material is treated separately.   1(g)

For a *manufacturer or processor* who has elected to use the dollar-value method—

    A pool shall consist of all items entering into the entire inventory for a "natural business unit" unless the taxpayer elects to use "multiple pools."   8(b)(1)

    Multiple pools may be established for inventory items which are not within a natural business unit pool. Each pool shall ordinarily consist of a group of items which are substantially similar.   8(b)(3)(i)(a)

    Where similar goods are inventoried in both natural business unit and multiple pools, the Commissioner may apportion or allocate the goods among the pools, if necessary to clearly reflect income.   8(b)(3)(i)(a)

    Materials of an unlike nature may be pooled even though they become part of otherwise identical finished products.   8(b)(3)(i)(b)

    The same class or type of finished goods and goods in process shall ordinarily be included in the same pool. Where the material used has changed (e.g., to conform with industry trends) a new pool will not ordinarily be required unless the result is a substantial change in the finished product.   8(b)(3)(i)(c)

    A miscellaneous pool may be used, but it shall consist only of items which are relatively insignificant by comparison with other inventory items and are not properly includable in another pool.   8(b)(3)(i)(d)

    Material-content pools may be used, but materials of an unlike nature may not be pooled even though they become part of otherwise identical finished products.   8(b)(3)(ii)

For a *wholesaler, retailer, jobber or distributor* who has
elected to use the dollar-value method inventory items
shall be pooled by major lines, types, or classes of goods,
and for this purpose customary classification of the particular business is *an* important consideration. In appropriate cases, however, the natural business unit pooling
principles may be used.   8(c)

The section specifically describing the dollar-value method of applying
LIFO, discussed in Chapter 12 was not added to the regulations until
January 20, 1961. In recognition of the fact that many unsatisfactory pooling practices had developed over the years because of this deficiency,
paragraph 1.472–8(h) of Appendix C provides that for the first taxable
year ending after April 15, 1961, a taxpayer using the dollar-value method
might change from one authorized pooling practice to another without
following the general rules for effecting a change. Also for this year, a
natural business unit pool could be established if a taxpayer had been
using the dollar-value principle with an authorized pooling method, or a
method of pooling which would be authorized if additional items were included, and could otherwise change to the use of a natural business unit
pool. Except for these special situations, the pools established for the first
LIFO year must be used for subsequent years unless a change is required
by the Commissioner to clearly reflect income or unless permission to
change is secured in advance.

Taxpayers using LIFO pools for which inventory quantities are measured
in terms of pounds, gallons, yards, and so forth, may not commence the
use of the dollar-value principle unless (a) steps are taken as prescribed
for obtaining the consent of the Commissioner to a change in accounting
method, (b) the same pools are continued, or (c) a new election is being
filed to use LIFO for a portion of the inventory not covered by a prior
election, and no change is contemplated for the existing LIFO inventories,
by inclusion in a natural business unit pool or otherwise.

A revenue ruling (Rev. Rul. 62–77, I.R.B. 1962–21, 9) has been issued
with respect to (a) changes to dollar-value LIFO inventory procedures
and (b) the use of a "natural business unit" pool by a wholesaler, retailer,
jobber, or distributor. The complete text of this ruling is quoted below:

Advice has been requested as to the various circumstances under which taxpayers, particularly wholesalers, retailers, jobbers and distributors, are required
to obtain the permission of the Commissioner of Internal Revenue to change to
the dollar-value last-in, first-out (LIFO) inventory method, using a natural business unit pool or pools, of valuing inventories, particularly in view of the respective provisions of section 1.472–8(c), 1.472–8(f)(1), and 1.472–8(h)(1) of the
Income Tax Regulations.

Section 1.472–8(a) of the regulations provides, in part, that any taxpayer may elect to determine the cost of his LIFO inventories under the so-called "dollar-value" LIFO method, provided such method is used consistently and clearly reflects the income of the taxpayer in accordance with the rules of that section. The dollar-value method of valuing LIFO inventories is a method of determining cost by using "base-year" cost expressed in terms of total dollars rather than the quantity and price of specific goods as the unit of measurement. Under such method the goods contained in the inventory are grouped in a pool or pools as described in paragraphs (b) and (c) of section 1.472–8 of the regulations with reference to manufacturers or processors and in paragraph (c) of that section with reference to wholesalers, retailers, etc.

Under section 1.472–8(c) of the regulations, items of inventory in the hands of wholesalers, retailers, jobbers, and distributors, shall be placed into pools by major lines, types, or classes of goods. In determining such groupings, it is provided that customary business classifications of the particular trade in which the taxpayer is engaged is an important consideration. An example of such customary business classification is the department in the department store. In such cases, practices are relatively uniform throughout the trade, and departmental grouping is peculiarly adapted to the customs and needs of the business. However, in appropriate cases, the principles set forth in paragraphs (b) (1) and (2) of section 1.472–8 of the regulations, relating to pooling by natural business units, may be used by wholesalers, retailers, jobbers, or distributors with the permission of the Commissioner.

Section 1.472–8(f)(1) of the regulations provides that, except as provided in section 1.472–3 of the regulations, in the case of a taxpayer electing to use a LIFO inventory method for the first time, or in the case of a taxpayer changing to the dollar-value method and continuing to use the same pools as were used under another LIFO method, a taxpayer using another LIFO method of pricing inventories may not change to the dollar-value method of pricing such inventories unless he first secures the consent of the Commissioner in accordance with paragraph (e) of section 1.446–1 of the regulations.

Section 1.472–8(g)(1) of the regulations provides that any method of pooling authorized by section 1.472–8 and used by the taxpayer in computing his LIFO inventories under the dollar-value method shall be treated as a method of accounting. Any method of pooling which is authorized by that section shall be used for the year of adoption and for all subsequent taxable years unless a change is required by the Commissioner in order to clearly reflect income, or unless permission to change is granted by the Commissioner as provided in paragraph (e) of section 1.446–1 of the regulations. Where the taxpayer changes from one method of pooling to another method of pooling permitted by that section, the ending LIFO inventory for the taxable year preceding the year of change shall be restated under the new method of pooling.

Under section 1.472–8(h)(1) of the regulations, it is provided, in part, that notwithstanding the provisions of paragraph (g) of section 1.472–8, a taxpayer, for his first taxable year ending after April 15, 1961, may change from one method of pooling authorized by section 1.472–8 to any other method of pooling authorized by that section, provided the requirements of subparagraph (2) of paragraph (h) are met. Also, it is provided that, for such year if a taxpayer is currently using only a method of pooling which would be authorized by that section if additional items were included in the pool, and could change to the natural business unit method except for the fact that he has not inventoried all items entering into the inventory investment for such natural business unit on the LIFO method, he may change to the natural business unit method if he elects, under the provisions of section 1.472–3, to extend the LIFO election to all items entering into the entire inventory investment for such natural business unit, provided the requirements of subparagraph (2) of that paragraph are met.

Since the natural business unit method of pooling is not an authorized method for wholesalers, retailers, jobbers and distributors without the Commissioner's prior permission under section 1.472–8(c) of the regulations, and since section 1.472–8(h) is applicable only to taxpayers changing from one authorized method of pooling to another authorized method of pooling under section 1.472–8, it is held that wholesalers, retailers, jobbers and distributors may not change from any other method of pooling to the natural business unit method without the Commissioner's prior permission.

A change from the unit or specific goods LIFO method using separate LIFO pools, to the dollar-value LIFO method, using the same LIFO pools as used under the unit or specific goods LIFO method, may be made by such a taxpayer without the Commissioner's permission under the exception provided in section 1.472–8 (f)(1) of the regulations.

With respect to all taxpayers using the unit or specific goods LIFO method, nothing in sections 1.472–8(f)(1) and 1.472–8(h)(1) of the regulations permits the change from such unit or specific goods LIFO method to the dollar-value LIFO method, using a natural business pool or pools, without the Commissioner's permission for the first taxable year ending after April 15, 1961.

However, wholesalers, retailers, jobbers and distributors electing to use the dollar-value LIFO method for the first time, utilizing a method of pooling by major lines, types or classes of goods, shall do so by filing an application, Form 970, Application for the Adoption and Use of the Elective Inventory Method, and by otherwise complying with the provisions of sections 1.472–3 of the regulations. In such case the appropriateness of the method of pooling used, as well as the propriety of all computations incidental to the use of such pools, will be determined by the Commissioner through the appropriate District Director in connection with the examinations of the returns of such taxpayers. See sections 1.472–3(d) and 1.472–8(d) of the regulations.

Where wholesalers, retailers, jobbers and distributors wish to use the natural business unit method of pooling in connection with a change to the dollar-value LIFO method from a method of valuation other than the LIFO method, the prior permission of the Commissioner to do so is required for any taxable year. See section 1.472–8(c) of the regulations. Such permission must be secured in accordance with section 1.446–1(e) of the regulations.

In each case where a wholesaler, retailer, jobber or distributor applies to the Commissioner for permission to change to the dollar-value LIFO method, using a natural business unit pool or pools, for valuing his inventories, he must clearly demonstrate that such natural business unit method of pooling is appropriate and clearly reflects income.

Particular attention is directed to the penultimate above-quoted paragraph holding the wholesalers, retailers, jobbers, and distributors wishing to use a "natural business unit" pool cannot do so merely by stating their position

X Clothing Company
Summary of Inventories at December 31, 19—

	Yards			Amount
	Piece goods*	Stock goods	Total	
Cotton goods on LIFO:				
Group I—Heavy weight	1,700,000 yds.	875,000 yds.	2,575,000 yds.	$ 417,500
II—Medium weight	1,800,000	950,000	2,750,000	305,000
III—Light weight	3,400,000	800,000	4,200,000	392,000
IV—Corduroys	5,250	5,000	10,250	4,940
	6,905,250 yds.	2,630,000 yds.	9,535,250 yds.	$1,119,440
Other yard goods on lower of FIFO cost or market:				
Wools and part wools	150,000 yds.			$ 180,000
Part rayon	100,000			65,000
Rayon	1,000,000			600,000
	1,250,000 yds.			$ 845,000†
Finished goods:				
Containing cotton piece goods:				
Total cost			$1,500,000	
Less: Cost of material content		2,630,000 yds.	800,000	
				700,000
Containing wool and rayon				750,000†
Other inventory factors:				
Trim				1,000,000†
Packing				100,000†
Labor and overhead on piece goods in process				155,000
Total inventory				$4,669,440

* Yardage shown as "Piece goods" includes material in process at end of year.
† Stated on lower-of-cost-or-market basis.

Inventories on LIFO

	Group I—Heavy weight			Group II—Medium weight			Group III—Light weight			Group IV—Corduroys		
	Yards	Unit cost	Amount	Yards	Unit cost	Amount	Yards	Unit cost	Amount	Yards	Unit cost	Amount
Closing inventory layers:												
Base	2,500,000	$0.16	$400,000	1,500,000	$0.10	$150,000	3,950,000	$0.09	$355,500	9,500	$0.47	$4,465
1941	50,000	.20	10,000	1,000,000	.105	105,000	100,000	.11	11,000	250	.50	125
1942	—			—			—			—		
1943	—			—			—			—		
1944	25,000	.30	7,500	250,000	.20	50,000	150,000	.17	25,500	500	.70	350
	2,575,000		$417,500	2,750,000		$305,000	4,200,000		$392,000	10,250		$4,940

in an original LIFO election, and must follow the procedure of applying in advance for permission to change an accounting method. This position of the Internal Revenue Service is based upon the statement in section 1.472–8(c) of Appendix C that, in appropriate cases, the principles relating to pooling by natural business units may be used, "with permission of the Commissioner," by wholesalers, retailers, jobbers, or distributors. Prior to the issuance of this ruling it was assumed that the required permission would be obtained if the use of a "natural business unit" pool was found to be appropriate when the LIFO procedures were reviewed in connection with an examination of the federal income tax return for the first year the method is used. There is no apparent justification for requiring wholesalers, retailers, jobbers, and distributors to anticipate a decision to elect to use LIFO and file Treasury Department Form 3115 during the first 180 days of the year.

APPLICATION OF LIFO WITH POOLING BY SPECIFIC GOODS

Where the relative volume of an inventory is not determined by application of the dollar-value principle, the procedure is commonly designated as pooling by specific goods.

In using specific goods pools, the possible combinations of items includable in a category of inventory are limited. In general only items of a homogeneous nature can be combined. It is not necessary, however, that the units of quantity represent the physical weight, measurement, or count. For many types of goods there can be combinations of items within a category by adjusting for differences of grade, so as to bring all items to common standard. This is particularly applicable where the goods are bought or sold at prices based on physical measurement but adjusted for variations in quality or chemical content.

One illustration of this principle of specific goods pooling is afforded by a manufacturer of gelatin. Gelatin is made principally from by-products of slaughterhouses and leather tanners, for example, skins, hides, and bones. By processing these materials, the manufacturer produces a salable gelatin product used in the making of photographic film, food products, pharmaceuticals, and other items. Measuring quantities in terms of pounds on hand in the various categories of raw materials, work in process, and finished stock would not produce satisfactory results. A pound of one type of raw material may yield considerably more or less gelatin than a pound of another type and have a different cost. It is practical, however, to measure the jelling consistency of the raw materials, referred to in the trade as *bloompoints*. All raw materials can thus be reduced to bloompoints, and the bloompoints contained in the in-process and finished goods can be added to those in raw materials for a material-content pool.

On page 258 is a summary analysis of the LIFO inventory of X Clothing Company, a manufacturer of shirts, work clothes, dresses, and sports attire. The company used material-content pools and classified the various types of cotton goods required in its business as heavy weight, medium weight, light weight, and corduroys. In addition to illustrating how specific goods pools may take into account similarly of character, quality, or price of each type of material, this is an example of LIFO being applied to only a portion of the total inventory. It is to be noted that the manufacturing costs for the finished goods containing cotton piece goods is stated at cost rather than the lower of cost or market. No market writedowns can be recognized as to the material content of the product, and it cannot be determined whether a writedown of finished products would be attributable to the material content or the manufacturing costs.

The principal disadvantage to pooling by specific goods is the inability to continue to avoid recognition of inflationary profits when a particular commodity for which LIFO has been elected is being displaced by another commodity either temporarily or permanently. Such displacement may occur for competitive reasons because of changes in manufacturing processes or requirements of customers, or merely because of a shortage of the raw material previously used. In many cases it is not practical to treat the new commodity as part of the old LIFO pool; so the profit previously deferred is reflected in income as the quantities of the old commodity are reduced.

TWELVE

Measuring LIFO Inventories By Dollar-Value Principle

This chapter and Chapter 11 review in detail tax rules relating to LIFO adoption and subsequent usage. Certain of the recommendations, particularly with respect to partial adoption of LIFO, may not be appropriate to a company which presents its financial statements in conformity with generally accepted accounting principles. Reference should be made to Chapter 15 for additional discussion of financial accounting considerations.

* * *

The possible uses of the dollar-value principle in measuring LIFO inventories are practically unlimited, but may be illustrated by the following descriptions of procedures, approved by representatives of the Internal Revenue Service, developed by three machinery manufacturers prior to the 1961 additions to the regulations which favor a single inventory pool for a natural business unit of a manufacturer or processor.[1] As emphasized in the regulations,[2] where inventories are measured by the dollar-value principle, the primary determination is an aggregate for the goods on hand at any particular time in terms of cost levels prevailing as of a specified base date.

---

[1] Second 1.472–8(b), Appendix C (discussed on p. 267 et seq.)
[2] Section 1.472–8(a), Appendix C.

Company A, a large manufacturer of heavy equipment, was able to analyze its inventory records so as to classify the raw material on hand and the material content of the' in-process and finished goods into six pools. The materials had sufficiently common basic characteristics to justify the assumption that price fluctuations would be approximately the same for the items in the respective pools. Direct labor was considered the seventh LIFO pool, and the overhead applicable to the inventory constituted the eighth pool. In this instance the company maintained its regular accounting records on a standard cost basis, and continued to use the same standards as were in effect at the beginning of the first LIFO year. Where necessary, these standards were adjusted at that time to the then current costs for the items in the opening inventory. By use of these fixed standards and standards computed on a comparable base for new items added to the inventory, the regular accounting records provided an extension of the inventory on hand at the cost level prevailing at the basic LIFO date. A comparison of the aggregate amounts of the standard costs provided a direct measure of the relative inventory quantities at each year end. If there was an increase in any pool, the basic LIFO cost was converted to the current cost for the year of the increment by reference to the percentage of variances from standard for the current year as reflected by the variance amounts compiled under the general accounting procedures.

Company B decided to reflect current costs rather than fixed standards in the detailed accounting records and merely supplement inventory determinations at current prices to establish LIFO cost.

Physical inventories at Company B's manufacturing plants are taken annually one month prior to the end of the year, and the book inventory balances at that date are adjusted to the amounts of the physical inventories. The inventories of the manufacturing plants at the year end are book figures based upon the amount of the physical inventories adjusted for purchases, usage, and the like, during the last month. Inventories at the various sales branches are taken annually as at the year end, and the book inventory balances at that date are adjusted to the amounts of the physical inventories. The procedures followed in determining the LIFO cost for the inventories were set up to minimize special computations.

Raw materials inventories at each plant as of one month prior to the year end, based on physical inventories taken as at that date, were extended at either (a) the unit cost used for the same material in the 1950 inventory or (b) a substitute cost. In the determination of substitute costs two principal methods were used:

1. Unit costs as at the 1950 inventory date, as shown by stock records, price lists, or other information available in the purchasing department.

2. Another item of the same general type of material purchased from the same supplier was selected from the 1950 inventory and a substitute cost was computed, based on the assumption that different items of the same general type of material purchased from the same supplied would increase in cost in the same ratio.

Company B's Dollar-Value LIFO Pools

Pool	Description	Pool	Description
I	Steel bars, shapes, and plates	VI	Foundry materials
	Sheet steel	VII	Product line A
	Steel pipe, pipe fittings, and tubing		Material
	Forgings—purchased rough		Labor
II	Lumber		Burden
	Paint	VIII	Product line B
	Belting		Material
	Other direct materials		Labor
III	Tires, tubes, valve cores, and caps		Burden
IV	Bolts, nuts, screws, and other hardware	IX	Product line C
			Material
	Bearings and bushings		Labor
	Gears—purchased rough		Burden
V	Hydraulic units and parts	X	Domestic freight applicable to products
	Electrical equipment		
	Engines and parts		

In certain instances a general ratio between prices as at the 1950 and current inventory dates was computed for each inventory account and applied, by accounts, to the items which had not been included in the 1950 inventory.

A percentage was computed for each raw material pool by calculating the relationship between the total current costs as at the inventory date (book values after adjustments to reflect physical inventories) and the total dollar amount computed on the basis of 1950 or substitute costs. These percentages were applied to the total dollar amounts of the respective pools as shown by the book inventory accounts at year end to state the inventories on a 1950 cost basis.

Finished and unfinished products, represented by work in process, finished goods at plants and branches, and repair parts at plants and branches, were classified into three major product lines. The material, labor, and burden content of the inventories were established as follows:

a) *Work in process:* The regular analyses of inventories showed the material, labor, and burden content of the work in process inventories.

b) *Finished goods:* The physical inventories of finished goods at the plants were split as between material, labor, and burden on the basis of computed costs at the inventory dates. The percentage of each of the three to the total amount of finished goods was determined and the year-end book inventories were split into material, labor, and burden by use of these percentages.

c) *Repair parts:* The percentages of material, labor, and burden to total cost of repair parts produced during the year were determined, and these percentages were applied to the cost of such parts to establish the material, labor, and burden content of the repair parts inventories.

Inventories at the branches at the year end are based on physical inventories as at that date. The physical inventories of finished goods at the branches were split as between material, labor, and burden on the basis of computed costs. Repair parts at the branches were combined with the repair parts at the plants for the purposes of determining material, labor, and burden content.

A material index was computed for each plant on the basis of the relationship between the aggregate raw materials inventories at physical inventory date extended at current costs and at 1950 costs. For purposes of this computation all raw materials inventories at each plant were considered together. The indexes were used to reduce the material content of the inventories of finished and unfinished products at each plant from current costs to 1950 costs. The material-content amounts by plants were then combined to arrive at a total for each of the three major product lines.

The average labor rates per hour were determined for each plant on the basis of the number of employees in each labor grade multiplied by the timing rate for each grade. A labor index was then computed for each plant on the basis of the relationship between the average rates per hour. The indexes were used to reduce the labor content of the inventories of finished and unfinished products at each plant from current costs to 1950 costs. The labor content amounts by plants were then combined to arrive at a total for each of the three major product lines.

The average burden rate applicable to the labor content of finished and unfinished product inventories for 1950 was determined by summarizing the labor and burden for each of the major product lines. These percentages were applied to the total labor, expressed on the basis of 1950 costs, included in the current inventories.

Domestic freight applicable to current finished product inventories (including repair parts) at the sales branches was computed by multiplying the total weight of the products by the average freight rates from the re-

Computation of Labor Rate Index

Labor grade	Number of employees in labor grade at end of current year	Beginning of first LIFO year		End of current year	
		Timing rate per hour	Timing rate multiplied by number of employees	Timing rate per hour	Timing rate multiplied by number of employees
10	25	$1.25	$ 31.25	$1.30	$ 32.50
9	150	1.30	195.00	1.40	210.00
8	100	1.40	140.00	1.50	150.00
	275		$366.25		$392.50
Average rate per employee per hour			$ 1.33		$ 1.43
Percentage of current average rate to 1950 average rate					107.5%

spective plants to the branches. Base-year cost was computed by multiplying the weight by the respective 1950 freight rates.

In applying the dollar-value principle, Company C, another machinery manufacturer, classified all raw materials in one pool and classified the in-process and finished goods into pools according to broad categories of end products. Since the various types of end products were manufactured in different plants, the end product classification was in general by plants. Its physical inventories were taken two months in advance at the end of the year. By pricing a substantial portion of a physical inventory at current costs and also at base-year costs, a percentage of change was secured. It was assumed that the composition of the year-end inventory was proportionately the same as at the date of the physical inventory, and that the percentage of cost change to the current year was fairly reflected by the percentage of change to the date of the physical inventory. For these computations a dual extension was made of approximately 60 per cent of the total inventory and after making this representative sampling an additional 5 per cent was extended to confirm the validity of the original computation. The fact that the perecntage of cost change was not modified materially by adding the additional 5 per cent was considered an indication of the fairness of the original sampling.

Although machinery manufacturers constitute a large proportion of the users of the dollar-value principle, there are many other instances in which the method has proved helpful. Enumeration of a few will indicate the possibilities in almost any type of inventory:

Breweries: The dollar-value method has been applied in inventorying returnable bottles where for federal income tax purposes they are considered as having been sold to and repurchased from customers.

Fertilizer manufacturers: The dollar-value method has been applied in inventorying material costs and processing expenses.

Newspapers: The dollar-value method has been applied in inventorying newsprint.

Paper manufacturers: The dollar-value method has been applied in inventorying pulpwood and the pulpwood content of in-process and finished goods.

Steel manufacturers: The dollar-value method has been applied in inventorying ores, coal, and other materials as well as products.

Textile manufacturers: The dollar-value method has been applied to the material content in all stages of production and in some cases to all elements of cost.

Wholesalers of hardware and industrial and farm supplies: The dollar-value method has been applied to inventories held for resale.

Wire rope manufacturers: The dollar-value method has been applied to finished goods and in-process inventories.

A ruling by the Internal Revenue Service [3] holds that a securities "specialist" may elect to use LIFO for his inventory of unsold securities in which he is a specialist. The term "specialist" refers to a stock exchange member who accepts orders in selected securities from other members for execution.

The fact that this revenue ruling is limited to a "specialist" does not preclude the use of LIFO by other dealers who inventory unsold securities. Possibly the dealer to whom the ruling was addressed carried an inventory of only one issue of stock so that the LIFO principle could be effectively applied on the basis of the number of shares owned at the end of each taxable year, but the dollar-value principle might be used to apply LIFO to a diversified portfolio.

The income tax regulations contain a special section pertaining to inventories by dealers in securities, and its scope is indicated by the following excerpt:

. . . For the purpose of this section, a dealer in securities is a merchant of securities, whether an individual, partnership, or corporation, with an established place of business, regularly engaged in the purchase of securities and their resale to customers; that is, one who as a merchant buys securities and sells them to customers with a view to the gains and profits that may be derived therefrom. If

---

[3] Rev. Rul. 60–321, 1960–2 C.B. 166.

such business is simply a branch of the activities carried on by such person, the securities inventoried as provided in this section may include only those held for purposes of resale and not for investment. Taxpayers who buy and sell or hold securities for investment or speculation, irrespective of whether such buying or selling constitutes the carrying on of a trade or business, and officers of corporations and members of partnerships who in their individual capacities buy and sell securities, are not dealers in securities within the meaning of this section. [Section 1.471–5, Appendix C.]

In the case of a large diversified business organization, a dealer in securities using the dollar-value principle of applying LIFO would presumably have pools by major lines, types, or classes of securities. For example, the operations of the business might be so departmentalized that three separate dollar-value pools would be appropriate for corporate stocks and stock rights, corporate bonds, and state and municipal bonds.

It is highly unlikely, however, that LIFO would be an acceptable method of valuing securities in financial statements prepared in conformity with GAAP.

LIFO POOL FOR NATURAL BUSINESS UNIT

With regard to establishing dollar-value pools for inventories of manufacturers and processors, the following statements are made in the income tax regulations:

A pool shall consist of all items entering into the entire inventory investment for a natural business unit of a business enterprise, unless the taxpayer elects to use the multiple pooling method . . . Thus, if a business enterprise is composed of only one natural business unit, one pool shall be used for all of its inventories, including raw materials, goods in process, and finished goods . . . [Section 1.472–8(b)(1), Appendix C.]

The regulations wisely avoid an exact definition of "natural business unit." Certain observations are made and several examples are given, but it is stated that whether an enterprise is composed of more than one natural business unit is a matter of fact to be determined from all the circumstances. As important considerations entering into the determination are mentioned, the "natural business divisions adopted by the taxpayer for internal management purposes, the existence of separate and distinct production facilities and processes, and the maintenance of separate profit and loss records"—unless such divisions, facilities, or accounting records are set up merely because of differences in geographical location.

Comments by interested parties on the regulations as published in proposed form, directed attention to the position of a producer of a basic material marketed in part at that stage and also transferred to manufacturing plants which individually constituted a natural business unit. A question was raised as to whether all the material owned by the corporation could be included in a LIFO pool separate from those established for the business units. The answer of the Internal Revenue Service is indicated by the addition of a specific sentence in the final regulations to the effect that where similar types of goods are inventoried in two or more natural business units, the Commissioner may apportion or allocate the goods among the various units, *if he determines* that such apportionment or allocation is necessary in order to clearly reflect income. The Service appears to favor establishing inventories along the lines of natural business units but is reserving the right to reallocate inventories between business units if it is determined that some artificial allocations have been made for the purpose of minimizing reported income.

Another sentence added in the final regulations specifically provides that where a manufacturer or producer is also engaged in the wholesaling or retailing of goods purchased from others, any pooling of such purchased goods shall be determined in accordance with the stated principles relative to pools for wholesalers and retailers. This provision may have been added to cover such goods as miscellaneous accessories handled by an oil company in connection with service station operations. The inventory considered as a single pool on the basis of a natural business unit might exclude the purchased accessories. There could be a separate LIFO pool for the miscellaneous items acquired for resale or, alternatively, the miscellaneous items could be inventoried on a lower-of-cost-or-market basis. The language in the regulations should not be extended to apply to parts which may be purchased by a manufacturer for inclusion in a finished product and carried in inventory for the purpose of effecting incidental sales for replacement purposes. Replacement parts under these circumstances would be part of the total LIFO pool for the business unit.

The fact that a natural business unit pool is to include all items entering into the entire inventory investment requires careful consideration of the scope of the term "inventory" for federal income tax purposes.

. . . The inventory should include all finished or partly finished goods and, in the case of raw materials and supplies, only those which have been acquired for sale or which will physically become a part of merchandise intended for sale, in which class fall containers, such as kegs, bottles, and cases, whether returnable or not, if title thereto will pass to the purchaser of the product to be sold therein. [Section 1.471–1, Appendix C.]

On the basis of this concept it has been contended by some Treasury Department representatives that materials and supplies consumed in manufacturing operations, but which do not physically go into the articles to be sold, are not to be inventoried. If taken literally, a question could be raised as to why expenditures made for the acquisition of such items should not be written off as they are incurred; however, the common practice is to consider the cost of supplies on hand either as a deferred charge comparable to prepaid insurance or as inventory. Since it has been the custom for business generally to inventory many types of operating supplies and apply the lower-of-cost-or-market rule to them, there should be no serious question concerning the application of LIFO to those items.

The statement by the Committee on Accounting Procedure of the American Institute of Certified Public Accountants (paragraph 3 of Appendix A) specifies that the term "inventory" embraces supplies to be *consumed* directly or indirectly in production of goods or services to be available for sale.[4]

There are several industries having goods which are sometimes thought of as supplies but which can be properly treated only under the provisions for inventories. One illustration is the cement industry. Coal is used in substantial quantities by that industry for firing the kiln during the burning operation. Although a large part of the coal may be discharged through the smokestack in the form of gas, all the solid residue (the ash) becomes part of the cement. Another illustration is the steel industry, which consumes refractories in its operations. A third is the electric power industry, where huge quantities of coal are consumed for the purpose of generating steam to turn the turbines. The burning of the coal is a step in providing the energy which produces the revenue, but it could be argued that the coal does not become part of the electric energy which is sold.

Some doubt has also been expressed as to whether or not LIFO can be applied to spare parts and supplies used for repair or construction purposes. To the extent that spare parts or supplies are capitalized, the use of LIFO would not have a material effect on the income account, as the current cost would rest in a fixed asset account and the LIFO cost would be retained in the supply account. Through depreciation, income would gradually be charged with the current cost for the year of replacement. The method of accounting for parts used for maintenance purposes does, however, directly affect income, and the parts represent an essential segment of the necessary investment for the business and, from an accounting standpoint, should be included in the natural business unit pool.

Inclusion of containers, crating materials, cartons, spools, and so forth in a natural business unit pool may require the compilation of additional

---

[4] Prior to 1933 the income tax regulations provided for including in inventories "raw material and supplies on hand that have been acquired for sale, consumption, or use in productive processes, together with all finished or partly finished goods." The earlier regulations were construed to permit the statement of inventories of supplies at the lower of cost or market in the case of *Aluminum Company of America v. United States* (24 F. Supp. 811 (1938)) involving the determination of tax for the calendar year 1920.

accounting detail. The adequacy of the procedures used for these items must be judged, however, from the standpoint of the relative significance of their possible effect upon the LIFO cost for the total inventory pool.

A somewhat unique question arises in applying the natural business unit concept to articles which are to be given away or sold at a nominal price to further the sale of the major product. Examples might include safety razors sold with a set of blades for but slightly more than the price of the blades themselves, novelties and toys sold at bargain prices at gasoline stations or with coupons packed in boxes of breakfast foods or detergents, magazines containing sewing patterns, and so forth. These items are being held for *sale* and are part of the inventory within the meaning of the federal income tax regulations.[5] Although they do have advertising value, it is doubtful that they should be considered in the same category as advertising brochures. Advertising supplies are generally accounted for as prepaid expenses or deferred charges, but any item being offered for sale would be part of the inventory investment.

PERMISSIVE USE OF MORE THAN ONE DOLLAR-VALUE POOL

The regulations specifically state that the formulation of detailed rules for selection of pools applicable to all taxpayers is not feasible, and cover in general terms the situation in which a taxpayer elects to establish multiple pools for items not within a business unit LIFO pool. A change in language was made in the final regulations because the regulations as originally proposed were susceptible of being interpreted in such manner as to preclude the establishment of a pool for a type of goods which would be common to more than one business unit.

With respect to multiple pools as an alternative to pooling based upon business units, the following significant statements are made:

. . . Each such pool shall ordinarily consist of a group of inventory items which are substantially similar. In determining whether such similarity exists, consideration shall be given to all the facts and circumstances. The formulation of detailed rules for selection of pools applicable to all taxpayers is not feasible. Important considerations to be taken into account include, for example, whether there is substantial similarity in the types of raw materials used or in the processing operations applied; whether the raw materials used are readily interchangeable; whether there is similarity in the use of the products; whether the

[5] If the business is expected to operate at a profit, it is doubtful that the inventory of these items should be written down below cost; however, in the case of magazines and pamphlets containing certain sales stimuli, the cost properly allocable to the quantities on hand should be determined on a marginal basis rather than a per-unit basis after the principal portion of a particular issue has been disposed of.

groupings are consistently followed for purposes of internal accounting and management; and whether the groupings follow customary business practice in the taxpayer's industry. The selection of pools in each case must also take into consideration such factors as the nature of the inventory items subject to the dollar-value LIFO method and the significance of such items to the taxpayer's business operations. [Section 1.472–8 (b) (3) (i) (a), Appendix C.]

In the regulations as issued in final form a sentence was added to the effect that where similar goods are inventoried in "natural business unit" pools and in "multiple" pools, the Commissioner may apportion or allocate such goods *if he determines* such apportionment or allocation is necessary in order to clearly reflect income. Although there is adequate basis for the Commissioner's reservation of the authority to reallocate inventories among LIFO pools,[6] such authority will presumably be used only in extreme cases, for example, where the taxpayer's computations are artificial and do not reflect an allocation of goods consistent with sound business management or are inconsistent with appropriations actually made by operating personnel.

Where the taxpayer elects not to use a single LIFO pool for a business unit, raw or unprocessed materials which are substantially similar may be pooled together, but materials of an unlike nature may not be placed in one pool merely because they become part of otherwise identical finished products.

Finished goods and goods in process in the inventory should be pooled by major classes or types of goods, and ordinarily the finished goods and goods in process will be included in the same pool. Where the material content of a class of products has been changed, for example, to conform with current trends in an industry, a separate pool will not ordinarily be required unless the change in material content results in a substantial change in the finished product.

The practical necessity of having a miscellaneous pool is recognized in the regulations, but such a miscellaneous pool should consist only of items which are relatively insignificant in dollar value by comparison with other inventory items, and which are not properly includable as part of another pool.

The dollar-value principle may be used in conjunction with the material-content method to which specific reference has been made in the regulations since 1944. The general intent of the section added to the regulations

---

[6] Section 1.472(a) of Appendix C provides that the use of LIFO "shall be in accordance with such regulations as the Secretary or his delegate may prescribe as necessary in order that the use of such method may clearly reflect income." Further, the LIFO election (Form 970) contains an agreement by the taxpayer to adjustments incident to the use of such method "as the District Director of Internal Revenue upon the examination of the taxpayer's returns . . . may deem necessary in order to clearly reflect income."

in January, 1961, appears to be to permit continuation of LIFO dollar-value pooling methods where the company does not elect to use a single pool for the inventory investment of a natural business unit.

MEASURING COST-LEVEL CHANGES

Except for taxpayers entitled to use retail price indexes prepared by the Bureau of Labor Statistics the regulations state that only the so-called double-extension method may ordinarily be used in measuring cost-level changes for the purpose of applying the dollar-value principle to a LIFO inventory pool.

Where the total base-year cost of a LIFO inventory pool at the end of a year does not exceed the corresponding total for the pool at the beginning of the year, there is no need for the total current-year cost. The LIFO cost for the ending inventory is merely a carryforward of all or some portion of the LIFO cost for the beginning inventory. If the total base-year cost of the ending inventory is greater than the corresponding total for the beginning inventory an additional cost figure must be computed. The general rule is that the LIFO cost for an inventory increment is determined by multiplying the amount of the increment measured in terms of base-year cost by the ratio of the total current-year cost of the pool to the total base-year cost of the pool.

In each case, therefore, it is necessary to determine the feasibility of extending inventories at *base-year costs* and *current-year costs* if needed because of increments.

Although considerable emphasis is placed upon the double-extension method, it is clear there is a need for an index or for more than one extension of even a portion of an inventory only if (a) there is an increment in the inventory pool during the year or (b) the complete extension of the inventory is at current-year costs rather than at base-year costs. Consequently, there are advantages from adopting accounting procedures under which extensions at base-year costs are the initial determinations. In such cases Treasury Department representatives are interested in the indexes used only to the extent they enter into the computation of the LIFO cost for the portion of the inventory representing an increment for the year. Indexes used to estimate the current cost for internal management purposes would not be significant for tax purposes.

The *base-year cost* for an inventory item is generally its cost as determined at the beginning of the taxable year for which LIFO was first adopted. For an item entering a pool for the first time subsequent to the beginning of the base year, the base-year cost may be established in any number of ways:

1. The taxpayer using reasonable means may determine what the cost of the item would have been had it been in existence in the base year.

2. The taxpayer using available data or records may determine what the cost of an item in existence on the base date would have been had he stocked the item.

3. If the taxpayer does not reconstruct or establish a base-year cost, but does reconstruct or establish the cost for some subsequent year, the earliest cost which is reconstructed or established may be used as the base-year cost for the item. [Section 1.472–8(e)(2)(iii), Appendix C.]

The examples of acceptable procedures set forth in the regulations do not preclude the use of other procedures appropriate in particular cases. The exercise of judgment is clearly contemplated.

The *current-year cost* of the items making up a pool may be determined under the specific provisions of the regulations as follows:

1. By reference to the actual cost of the goods most recently purchased or produced;

2. By reference to the actual cost of the goods purchased or produced during the taxable year in the order of acquisition;

3. By application of an average unit cost equal to the aggregate cost of all of the goods purchased or produced throughout the taxable year divided by the total number of units so purchased or produced; or

4. Pursuant to any other proper method which, in the opinion of the Commissioner, clearly reflects income. [Section 1.472–8(e)(2)(ii), Appendix C.]

The full meaning of the alternative of "any other method" is not readily apparent, but it does permit accounting procedures which involve some variation from the general statements of how current-year cost is to be computed. These procedures for establishing current-year costs represent one approach to adapting the dollar-value principle to the methods of costing inventory increments discussed in the section starting on page 247.

Complete double extensions are frequent in the case of relatively small inventories and sometimes in the case of large companies; however, complete double extension of an inventory is not practical in the majority of instances.

Businesses using the dollar-value principle are generally those having on hand at all times a wide variety of materials and a large number of items, parts, subassemblies and products. Further, the items required are constantly changing. Among the characteristics of a competitive economy is the constant endeavor to provide customers with a better product at a lower price. The materials used may be changed because of variations in public taste (e.g., heavy work clothing has been replaced to a large extent by garments made of lighter-weight materials and sports-type garments), because of improved manufacturing techniques (e.g., machines are constantly being developed which can process a lighter or less expensive metal), or because of limitless other factors. End products and individual component parts are being changed all the time, and most business units maintain market research and engineering specialists to further these changes.

Where the "double extension" method is not used in applying the dollar-value principle to LIFO inventories, the more frequently encountered alternative procedures for measuring the relative quantity of goods included in an inventory and the current cost for an increment are as follows:

1. Measuring the relative quantity of goods on hand by applying to the total current cost of the inventory:
   a) An index developed by double-extending less than all of the items
   b) An index developed from published statistics
   c) An index developed by double-extending all or a portion of each inventory at current-year costs and at costs for a year subsequent to the base year
   d) A link-chain index developed by double-extending all or a portion of each inventory at beginning-of-year and end-of-year costs and computing a cumulative index
2. Establishing the current cost for an inventory increment by applying to the amount of the increase measured in terms of base-year cost:
   a) A ratio developed by comparing current-year acquisition costs with extensions at base-year costs for quantities acquired during the year rather than for quantities in the year-end inventory
   b) A ratio developed by comparing the amount of the total current-year cost as computed for the closing inventory of the preceding year with the amount of the total base-year cost for that inventory.
   c) A ratio developed by comparing the amount of the total current-year cost as computed for the physical inventory taken in advance of the end of the year with the amount of the total base-year cost for that inventory.

All the foregoing procedures will result in income being clearly reflected under appropriate circumstances and others not referred to may be equally acceptable. The primary test which has been stated in the regulations since 1949 is that the method of computation be established to the satisfaction of the Commissioner as "reasonably adaptable to the purpose and intent" of LIFO.[7] The general rules added to the regulations in 1961 are not absolute, and accounting procedures must take into consideration the practicability of compiling basic data.

Because LIFO determinations are dependent upon a comparison of inventories at the beginning and end of the year without regard to interim fluctuations, many businesses electing LIFO continue to maintain their accounting records on a FIFO basis. This means that the starting point for year-end LIFO computations is the total current cost for the goods on hand. The relative quantity of goods represented by the inventory can be established under these circumstances by applying to the total current cost an index developed by double-extending less than all the items. The mechanics of this type of computation can be illustrated by assuming an inventory for which the total current cost is $1 million. The quantities on hand of items having an aggregate current cost of $600,000 are extended at base-year costs and found to have an aggregate base-year cost of $500,000. This produces an index of 120 per cent, that is $600,000/$500,000. The total base-year cost for the inventory is then established at $833,333 by dividing $1,000,000 by 120 per cent.

Generally, it is not difficult to establish the extent to which double extensions need to be made to construct a valid index to be applied to the total of any particular inventory. Depending upon the types of goods included in the inventory, a valid index can frequently be determined by extending quantities which represent just the major items. In the aggregate these items may represent a small fraction of the total value of the inventory, but where the remaining items are relatively unimportant individually and are generally similar in character to the major items, there is little likelihood that the conversion index would be modified significantly by expanding the volume of the double extensions. It is not practical to specify a percentage of inventory which should be double extended because the circumstances will vary in each instance. Ordinarily an extension of as much as fifty per cent of an inventory will result in a valid conversion index provided no single material item is omitted which would obviously affect the result.

In some cases the volume of the inventory items is so great that it is not practical to compute an index by even partial double-extension. Where the items fall within a distinct class of goods for which published statistics are available, a valid index may be obtained without making any individual

[7] A discussion of the purpose and intent of LIFO is included in a memorandum entitled "Pooling of LIFO Inventories by Use of Dollar-Value Method" prepared by Carman G. Blough, Samuel J. Broad, and Robert M. Trueblood, and submitted to the Treasury Department under date of Feb. 23, 1960. See 110 *J. Accountancy* 1, 77 (July 1960).

extensions at base-year costs. Where such an index is used, the burden is on the taxpayer to establish that the statistics are appropriate. If the index is based upon data secured from the Department of Labor or other governmental agency, the taxpayer avoids the necessity of proving the consistent use of acceptable statistical methods in the basic compilations. Occasionally the Bureau of Labor Statistics has assisted taxpayers in establishing an index to be applied to their particular inventories. This procedure can generally be used only where the character of the inventories makes it practical to obtain the relative aggregate weight of the items on hand falling within established Wholesale Price Index groupings. With this information it is possible to compute an index reflecting a weighted average of all the product classes represented in the inventory.

Where base-year costs can be used as standard costs in the accounting records, it is possible in some cases to compile information which is significant for management purposes as well as for making LIFO computations. Over the years, however, the number of theoretical base-year costs increases because of changes in the components of the inventory pool and the base-year cost amounts lose their utility. For this reason the standard costs must be revised periodically—after the elapse of five, eight, or ten years, depending upon the circumstances—and the relative quantity of the goods in subsequent inventories can be measured for LIFO purposes by using these unit costs in place of the original base-year costs. The principle underlying this type of revision of base-year costs is recognized in section 1.472–8(g)(3) of Appendix C. For some situations it is specifically provided that a later year may be used as the base year instead of the earliest year for which LIFO was adopted for items in a pool.

The transition to the use of later unit costs as base-year costs requires the extension of at least the major portion of one inventory at both the old and the new costs. The mechanics of developing a revised index are shown on page 278 by a simplified example in which it is assumed that the total for an inventory at December 31, 1961, was $305,500 when extended at 1959 base-year costs and $600,000 when extended at current costs. It will be noted that the originally established LIFO cost for each segment of the inventory is carried forward unchanged so long as it remains intact. The conversion factors are actually used only when a segment has been partially liquidated.

One of the techniques developed to cope with the ever changing character of inventories is the link-chain index. Under this procedure the change in cost levels is measured first on an annual basis, and then the cumulative change is reflected by multiplying the annual index and the last previously determined cumulative index. This is the procedure used in compiling the Bureau of Labor Statistics, Department Store Inventory Price Indexes approved by the Treasury Department for the computation of LIFO inventories by retail stores.

A simplified example of the mechanics of the link-chain index is set forth on pages 280–81. For the purpose of this example the following assumptions have been made:

1. The inventory for the business unit consisted of just two items at the beginning of the first year for which LIFO was used—10 units of Item A and 5 units of Item B.

2. Item A was maintained at a constant level of 10 units; however, over a three-year period Item C was substituted for Item B, even though an aggregate of 5 units was constantly maintained for Items B and C.

3. A theoretical cost for Item C as of the beginning of the first year has been computed although none was actually included in the inventory.

4. The cost of the goods in the closing inventory in excess of those in the opening inventory of the year is determined by reference to the year's acquisitions in the order thereof, and the current costs for the inventory at the close of the preceding year reflects such acquisition costs.

It will be noted that in this illustration the inventory determinations are substantially the same whether the computations use the base-year unit costs or use the beginning-of-the-year unit costs and a link-chain index. In view of the fact that larger differences could result under certain circumstances, however, consideration must be given to whether one method can be said to be more appropriate in implementing the determination of the annual income of a business.

A procedure whereby the quantity of goods in each inventory is measured by using unit costs as of the beginning of the year for which LIFO was initially adopted is comparable to the mechanics of computations which do not involve the dollar-value principle, that is, where the inventories are measured in units such as gallons, pounds, or yards rather than dollars as reflected by extensions of physical quantities at unit costs prevailing at a particular date. The procedure cannot be said to be wrong, but neither can it be said to be the only proper method of applying LIFO. It becomes increasingly difficult in application as time goes by because more theoretical costs have to be computed for new items not represented in the basic inventory, and the comparisons are between what the aggregate cost would have been had the goods included in the opening and closing inventories for the year been on hand at the basic date. The full impact of a change in inventory mix between items, for which the unit cost has fluc-

Mechanics for Using Current Costs as Base-Year Costs

Inventory at December 31, 1961, using original base-year costs:

	Extensions at Dec. 31, 1949, unit costs	Conversion factor	LIFO cost
1949 base	$ 30,500	100%	$ 30,500
Increments:			
1950	40,000	110	44,000
1956	200,000	180	360,000
1959	5,000	200	10,000
1960	30,000	185	55,500
Total	$305,500		$500,000

Proration of total December 31, 1961, cost:

	Extensions at Dec. 31, 1949, unit costs Amount	%	Proration of extensions at Dec. 31, 1961, unit costs
1949 base	$ 30,500	10	$ 60,000
Increments:			
1950	40,000	13	78,000
1956	200,000	65	390,000
1959	5,000	2	12,000
1960	30,000	10	60,000
Total	$305,500	100	$600,000

Using revised base-year costs:

	Extensions at Dec. 31, 1961, unit costs	Conversion factor	LIFO cost
1949 base	$ 60,000	51%	$ 30,500
Increments:			
1950	78,000	56	44,000
1956	390,000	92	360,000
1959	12,000	83	10,000
1960	60,000	93	55,500
Total	$600,000		$500,000

Inventory at December 31, 1962:

	Extensions at Dec. 31, 1961, unit costs	Conversion factor	LIFO cost
1949 base	$ 60,000	51%	$ 30,500
Increments:			
1950	78,000	56	44,000
1956	390,000	92	360,000
1959	12,000	83	10,000
1960	45,000	93	41,850
Total	$585,000		$486,350

Simplified Inventories Extended at Alternative Cost Levels for Purpose of Illustrating Mechanics of Dollar-Value LIFO Computations

	Goods on hand measured in terms of					
	Current unit costs		Base-year unit costs		Beginning-of-year unit costs	
	Per unit	Total	Per unit	Total	Per unit	Total
First year:						
Opening inventory:						
Item A—10 units........	$50	$500				
Item B— 5 units........	10	50				
Item C— – units........	12	—				
		$550				
Closing inventory:						
Item A—10 units........	$52	$520	$50	$500	$50	$500
Item B— 4 units........	12	48	10	40	10	40
Item C— 1 unit.........	14	14	12	12	12	12
		$582		$552		$552
Second year:						
Closing inventory:						
Item A—10 units........	$55	$550	$50	$500	$52	$520
Item B— 2 units........	13	26	10	20	12	24
Item C— 3 units........	16	48	12	36	14	42
		$624		$556		$586
Third year:						
Closing inventory:						
Item A—10 units........	$60	$600	$50	$500	$55	$550
Item B— – units........	15	—	10	—	13	—
Item C— 5 units........	16	80	12	60	16	80
		$680		$560		$630

tuated differently during the period that LIFO has been used, is reflected in the income of the year in which the change in mix occurs.

The LIFO section of the Internal Revenue Code stipulates the taxpayer shall treat those goods remaining on hand at the close of the taxable year as being: first, those included in the opening inventory of the taxable year

| | Computations using base-year unit costs | | |
	Goods on hand measured in terms of base-year unit costs	Conversion index	LIFO inventory cost
	Total — Segments		
First year (closing inventory):			
Total goods on hand................	$552		
Goods included in opening inventory..	550	$550 — 1.00(a)	$550.00
Goods acquired during year.........	$ 2	2 — 1.00(b)	2.00
LIFO inventory cost................			$552.00
Second year (closing inventory):			
Total goods on hand..............	$556		
Goods included in opening inventory..	552	{ 550 — 1.00	$550.00
		{ 2 — 1.00	2.00
			552.00
Goods acquired during year.........	$ 4	4 — 1.054(c)	4.22
LIFO inventory cost................			$556.22
Third year (closing inventory):			
Total goods on hand..............	$560		
		{ 550 — 1.00	$550.00
Goods included in opening inventory..	556	{ 2 — 1.00	2.00
		{ 4 — 1.054	4.22
			556.22
Goods acquired during year.........	$ 4	4 — 1.122(d)	4.49
LIFO inventory cost................			$560.71

Explanation of Factors Designated "Conversion Index" in Illustration Above

(a) LIFO cost of basic segment is 550/550 (or 1.00) times actual cost of opening inventory for first year.

(b) LIFO cost of first-year increment is 1.00 times the quantity measured in terms of base-year unit costs because the relationship of the aggregate of the extensions of the opening inventory for the first year (550/550, or 1.00) establishes acquisition cost.

(c) LIFO cost of second-year increment is 1.05435 times the quantity measured in terms of base-year unit costs because the relationship of the aggregate of the extensions of the opening inventory for the second year (582/552, or 1.05435) establishes acquisition cost.

(d) LIFO cost of third-year increment is 1.1223 times the quantity measured in terms of base-year unit costs because the relationship of the aggregate of the extensions of the opening inventory for the third year (624/556, or 1.1223) establishes acquisition cost.

(e) Goods on hand measured in terms of base-year unit costs at end of first year has been determined by direct computation, giving a factor of 552/552, or 1.00.

(f) Goods on hand measured in terms of base-year costs at end of second year is 0.94845 times the quantity measured in terms of beginning-of-year unit costs because the relationship of the aggregate of the extensions of the opening inventory for the

Computations using beginning-of-year unit costs and link-chain index

Goods on hand measured in terms of beginning-of-year unit costs	Conversion index	Goods on hand measured in terms of base-year costs		Conversion index	LIFO inventory cost
		Total	Segments		
$552	1.00(e)	$552.00			
550		550.00	$550.00	1.00(a)	$550.00
$ 2		$ 2.00	2.00	1.00(b)	2.00
					$552.00
$586	0.94845(f)	$555.79			
582		552.00	{ 550.00	1.00	$550.00
			{ 2.00	1.00	2.00
					552.00
$ 4		$ 3.79	3.79	1.054(h)	4.00
					$556.00
$630	0.89069(g)	$561.13			
624		555.79	(550.00	1.00	$550.00
			{ 2.00	1.00	2.00
			(3.79	1.054	4.00
					556.00
$ 6		$ 5.34	5.34	1.123(i)	6.00
					$562.00

second year (552/582, or 0.94845) establishes the cost-level change of the first year.

(g) Goods on hand measured in terms of base-year costs at end of third year is 0.89069 times the quantity measured in terms of beginning-of-year unit costs because the relationship of the aggregate of the extensions of the opening inventory for the third year at second year's beginning unit costs and at current unit costs (586/624, or 0.9391) establishes the cost-level change during the second year, and this factor multiplied by the factor for the prior year establishes the cost-level change through the second year (0.9391 × 0.94845, or 0.89069).

(h) LIFO cost of second-year segment is 1.05435 times the quantity measured in terms of base-year costs because the relationship of the aggregate of the extensions of the opening inventory for the second year (582/552, or 1.05435) establishes the cost-level change during the first year and the acquisition cost.

(i) LIFO cost of second-year segment is 1.1227 times the quantity measured in terms of base-year costs because the relationship of the aggregate of the extensions of the opening inventory for the third year at current unit costs and at second year's beginning unit costs (624/586, or 1.06485) establishes the cost-level change during the second year, and this factor multiplied by the factor for the prior year establishes the cost-level change through the second year (1.06485 × 1.05435, or 1.1227) and the acquisition cost.

(in the order of acquisition) to the extent thereof; and second, those acquired in the taxable year. Under the dollar-value principle it can be argued that a better comparison of the relative quantity of goods on hand at the beginning and end of any particular year can be made by extending both inventories at beginning-of-the-year unit costs than by comparing extensions at base-year unit costs. Differences in the two comparisons as illustrated in the example on pages 280–81 are as follows:

1. There is no change in the computation of the closing inventory for the first year.

2. In the second year two units of Item C were substituted for Item B, and

   a) In the computation using base-year unit costs, the quantity of goods on hand increased $4 in terms of base-year costs. The $4 increase is attributable to the fact that the cost of Item C as of the basic date was $12—$2 per unit more than the concurrent cost of Item B. The conversion index measured by reference to the total inventory (1.054) is applied to include the additional goods in the LIFO cost at $4.22.

   b) In the computation using beginning-of-the-year unit costs and a link-chain index, the quantity of goods on hand increased $4 in terms of the beginning-of-year costs. The $4 increase is attributable to the fact that the cost of Item C as of the beginning of the second year was $14—$2 more than the concurrent cost of Item B. The conversion is made in a manner which reflects the actual additional cost of $4 in the LIFO cost.

3. In the third year two additional units of Item C were substituted for Item B, and

   a) In the computation using base-year unit costs, the quantity of goods on hand increased $4 in terms of base-year costs. The $4 increase is again attributable to the fact that the cost of Item C as of the basic date was $12—$2 per unit more than the concurrent cost of Item B. The conversion index measured by reference to the total inventory (1.122) is applied to include the additional goods in the LIFO cost at $4.49.

   b) In the computation using beginning-of-the-year unit costs and a link-chain index, the quantity of goods on hand increased $6 in terms of the beginning-of-the-year costs. The $6 increase is attributable to the fact that the cost of Item C as of the beginning of the third year was $16—$3 more than the concurrent cost of Item B. The conversion is made in a way that reflects the actual cost of $6 in the LIFO cost.

It will be noted that in the computations using beginning-of-the-year unit costs and a link-chain index, the increment in the quantity of goods is included in the LIFO costs at the actual cost of the increment. In both cases the quantity of goods in the closing inventory to the extent of the goods on hand at the beginning of the year is included in the LIFO cost at the amount attributed thereto in the prior inventory. The link-chain method conforms, therefore, with the explicit requirement of the statute.

Permitting the use of the alternative amounts for current-year costs, discussed on page 273, is recognition of the various procedures for costing inventory increments. Only in the exceptionally simple case, however, would it be practical to extend the closing inventory quantities at the cost of the first acquisitions during the year for a comparable quantity on an item-by-item basis. Similarly, it is unrealistic to contemplate establishing a current-year cost for each item by computing the average cost for the entire year's acquisitions. It seems doubtful that any company would know the total current-year cost of its closing inventory under either of these methods, and the effect upon income of using one of these procedures for costing an increment rather than more practical alternatives would not justify the expense of making an additional extension of the inventory.

There is no implication in the regulations that the use of per unit current-year costs for the inventory items is the only way in which the cost of increments can be computed. Doubtless procedures similar to those described on page 274 will be generally adopted, but technically their use constitutes a variation from the complete double-extension method.

The regulations provide, "Where the use of the double-extension method is impractical, because of technological changes, the extensive variety of items, or extreme fluctuations in the variety of the items, in a dollar-value pool, the taxpayer may use an index method for computing all or part of the LIFO value of the pool. An index may be computed by double-extending a representative portion of the inventory in a pool or by the use of other sound and consistent statistical methods." A taxpayer using an index method must be able to demonstrate to the satisfaction of revenue agents in connection with the examination of his tax returns the appropriateness of the method of computing the index and the suitability of the use of the index.

The regulations further provide, "The use of any so-called 'link-chain' method will be approved for taxable years beginning after December 31, 1960, only in those cases where the taxpayer can demonstrate to the satisfaction of the district director that the use of either an index method or the double-extension method would be impractical or unsuitable in view of the nature of the pool." As with an index method, a taxpayer *may* request the Commissioner's office to approve in advance the appropriateness of the link-chain method; however, advance approval is not mandatory.

Since 1976 the Service has held in suspense many applications requesting permission to change from the double-extension or index method to the link-chain method. The Service appears to be requiring a representation or proof of 90 to 100% turnover of items comprising a pool during the five year period preceding the year of requested change. The 90-100% turnover is understood to be met if the aggregate of added and/or deleted items within a year approximates 20% of all items in the pool.

The Service's attitude seems to be contrary to that of the S.E.C., at least as evidenced in the 1974–7 restatement of earnings by Jones & Laughlin Steel Corporation. It is suggested that permitting the use of the link-chain method will minimize problems which could arise in accounting for "new items" entering single LIFO pool, the value of which is calculated by use of the dollar-value, double-extension method.[8]

The regulations impose an additional requirement if the complete double-extension method is not used:

> . . . A taxpayer using either an index or link-chain method shall attach to his income tax return for the first taxable year beginning after December 31, 1960, for which the index or link-chain method is used, a statement describing the particular link-chain method or the method used in computing the index. The statement shall be in sufficient detail to facilitate the determination as to whether the method used meets the standards set forth in this subparagraph. In addition, a copy of the statement shall be filed with the Commissioner of Internal Revenue, Attention: T:R, Washington 25, D.C. The taxpayer shall submit such other information as may be requested with respect to such index or link-chain method. Adequate records must be maintained by the taxpayer to support the appropriateness, accuracy, and reliability of an index or link-chain method. A taxpayer may request the Commissioner to approve the appropriateness of an index or link-chain method for the first taxable year beginning after December 31, 1960, for which it is used. Such request must be submitted within 90 days after the beginning of the first taxable year beginning after December 31, 1960, in which the taxpayer desires to use the index or link-chain method, or on or before May 1, 1961, whichever is later. [Section 1.472–8(e)(1), Appendix C.]

Although decisions to elect LIFO are generally made only at the end of the year, this provision in the regulations requires that, if a complete double extension is not to be made and advance approval of the Commissioner's office is desired, a request for approval of the contemplated statistical index method be filed during the first ninety days of the initial LIFO year. This

---

[8] See further discussion in Chapter 15.

sentence in the regulations should be deleted or modified to recognize the practicality of timing in LIFO adoptions.

CHANGING SPECIFIC GOODS POOLS TO DOLLAR-VALUE POOLS

When a change is made to a LIFO inventory procedure based upon the dollar-value principle after some other procedure has been in use for some time, there is commonly occasion to combine a number of the previously established pools. Further, it is frequently appropriate, incidental to the change, to include in a dollar-value LIFO pool one or more classes of items for which the cost has been computed under the FIFO assumption as to flow of costs.

The primary consideration in this type of change-over is that the dollar amounts assigned to the opening inventory for the year are not to be modified or adjusted. Similarly, the cost attributable to each segment of the LIFO inventory will remain the same.

The only change which is being made as a matter of basic principle is that the quantity of goods on hand at the respective inventory dates is to be measured in terms of dollars by applying to the various items the unit costs applicable thereto as of a specific date rather than in terms of tons, gallons, yards, and so forth. The date chosen for this purpose has little significance in considering the appropriateness of the computations. It should be the date which is the most practicable in each individual case, and it will generally be either the beginning of the year LIFO was first used or the beginning of the year the change in procedure is being effected.

The computations required in making the change in inventory procedure include:

1. A recapitulation of costs assigned to the various segments of the opening inventory by years of acquisition.
2. A statement of the quantity of goods represented by the various segments of the opening inventory expressed in terms of the unit costs adopted for the purpose of comparing future inventory quantities.
3. A set of conversion factors, determined from the computations referred to in (1) and (2), required to assign to the corresponding segments of future inventories included in the dollar-value LIFO pool, the same costs as have been previously established.

The complexity of these computations will depend primarily upon the number of different items included in the previously established LIFO pools and the ability to obtain unit costs for the various items as of the selected date. The difficulties involved in obtaining accurate unit costs as of an earlier date generally make it more practical, and in some instances absolutely necessary, to use unit costs as of the beginning of the year in which the change in procedure is being effected.

A previously established LIFO pool may include items which have a range of unit costs, and it will not be possible to extend the pounds included in each inventory layer on a precise item basis. For example, where different staple lengths or grades of cotton are used at different times in the same mill to produce the same class of goods, the cotton may have been inventoried as a single LIFO pool measured in terms of pounds. As demonstrated by the following illustration, only the average cost of the goods included in such a pool as of the selected inventory date can be used under these circumstances because it is impossible to identify the individual items accounting for a specific segment of the inventory:

	Quantities in inventory at	
	Beginning of year	End of year
Grade 1.........	10x lb.	7x lb.
Grade 2.........	3x	7x
Grade 3.........	7x	11x
Total.......	20x lb.	25x lb.

The quantity of goods in this inventory pool increased $5x$ lb., but it cannot be said that the increase is attributable to Grade 2 or Grade 3, or any particular combination of the two. The inventory at the end of the year contains $4x$ lb. more of both Grade 2 and Grade 3 than did the inventory at the beginning of the year.

The federal income tax regulations (section 1.472–8(f)(2) of Appendix C) contain an example intended to illustrate the mechanics of changing to a LIFO inventory procedure based upon the dollar-value principle. This example does not, however, expressly recognize differing grades of goods within any of the previously established pools. It either assumes there are no differences between the units within a pool or is intended specifically to recognize that an average unit cost as of the date LIFO was first adopted is to be used.

One alternative to using an average unit cost for the various pools as of the date LIFO was first adopted is illustrated below by computations for ABC Company which give recognition to the existence of various grades within each pool, using unit costs as of the beginning of 1978, the year in which the dollar-value principle is first applied.

Analysis of December 31, 1977, Inventory of ABC Company

1. Recapitulation of LIFO costs by years of inventory acquisition:

	1974 base	Increments 1975	Increments 1976	Increments 1977
Item A	$ 100	$ 400	$ 400	$ 600
Item B	1,800	800		500
Item C	4,000	1,200	2,400	
	$5,900	$2,400	$2,800	$ 1,100
Total LIFO cost				$12,200

2. Statement of quantity of goods represented by LIFO layers, expressed in terms of unit costs adopted for the purpose of comparing future inventory quantities:

December 31, 1977, inventory at current costs—

	Quantity	Dec. 31, 1977 unit cost	Amount
Item A:			
Grade 1	300	$ 5.75	$ 1,725
Grade 2	200	6.10	1,220
Total	500		$ 2,945
Average		5.89	
Item B:			
Grade 1	250	10.00	$ 2,500
Grade 2	100	10.50	1,050
Grade 3	100	9.75	975
Total	450		$ 4,525
Average		10.06	
Item C:			
Grade 1	700	9.00	$ 6,300
Grade 2	150	9.50	1,425
Grade 3	250	8.70	2,175
Grade 4	400	9.25	3,700
Total	1,500		$13,600
Average		9.07	
Total December 31, 1977 value			$21,070

Segments of December 31, 1977, inventory—
Quantities:

	1974 base	Increments		
		1975	1976	1977
Item A..................	100	200	100	100
Item B..................	300	100		50
Item C..................	1,000	200	300	

Extensions at average of 1977 costs:

	1974 base	Increments		
		1975	1976	1977
Item A ($ 5.89)	$ 589	$1,178	$ 589	$ 589
Item B ($10.06)	3,018	1,006		503
Item C ($ 9.07)	9,070	1,814	2,721	
	$12,677	$3,998	$3,310	$ 1,092
Total December 31, 1977, value				$21,077

3. Conversion factors for assigning to corresponding segments of future inventories the previously established LIFO costs:

	Dec. 31, 1977 values	Conversion factor	LIFO cost
Segments of 1977 inventory—			
1974 base	$12,677	46.54%	$ 5,900
Increments:			
1975	3,998	60.03	2,400
1976	3,310	84.59	2,800
1977	1,092	100.73	1,100
Total	$21,077		$12,200

On the basis of the foregoing, the LIFO cost for the inventory at December 31, 1978, would be determined as follows:

Computation of LIFO Cost for December 31, 1978, Inventory of ABC Company

	1978 inventory quantities extended at Dec. 31, 1977, unit costs		
	Quantity	Unit cost	Amount
Item A:			
Grade 1	400	$ 5.75	$ 2,300
Grade 2	250	6.10	1,525
Item B:			
Grade 1	378	10.00	3,780
Grade 2	110	10.50	1,155
Grade 3	200	9.75	1,950
Item C:			
Grade 1	500	9.00	4,500
Grade 2	10	9.50	95
Grade 3	300	8.70	2,610
Grade 4	100	9.25	925
			$18,840

	Dec. 31, 1977, values	Conversion factor	LIFO cost
Segments of 1978 inventory:			
1974 base	$12,677	46.54%	$ 5,900
Increments:			
1975	3,998	60.03	2,400
1976	2,165	84.59	1,831
Total	$18,840		$10,131

Unit costs as of the beginning of the year in which LIFO was first adopted could similarly be used, but that procedure is generally not practicable because earlier costs are seldom available for each of the individual items in the current and future inventories.

The mechanics of changing to a procedure based upon the dollar-value principle where additional items are included in the pool and where it is practicable to determine unit costs as of the beginning of the year in which LIFO was first adopted may be illustrated by the XYZ Company.

Analysis of December 31, 1977, Inventory of XYZ Company

1. Recapitulation of LIFO costs by years of inventory acquisition:

	1965 base	Increments		
		1969	1973	1977
Commodity W	$400	$10	$	$ 10
Commodity X	150		120	
Commodity Y	4	1		5
Commodity Z				400*
	$554	$11	$120	$ 415
Total LIFO cost				$1,100

* Commodity Z was not part of the LIFO inventory prior to 1978.

2. Statement of quantity of goods represented by the LIFO layers, expressed in terms of unit costs adopted for the purpose of comparing future inventory quantities:

December 31, 1977, inventory at 1965 unit costs—

	Quantity	Dec. 31, 1965, unit cost	Amount
Commodity W:			
Item A	1,075 yd.	$0.15	$161.25
Item B	1,500	.16	240.00
Total	2,575 yd.		$401.25
Average		.156	
Commodity X:			
Item C	1,400 lb.	.095	$133.00
Item D	700	.10	70.00
Item E	400	.11	44.00
Total	2,500 lb.		$247.00
Average		.099	

Commodity Y:			
Item F	2 gal.	.40	$ 0.80
Item G	6	.38	2.28
Item H	5	.41	2.05
Item I	4	.39	1.56
Total	17 gal.		$ 6.69
Average		.394	
Commodity Z:			
Item J	80 tons	3.00	$240.00

Segments of December 31, 1977, inventory—
Quantities:

	1965 base	Increments		
		1969	1973	1977
Commodity W	2,500 yd.	50 yd.		25 yd.
Commodity X	1,500 lb.		1,000 lb.	
Commodity Y	10 gal.	2 gal.		5 gal.
Commodity Z				80 tons

Extensions at average of 1965 costs:

	1965 base	Increments		
		1969	1973	1977
Commodity W ($0.156)	$390.00	$7.80	$	$ 3.90
Commodity X ($0.099)	148.50		99.00	
Commodity Y ($0.394)	3.94	.79		1.97
Commodity Z ($3.00)				240.00
	$542.44	$8.59	$99.00	$245.87
Total December 31, 1965, value				$895.90

3. Conversion factors for assigning to corresponding segments of future inventories the previously established LIFO costs:

	Dec. 31, 1965, values	Conversion factor	LIFO cost
Segments of 1977 inventory:			
1965 base	$542.44	102.13%	$ 554
Increments:			
1969	8.59	128.05	11
1973	99.00	121.21	120
1977	245.87	168.79	415
Total	$895.90		$1,100

On the basis of the foregoing, the LIFO cost for the inventory at December 31, 1978, would be determined as follows:

Computation of LIFO Cost for December 31, 1978, Inventory of XYZ Company

	1978 inventory quantities extended at December 31, 1965, unit costs		
	Quantity	Unit cost	Amount
Commodity W:			
Item A	1,600 yd.	$0.15	$240.00
Item B	800	0.16	128.00
Commodity X:			
Item C	1,200 lb.	0.095	114.00
Item D	750	0.10	75.00
Item E	300	0.11	33.00
Commodity Y:			
Item F	5 gal.	0.40	2.00
Item G	10	0.38	3.80
Item H	8	0.41	3.28
Item I	7	0.39	2.73
Commodity Z:			
Item J	75 tons	3.00	225.00
Total			$826.81

	Dec. 31, 1965 values	Conversion factor	LIFO cost
Segments of 1978 inventory—			
1965 base	$542.44	102.13%	$554.00
Increments:			
1969	8.59	128.05	11.00
1973	99.00	121.21	120.00
1977	176.78	168.79	298.39
Total	$826.81		$983.39

The extension of the December 31, 1977, inventory quantities at 1965 unit costs on an item-by-item basis should not be necessary. Use of the average costs previously established with respect to the 1965 inventory will produce acceptable results in most cases. Had such average costs been applied in the foregoing computations, the analysis of the 1977 inventory and the conversion factors would have been as at the top of the next page.

**Alternative Analysis of December 31, 1977,
Inventory of XYZ Company**

	1965 base	Increments 1969	Increments 1973	Increments 1977
Extensions at 1965 costs:				
Commodity W (16¢)	$400.00	$8.00	$	$ 4.00
Commodity X (10¢)	150.00		100.00	
Commodity Y (40¢)	4.00	.80		2.00
Commodity Z ($3.00)				240.00
	$554.00	$8.80	$100.00	$246.00
Total December 31, 1965, value				$908.80

Conversion factors:

	Dec. 31, 1965 values	Conversion factor	LIFO cost
Segments of 1977 inventory—			
1965 base	$554.00	100.00%	$ 554.00
Increments:			
1969	8.80	125.00	11.00
1973	100.00	120.00	120.00
1977	246.00	168.70	415.00
Total	$908.80		$1,100.00

The 1978 inventory will presumably be extended on a detailed basis so the aggregate 1965 value of $826.81 would be converted to a LIFO inventory cost of $961.68, as follows:

**Alternative Computation of LIFO Cost for December 31, 1978,
Inventory of XYZ Company**

	Dec. 31, 1965 values	Conversion factor	LIFO cost
Segments of 1978 inventory—			
1965 base	$554.00	100.00%	$ 554.00
Increments:			
1969	8.80	125.00	11.00
1973	100.00	120.00	120.00
1977	164.01	168.70	276.68
Total	$826.81		$ 961.68

The difference of $21.71 ($983.39—$961.68) is not material and will not increase because all subsequent inventories will be extended on a basis comparable to the 1978 inventory.

THIRTEEN

Retail Method of Computing Inventories

Few customers realize the tremendous amount of paper work required to operate a retail department store of any size, or even a specialty store. Although the customers are aware that there are different departments, each of which handles a specific type of merchandise, they probably do not reflect upon the subject sufficiently to realize that the store may have thousands of individual items on display or concealed from view in the reserve stock rooms, receiving departments, and warehouse. The task of designing appropriate accounting records for these inventories is not simple and may range from tracking the movement of each type of merchandise sold by the use of point of sale terminals supported by sophisticated computer software systems to the taking of annual physical inventories with no attempt made throughout the year to account for changes in inventory levels. For those companies that find the use of point of sale terminals and related computer systems to account for the movement in each product offered for sale too expensive, the retail method offers an approach to obtaining adequate control over inventories at a minimum effort.

The basic difference between the inventory procedures commonly used by retailers and by industrial concerns is indicated by the following general statements:

1. Under the retail method, the inventory control records are maintained by departments on the basis of total retail dollars (selling prices). Markup percentages are determined for each department and used subsequently to reduce the retail value to cost. In many instances stores do maintain a unit control or perpetual inventory record, but these unit

records are used primarily by buyers or for special purposes and are seldom used in computing cost for inventory purposes.

2. Industrial concerns usually maintain inventory control accounts on a cost basis. They will also maintain statistical records on a unit basis or list the units of individual items on hand periodically at the time of taking a physical inventory. The dollar amounts assigned to such inventories are computed by multiplying the quantities by the appropriate unit costs.

DEPARTMENTAL INVENTORY CONTROLS

In the operation of the departmental control records maintained under the retail inventory method, four sets of basic figures must be available: (1) merchandise purchases at retail value and at cost, (2) inbound transportation costs, (3) adjustments in retail prices (markups, markdowns, etc.), and (4) sales of merchandise.

The accounting procedures followed in a typical store are:

1. *Purchases:* Purchases of merchandise for resale are recorded on a departmental basis. Posting information is obtained from previously approved vendor invoices which have been marked with the total retail price for the various merchandise items on the invoice. Postings are made for the retail value and the invoice cost price. At the month end, a summary of purchases at both retail value and invoice cost price is prepared. The total invoice cost price for purchases of all departments becomes the basis of an entry in the general ledger to record the merchandise purchases and vendor invoices payable with respect to merchandise received during the month.

2. *Inbound transportation costs:* The freight and express costs on inbound shipments are recorded in the expense accounts payable ledger, maintained, as in the case of the purchase ledger, by departments. Alternatively, the inbound freight may be entered in a separate column in the departmental purchase ledger. At the month end, a summary of all such inbound transportation costs becomes the basis of an entry in the general ledger debiting Freight and Express and crediting Accounts Payable.

3. *Adjustments in retail prices:* The retail prices originally placed on incoming merchandise may be subsequently adjusted for a variety of reasons. Because, under the retail method, the relief of inventory balances for goods sold is based on the retail value of sales, a record must be maintained of all such changes. This record of adjustments to retail prices becomes an integral part of the computation of the actual markup percentage used to translate ending inventories at retail to their corresponding cost value. The record of retail price adjustments also provides required information to measure stock shortages. These adjustments are also compiled on a departmental basis and are commonly

segregated as to additional markups, markdowns, outright "adjustments," and discounts allowed.

4. *Sales:* Sales at retail must be accumulated by department in order to relieve the retail value of inventories available for sale by the total retail value of merchandise sold. The same summary of retail sales can serve as a basis for various analyses of departmental sales and as the source document for posting the sales entries to the general ledger.

The monthly totals of (1) the retail value and invoice cost price of merchandise received, obtained from the individual departmental purchase ledgers, (2) the departmental freight and express costs, (3) the retail price adjustments made with reference to the merchandise in the various departments, and (4) the departmental sales, are posted to the inventory controls, a sample from of which is shown on page 297.

The departmental inventory control is a vital part of the accounting records. Normally, this inventory control computation is part of a departmental operating report which contains also the income and expenses of the department. For the present purpose, however, only the inventory control need be considered and only that portion of the operating report relative to inventory control is shown. Columns are provided for information at retail value and cost price, on a year-to-date basis and on a monthly basis. Except for the beginning inventory amounts, the information required is inserted in the monthly columns first. The year-to-date figures are obtained by adding the current month's figures to the year-to-date figures at the previous month end. The following comments explain the various lines on the form:

1. *Beginning inventory and markup %:* The amounts to be inserted on this line in the year-to-date columns are copied from the closing inventory lines of the prior year's control sheet, and the beginning inventory amounts in the month columns are copied from the closing inventory lines of the previous month's control sheet. The manner in which these figures would have been determined will be revealed as the closing inventory for the current month is explained below. The total of the year-to-date beginning inventory at cost for all departments agrees, of course, with the general ledger inventory control amount.

2. *Purchases:* The retail value and cost price of merchandise purchased during the month are entered from the respective monthly departmental totals shown by the departmental purchase ledgers. Obviously, the total of all department purchases at cost must agree with the general ledger journal entry for the month recording total purchases and the related credit to accounts payable.

3. *Freight and express:* Only the cost column is used to record the inbound transportation costs as the original markup made on the mer-

Departmental Inventory Control

No. _____   Month of: _____ 19__
     (Department)

Line		RETAIL Year to date	%	Month	%	COST Year to date	Month
1	Beginning inventory and markup %	$ ____		$ ____		$ ____	$ ____
	Add:						
2	Purchases......................						
3	Freight and express...........	**		**			
4	Additional markups............					**	**
5	Retail adjustments.............	____		____		** ____	** ____
6	Total: Purchases and markup %....	____		____		____	____
7	Total: Inventory plus purchases, and markup %...................	____		____			
	Less:						
8	Markdowns..................						
9	Employees' discounts...........						
10	Other discounts...............						
11	Shortages....................	____		____			
12	Total reductions..............	____		____			
13	Total: Inventory available for sale						
14	Less: Sales....................	____		____		____	____
15	Closing inventory (retail)..........	$ ____		$ ____			
16	Closing inventory (cost)..........					$ ____	$ ____

chandise purchase cost should be sufficiently high to cover the transportation costs.

4. *Additional markups:* There are instances when the retailer realizes that the retail value of merchandise should be increased. This may result, for example, from a revised appraisal of the quality of or demand for the merchandise or from ascertaining that an error was made in determining the original retail value. These increases in retail value do not affect the cost of the merchandise but must be recognized as an addition to the inventory at retail.

5. *Retail adjustments:* Occasionally, the retailer may find it advantageous to adjust the retail value of certain merchandise but realizes that such adjustments may not be classified properly as either an additional markup or a markdown. These adjustments usually result in a reduction in the retail value. Markdowns, explained in detail in a later section, frequently reflect on the ability of the departmental buyer; therefore, although the adjustments are a form of markdown, they are treated separately. This line is most commonly used for markup cancellations; however, it might also be used where the retailer decides to stage a special sale, reducing the retail value of the regular merchandise. The reduction of this type could be entered as an inventory adjustment, and, in this manner, it would not be chargeable to the buyer. This adjustment does not affect the cost of the merchandise, so only the retail column is used.

6. *Total purchases, markups, and adjustments:* The amounts on the previously described four lines are totaled and a markup percentage, sometimes referred to as markon percentage, may be computed for the month and year to date. The markup percentage is stated on the basis of the retail value, and actually represents the percentage of the retail value in excess of cost price. Assuming a retail value of $58,900 and a cost price of $34,340, the computation of the markup percentage may be made by subtracting the cost price from the retail value and dividing the excess by the retail value, as follows:

$$
\begin{array}{lr}
\text{Retail value} & \$58,900 \\
\text{Cost price} & 34,340 \\
\hline
\text{Excess} & \$24,560 \\
\end{array}
$$

$$\frac{\$24,560}{\$58,900} = 41.70\%, \text{ markup percentage}$$

Both the markup percentage and the complement cost percentage (100%—markup percentage) are used extensively in the retail inventory method.

7. *Total opening inventory, purchases, markups, and adjustments:* As the caption indicates, the amounts to be entered on this line represent the sum of the opening inventory and the total on the previous line. This represents the total merchandise to be accounted for. A cumulative markup percentage calculation is required at this point, for it is this cumulative markup percentage which will be used later to compute the cost price of the closing inventory. The rationale explained above also applies to this calculation; however, an alternative procedure arriving at the same result can be illustrated, assuming that the totals of opening inventory were $6,220 and $3,700, purchases, and so forth, were $58,900 and $34,340 and the sum totals were $65,120 and $38,040, each at retail value and cost price, respectively.

$$\frac{\$38,040}{\$65,120} = 58.42\%$$

$$100\% - 58.42\% = 41.58\%, \text{ markup percentage}$$

Under this procedure a direct computation of the cost percentage (58.42%) is the first step.

8. *Markdowns:* At frequent intervals, it is necessary to reduce the retail value of merchandise in an effort to move it from stock. The causes which give rise to the necessity of reducing the retail value are numerous, and only a few are given to illustrate the more common types:

   a) Seasonal goods that the retailer does not desire to carry over until next year may still be on hand.

   b) Impending style or model changes, for example, the retailer desires to move the old items before the new ones become available.

   c) Soilage and damage, which reduce the attractiveness of the merchandise at full retail value.

   d) Odds and ends of a complete line, which the retailer desires to move.

   e) Competitive condition, for instance, another area retailer may be selling the same or a similar product at a lower price.

   The markdowns are summarized for the month by departments, and the total is entered on this line of the control record.

   The age analysis of the inventory, as hereinafter explained, is frequently used as a basis for markdowns. There is nothing to prevent a second or additional markdown from being made if the merchandise does not move after the first markdown.

   There are instances when a markdown cancellation may be prepared. This may occur when a markdown is made for a short period and, after a portion of the merchandise has been disposed of at the reduced retail value, the original retail value is restored on the remaining merchandise. The markdown cancellations are used as a deduction from the markdowns, so that a net figure is taken into account.

9. *Employees' discounts:* Most department stores offer discounts to employees on merchandise purchased. The rate of discount varies between stores and frequently varies between departments, reflecting the fact that the store has varying markup percentages in many of its departments. Since the sales figure will relieve inventory only at the discounted sales value, it is necessary to accumulate total discounts allowed employees by departments in order to remove the entire retail value from the inventory control. The accumulation of information relating to employee discounts may also be of interest to the retailer in evaluating the costs associated with the policy of allowing such discounts.

10. *Other discounts:* Discounts are sometimes allowed to religious organizations and members of the clergy, and the like. The total of such discounts allowed must be recognized for the same reason as for employees' discounts.

11. *Shortages:* Shortages or shrinkage in inventories occur even though every attempt is made to reduce them to a minimum. They exist for several reasons, a few of which are errors in the preparation of the sales check, pilferage, breakage, and unreported markdowns. The amount of shortage varies between departments, depending upon the type of merchandise carried. Based on the retailer's past experience for shortages by department, a percentage of sales is developed for each department that is then applied to monthly sales to provide for the anticipated shortage. Of course, this estimated shortage is adjusted periodically, based on actual physical inventories of merchandise on hand at its retail value.

12. *Total reductions:* The amount entered on this line, as indicated by the caption, represents the sum of the four reductions in inventory at retail just explained. These items are not entered in the cost columns and are not reflected by entries in the general ledger.

13. *Total inventory available for sale:* The amount to be entered on this line represents the result of subtracting the amount on line 12 from the amount on line 7. Line 7 represents the opening inventory at retail plus purchases and certain adjustments to retail values. Line 12 represents various factors reducing the retail value. The difference between the two is the merchandise to be accounted for at retail, immediately prior to the deduction for sales made. This amount is not itself significant and could be omitted.

14. *Sales:* The net sales for the month are entered in the retail column. If an amount is entered in the cost column for the sake of completeness, it is a balancing figure determined after the closing inventory at cost (line 16) is computed.

15. *Closing inventory (retail):* Deducting the total sales should develop a figure approximating the retail value of a physical inventory if one were to be taken. Naturally the amount in the year-to-date column must agree with the monthly column figure; if the amounts differ, an error (which should be located and corrected) has occurred in entering one or more figures on other lines.

16. *Closing inventory (cost):* The last operation is to reduce the inventory from retail value to cost. The markup percentage is developed on line 7. In the completed example of this Departmental Inventory Control form, shown on page 301, attention is directed to the fact that the markup percentage in the year-to-date column differs from that in the month column. This is a result of monthly variations in the markup on purchases. In reducing the retail value to cost, the complement cost per-

centage to the cumulative markup percentage is used for both the year-to-date and month columns. Naturally, there should not be two different amounts assigned as cost for the closing inventory, and since the year-to-date markup percentage levels off monthly variations, it is used.

The Departmental Inventory Control computations are an essential part of the accounting records and provide an important part of the monthly operating statement required by management.

From the Departmental Inventory Control form it will be noted that three of the four items deducted in arriving at the retail value of the closing

Departmental Inventory Control

No. 11–00   Piece Goods   Month of: March, 19—
     (Department)

Line		RETAIL				COST	
		Year to date	%	Month	%	Year to date	Month
1	Beginning inventory and markup %............	$ 6,220	40.52	$ 5,000	41.00	$ 3,700	$ 2,950
	Add:						
2	Purchases.............	58,795		31,225		34,040	18,722
3	Freight and express.....	**		**		300	175
4	Additional markups.....	150		60		**	**
5	Retail adjustments......	(45)		—		**	**
6	Total: Purchases and markup %..................	58,900	41.70	31,285	39.60	34,340	18,897
7	Total: Inventory plus purchases, and markup %..	65,120	41.58	36,285	39.79	38,040	21,847
	Less:						
8	Markdowns............	255		105			
9	Employees' discounts....	75		30			
10	Other discounts........	20		—			
11	Shortages.............	150		60			
12	Total reductions........	500		195			
13		64,620		36,090			
14	Less: Sales..............	54,620		26,090			
15	Closing inventory (retail)...	$10,000	41.58	$10,000			
16	Closing inventory (cost)....					$ 5,842	$ 5,842

inventory (employees' discounts, other discounts, and shortages) definitely do not pertain to merchandise still on hand. Of the deduction items only the markdowns might apply, at least in part, to the closing inventory. It is not generally feasible to establish the amount of the markdowns specifically applicable to the goods on hand, so the alternative recognized procedures are to assume either that a proportionate part of the total markdowns is applicable to the inventory items or that none is applicable.

If a proportionate part of the total markdown is actually applicable to merchandise on hand, the *cost* of the Piece Goods Department inventory reflected in the statement n opage 303 could be determined as shown below.

Determining Cost of Inventory by Restoring Markdowns

		Merchandise	
	Sold, etc.	On hand	Total available
Sales...................................	$54,620		
Employees' discounts......................	75		
Other discounts..........................	20		
Shortages...............................	150		
	54,865		
Sales value of merchandise on hand..........		$10,000	$64,865
Markdowns:			
54,865/64,865 × $255..................	216		
10,000/64,865 × $255..................		39	255
Retail value of beginning inventory plus purchases and markups.....................	$55,081	$10,039	$65,120
Markup %—41.58%......................			
Cost.....................................	32,175	5,865	38,040

Because the computation of the markup percentage as shown on page 303 is based on the original (before markdown) retail value assigned to the merchandise, the restoration of the markdowns applicable to the ending inventory is appropriate to arrive at a more accurate approximation of the cost of the merchandise on hand. In practice the cost of the closing inventory is determined by taking the markdowns into account in computing the markup percentage. The amount computed in this manner as the cost of the merchandise on hand is reasonably accurate. Regardless of which of the two methods for reflecting the effect of markdowns is used, if less than a proportionate part of the total markdowns is actually applicable to the goods in the inventory, the cost will be overstated. Conversely, if more than a proportionate part of the total markdowns is in fact applicable to the inventory, the amount computed as the cost will be understated.

In most instances in which the procedure illustrated on page 301 is followed, it is used in order to apply the principle of assigning an amount to the inventory that represents the lower of cost or market. Mechanically, this procedure assumes that no part of the markdowns is applicable to the merchandise on hand, whereas in fact if merchandise on hand includes items that have been marked down, the application of the percentage markup that does not take into consideration the effect of markdowns will result in stating these items at below their original cost price. However, the objective is to avoid stating the inventory at its full cost when some of the merchandise will not be sold at its regular retail price.

Determining Cost of Inventory by Adjusting Markup Percentage

		Retail	Markup %	Cost
Beginning inventory plus purchases...........		$65,120	41.58	$38,040
Markdowns.............................		255		
		64,865	41.35	
Less:				
Employees' discounts...............	$ 75			
Other discounts...................	20			
Shortages.......................	150	245		
		64,620		
Less: Sales............................		54,620		
Closing inventory (retail)..................		$10,000		
Closing inventory (cost)..................				$ 5,865

A more accurate approach to recognizing the lower of cost or market for merchandise on hand would be to specifically identify those items that have been marked down below cost in order to provide the necessary reserve to reduce the overall value of the inventories to the lower of cost or market.

Where selling prices have been reduced, the calculation will approximate cost only if appropriate allowance for price reductions is included in fixing the gross profit margin to be deducted. If no such allowance is made, the result of the calculation will tend to approximate replacement price. This difference in result is specifically recognized in the federal income tax regulations (section 1.471–8 of Appendix C). The regulations provide that a taxpayer using the LIFO inventory method in conjunction with retail computations must adjust retail selling prices for markdowns as well as markups, in order that there may be reflected the approximate cost of the goods on hand regardless of market values. This tax consideration is discussed in Chapter 14.

PHYSICAL INVENTORIES

Physical inventories should be taken at least once a year either on or near to the fiscal year-end, commonly January 31. Some stores follow the practice of taking an interim physical inventory at midyear. Others take interim physical inventories for only specific departments whose shortage or overage at a previous fiscal year-end was not fully explained. The inventory control records may or may not be adjusted for these interim physical inventories. In the absence of significant recurring differences at the time of the physical inventories there is a question as to whether the expense of interim physical inventories is justified by the benefits derived. However, interim physical inventories are usually taken when a change in a departmental buyer occurs, in order to establish a sound inventory for the new buyer. Also certain "trouble departments" may be inventoried regularly at the end of each month or thirteen-week operating period.

Even where unit control or perpetual inventory records are maintained, it may not be practical to maintain such records for all departments. A continuous record of units on hand, however, is generally considered important for departments handling merchandise with relatively high unit value. Furthermore, the information available from perpetual inventory card records is valuable from a management viewpoint where style, model, or color are of prime significance.

Merchandise is marked when placed in stock with a ticket, tag, or sticker to indicate the retail value. When markdowns are taken, the original retail price may be crossed out by a marking pencil and the reduced retail price marked in, or the original marker may be removed entirely and a new one substituted. Stores differ as to the manner of marking merchandise, and more than one plan may be in effect in the same store.

In addition to the retail value, the marker will have sundry symbols imprinted thereon. Again, no one rule necessarily applies even within a given store; but these symbols may reveal, in code form, such information as the date the merchandise was purchased, the manufacturer or supplier, and the individual classification within a department. A buyer for the Sporting Goods Department may desire to have a recapitulation of his departmental inventory by basketball, football, baseball, golf, fishing, and similar equipment, and, by means of a coding system, this may be accomplished.

The physical inventories are generally taken under the supervision and instructions of the controller's department by sales employees of the particular department, with additional help as required. The record of the count is made on prenumbered inventory sheets appropriately identified as to department and location of merchandise. Columns are provided to record the age of merchandise, classification, description, quantity, and retail value. Like items, with the same date of purchase and same retail value, are usually counted and entered in total; however, like items with the same retail value but with different dates of purchase are listed by groups according to age of merchandise.

Upon completion of the inventory, all sheets are accounted for and turned over to the controller's department. The clerical work involved in extending, footing, and summarizing the inventories is frequently performed by outside help either with the aid of comptometers or tabulating equipment. The total retail value of each department's inventory is completed first. Next, an age analysis may be prepared, for example, 0-6 months old; 7-12 months, 13-18 months, and over 18 months. Finally, if the departmental buyer has requested it, the inventories will be summarized in classification groupings.

Aside from the grand total of the inventory, the other statistical information is not required by the controller's department for comparing with book controls; however, the age analysis is very useful in comparing the age with previous inventories. It affords management and the departmental buyer with an instrument to appraise the over-all inventory and determine policy in respect of disposing of old merchandise, and to some extent it provides the basis for an appraisal of the buyer's efforts.

The inventory, stated at retail, is then compared with the Departmental Inventory Control previously explained. To make the proper comparison, the deduction for provision for shortage is added back to the amount of inventory computed at retail. The true shortage is thus obtained. Investigation of unusual shortages or overages is required in order to establish responsibility and to provide for corrective measures.

The final physical inventory at retail is entered on the inventory control form at the fiscal year-end closing, and the difference between the actual shortage and the shortage provided for during the year is taken into account. Should the physical inventory be taken at a date other than a month end, it is essential that proper cutoffs be made of sales, purchases, markdowns, and all the other information necessary to construct an inventory as of the date of the physical count.

SELECTION OF DEPARTMENTS

The type and extent of departmentalization in a retail establishment is generally an expression of the business management and merchandising policies of the retailer. Management usually controls operations by assigning responsibility to individual buyers for specific classes of merchandise, for example, women's wear, sporting goods, major appliances, and the like. The buyer is responsible for purchasing merchandise and the control of inventory quantities. Depending upon the circumstances, he may individually, or with the aid of a department manager, control the selling and operational functions of the department. This pattern of management is evident to the consumer as he visits the various departments of a large retail store. Where management reporting follows assigned responsibilities, inventory control follows the same lines.

Although a precisely uniform markup percentage is seldom used, the markup on different classes of merchandise tends to fall within a limited range. The retail method is an averaging process, and it is desirable for calculations of markup percentages to be made for groups of merchandise with similar characteristics. In general, these group classifications follow the departmental lines. If departmental responsibilities cover a class of merchandise with several price lines and varying markups, retail inventory calculations along price lines may be necessary to give proper recognition to the averaging process. In other instances, it may be possible to group certain departments that have merchandise with similar characteristics.

COMPARISON WITH OTHER METHODS

Although the retail inventory method is widely applied by retail organizations, other methods are used and may be more appropriate in certain circumstances.

The simplest of these alternative procedures is the physical inventory method whereby cost of sales is determined periodically by computation, that is, beginning inventory, plus purchases, less ending inventory. No record is made in the inventory account of current transactions as they occur. The summaries of sales and purchases and periodic physical inventories are the essentials required for the determination of income. This procedure is most effective from a management control viewpoint when physical inventories are frequently taken—monthly, weekly, or even daily—which may be practical in small or specialized businesses where the inventory is limited and can be compiled readily (e.g., cigar stands, taverns, small grocery stores and restaurants).

The specific cost method, whereby book inventory controls are established on a unit-cost basis, may be preferable for retail operations which have only a few types of merchandise with a limited number of price lines. Examples of merchandise for which this procedure may be practical include pianos, automobiles, phonograph records, and expensive furs.

Purchases, including transportation, are added to the beginning inventory, and from this total are deducted the cost of goods sold and any markdowns required by the fact that the market value of the units on hand is less than cost. There are numerous ways in which this cost method may be operated to permit a determination of the cost of the units sold. A two-part price tag with the cost indicated in code may be placed on the merchandise and removed at the time of sale. As an alternative to the coded cost, there may be a reference on the detachable portion of the price tag to the page in the unit-control record where cost information is available.

A cumulative book inventory record is maintained showing the cost of the units on hand and the amount of any markdowns recorded to recognize a lower market value. This book inventory is checked by the taking of physical inventories on a periodic basis or as may be practical.

Although another procedure may be appropriate in certain instances, the reasons for the popularity of the retail method include:

1. Physical inventories are taken at retail prices, which is generally much easier than obtaining cost prices.
2. The accounting system can accommodate any volume of transactions with ease.
3. The method allows for the periodic determination of inventories and profits without the necessity of taking a physical inventory.
4. Identification and segregation of stock shortages by departments is simplified.
5. The effect of markdowns on departmental profits is readily ascertainable.

The retail method is recognized as an acceptable inventory procedure in each of the statements attached as appendices, even though the amount assigned to any particular inventory is merely an approximation of the amount which might be arrived at under a method that determines the actual cost of merchandise on hand. The accuracy of the retail method in approximating actual cost depends to a large extent on the care taken in designing the system so that items with similar markup percentages are included in departmental groupings. Probably the most frequent inaccuracy in applying the retail method occurs from mixing high volume, low markup items in the same retail grouping as items that have a higher markup and lower volume. Because the high volume, low markup items would tend to reduce the computed markup percentage for the grouping, its application to the retail value of merchandise on hand (which would probably have a higher proportionate value of slower moving, high markup items) would tend to overstate the true cost of the merchandise.

FOURTEEN

Adapting LIFO to the Retail Method

The procedures for adapting the LIFO concept to the determination of amounts to be assigned to retail store inventories were developed to meet a specific business need. It was necessary to superimpose the LIFO principle upon the highly specialized costing system commonly referred to as the "retail inventory method" described in Chapter 13. This is generally done by adjusting for price fluctuations through application of a series of nationwide price indexes supplied by the Bureau of Labor Statistics of the U.S. Department of Labor to the total dollar value of each departmental inventory.

The LIFO problem peculiar to retailers basically arose from the fact that there is rarely a record of the specific cost for individual inventory items. Having thousands of different items in various departments, and selling them at a rapid rate of turnover for a relatively small dollar amount per item and per transaction has generally rendered impractical the maintennance of inventory accounting records on a unit-cost basis, as would be required to apply either unit or conventional dollar value LIFO. The retail inventory method was developed many years ago to cope with just this situation, and, through the use of government supplied indexes, has been adapted to the LIFO concept.

Fundamentally, the retail method consists of accumulating the aggregate retail value of all items in a department at the inventory date and reducing this departmental total to its estimated cost determined by applying an adjustment representing the average gross markup for the year on that department's goods. The LIFO calculations may be made at the end of interim accounting periods or only once a year. If the LIFO calculations are made on an interim basis, care must be taken so as not to recognize the effect of a decrement in a LIFO pool if no decrement is anticipated at the end of the year. LIFO interim reporting considerations are discussed in Chapter 8 beginning at page 166. The discussion and examples which follow are based upon methods used by a fairly large and reasonably typical department store for which the records are maintained throughout the year on the retail method, and at the close of the year the LIFO computations are made to adjust the amount assigned to the inventory from current cost to cost on the LIFO basis.

DETERMINING CHANGE IN QUANTITY OF GOODS IN THE INVENTORY

The procedures usually followed by retailers on LIFO rely upon an approximation of the extent of changes in *physical quantities* of the goods represented by inventory dollar amounts through the use of a retail price index. The purpose of this index is to eliminate from inventory dollar amounts the effect of year-to-year price changes so that inventories of different periods may be reduced to a comparable price base. Once the price difference factor has been eliminated by the index, the differences between dollar amounts of inventories are considered to reflect quantity changes.

The Treasury Department has approved a series of price indexes for federal income tax purposes based on data furnished by the Bureau of Labor Statistics. Because of the IRS book-tax conformity requirements relative to the use of LIFO, the same indexes are also used for computing the LIFO inventory values for financial reporting purposes. To January 1954, an index was computed for each of ten groups, two combinations of groups, and a store total. In January 1954, the former groups were revised into twenty-one departmental groups, including one group for which no index is computed. Each of the modified groups was identified with one of the former groups, however, to permit continuity. The indexes are all stated in terms of January 1941, equaling 100.

Generally recognized departments as established by the Controllers Congress of the National Retail Merchants Association constitute the basis for the B.L.S. groups. On pages 312–13 are listed the B.L.S. groups for which price data are provided semiannually, with an indication of the corresponding departments recommended by the Controllers Congress. For departments included in the group for which no specific index is computed, the Treasury Department has approved the use of a storewide index. The store total index reflects data on a national basis for all departments, including some not listed separately, with the following exceptions: candy, foods, liquor, tobacco, paints, and wallpaper, as well as contract departments.

It should be noted that B.L.S. indexes are issued semiannually as of January 15 and July 15, and the mid-month figure of January 15, for example, may be used at December 31 or January 31.

Use of the B.L.S. indexes is generally considered restricted to department stores employing the retail method of inventory valuation. Department stores or departments of retail stores using some other-than-retail method of valuation may elect LIFO and find the dollar-value principle discussed in Chapter 12 provides the most convenient and practical procedure for costing the inventory for LIFO purposes. It may be easier, however, to compute the retail value of the inventory than to make extensions of inventory quantities at the unit costs prevailing at a basic LIFO date. Under such circumstances, where the cost and retail value of each year-end inventory can be determined (which will permit a computation of the gross profit percentage for each department for the year), consideration might be given to using the B.L.S. price index to determine a cost price index and the relative inventory quantities from year to year. Such possible uses of B.L.S. price indexes are discussed in the concluding sections of this chapter in connection with the comments relative to inventories of specialty and variety stores.

Since the tabulations published by the Bureau of Labor Statistics all use January 1941 as the base year, taxpayers electing LIFO in subsequent years must compute their own cumulative percentage of price change from the beginning of the year in which LIFO was adopted for the respective departments. The government statistics do show the percentage of price change during the year. If LIFO was adopted for a piece goods department commencing with the fiscal year ended January 31, 1974, the cumulative price change from 1941 to the beginning of the year of LIFO election (February 1, 1973) would be read from the government tables to be 226.3%, and the price change during the year ended January 31, 1974 would be read from the tables to be 15.5%. In the computations 100% will be used for the inventory at the beginning of the 1974 fiscal year. The price index at January 31, 1974 will be 115.5 (100.0%) + (100.0% × 15.5%), and the cumulative price index at January 31, 1975, will be 121.4 (115.5%) + (115.5% × 5.1%). The commonly used form of work sheet hereafter explained for the compilation of LIFO inventories by departments is designed to provide for the cumulative computation of the price change regardless of the year for which LIFO is first used. The same result can also be obtained by dividing the index for the end of the year of adoption and for each subsequent year end by the index at the beginning of the year of adoption of LIFO. In our example above, the compu-

Grouping of Controllers Congress Departments for Purposes of Inventory Price Indexes

B.L.S. Group No.	Name	Pre-1954 Controllers Congress Department[1] No.	Name	Revised Controllers Congress Department No.	Name
I.	Piece goods	11.	Silks, velvets, and synthetics (I)	11–00	Piece goods
		12.	Woolen dress goods (I)		
		13.	Wash goods and linings (I)		
II.	Domestics and draperies	14.	Linens (I)	15–00	Household textiles
		15.	Domestics—muslins, sheetings, etc. (I)	64–11	Curtains, draperies, and decorator fabrics
		18.	Blankets, comfortables, and spreads (I)		
		74.	Draperies, curtains, and upholstery (I)		
III.	Women's and children's shoes	47.	Women's and children's shoes (II)	39–00	Women's and children's shoes
IV.	Men's and boys' shoes	67.	Men's and boys' shoes (II)	53–00	Men's and boys' shoes
V.	Infants' wear	43.	Infants' wear (III)	44–12	Infants, apparel and furniture
VI.	Women's underwear	36.	Corsets and brassieres (III)	36–00	Corsets and brassieres
		38.	Knit underwear (III)	38–00	Underwear and negligees
		39.	Silk and muslin underwear and slips (III)		
		42.	Negligees and robes (III)		
VII.	Women's and girls' hosiery	37.	Women's and children's hosiery (III)	37–00	Women's and children's hosiery
VIII.	Women's and girls' accessories	31.	Neckwear and scarfs (X)	32–00	Neckwear and accessories
		33.	Handkerchiefs (X)	33–00	Handbags and small leathers
		35.	Women's and children's gloves (X)	35–00	Women's and children's gloves and mittens
		46.	Handbags and small leather goods (X)		
IX.	Women's outerwear and girls' wear	34.	Millinery (IV)	34–00	Millinery
		51.	Women's and misses' coats and suits (IV)	41–00	Coats and suits, women's, misses', and juniors'
		52.	Junior miss coats, suits, and dresses (IV)	42–00	Dresses, women's, misses', and juniors'
		53.	Women's and misses' dresses (IV)	45–00	Housedresses, aprons, and uniforms
		54.	Blouses, skirts, and sportswear (IV)	43–00	Blouses and sportswear
		55.	Girl's wear (IV)	46–00	Furs
		57.	Aprons, housedresses, and uniforms (IV)	44–11	Girls' and teen-age apparel
		59.	Furs (IV)		
X.	Men's clothing	61.	Men's clothing (V)	51–11 or {51–14, 51–26	Men's clothing / Men's clothing, Men's sport clothing
XI.	Men's furnishings	62.	Men's furnishings (V)	51–12 or {51–15, 51–27	Men's furnishings / Men's furnishings, Men's casual furnishings
		65.	Men's hats (V)		

XII. Boys' clothing and furnishings	66C. Boys' clothing (V)	52–00 Boys' clothing and furnishings
	66F. Boys' furnishings (V)	
XIII. Jewelry and silverware	25S. Silverware and clocks (IX)	24–00 Jewelry and silverware
	25C. Costume jewelry (IX)	
	25F. Fine jewelry and watches (IX)	
XIV. Notions	21. Laces, trimmings, and ribbons (IX)	12–00 Patterns
	23. Notions (IX)	21–00 Notions, laces, trimmings, and ribbons
	26. Umbrellas (IX)	25–00 Art needlework
	27. Art needlework (IX)	31–00 Umbrellas
XV. Toilet articles and drugs	24. Toilet articles and drug sundries (IX)	22–00 Toilet articles and drug sundries
XVI. Furniture and bedding	71M. Mattresses, springs, and studio beds (VI)	61–00 Furniture and beds
	71U. Upholstered furniture (VI)	
	71O. Other furniture (VI)	
XVII. Floor covering	72. Oriental rugs (VII)	62–00 Oriental rugs
	73. Domestic floor covering (VII)	63–00 Domestic floor covering
XVIII. Housewares	76. China and glassware (VII)	65–00 China, glassware, and gift shop
	78. Housewares (VII)	66–21 Housewares
	79. Gift shop (VII)	67–00 Pictures, frames, and mirrors
	81. Pictures, frames, and mirrors (VII)	
XIX. Major appliances	75. Lamps and shades (VIII)	64–12 Lamps and shades
	77. Major appliances (VIII)	66–12 Major appliances
XX. Radios and television sets	84. Radios, phonographs, and records (VIII)	68–00 Radio, television, and records
XXI. No separate index computed	28. Books and stationery (XI)	69–00 Pianos and musical instruments
	91. Toys and games (XI)	26–00 Books and stationery
	92S. Sporting goods (XI)	66–22 Wallpaper and paint
	92C. Cameras and photographic equipment (XI)	71–00 Flower shop
	93. Luggage (XI)	72–00 Automobile accessories
		73–00 Pet accessories and pet shop
		74–00 Toys, sporting goods, and cameras
		75–00 Luggage
		76–00 Candy
		77–00 Foods and groceries
		78–00 Fresh and smoked meats
		79–00 Liquor shop
		81–00 Smoke shop

[1] Roman numerals in parentheses represent pre-1954 B.L.S. group with which the department was identified.

tation would be 261.4% (index for January 1974 from the government tables), divided by 226.3% or 115.5%.

In practically all instances the actual departmentalization of retail inventories is in accord with an accepted grouping for which a specific index is computed by the Bureau of Labor Statistics. In diversified goods departments, particularly in small branch stores, the selection of the index requires careful thought. Generally the index applicable to the major portion of the inventory in the department is used for LIFO computation purposes. In cases where there is no one major class of inventory in the department, the soft goods total index, the durable goods total index, or the storewide index may be appropriate.

COMPUTATION OF LIFO INVENTORIES

The steps involved in the application of LIFO to retail inventories can best be shown by an example with supporting explanations, but the following basic principles concerning the combining of LIFO computations with the retail inventory method are significant:

1. Each closing departmental inventory at *retail value* is reduced to its base-year price level (the year the department elected LIFO) by the application of the B.L.S. index number appropriate for the merchandise group within which the departmental goods may be generally classified. This process eliminates the effect of price changes from the base year to the current year and puts the base year and current year on a comparable dollar basis.

2. The closing *retail* inventory is adjusted to eliminate price changes and is compared with the previous year's closing *retail* value (also at the base-year price level).

   a) If this comparison indicates an increase in inventory, such increase, for LIFO purposes, is considered an increase in physical quantity and is multiplied by the index number applicable to the current year to get the retail value of the increase.

   b) If this comparison indicates a decrease in inventory, for LIFO purposes, it is considered a decrease in physical quantity and to have come from the most recently added merchandise. Therefore, deductions to cover the decrease are made from the latest period in which there were additions to inventory and at the prices at which they were previously added to the retail value of the inventory. If there have been no increases, the deductions are taken from the base year at the base retail prices.

3. The adjusted increase or decrease in a retail layer on a LIFO basis is then reduced to LIFO cost through the use of the applicable cost complement percentage (the complement of the departmental "net" markon) for the current year if an increase; for the year(s) of the latest offsetting

addition(s) if a decrease. It should be noted that IRS regulations require the recognition of the effect of markdowns in the computation of the markon percentage.

4. The adjusted increase or decrease in (3) above (now reduced to LIFO cost) is applied to the closing LIFO inventory of the previous year to obtain the LIFO closing inventory of the current year.

5. The current cost of the inventory under the retail method as determined by the inventory control records is compared with the LIFO closing inventory figure obtained in (4) above. The difference is the cumulative LIFO adjustment at that year end and represents the net difference between LIFO and FIFO since the base year.

6. The cumulative LIFO adjustment at the end of the current year is compared with the cumulative LIFO adjustment at the end of the previous year, and the difference represents the annual LIFO adjustment which is the effect on pre-tax income for the current year.

Several basic forms of work sheets have been developed to accumulate the LIFO calculations by departments by years. Some contain slight variations in presentation of figures, but they all produce the same answer, that is, the LIFO cost of the merchandise inventory determined by application of the retail method of accounting. Two forms have been included herein for illustrative purposes, but the explanatory comments which follow are directed toward the first of these forms. It will be seen that the second type (page 318) is similar to the first in its application. The first form will be used to illustrate the mechanics involved. On page 317 is a blank form with explanatory comments.

Since the Internal Revenue Code requires that for LIFO purposes cost be used in lieu of the lower of cost or market, a new amount must be determined, in most instances, for the closing inventory of the year prior to adoption of the LIFO basis. As discussed in Chapter 13, the retail method commonly used tends to provide for a computation of the lower of cost or market. Assuming the facts given in the following table for the woolen dress goods department, the markup percentage used at the end of the preceding fiscal year for valuing the merchandise inventory, if computed in the commonly used manner of not reflecting the effect of markdowns, would have been 41.62%.

	Retail	Cost	Markup %
Beginning inventory..........	$125,500	$ 75,551	39.80%
Purchases.................	435,200	257,520	40.83%
Inbound transportation.......		3,000	
Additional markups..........	14,961		
	$575,661	$336,071	41.62%

$575,661 − $336,071 = $239,590 ÷ $575,661 = 41.62%

However, to determine the inventory cost on the basis required for the adoption of LIFO, it is necessary to recognize the effect of markdowns taken during the year preceding its adoption. For purposes of illustration, assume the same basic figures but, in addition, assume that markdowns amounted to $31,491. The markup percentage for LIFO purposes would be computed by recognizing the markdowns, and a LIFO markup percentage of 38.24 per cent determined as follows:

	Retail	Cost	Markup %
Beginning inventory..........	$125,500	$ 75,551	39.80%
Purchases.................	435,200	257,520	40.83%
Inbound transportation.......		3,000	
Additional markups..........	14,961		
Markdowns................	(31,491)		
	$544,170	$336,071	38.24%

$$\$544,170 - \$336,071 = \$208,099 \div \$544,170 = 38.24\%$$

The closing inventory at retail (for the year preceding adoption of LIFO) aggregated $132,350, and this amount is multiplied by the cost markup complement percentage (100%—markup percentage). The computations under the commonly used retail method indicate a lower-of-cost-or-market inventory value of $77,266, while the cost for LIFO purposes is $81,739.

		Cost
Retail	%	Amount
$132,350	58.38%	$77,266 on retail basis
132,350	61.76%	81,739 on retail basis for LIFO

The cost for LIFO is $4,473 ($81,739 − $77,266) greater than the value arrived at when markdowns are not taken into consideration. An adjustment for this amount would be made for tax purposes retroactively to the close of the year preceding the adoption of LIFO and additional taxes would be payable on the resulting increase in income. For financial reporting purposes, such adjustment would have no effect on the beginning inventory or on net income for the year of the change since a deduction equal to the adjustment would be recognized for tax purposes in the year of the change.

When the LIFO work sheet is completed for the opening inventory of the base year, the form will appear as shown on page 318.

Assume next that the final inventory control records have been closed for the first LIFO year, and they show that the inventory at retail

Departmental LIFO Inventory Calculations

Line	Base year	First year	Second year	Third year	Fourth year	Fifth year	Sixth year
1—Physical retail inventory........	This represents the actual physical inventory at the end of each year at retail.						
2—Percentage of price index change for the year........	This is the percentage of price increase for the year only. Furnished by Bureau of Labor Statistics.						
3—Price index reflecting change accumulated since basic LIFO date	This is the cumulative price increase plus 100% from base period (line 2 × line 3 of previous year plus line 3 of previous year = line 3 to date). When the basic LIFO date is January or July, 1941 (or approximately such months), the price index reflecting the cumulative percentage of price change is available directly in the tables furnished by Bureau of Labor Statistics.						
4—1 ÷ 3 Retail inventory units.......	This represents actual inventory at base prices.						
5—Increase or (decrease) on base.....	Subtract line 4 from previous year figure on line 4, and result is either increase or decrease of base in units assuming that $1 equals 1 unit.						
Decrease calculation:							
A—Unit decrease..........	As any decrease will use up a full year or years plus part of a year, or only part of a year, it is only necessary to calculate the part of the year. The amount of decrease if a whole year is depleted will show on line 8 for the particular year depleted. In order to obtain the cost of the part decrease, that amount must be multiplied by the cumulative price index (line 3) for the year in which the part decrease occurs and the result multiplied by 100% minus LIFO markup (line 7) (for years of decrease).						
B—Index for decrease......							
C—A × B..........							
D—100 minus LIFO markup %......							
E—LIFO decrease..........							
F—Unit decrease..........	This space to be used only for additional decreases.						
G—Index for decrease..........							
H—F × G..........							
I—100 minus LIFO markup %......							
J—LIFO decrease..........							
6—Increase at current retail.........	As increases (line 5) are at base prices, the amount of increase must be multiplied by cumulative price index (line 3) to get the retail value of the increase for the year.						
7—Cost complement to LIFO markup %	This is the purchase markup and is computed as discussed on page 330, taking into consideration the effect of markdowns.						
8—Increase or (decrease) over base...	For increases this is line 6 × line 7. For decreases it is line E (and line J, if applicable) plus line 8 of those years decreased for the period.						
LIFO closing inventory.........	This is previous year closing inventory plus or minus line 8.						
Cost of inventory, retail method........	Obtained from inventory control record.						
Cumulative LIFO adjustment...........	Represents the net difference between LIFO and FIFO since the base year (difference between LIFO closing inventory and cost of inventory, retail method).						
Annual LIFO adjustment.............	Represents the effect on income for the current year.						

value equals $195,500. It is found that the B.L.S. index figure has increased 20.3 per cent over the 100 per cent base period index, so that the cumulative index at the end of the first year is 120.3 per cent. The ending inventory must be reduced to base price (100%) for the purpose of comparing that inventory with the beginning inventory. The reduction of the ending inventory at retail value ($195,500) to the base price is accomplished by dividing $195,500 by 120.3 per cent. The resulting amount ($162,510) reflects the ending inventory in terms of the same dollar basis as the opening inventory.

The opening inventory ($132,350) subtracted from the ending inventory at the same base year dollar value ($162,510) gives $30,160 as the increase in the ending inventory over the beginning inventory in units of base year dollars. Since this increase is stated at 100 per cent dollars and

Departmental LIFO Inventory Calculations

No. 12—Woolen Dress Goods
(Department)

Line	Base year
1—Physical retail inventory......................................	$132,350
2—Percentage of price index change for the year...................	
3—Price index reflecting change accumulated since basic LIFO date.....	100.0%
4—1 ÷ 3 Retail inventory units...................................	132,350
5—Increase or (decrease) on base...............................	—
Decrease calculation:	
A—Unit decrease...	
B—Index for decrease..	
C—A × B..	
D—100 minus LIFO markup %.....................................	
E—LIFO decrease..	
F—Unit decrease..	
G—Index for decrease..	
H—F × G..	
I—100 minus LIFO markup %.....................................	
J—LIFO decrease...	
6—Increase at current retail......................................	
7 Cost complement to LIFO markup %..........................	
8—Increase or (decrease) over base..............................	
LIFO closing inventory...	81,739
Cost of inventory, retail method...................................	77,266
Cumulative LIFO adjustment......................................	(4,473)
Annual LIFO adjustment...	(4,473)

the current index is 120.3 per cent, the 100 per cent dollars ($30,160) must be raised to the basis of 120.3 per cent dollars ($36,282) by multiplying $30,160 by 120.3 per cent. The increase of $36,282 at retail must then be reduced to cost. The markup percentage for LIFO is computed by a procedure similar to that shown for the opening inventory of the first year except that the opening inventory is not used either at retail or at cost. After making the necessary calculations the markup for LIFO purposes is determined to be 38.87 per cent. The cost complement to this markup percentage is 61.13 per cent, and the retail value of the increase ($36,282) is multiplied by the cost complement (61.13 per cent) to arrive at an increase in inventory at cost of $22,179.

There are now two "layers" of inventory. The first "layer" represents the cost of the base stock, the second represents the cost of the increase in inventory for the first LIFO year. By adding the two together, the cost under LIFO of the ending retail value inventory of $195,500 is determined to be $103,918. This figure can be compared with the value under the normal retail method which is available from the inventory control records. It is found that under the normal retail method $115,345 would be considered as representing the lower of average cost or market.

Subtracting the LIFO cost basis ($103,918) from the retail basis ($115,345), it is found that under LIFO the inventories are $11,427 less than under the retail method at the end of this first year. This requires an adjustment to the general ledger to reduce the general ledger merchandise account to cost under the LIFO basis. There are two basic ways of reducing the general ledger balance to LIFO. One method is to reduce the inventory account directly, and an entry for this purpose might be as follows:

```
P & L—Cost of merchandise sold—
    LIFO adjustment                    $11,427
        Merchandise inventory                      $11,427
```

The alternative, and more commonly used, procedure would be to provide an adjustment account which when deducted from the merchandise inventory account would equal the inventory value on the LIFO basis. Such an entry might be stated as follows:

```
P & L—Cost of merchandise sold—
    LIFO adjustment                    $11,427
        LIFO inventory adjustment                  $11,427
```

It will be observed that the cumulative effect is used as the basis for this entry, and it recognizes the effect on both the opening and closing inventories in the initial LIFO year. In all subsequent years the annual LIFO adjustment would be used as the basis for the entry.

The application of the figures stated above, which have been entered on the form on page 321, shows how the inventory work sheet would appear at the end of the first LIFO year.

Assume now that the inventory control records are closed for the second LIFO year, and the ending inventory at retail value equals $207,670. Development of the LIFO inventory at the end of the second year is illustrated on page 324. The B.L.S. index has increased 13.7 per cent as compared to the index at the end of the prior year, so there is a cumulative index at the end of the second year of 136.8 per cent. Reducing the retail value to the base period retail value level, the inventory is stated at $151,806 as compared with $162,510 at the end of the first LIFO year. This represents a decrease of $10,704 at base period retail value level.

The LIFO inventory at base period retail value level had increased $30,160 during the first year, and applying the principle of the last-in first-out method, the decrease in inventory during the second year represents a reduction from that increase. There should be entered in the first LIFO year column under the $30,160 increase, the figure of $10,704, circled and dated second LIFO year. This indicates that $10,704 of the increase during the first LIFO year was eliminated by the amount of the inventory decrease during the second LIFO year. From this point on, all entries will be made in the second LIFO year column.

The following steps are taken in determining the LIFO cost represented by the decrease in inventory. On line A is entered the $10,704 decrease. If the decrease had been greater than the increase of the prior year, only the excess would be entered here. For an example of the procedure to be followed in this type of situation, reference can be made to the decrease in the fourth year as reflected on page 326. Since the $10,704 is at the base period retail value and the decrease represents part of an increase during the first LIFO year, the cumulative index for the first LIFO year of 120.3 per cent is entered on line B. Multiplying $10,704 by 120.3 per cent, the decrease at retail value of the first year (year of the layer to which the decrease applies) is determined to be $12,877. The LIFO cost complement of 61.13 per cent, secured from line 7 of the first LIFO year column, multiplied by $12,877 determines the LIFO cost of the inventory liquidated in the second LIFO year.

The closing LIFO inventory at the end of the second year is $96,046, arrived at by deducting the cost of the liquidated inventory ($7,872) from the closing LIFO inventory at the end of the first year ($103,918). The lower of cost average or market value reflected by the inventory control records is $124,602, and the difference of $28,556 represents the cumulative LIFO adjustment. Since $11,427 of this cumulative adjustment had been reflected at the end of the first year, the entry for the second year would be as follows:

P & L—Cost of merchandise sold—		
LIFO adjustment	$17,129	
LIFO inventory adjustment		$17,129

Inasmuch as the general ledger merchandise inventory account prior to the entry above represents the value normally determined under the retail

Departmental LIFO Inventory Calculations

No. 12—Woolen Dress Goods
    (Department)

Line	Base year	First year
1—Physical retail inventory..........................	$132,350	$195,500
2—Percentage of price index change for the year.......		20.3%
3—Price index reflecting change accumulated since basic LIFO date...................................	100.0%	120.3%
4—1 ÷ 3 Retail inventory units......................	132,350	162,510
5—Increase or (decrease) on base....................	—	30,160
Decrease calculation:		
A—Unit decrease..................................		
B—Index for decrease.............................		
C—A × B..		
D—100 minus LIFO markup %........................		
E—LIFO decrease..................................		
F—Unit decrease..................................		
G—Index for decrease.............................		
H—F × G..		
I—100 minus LIFO markup %........................		
J—LIFO decrease..................................		
6—Increase at current retail........................		36,282
7—Cost complement to LIFO markup %...............		61.13%
8—Increase or (decrease) over base.................		22,179
LIFO closing inventory.............................	81,739	103,918
Cost of inventory, retail method......................	77,266	115,345
Cumulative LIFO adjustment.........................	(4,473)	11,427
Annual LIFO adjustment............................	(4,473)	15,900

method less the cumulative LIFO adjustment through the first year, after the entry the general ledger merchandise inventory account will represent the merchandise inventory on the basis of LIFO at the end of the second year.

At the end of the third year, the inventory control record showed a retail value of $236,750, and on page 324 is set forth the LIFO work sheet completed through the end of that year. It will be observed that line 4 under the third LIFO year column shows a closing inventory of $164,296 in base year retail dollars as compared with $151,806 for the previous year end, an increase of $12,490 as shown on line 5.

The cumulative effect of LIFO at the end of the third year is $37,204, and the LIFO adjustment chargeable to the third year is $8,648. The entry would be:

```
P & L—Cost of merchandise sold—
    LIFO adjustment                        $ 8,648
        LIFO inventory adjustment                    $ 8,648
```

After posting the entry to the general ledger, the merchandise inventory account balance would be $107,214.

The retail value of the closing inventory for the fourth LIFO year has been purposely assumed to reflect a reduced amount, so that the reduction, when restated in terms of the base period retail level, would not only extinguish all increases in inventories since the base year but also reduce the inventory below that of the basic date.

The starting point is again the retail value of the closing inventory, which, in this case, is shown by the inventory control records to be $196,750. This retail value is reduced by the cumulative index of 151.0 per cent to arrive at a basic price level of $130,298. Comparison with the comparable figure at the end of the third year ($164,296) reveals a reduction of $33,998 at the base-year price level. The LIFO inventory layers present in the inventory at the end of the third year are analyzed in the following tabulation:

	Retail value at base-year price	LIFO cost
Base stock still consists of..........................	$132,350	$ 81,739
During the first LIFO year there was added $30,160 and $22,179, respectively, but in the second year this increase was reduced by $10,704 and $7,872, respectively, so there is a balance of.............................	19,456	14,307
During the third LIFO year there was added $12,490 and $11,168, respectively.............................	12,490	11,168
At the end of the third LIFO year the inventory consisted of	$164,296	$107,214

In practice it is not necessary to prepare a separate table since the information is obtainable from the work sheet.

The first entries on the LIFO work sheet (page 326) are as follows:

1. Enter $12,490 circled in the third-year column under the $12,490 figure shown on line 5. Indicate to left of circled figure that entry was made at end of fourth year. Draw a double line under the circled figure to indicate that the increase in the third year has been completely liquidated and further reference to this increase is unnecessary.

2. Enter $19,456 circled under the $10,704 circled figure in the first-year column. In arriving at the $19,456 amount, it is recognized that the inventory during the first year increased $30,160 but $10,704 of this

Departmental LIFO Inventory Calculations

No. 12—Woolen Dress Goods

(Department)

Line	Base year	First year	Second year
1—Physical retail inventory..................	$132,350	$195,500	$207,670
2—Percentage of price index change for the year		20.3%	13.7%
3—Price index reflecting change accumulated since basic LIFO date..................	100.0%	120.3%	136.8%
4—1 ÷ 3 Retail inventory units...............	132,350	162,510	151,806
5—Increase or (decrease) on base	—	30,160	(10,704)
		2d LIFO (10,704) year	
Decrease calculation:			
A—Unit decrease..........................			(10,704)
B—Index for decrease......................			120.3%
C—A × B.................................			(12,877)
D—100 minus LIFO markup %...............			61.13%
E—LIFO decrease..........................			(7,872)
F—Unit decrease..........................			
G—Index for decrease......................			
H—F × G.................................			
I—100 minus LIFO markup %...............			
J—LIFO decrease..........................			
6—Increase at current retail................		36,282	
7—Cost complement to LIFO markup %........		61.13%	
8—Increase or (decrease) over base..........		22,179	(7,872)
LIFO closing inventory......................	81,739	103,918	96,046
Cost of inventory, retail method..............	77,266	115,345	124,602
Cumulative LIFO adjustment.................	(4,473)	11,427	28,556
Annual LIFO adjustment.....................	(4,473)	15,900	17,129

Departmental LIFO Inventory Calculations

No. 12—Woolen Dress Goods
(Department)

Line	Base year	First year	Second year	Third year
1—Physical retail inventory	$132,350	$195,500	$207,670	$236,750
2—Percentage of price index change for the year		20.3%	13.7%	5.3%
3—Price index reflecting change accumulated since basic LIFO date	100.0%	120.3%	136.8%	144.1%
4—1 ÷ 3 Retail inventory units	132,350	162,510	151,806	164,296
5—Increase or (decrease) on base		30,160	(10,704)	12,490
		2d LIFO (10,704) year		
Decrease calculation:				
A—Unit decrease			(10,704)	
B—Index for decrease			120.3%	
C—A × B			(12,877)	
D—100 minus LIFO markup %			61.13%	
E—LIFO decrease			(7,872)	
6—Increase at current retail		36,282		17,998
7—Cost complement to LIFO markup %		61.13%		62.05%
8—Increase or (decrease) over base		22,179	(7,872)	11,168
LIFO closing inventory	81,739	103,918	96,046	107,214
Cost of inventory, retail method	77,266	115,345	124,602	144,418
Cumulative LIFO adjustment	(4,473)	11,427	28,556	37,204
Annual LIFO adjustment	(4,473)	15,900	17,129	8,648

was liquidated in the second year; therefore, only the difference between the $30,160 and $10,704, or $19,456, can be charged to this increase. Indicate that the $19,456 represents an entry made at end of fourth year, and draw a double line under the $19,456 to indicate that entire increase of $30,160 has been liquidated.

3. At this point there has been taken into account $31,946 ($12,490 + $19,456) of the total decrease of $33,998, leaving $2,052 which is now entered in the base-year column by circling and indicating the entry was made at end of the fourth year.

The next operation is to compute the LIFO cost of these liquidations. The liquidation in the fourth year covers three different layers of inventory, and each provides slightly different considerations:

1. First to be considered is the portion of the liquidation to the LIFO layer applicable to the third year. Since it liquidates this layer completely and since the LIFO cost of the layer has been determined in the third-year computations, reference can be made to line 8 under the third-year column to find the LIFO cost was $11,168. This cost is then entered on line 8 in the fourth-year column and circled to indicate the reduction on the LIFO cost basis.

2. The next calculation required is to determine the LIFO cost of the portion of the liquidation attributable to the increase in inventory which occurred in the first year. During the second year inventories had been reduced $10,704 at the basic price level, and this reduction was applied against the LIFO layer applicable to the first year. The LIFO cost of the reduction during the second year had been computed to be $7,872. The total layer for the first year amounted to $22,179 at LIFO cost, and deducting the $7,872 from $22,179 leaves $14,307, which is determined to be the LIFO cost of the portion of the fourth-year liquidation applicable to the LIFO inventory layer remaining for the first year. This figure ($14,307) is then entered in the fourth-year column directly under the ($11,168) previously entered.

3. The last computation needed to determine the LIFO cost of inventory liquidated applies to the $2,052 liquidation at the basic price level which reduces the base stock. The computation is shown on lines A through E in the fourth-year column, and the mechanics are similar to those previously outlined in connection with computing the LIFO cost of the inventory reduction during the second year. Since it is base stock that is now being considered, the index number is 100.0 per cent. Following the computations through, it is found that the LIFO cost of the reduction in base stock is $1,267. This is entered and circled directly under ($14,307) referred to above.

The factors have now been established to determine the LIFO cost of the closing inventory. From the LIFO cost at the end of the previous year

Departmental LIFO Inventory Calculations

No. 12—Woolen Dress Goods
(Department)

Line	Base year	First year	Second year	Third year	Fourth year
1—Physical retail inventory	$132,350	$195,500	$207,670	$236,750	$196,750
2—Percentage of price index change for the year		20.3%	13.7%	5.3%	4.8%
3—Price index reflecting change accumulated since basic LIFO date	100.0%	120.3%	136.8%	144.1%	151.0%
4—1 ÷ 3 Retail inventory units	132,350	162,510	151,806	164,296	130,298
5—Increase or (decrease) on base	4th(2,052)	30,160 / 2d(10,704) / 4th(19,456)	(10,704)	12,490 / 4th(12,490)	(33,998)
Decrease calculation:					
A—Unit decrease			(10,704)		(2,052)
B—Index for decrease			120.3%		100.0%
C—A × B			(12,877)		(2,052)
D—100 minus LIFO markup %		61.13%	61.13%		61.76%
E—LIFO decrease			(7,872)		(1,267)
6—Increase at current retail		36,282		17,998	(11,168)
7—Cost complement to LIFO markup %		61.13%		62.05%	(14,307)
8—Increase or (decrease) over base		22,179	(7,872)	11,168	(1,267)
LIFO closing inventory	81,739	103,918	96,046	107,214	80,472
Cost of inventory, retail method	77,266	115,345	124,602	144,418	119,034
Cumulative LIFO adjustment	(4,473)	11,427	28,556	37,204	38,562
Annual LIFO adjustment	(4,473)	15,900	17,129	8,648	1,358

(the third year) are deducted the three decreases on the LIFO cost basis shown in the fourth-year column. When this is done, the LIFO cost of the inventory at the end of the fourth year $80,472 ($107,214 − $11,168 − $14,307 − $1,267) can be entered on the work sheet.

The inventory cost under the normal retail method, obtained from the inventory control records, is entered as $119,034, and the cumulative LIFO adjustment of $38,562 ($119,034 − $80,472) is entered on the proper line. Deducting the cumulative adjustment of $37,204 at the end of the third year from $38,562 at the end of the fourth year gives the adjustment of $1,358 required to be made at the end of the fourth year. The general ledger entry would be as follows:

P & L—Cost of merchandise sold—
    LIFO adjustment $1,358
        LIFO inventory adjustment $1,358

It will be observed from an analysis of the LIFO work sheet on page 326 that at the end of the fourth year there is only one "layer" of inventory, that being the base stock "layer," and it has been reduced from $132,350 at the basic price level in the initial LIFO year to $130,298 in terms of the same base year dollars.

The appearance of the LIFO work sheet at the conclusion of the fifth year is shown on page 328. It will be noted that the inventory increased $26,703 on the base price level over the inventory at the close of the fourth year. The entry required after the computations have been completed would be:

P & L—Cost of merchandise sold—
    LIFO adjustment $10,859
        LIFO inventory adjustment $10,859

The foregoing discussion covers the mechanics of computing the cost of inventories under the LIFO principle in most of the situations encountered. When the index decreases below that applicable to the previous year, no change in method of computation is required. The retail value is always reduced by the cumulative index to arrive at the base price level. Should the cumulative LIFO adjustment fall below the cumulative adjustment at the end of the previous year, the effect will be to increase income, or the opposite from the effect shown by the entries in the illustration.

Liquidation from time to time of one or more LIFO pools is to be expected in the retail industry. Therefore, disclosure of the effect of liquida-

Departmental LIFO Inventory Calculations

No. 12—Woolen Dress Goods
(Department)

Line	Base year	First year	Second year	Third year	Fourth year	Fifth year
1—Physical retail inventory	$132,350	$195,500	$207,670	$236,750	$196,750	$261,720
2—Percentage of price index change for the year		20.3%	13.7%	5.3%	4.8%	10.4%
3—Price index reflecting change accumulated since basic LIFO date	100.0%	120.3%	136.8%	144.1%	151.0%	166.7%
4—1 ÷ 3 Retail inventory units	132,350	162,510	151,806	164,296	130,298	157,001
5—Increase or (decrease) on base	30,160	(10,704)	12,490	(33,998)	26,703
	4th(2,052)	2d(10,704)		4th(12,490)		
		4th(19,456)				
Decrease calculation:						
A—Unit decrease			(10,704)		(2,052)	
B—Index for decrease			120.3%		100.0%	
C—A × B			(12,877)		(2,052)	
D—100 minus LIFO markup %			61.13%		61.76%	
E—LIFO decrease			(7,872)		(1,267)	
6—Increase at current retail		36,282		17,998		44,514
7—Cost complement to LIFO markup %		61.13%	62.05%	61.76%	61.85%
8—Increase or (decrease) over base		22,179	(7,872)	11,168	(11,168)	27,532
					(14,307)	
					(1,267)	
LIFO closing inventory	81,739	103,918	96,046	107,214	80,472	108,004
Cost of inventory, retail method	77,266	115,345	124,602	144,418	119,034	157,425
Cumulative LIFO adjustment	(4,473)	11,427	28,556	37,204	38,562	49,421
Annual LIFO adjustment	(4,473)	15,900	17,129	8,648	1,358	10,859

Departmental LIFO Inventory Calculations

(Alternative Form)

No. 12—Woolen Dress Goods
(Department)

Line	Base year	First year	Second year	Third year	Fourth year	Fifth year	Cumulative through fifth year
1. Opening inventory at basic price retail level		$132,350	$162,510	$151,806	$164,296	$130,298	
2. Opening inventory at LIFO		81,739	103,918	96,046	107,214	80,472	
3. Cost complement to LIFO markup %	61.76%	61.13%	N/A	62.05%	N/A	61.85%	
4. Closing inventory at retail	132,350	195,500	207,670	236,750	196,750	261,720	$261,720
5. Price index reflecting change accumulated since basic LIFO date	100%	120.3%	136.8%	144.1%	151.0%	166.7%	166.7%
6. Closing inventory at basic price retail level (4 ÷ 5)	132,350	162,510	151,806	164,296	130,298	157,001	$157,001
7. Increase or (decrease) attributable to:							
Basic inventory	132,350				(2,052)		$130,298
First year's increment		30,160			(19,456)		—
Second year's increment			(10,704)				—
Third year's increment				12,490	(12,490)		
Fourth year's increment							
Fifth year's increment					$(33,998)	$ 26,703	$ 26,703
							$157,001
8. Increase or (decrease) at prices existing when acquired	(100%) 132,350	(120.3%) 36,282	(120.3%) (12,877)	(144.1%) 17,998	(144.1%) (17,998) (120.3%) (23,405) (100%) (2,052)	(166.7%) 44,514	(166.7%) $ 44,514 (100%) 130,298
9. Cost of increases or (decreases)	(61.76%) 81,739	(61.13%) 22,179	(61.13%) (7,872)	(62.05%) 11,168	(62.05%) (11,168) (61.13%) (14,307) (61.76%) (1,267)	(61.85%) 27,532	(61.85%) 27,532 (61.76%) 80,472
10. LIFO closing inventory	81,739	103,918	96,046	107,214	80,472	108,004	108,004
11. Cost of inventory, retail method	77,266	115,345	124,602	144,418	119,034	157,425	157,425
12. Cumulative LIFO adjustment	(4,473)	11,427	28,556	37,204	38,562	49,421	49,421
13. Annual LIFO adjustment	(4,473)	15,900	17,129	8,648	1,358	10,859	49,421

329

tions (discussed in Chapter 9) would ordinarily be unnecessary unless operating results or trends are unduly affected in a particular period. On page 329 a second form of LIFO work sheet is shown which is quite similar to the previously discussed type in its application. This form is an adaptation of the method outlined in Treasury Department Mimeograph 6244, issued March 9, 1948. Some retailers consider this form preferable because the computation of the net result (cumulative column) may be readily checked on the form to uncover possible errors in the annual calculations.

The Treasury Department has approved for federal income tax purposes the following additional alternative treatments of markdowns in computing the cost complement percentage: (1) eliminate from the annual net markon computation all markdowns specifically relating to goods in the opening inventory (which may be identified by the use of seasonal letters on the markdown notices or other identification procedures) and (2) where specific segregation of markdowns is not possible, include in the computation a portion of the total markdowns in the ratio that purchases at retail for the period relate to the opening retail inventory plus purchases at retail as shown in the following formula:

$$\frac{\text{Purchases at retail}}{\substack{\text{Opening inventory} \\ \times \text{ purchases}}} \times \text{Total markdowns}$$

Application of the second of these alternative procedures to a computation of the markup percentages reflected by the factors in the examples on pages 301 and 302 may be illustrated as follows:

Determining Markup Percentage by Adjusting Markups for Proportion of Markdowns

	Retail	Markup %	Cost
Beginning inventory..............	$ 6,220	40.52	$ 3,700
Purchases	58,795		34,040
Freight and express.............	—		300
Additional markups..............	150		—
Retail adjustments...............	(45)		—
	58,900		
Markdowns— $\frac{58,900}{65,120} \times \$255$..............	231		—
Current-year purchases..........	$58,669	41.47	$34,340

On the basis of the foregoing, the cost complement percentage for the year is 58.53 per cent. As stated on page 319, the markup percentage for LIFO purposes is computed without the use of the opening inventory.

The procedures described in this chapter and commonly used by retailers have the effect of pricing LIFO inventory increments at the average cost for the year during which the increment occurred. The general provisions of the federal income tax regulations are to the effect that taxpayers have a right of election to cost inventory increments by reference to earliest or latest purchases in the year, as alternatives to the average cost. The available statistics lend themselves to developing such alternative procedures, and they should receive careful consideration.

IN-TRANSIT AND WAREHOUSE INVENTORIES

Inventory in transit and in warehouses at the end of each year will ordinarily be treated under the LIFO method the same as all other merchandise owned by the taxpayer. The usual practice is to record such goods as a part of each department's inventory and include it in the computation of the markon percentage. The data used in determining in-transit inventory at the year end are frequently obtained by an analysis of the departmental purchase ledgers and unposted invoices in the following month, and a journal entry made to set up the amount of the inventory and the liability for its cost. This year-end entry may be reversed in the month following closing, since the shipments will be included in the regularly compiled total purchases. The in-transit and warehouse inventories are used in the departmental LIFO work sheets but do not appear as a separate item.

The inclusion of the in-transit inventory increases the departmental merchandise pools and provides a larger base. In some instances, however, retailers have chosen to ignore in-transit goods for LIFO purposes and merely show the total in-transit inventory cost as an addition to inventory in a manner similar to stores not on LIFO. If a consistent practice is followed, the Treasury Department representatives should have no objection regardless of which procedure is followed. The same latitude is not generally recognized, however, as regards warehouse stock. Even though a consistent practice is followed, the facility with which goods could be transferred from the warehouse inventory (if it is carried at specific invoice cost) to the store inventory (where it enters into the retail computation) places the control of the inventory in the hands of the retailer almost as a matter of compilation of figures rather than as a result of the exercise of business judgment in the timing of merchandise purchases.

Regardless of the benefits which may flow from including the in-transit inventory in the LIFO base, situations have arisen in practice where, at the time it was decided that the LIFO method would be adopted (generally near or after the end of the year), there was no practical procedure by which the cost of the goods in transit at the beginning of the year could be classified by departments. Wherever the possibility of adopting LIFO can be anticipated, it may be advisable currently to analyze the in-transit inventory on a departmental basis even though there would be no advantage therefrom if the ultimate decision is against adoption of LIFO. If this is not practicable, there is no reason why LIFO cannot be extended to cover the in-transit inventory at the end of the year. The result would merely be to have the in-transit merchandise reflected in the LIFO inventory as a factor determining an increase or decrease for the year rather than as part of the LIFO base. Procedurally, an additional election on Treasury Department Form 970 should be filed with the federal income tax return covering the year for which in-transit merchandise is first included in the LIFO computations of both the beginning and ending inventories. The LIFO method can thus be extended to cover the in-transit inventory at any time at the retailer's election, but if the election is once made a consistent practice must be subsequently followed.

In many cases the retail value of the in-transit inventory is not specifically computed, but the amount to be used in the LIFO computations as the retail value is determined by applying to the cost the markon percentage for the month following the close of the year. There are also circumstances where this procedure can appropriately be followed with respect to the warehouse stock.

RESERVE FOR CASH DISCOUNTS

Fundamentally, the reserve for cash discounts represents a valuation account which reduces inventory to the cost after discounts have been taken into account. Department stores normally post their purchase invoices before discount, the effect of which overstates the true cost. The conventional method is to maintain a reserve for discount for each department on the basis of experience, and the actual discount is taken up when earned.

The treatment of cash discount reserves for LIFO purposes varies with retailers and is not too significant in relation to other LIFO factors. A good theoretical, but generally impractical, treatment is to include in each departmental inventory layer a portion of the discount reserve applicable to that year. This, of course, involves additional calculations and record-keeping. Among alternative practical procedures is to deduct the discount reserve (at retail) from the closing retail inventories *before* application of the LIFO computation. The effect of this procedure is to take into consideration a logical reduction in the inventory for cash discounts without getting involved in computations that would produce immaterial adjustments. Another practice is to ignore the effect of the reserve for cash discounts for LIFO purposes and compute LIFO on the "gross" cost. In the departmental operating statements for some stores, however, the discount earned is offset against the cost of sales to determine the gross margin.

LIFO GROUPINGS ON DEPARTMENTAL BASIS

As previously noted, department stores are required generally to make separate LIFO computations for each department even though the same price index will be applied to several of the departments. For LIFO purposes, a department is commonly regarded as being comprised of any group of merchandise items for which a separate stock ledger is maintained under the retail inventory method. As with other accounting and tax questions, however, recognition must be given to the circumstances of each individual case, and a sounder application of the LIFO principle may result from the combining of several departments into a single LIFO group. Approximately ninety departments in one store were found to be susceptible of classification into less than forty groups for which the LIFO computations were made. Combining of inventories with from one to five other departments was appropriate for approximately 80 per cent of the total number. The prime consideration in combining the departments was the interchangeability of merchandise for sale, although such factors as price range, homogeneity of buying or merchandising control, and department location afforded some support for certain combinations. Examples of groupings include the combining of basement departments with regular store departments selling like goods and the pooling of summer furniture with regular furniture. Generally, in the case of retailers operating several stores in different locations, the similar departments should be combined for LIFO purposes in order to preserve, through offsets, the base inventory volume of layers which might be lost in yearly fluctuations of individual departments.

A retailer need not place all his departmental inventories on LIFO; but once the LIFO method is elected for a particular department, it may not be changed without permission from the Commissioner of Internal Revenue. Certain "cost" and "contract" departments (e.g., alteration and wholesale departments) usually do not determine their inventories under the retail method or use LIFO, but the great majority of other departments are suitable for LIFO.

Based on forecasts of price movements in particular lines of goods and the extent of turnovers and resultant inventory changes, management must decide which departments will apply the LIFO principle. Some retailers who adopted LIFO in 1941 excluded from their election such departments as electrical appliances, hosiery, and toys because of the uncertainty of war restrictions and government allocations. The greatest tax benefit from LIFO is secured if the election is made when faced with increasing prices and taxes; however, an actual tax detriment may be sustained if income deferred by reason of applying LIFO must be recognized because of an inventory liquidation in a higher tax-rate year.

Continuity of departments is a problem that arises frequently with retailers. In the usual department store there are frequent changes in departmental structure, due to establishing new departments, discontinuing old departments, and combining or subdividing existing departments. Continuity may also be affected by leasing a department or otherwise placing its operations in the hands of a concessionaire. Conversely, a retailer may take over a department which has been operated by a concessionaire.

The problem created by lack of continuity is especially significant since, under the retail method, there is no specific identity of goods and dollar units only are used.

If the election is made to put a new department on LIFO, the base is established by using the year-end figures for the inventory and price level as of the beginning of the initial LIFO year for the new department, and subsequent quantity and price-level changes are determined from this base. The discontinuance of a department results in reflecting in the income statement the departmental cumulative LIFO adjustment.

Combining two or more existing departments after a period of operation of LIFO can be achieved by combining the corresponding dollar figures to date for each departmental retail layer. Each retail layer making up the total remains intact on the combined basis; but it is necessary to recompute the LIFO markon complement percentage, using the combined figures. In most cases the departments being combined will be similar, at least to the extent that they have been within the same B.L.S. price index grouping; however, the same procedure can be used in the case of two departments in different price index groups. The index covering the greater portion of the merchandise would be used for the department after the consolidation.[1]

---

[1] The procedure for combining dollar-value LIFO pools is commented upon in section 1.472–8 (g) (2) of the regulations, Appendix C.

Continuing to record the data on a combined basis after a previously existing department has been split may be the only practical procedure. This is a logical exception to the general rule that each departmental computation should be carried out separately. If separate computations are to be made, however, each of the LIFO inventory layers may be apportioned on the basis of the relative volume of the inventories of the split departments at the time of the separation.[2]

SPECIALTY STORES

Every retail store does not automatically qualify as a department store under the rulings which have been used by the Treasury Department with respect to the use of the B.L.S. price indexes. Generally, a retail store may use the B.L.S. indexes for federal income tax purposes if it has a reasonable number and variety of departments and if the goods carried in the various departments are reasonably similar to those carried in the corresponding departments by a typical department store in the particular locality. It is not necessary that all the departments of the most elaborate store be represented.

The Treasury Department has not yet conceded that an extremely specialized store carrying a single line of goods, such as a shoe store, a radio and television store, or an electrical appliance store, could elect LIFO and use a single B.L.S. index. In such a situation the burden would be upon the retailer to show that the B.L.S. index is adequately representative of its whole inventory. On the other hand, a retail establishment known in the trade as a *specialty store*, may use the appropriate B.L.S. index if it employs the retail inventory method and its departmental inventories are reasonably similar to those carried by department stores. Types of recognized specialty stores include establishments carrying a variety of ladies' wear and accessories or men's clothing and furnishings, or a reasonably full line of furniture and home furnishings.

There have been cases where specialty stores chose to use the B.L.S. indexes even though the inventory records are kept on the basis of cost, rather than the retail method. For this purpose cost price indexes may be computed from the department store inventory (retail) price indexes. The theory is that the difference between the movements of wholesale (or cost) and retail prices for any given year will be reflected in a change in the markon percentage. If the markon is uniform within any particular de-

---

[2] This procedure for separating a dollar-value LIFO pool is illustrated in section 1.472–8 (g) (2) (ii) of the regulations.

partment or line of merchandise, the cost and retail prices for the goods handled will necessarily change in the same relative amount.

The computed cost indexes for various inventory dates will be equal to the retail price indexes multiplied by the fraction representing the ratio of the cost percentages. A good merchandiser will know his average net markon and cost percentages even though he does not use the retail method. The LIFO inventory computations in this situation may be illustrated as follows:

	Base year	First year	Second year
Cost indexes:			
1. Retail price index..................	100	105	115
2. Net markon %.....................	40.5%	42.0%	39.1%
3. Cost %...........................	59.5%	58.0%	60.9%
4. Ratio of cost %...................	59.5/59.5	58.0/59.5	60.9/59.5
5. Cost index (1 × 4)................	100	102.3	117.7
LIFO inventories:			
6. Inventory at cost (FIFO)...........	$50,000	$70,000	$55,000
7. Inventory at base-year cost (6 ÷ 5 × 100)..................	$50,000	$68,426	$46,729

8. LIFO inventories—

$50,000 × 100 =	$50,000		
$50,000 × 100 =		$50,000	
18,426 × 102.3 =		18,850	
$68,426 =		$68,850	
$46,729 × 100 =			$46,729

The net markon and cost percentages (lines 2 and 3 above) are determined for each department on the basis of the retailer's own average for the year. These percentages will be based upon the year's sales (rather than being based upon purchases as under the retail inventory method), but any differences will tend to average out over a few years.[3]

VARIETY STORES

For June and December, 1953, the Treasury Department published special price indexes for use by *variety stores*. These establishments are those engaged primarily in selling at retail a variety of merchandise in the low and popular price ranges, such as stationery, gift items, women's acces-

[3] The application of B.L.S. indexes to specialty stores is discussed in Rev. Rul. 23, 1953–1 C.B. 34; and Rev. Rul. 54–49, 1954–1 C.B. 32.

sories, toilet articles, light hardware, toys, housewares, confectionary, and so forth. They are commonly known as *5 and 10 cent stores* and *5 cents to a dollar stores*, although higher-priced merchandise is usually carried.

Twenty-seven departments were grouped for the purpose of establishing eleven B.L.S. indexes in a manner somewhat similar to the indexes for retail department stores. The use of the indexes was not mandatory; and for federal income tax purposes stores were permitted to prepare their own indexes provided sound statistical methods were used. When the Bureau of Labor Statistics discontinued publication of variety store inventory price indexes, retailers were permitted to use indexes prepared from their own data.[4]

---

[4] The development of price indexes for variety stores is discussed in Rev. Rul. 54–63, 1954–1 C.B. 33; and Rev. Rul. 55–220, 1955–1 C.B. 247.

FIFTEEN

Certain Considerations— Generally Accepted Accounting Principles

As mentioned in the first chapter, Chapter 4 of ARB 43 (issued in 1953) is the authoritative pronouncement regarding "inventory pricing." Subsequent to the issuance of ARB 43, there have been pronouncements of the AICPA Committee on Accounting Procedures and its successor organizations—the Accounting Principles Board and Financial Accounting Standards Board—and by the Securities and Exchange Commission which must be considered if inventory accounting and financial reporting are to conform with generally accepted accounting principles (GAAP).

Throughout this book references are made to various GAAP requirements. The purpose of this chapter is to discuss certain GAAP requirements not treated elsewhere and to direct the reader's attention to important GAAP considerations in other chapters.

ARB 43 was issued over twenty-five years ago. Since then, many authoritative bulletins, opinions, statements, releases, and interpretations relating to GAAP have been issued in the United States. Not all of them relate to or affect accounting for inventories. Set forth below is a listing of the pronouncements that are believed to be pertinent to current accounting for and reporting of inventories and inventory transactions.

Number and Title	Issue Date	Subject Matter Relating to Inventories
Accounting Research Bulletins:		
No. 45 Long-Term Construction-Type Contracts	10/55	Accounting for uncompleted contracts
51 Consolidated Financial Statements	8/59	Elimination of intercompany profits and losses
Accounting Principles Board Opinions:		
No. 16 Business Combinations	8/70	Basis of recording assets
18 Equity Method of Accounting for Investments in Common Stock [1]	3/71	Elimination of intercompany profits and losses
20 Accounting Changes [2]	7/71	Changes from one method of accounting to another
21 Interest on Receivables and Payables	8/71	Imputing interest on note exchanged for inventories
22 Disclosure of Accounting Policies	4/72	Disclosure of inventory pricing method
28 Interim Financial Reporting [3]	5/73	Determining cost of goods sold during interim periods
29 Accounting for Nonmonetary Transactions	5/73	Exchanges of nonmonetary assets, including products held for sale in the ordinary course of business for other products to be sold in the same line of business to facilitate sales to customers
30 Reporting the Results of Operations [1]	6/73	Disclosure of unusual or infrequently occurring items
Statements of Financial Accounting Standards (promulgated by the Financial Accounting Standards Board):		
No. 2 Accounting for Research and Development Costs	10/74	Elements of cost to be identified with research and development activities
3 Reporting Accounting Changes in Interim Financial Statements (an Amendment of APB Opinion No. 28)	12/74	Reporting changes to LIFO and other accounting changes in interim financial statements
8 Accounting for the Translation of Foreign Currency Transactions and Foreign Currency Financial Statements [2]	10/75	Translation of inventory
33 Financial Reporting and Changing Prices	9/79	Measuring the effects of changing prices on inventories

[1] See subsequent APB Interpretation.
[2] See subsequent FASB Interpretation.
[3] See subsequent FASB Amendment.

The following Accounting Series Releases have been issued by the Securities and Exchange Commission:

Number	Title/Subject	Issue Date
No. 138	Increased Disclosure of Unusual Charges and Credits to Income	1/73
141	Determination of Replacement or Current Cost for Disclosing Excess over Stated LIFO Value	2/73
151	Disclosure of Inventory Profits	1/74
164	Nature of Costs Accumulated in Inventories	11/74
169	Disclosure Problems Relating to Adoption of LIFO Method and SEC/IRS Agreement Relating Thereto	1/75
190	Requirement for Footnote Disclosure of Estimated Current Replacement Cost of Inventories	3/76

OTHER INFORMATION SOURCES

Other important sources of information which may be pertinent in particular fact situations include the following:

Accounting Principles Board Statement No. 4—Basic Concepts and Accounting Principles Underlying Financial Statements of Business Enterprises (10/70)

Accounting Research Study No. 13—The Accounting Basis of Inventories (published in 1973 by the AICPA)

Statements of Position (issued from time to time by the Accounting Standards Division of the AICPA)

Staff Accounting Bulletins (issued from time to time by the staff of the Securities and Exchange Commission)

Industry Audit Guides (published by the AICPA):

Audits of Government Contractors (contract costs included in inventory and financial reporting and disclosure of inventories) (1975)

Audits of Construction Contractors (accounting for and disclosure of contract costs) (1965)

INVENTORY COSTING

Chapter 4 of ARB 43, and various sections of this book, set forth general principles applicable to the determination of the cost of inventories. The principal cost methods in general usage are specific and average cost (discussed in Chapter 6), first-in first-out (FIFO), and last-in first-out (LIFO) (both discussed in Chapter 8). The LIFO method and various considerations incident to its use are also extensively discussed in Chapters

9 through 12 and in Chapter 14. Such chapters are, however, primarily in the context of tax planning and acceptability; GAAP considerations, as discussed below, may conflict with these tax objectives.

The treatment of overhead in determining inventory costs is discussed in Chapter 6. As a general rule, all usual material, labor, and overhead elements related to production should be included in inventory costs. Exceptions are rare and usually result from long-standing industry practice.

LOWER COST OR MARKET

The history, application, and other aspects of the "lower of cost or market" concept are discussed in Chapter 7. Because it is a concept that is not universally understood, the following commentary may be helpful in its application.

ARB 43, Chapter 4, Statement 6 sets forth the lower of cost or market rule in terms of current replacement cost, but paragraph 10 notes that ". . . Statement 6 is intended as a guide rather than a literal rule." Generally, in practice, the guiding principle in arriving at a market valuation is subsequent net realizability, particularly for finished goods; usually for work in progress; and not infrequently for raw materials. If there should be evidence that a drop in market quotations will reduce subsequent sales prices of a company's products, cost-to-complete will have to be estimated for raw materials and work in progress. In determining the net amount to be realized on subsequent sales, selling costs need include no items other than clearly direct items, such as shipping costs and salesmen's commissions, and no allowance need be made for an appropriate profit margin. A write-down below market, to the point of reinstating a potential normal profit margin in a subsequent period, while acceptable, is not necessarily desirable. Moreover, what might be considered "normal" is somewhat arbitrary.

Inventories may be written down to net realizable value on an item basis, by inventory product class, by disclosed class of business, or on an all-inclusive basis. Whatever method is used should be consistently applied. Inventories related to a single finished product should preferably be grouped for the purpose of evaluating the need for a market write-down. For example, there is no need to write down individual components of a particular finished product if the net realizable value of the finished product is greater than the aggregate costs of the components, the costs of production, and the direct selling expenses.

Reference should be made to the section entitled "Inventories in Translated Financial Statements" later in this chapter, for application of the lower of cost or market rule in translated financial statements.

When cost is determined on a LIFO basis and such cost exceeds the estimated net amount subsequently realizable, provision should be made to reduce the LIFO cost to market. This provision should be made through a reserve account to avoid affecting the basic LIFO cost calculations, but separate disclosure of the reserve amount in the financial statements is not required. Subsequent to providing a reserve, when market rises to the original LIFO cost, the reserve is no longer required and should be restored to income.

A write-down of LIFO cost to market in accordance with generally accepted accounting principles is not an allowable deduction for tax purposes. Questions have arisen as to whether the difference between LIFO inventories on a book versus a tax basis and the resulting difference between income reported for tax purposes and that reported to shareholders causes a potential conflict with the conformity requirements of Section 472 of the Internal Revenue Code. Such market write-downs have often been accepted by the IRS in the past, but its position has varied. It is believed that market write-downs in the financial statements are supported by a provision in the LIFO regulations which, in effect, states that a taxpayer's use of market value in lieu of cost for reporting to shareholders is not considered at variance with the conformity requirement [Reg. 1.472-2(e)]. This view was confirmed by the IRS in Revenue Ruling 77–50. However, since the conformity rules are under constant review by the IRS, it is suggested that all market write-down situations involving LIFO inventories be considered in light of more recent rulings, if any, and the income tax regulations (see Appendix D for regulations proposed on July 17, 1979).

CHANGES IN ACCOUNTING PRINCIPLES

APB Opinion No. 20 (APB 20) is the authoritative pronouncement dealing with changes in accounting principles and requires management to justify a change on the basis that the new principle is preferable. The SEC, through Accounting Series Release No. 177, has formalized the justification process beyond the disclosure requirements of APB 20. In the first quarterly report on Form 10-Q filed subsequent to the date of an accounting change, the registrant is required to include a letter from its independent accountants indicating whether the change is to an alternative principle which in their judgment is preferable under the circumstances. A preferability letter is also required to be filed with the registrant's annual report on Form 10-K when a change is adopted in the fourth fiscal quarter. No letter from the accountants need be filed when a change is made in response to a standard adopted by the FASB which requires such changes.

FASB Interpretation No. 1 deals with accounting changes related to the cost of inventory. It states that a change in the composition of inventory costs to conform financial and tax reporting is an accounting change covered by APB 20. Justification for the change on the basis of preferability cannot rest solely on income tax effect but must provide for improved financial reporting. Issuance of this Interpretation followed the adoption in 1973 of Internal Revenue Service Regulation 1.471-11 which requires book and tax conformity for certain items of overhead.

APB 20 provides that accounting changes are generally recognized by reflecting the cumulative effect of changing to the new principle in results of operations of the period of change. Important exceptions to this general rule include certain changes in inventory pricing methods. When the cumulative effect of a change is not determinable, the change is made entirely prospectively, and adoptions of LIFO are generally made in this fashion (if the restoration of market write-downs coincident with the initial adoption of LIFO is deemed to be a separate accounting change, it would be effected by a cumulative effect adjustment as of the date of adoption of LIFO). APB 20 specifically requires that a change from the LIFO method of inventory pricing to another method be effected by restating the financial statements of all prior periods presented.

ACCOUNTING FOR INTERCOMPANY PROFITS

Sales of inventory to affiliated companies included in consolidated financial statements normally give rise to a profit in the financial statements of the selling company in the period in which the intercompany sale occurs. An offsetting charge against income in the financial statements of the buying company will be deferred to a subsequent period if the transferred inventory has not been sold by the end of the current period. While profit recognition may be appropriate in the separate financial statements of the selling company, from a consolidated point of view profits cannot be recognized until realized by a sale to parties outside the consolidated entity.

Concept of Intercompany Profit

The term "intercompany profit" as used in this discussion refers to profit arising from transfer of inventories (1) between companies included in consolidated financial statements, (2) between such companies and investee companies accounted for under the equity method of accounting, or (3) between investee companies accounted for under the equity method.

The general objective of intercompany profit elimination in consolidated statements is to exclude from consolidated income and consolidated shareholders' equity the profit or loss arising from transactions *within* the consolidated entity and to reduce correspondingly the carrying amount of assets remaining in the consolidated entity. Generally, the gross profit of the selling company is used.

Intercompany profits should be eliminated from the applicable asset reflected in the consolidated balance sheet on a before-tax basis with a corresponding increase in net deferred tax debits or decrease in net deferred tax credits in order to reflect the tax effects of the timing difference that arises when the selling company reports income from an intercompany transaction for tax purposes in its separate income tax return in a period prior to the reporting of the income in the consolidated financial statements.

Literature and Practice

ARB 51 establishes as basic consolidation principles (1) that any intercompany profit or loss on assets remaining within a consolidated group of companies should be eliminated and (2) that the amount of intercompany profit or loss to be eliminated is not affected by the existence of a minority interest. Where the sale is made by the parent, the entire gain or loss is charged to the parent (consolidated) interest. Where the sale is made by a subsidiary with a minority interest, the entire gain or loss eliminated may be either charged entirely to the parent (majority) interest or prorated between the majority and minority interests. (See ARB 51, paragraphs 6 and 14.) In any event, the amount of profit eliminated from the asset is not affected by the existence of a minority interest in the subsidiary.

APB Opinion No. 18 (APB 18) discusses the equity method of accounting as it applies to unconsolidated subsidiaries, corporate joint ventures, and investees and provides that "Intercompany profits and losses should be eliminated until realized by the investor or investee as if a subsidiary, corporate joint venture or investee company were consolidated."

Following Interpretation No. 1 of APB 18, a partial elimination procedure is generally followed for less than majority-owned companies accounted for by the equity method. In such situations, profit is normally eliminated by the investor on a sale to the investee only to the extent of the investor's ownership interest in the investee. When the investee sells to the investor, the investor eliminates until realized only its share of the profit earned by the investee on the sale. There are examples in practice, however, where (1) profits are entirely eliminated or (2) profits are entirely recognized. The former reflects a literal application of the official pronouncements, whereas the latter is usually justified on the grounds that an arm's-length transaction has occurred with an independent and non-controlled party or that realization has occurred to a sufficient degree to "seal" the transaction.

Lower of Cost or Market Test

The following procedures should be followed in testing for lower of cost or market and adjusting the accounts when a market reduction is indicated.

Intercompany Transactions at a Profit. When intercompany transactions result in a profit, the new basis (cost) of the inventories on the books of the company holding the inventories will include the entire intercompany profit. Some or all of the intercompany profit and related income taxes would normally be eliminated in consolidation; the actual amount would depend on which acceptable accounting procedure is followed in the circumstances.

Normally, the market test is made by the company holding the inventories and, if cost exceeds market, a market reduction is provided as part of closing its separate books. To the extent that the write-down gives rise to an immediate or a future (upon realization of the market loss) tax deduction (which is assured of realization), the company making the write-down will record a tax benefit as part of its normal calculation of income tax expense. These adjusted amounts should be used for consolidation purposes, which means that the parent and minority interests in the company holding the inventories will reflect their respective shares of the recorded market reduction net of any tax benefit recorded.

Intercompany Transactions at a Loss. When an intercompany transaction results in a loss to a seller affiliate, the investor (parent) company should take into account the ultimate selling price in determining the extent to which its share of the loss (before taxes) should be deferred in consolidation. To the extent that market does not permit deferral of the loss, an adjustment should be made in consolidation to reduce the investor company's share of the loss which would otherwise be deferred in consolidation.

INVENTORIES IN TRANSLATED FINANCIAL STATEMENTS

Preparation of financial statements by United States companies with foreign operations, subsidiaries, or other affiliates generally involves translation of foreign currency financial statements. Translation is the process of expressing foreign currency amounts in U.S. dollars. Statement No. 8 of the Financial Accounting Standards Board (FAS 8) and subsequent interpretations of that statement set forth the principles applicable to the translation process. Like any other accounting process, translation calls for skill and judgment to attain practical objectives: fair presentation and an adequate matching of costs and revenues in conformity with GAAP, giving due consideration to materiality.

FAS 8 generally requires translation of inventories at historical (rather than current) rates. However, the Financial Accounting Standards Board is reconsidering certain provisions of FAS 8, including those relating to appropriate rates to be applied to specific items, and has tentatively concluded that the current rate method best achieves translation objectives in most circumstances. As long as it is effective, reference to FAS 8 is essential to assure compliance with GAAP. Set forth below is certain information which should be helpful in applying the concepts of FAS 8.

Translation of Raw Materials, Work in Process, and Finished Goods

General. When exchange rates weaken during the period of inventory accumulation, local currency selling prices generally tend to increase enough to recover the equivalent dollar cost of the inventory to be sold and to provide sufficient funds to purchase (or manufacture) inventory replacements. This, of course, may not be true either in those cases where government price controls are in effect or in instances where local market conditions do not permit price increases.

As a practical matter, FIFO inventories may be translated at the closing free exchange rate at the end of each period when the free exchange rate is fairly stable and purchases (or manufacturing) are fairly consistent from month to month during the period of inventory accumulation, unless inventory cost includes significant amounts of depreciation or other charges translatable at historical exchange rates differing significantly from the current rate. However, when the free exchange rate has fluctuated significantly during the period of inventory accumulation, inventories should be translated at the rates in effect during their periods of accumulation (i.e., at the average free exchange rate for each month in which the inventories were deemed to have been accumulated) whether selling prices have or have not fluctuated with significant exchange rate changes.

If the inventory at the end of the period is Foreign Currency (FC) 1,000,000, the following translation, usually referred to as the FIFO accumulation approach, based only on local currency control account entries, usually gives a reasonable result for FIFO inventories:

Purchases:

	FC	Rate	Dollars
December	450,000	.200	90,000
November	500,000	.215	107,500
October *	50,000	.230	11,500
	1,000,000		209,000

* Total October purchases were FC 400,000.

Lower of Cost or Market. When inventories are translated at historical exchange rates, even when there is no allowance for losses in local currency, an allowance for losses may be required in dollars and a lower of
cost of market test should be applied to the inventories *after translation* to
ensure that dollar equivalent inventories are not overstated (see paragraph
46 of FAS 8). When translated historical cost is less than translated market,
an allowance for losses in dollars may not be necessary even though an allowance for losses has been recognized in the local currency financial statements. An appropriate measure of the market value of the inventories
expressed in dollars is local currency net realizable value (see below) translated at the closing free exchange rate. It is important that the dollar
equivalent of the effect of foreign income taxes paid or payable on sales
should be considered in making the net realizable value test of inventory
items translated at historical rates. An illustration of a market value test for
finished goods follows:

Market Value Test	FC (Credit)	Rate	Dollars (Credit)
Inventory cost	10,000	1.00	10,000
Estimated:			
Selling price	(12,000)	.80	(9,600)
Selling expenses	500	.80	400
Income tax on FC 1,500			
profit at 40%	600	.80	480
Net realizable value	(10,900)		(8,720)
Allowance for loss	—x—		1,280

Cost-to-complete will have to be estimated for raw materials and work
in process. Application of the cost or market test will result in immediate
recognition of the estimated loss which will actually occur when selling

prices cannot be advanced sufficiently to offset the effect of a declining exchange rate.

FASB Interpretation No. 17 deals in some detail with the application of the lower of cost or market rule set forth in Statement 6 of ARB 43, Chapter 4, to inventories translated in accordance with FAS 8. ARB 43, Chapter 4, notes that ". . . Statement 6 is intended as a guide rather than a literal rule" and the last sentence of the Interpretation should be viewed as acknowledging the need for judgment in inventory pricing. The emphasis in the Interpretation on applying Statement 6 should not be construed as requiring that market be equated with current replacement cost. Net realizable value continues to be acceptable as a measure of market in instances where this measure is judged to be appropriate.

The FASB Interpretation specifically precludes including an inventory write-down in the aggregate exchange gain or loss disclosed in accordance with FAS 8. If a substantial and unusual loss results from the application of the lower of cost or market rule, it may be appropriate to exclude such amount from cost of sales, in which case it should be reported as an unusual item in accordance with paragraph 26 of APB Opinion No. 30.

Translation of LIFO Inventories

Individual LIFO layers in the balance sheet are translated at historical rates applicable to the years when the layers were created. Rates used should correspond with the method of pricing layers, i.e., based on first or last acquisitions or average cost during the year. The foreign money price (cost) is multiplied by the foreign exchange rate in effect at the date to which the foreign money price pertains.

The so-called LIFO adjustment is not translated separately. The foreign currency (FC) LIFO reserve is a derived figure calculated as the difference between the FC inventory at FIFO, average, standard, or some other valuation and the FC inventory at LIFO; the FC LIFO adjustment is the difference between ending and beginning FC LIFO reserves. Similarly, the dollar LIFO reserve is a derived figure calculated as the difference between the dollar equivalent of the FC inventory at FIFO, average, standard, or some other valuation and the dollar equivalent LIFO inventory calculated as indicated above; the dollar LIFO adjustment is the difference between the ending and beginning dollar LIFO reserves.

The effect of the specified procedures is to translate the entire FC cost of sales (including the LIFO adjustment) at rates in effect when the costs were incurred. If a LIFO layer arising in the current year is priced based on first (last) acquisitions, rates to translate cost of sales are weighted toward rates in effect in the latter (early) part of the year.

Cost of Sales

Beginning and ending inventories used in calculating cost of sales should be the amounts used in the beginning and ending balance sheets. Purchases and other current costs should be translated at the average free exchange rate for the applicable period. It is not appropriate to simply translate cost of sales at the average rate for the period, a procedure which distorts exchange gains and losses. When the dollar equivalent cost of the inventory has been written down to market value, the write-down usually is (or should be) included in cost of sales; it is *not* an exchange loss.

LIFO PROBLEMS

General

Since the acceptance of LIFO for U.S. income tax purposes in 1939, the principal basis for its popularity has been its usefulness in minimizing tax payments. Accountants support the soundness of the LIFO theory particularly in an era of persistent inflation; as users of financial statements become more and more aware of the limitations of the historical cost framework and debate the merits of different techniques for reporting the effects of inflation and changing prices, LIFO is considered to eliminate the more severe distortions of rising prices. However, its reduction in reported earnings frequently makes managements reluctant to adopt LIFO, and for them the decision to adopt LIFO may involve a trade-off between tax savings and reported earnings per share.

In general, little attention has been focused upon the various LIFO techniques, their relative merits, or their theoretical soundness. A method that is acceptable for tax purposes is generally considered acceptable under GAAP, an attitude reinforced by the book-tax conformity rule. However, since 1974, which saw a wide-scale adoption of LIFO by U.S. industry in response to a renewed outbreak of inflation, the propriety of certain LIFO techniques has been questioned.

It has been charged, for example, that certain LIFO applications result in fairly arbitrary determinations of periodic income. While the LIFO concept is fairly well understood among preparers and users of financial information, application of dollar-value LIFO involves selection of inventory pools and methods of constructing an index or indices which may be quite arbitrary and which may potentially yield dramatically different amounts for inventory and income.

One problem in LIFO application that deserves elaboration because of the recent interest of the Securities and Exchange Commission, the Internal

Revenue Service, and the courts involves accounting for "new items"; this is discussed at length commencing at page 351.

Moreover, particular attention has been paid to the selective use of LIFO, i.e., its application to only a portion of the inventory. GAAP has traditionally tolerated several inventory methods within the same reporting entity, as long as the different methods are applied consistently to physically segregated inventories. However, when LIFO and FIFO result in such radically different income determinations and when they are based on radically different accounting concepts, the application of both methods in a single set of statements may be considered arbitrary unless compelling reasons for the different methods are provided by different characteristics of the different inventories to which they are applied. With the requirement of APB 20 that management justify an accounting change as being to a preferable method and ASR 177's requirement that auditors concur in the preferability judgment, the question has been raised whether the adoption of LIFO can be justified on the basis that it is preferable without applying it to the entire inventory of the reporting entity. Piecemeal adoption of LIFO—its extension to the entire inventory gradually over a period of years as management believes it can afford the impact on reported earnings—is viewed as particularly offensive.

Because LIFO is rarely accepted by foreign tax authorities, it is fairly common for domestic inventories to be carried at LIFO while foreign inventories are stated at FIFO, average, or other current cost. In addition to the theoretical difficulty of justifying different methods, this situation raises the possibility of income manipulation or involuntary distortions by transfers of inventory from LIFO to current cost jurisdictions. The most severe distortion would result when liquidation of domestic LIFO inventories is offset by an increment of foreign inventories carried at current cost. Less dramatic but still significant differences in income could result from accidental or intentional location of the inventory, i.e., whether it is held by a domestic or foreign company, at the fiscal year end when the effect is to reduce the current year's LIFO layer.

To avoid this type of problem, some multinational companies have adopted LIFO worldwide for GAAP reporting purposes. Such an endeavor obviously involves severe computational complexity. While a number of approaches might be acceptable, it would generally be most theoretically sound to have a worldwide LIFO computation superimposed on the domestic LIFO computation, i.e., a computation made in the same fashion—same choice of pools and methods of index construction—as the domestic computation, adjusted to reflect foreign cost as necessary in pricing increments but otherwise not distinguishing overseas from domestic inventories. (If, in the FASB reconsideration of FAS 8, current rather than historical rate is adopted for translation of inventories carried in foreign currency accounts, use of a worldwide LIFO computation may be impractical.)

Similar possibilities for aberrations in income exist when a purely domestic LIFO company utilizes numerous pools with transfers among the pools in the production process, sometimes offsetting liquidations in some pools with increments in others.

Possible aberrations in income determination resulting from the use of LIFO are receiving increasing attention from the SEC; with some remote possibility existing for examination by that standards-setting authorities. In general, however, the myriad of LIFO applications extant in practice continue to be considered as GAAP, buttressed by the conformity requirement and having the merit of consistent year-to-year application.

New Items

Users of either the double-extension or the index method of dollar-value LIFO need to be aware of and understand how the accounting for "new items" may impact LIFO inventory value. Fundamental to this understanding is the recognition that what is perceived to be the current IRS view may be 180 degrees removed from that of the SEC.

Current problems with new item accounting are directly due to the lack of either authoritative definitions or guidelines, under either generally accepted accounting principles or the tax rules, for the words "item" and "new." Such lack has caused necessary interpretations of what a new item is and how it should be accounted for, with subsequent second-guessing by both the SEC and the IRS in certain reported instances. A review of the rules that seem to exist and an analysis of certain recent developments may offer a better understanding of this developing problem area in LIFO accounting.

Users of the double-extension (or index) method of dollar-value LIFO are required, under the federal income tax regulations, to ascertain a base-year unit cost for each item that enters the LIFO pool for the first time subsequent to the beginning of the base year. The regulations [Section 1.472-8(e)(2)(iii)] require that: "In such a case, the base-year unit cost of the entering item shall be the current cost of that item unless the taxpayer is able to reconstruct or otherwise establish a different cost."

If the new item is a product or raw material which did not exist on the base date, the taxpayer may use any reasonable means to determine what the cost of the item would have been if it had been in existence in the base year. If unable to establish a reconstructed base-year unit cost to the IRS's satisfaction, a taxpayer may, under the regulations, use the earliest cost which can be satisfactorily reconstructed. The regulations thus appear to offer flexibility in accounting for new items.

Because, for the purpose of determining whether an increment has occurred, many companies derive the base year cost of LIFO inventory by applying the price change index for the year to the closing inventory's current cost, the impact of the alternative methods of determining and accounting for new items on LIFO value becomes apparent. If new items are many in number and have an aggregate current cost which is a significant portion of the entire LIFO inventory, there could be a material difference in value obtained by the use of current cost, rather than reconstructed base year cost, in the index calculation. In a period of rising prices such as most taxpayers have experienced consistently since 1973, it can be stated generally that the failure to reconstruct base year costs produces a higher inventory value, presumably a higher tax bill, and higher reported net income.

The following example illustrates the difference in LIFO value if current cost, rather than reconstructed base year cost, is used for a new item:

ILLUSTRATION OF DIFFERENCE—NEW ITEM ENTERED AT FIFO COST (CURRENT) vs. RECONSTRUCTED 1960 BASE YEAR COST

Assume that a manufacturing company adds to its LIFO natural business unit pool in 1979 only new items with an aggregate cost of $8 million valued on a FIFO, or current cost, basis. Assume further that the company adopted LIFO in 1960 and has the capability to reconstruct 1960 costs for these new items to the satisfaction of the IRS. Assume also that the price relationship of the new items entering in 1979 is the same as the remaining items in the pool, and that the aggregate cost (both in base and current dollars) of the remaining items in the pool at the end of 1979 is unchanged from the end of 1978, except for 10 per cent inflation experienced during 1979.

LIFO Calculation at 12/31/79:

	"New Items" Entered at		
	Current Cost		Reconstructed Base Year Cost
	(000's omitted)		
Base dollars—12/31/78	$ 54,000		$ 54,000
Base dollars—1979 new items (c)	8,000		3,570
Base dollars—12/31/79 (a)	62,000		57,570
Index for the year:			
12/31/78 FIFO:			
$110,000 × 1.10	121,000		121,000
Add: New items, 1979	8,000		8,000
12/31/79 FIFO (b)	129,000		129,000
Current year's index:			
[(b) ÷ (a)] (d)	2.0806		2.2407
LIFO value of 1979 layer:			
[(c) × (d)]	$ 16,644		$ 8,000
Difference		$8,644	

Obviously, when the effect is as dramatic as in the foregoing example, it is questionable whether use of the current-year cost of "new items" would be acceptable under GAAP.

The lack of settled, authoritative guidelines, both accounting and tax, for determining what is a new item makes the accounting for it a difficult matter, particularly in view of the apparent divergence of views and interests between the SEC and the IRS. The LIFO Training Manual, issued by the IRS as a training tool for its examining agents in June 1976, suggests that a taxpayer has a choice under the regulations of using either a base year cost or the current cost for a new item. A leading tax reference service makes the same suggestion. In the examples offered by each of these published sources, however, the current cost of the entering item is appreciably less than the determinable base year cost. In a period of rising prices, as experienced since 1973, it is doubtful that such condition, which in the examples produces a favorable tax result, would arise in normal circumstances.

The SEC's recent interest in the effect on income of "new item" accounting is evidenced in the restatements of earnings (presumably with amendments of tax returns) by Sharon Steel Corporation for 1975 and by Jones & Laughlin Steel Corporation for the years 1974 through 1977. Both Sharon Steel and Jones & Laughlin Steel Corporation had valued inventories under the dollar-value LIFO method using the single-pool (natural business unit), double-extension method. Being integrated steel producers, the inventory of each of the companies was comprised of a substantial variety of materials and products.

Sharon had treated a blend of iron ores, received and used for the first time in 1975, as a new item and entered such ore blend in its LIFO pool at current cost, rather than reconstructed base cost. The blend was comprised of a new pellet ore from a new source of supply, and two pellet ores from other old sources of supply (these two sources had been blended previously). In the restatement of earnings, only the unblended ore from the source of supply which was new in 1975 was permitted to be valued at current cost. A reconstructed base year cost was required for the portion of the blend which consisted of ores from the two old sources of supply.

The restatement of earnings of Jones & Laughlin Steel for 1974 through 1977 indicates that the company had followed a consistent policy since 1960 of using the current year cost of new items as their base year costs; no attempt was made to reconstruct or otherwise establish base year costs. It should be noted that the restatement required a correction in accounting only for certain of the items which were allegedly incorrectly treated as new items. Although the use of current cost to enter new items was apparently accepted for the purpose of the restatement of earnings, there is interesting disclosure in the financial report accompanying the restatement of earnings for 1974–1977 of what the effect on inventory valuation and earnings for the period would have been if the company had updated its base year beginning in 1974. This method is probably the same as the "link-chain" method.

It has been reported that the SEC proposes to issue either a Staff Accounting Bulletin or an interpretative Accounting Series Release on new item accounting by a double-extension, dollar-value, natural business unit LIFO user and that the SEC is of the view that tax rules should not dictate what is appropriate accounting under GAAP. Although it is pure conjecture as to what such bulletin, if issued, will contain, the perceived need for an SEC pronouncement is said to have resulted from the experiences in both the Sharon Steel and Jones & Laughlin Steel situations.

One way of minimizing the difficulty of determining a reconstructed base year cost, and the controversy that may arise if current cost is used for new items, is to use the "link-chain" method to determine the price change for the year. It will be recalled that, under the link-chain method, items in the closing inventory are valued at current costs (rather than base year) at the beginning and end of the year to derive the current year's index. Such index is then linked to the cumulative index at the end of the preceding year. A LIFO user who uses the link-chain method would thus appear to minimize the problem of possible required reconstruction of base year costs for a new item entering the inventory for the first time subsequent to the base year. The task of reconstructing base year costs to the IRS's satisfaction may become more difficult the longer dollar-value LIFO is used. The adoption or change to the link-chain method would be an accounting change for financial reporting purposes, which would entail the "preferability" considerations discussed on page 342.

Some recent developments in tax accounting for "new items" also merit attention. The Tax Court of the United States decided the *Wendle Ford Sales, Inc.* case in June 1979. This taxpayer had adopted LIFO in 1974 for new cars and new trucks. At issue was whether catalytic converters and solid-state ignition systems which were added to the new models between 1973 and 1974 represented "items" of inventory which were not present in the base year, thus requiring an adjustment to the base cost of the inventory for purposes of calculating price change for the year. The Tax Court held for the taxpayer on the basis that the catalytic converters and solid-state ignition systems were minor modifications: (1) which had no appreciable effect on the 1975 model vehicle's performance, value, or otherwise, when compared with the 1974 model vehicle; and (2) the cost of which represented only an insignificant percentage of the total cost of the parts of an unassembled automobile. The court suggested, however, that there may be circumstances in which modifications, either viewed individually or taken collectively, may be so substantial and significant (particularly with the passage of time and frequent modifications) as to require the redesigned product to be treated as a "new item" with a required adjustment to the base year cost of the inventory pool. The point at which such threshold is passed would require a case-by-case factual analysis.

Before closing discussion of the "new item" question it should be noted that the IRS has also ruled privately that it is necessary to correct the base year costs where the relationship between the costs at the base date and the current year is affected by something other than inflation, such as technological changes. In this regard, the IRS issued a technical advice memorandum in early 1979, published as Private Letter Ruling 7920008, which proposes to deny the use of the "cost component" method of determining the annual inflation rate change to a dollar-value LIFO taxpayer which had used such method consistently without challenge by the IRS over a twenty-year period.

There are instances, particularly in certain industries which either must employ a process cost system or which do not manufacture "shelf items," where the "cost component" method of LIFO is the only feasible method. "Cost component" LIFO has been used for many years for tax and financial reporting, and its validity has not previously been subjected to question by the IRS, the SEC, or accounting standard-setting bodies.

Year-end Transactions

Another area of interest to LIFO users is the problem of managing year-end quantities of inventory to preserve the LIFO benefits by avoiding liquidations. Such actions should be considered as having a valid business purpose provided that the inventory acquired will be used in the operations within a reasonable time frame.

One case and a recent IRS ruling merit mention in this regard.

SuCrest Corporation which determined the cost of its raw sugar inventory on a LIFO basis, originally included certain raw sugar purchased prior to the end of 1975 in its 1975 inventory. However, because the Company did not require this sugar in its declining operations, it never took delivery and immediately after year-end resold the sugar to the supplier. After a special investigation it was concluded that SuCrest should be treated as a borrower, rather than owner, of the sugar and the Company restated its 1975 financial statements accordingly.

A similar conclusion is expressed by the IRS in Revenue Ruling 79-188. The facts disclose a taxpayer used LIFO since 1969 for the gold content of raw materials, work in process, and finished goods inventories used in its jewelry manufacturing operations. During calendar 1977, the taxpayer's sales of finished gold jewelry declined substantially, as did the level of gold inventory. The taxpayer's LIFO gold layers were at $35 per ounce. On December 28, 1977 the taxpayer made a substantial year-end purchase of $200 per ounce to avoid penetrating its LIFO layers. All of the year-end purchase was sold back to the supplier in January, 1978. The IRS held that the December 28, 1977 purchases of gold were not properly includible in December 31, 1977 inventory because the gold was never used in the manufacturing process.

BUSINESS COMBINATIONS

Accounting for inventories in business combinations involves complex considerations, particularly with respect to LIFO inventories and differences between book and tax bases not only in "purchase" transactions but also in "pooling of interests" transactions.

The example on page 357 presents what is believed to be the appropriate method of assigning cost to FIFO inventories acquired in a tax-free "purchase" transaction.

APB 16 requires inventories acquired in a business combination accounted for as a purchase to include manufacturing profit to the point of completion on the premise that the acquiring company is not entitled to preacquisition manufacturing profit. When the acquired inventory "turns over" under the normal application of the FIFO method, comparability of current gross profit margins with those of prior periods and with those anticipated for future periods may be significantly affected. In such instance the lack of comparability should be disclosed for fair presentation. The subsequent liquidation of a substantial portion of a purchased LIFO base requires the same disclosure as a substantial liquidation of any LIFO layer.

Chapter 10 includes extensive discussion of accounting for "purchased" LIFO inventories (pages 222 to 228) and of accounting for LIFO inventories in a taxable transaction accounted for as a "pooling of interests."

FINANCIAL REPORTING AND CHANGING PRICES

The SEC's Accounting Series Release No. 190 requires certain registrants to disclose the replacement cost of inventories at year end and of cost of sales for the year based on the replacement cost of the goods at the time

Recording FIFO Inventories in a Purchase Transaction:

(a)	Finished goods:	
	Selling price to customers	$1,600,000
	Less:	
	Cost of disposal	(80,000)
	Selling profit (10% of sales price)	(160,000)
		1,360,000
(b)	Work in process (60% complete):	
	Selling price of finished goods	1,000,000
	Less:	
	Cost to complete	(220,000)
	Cost of disposal	(50,000)
	Selling profit (10% of sales price)	(100,000)
	Manufacturing profit (gross profit of 40% less selling profit of 10% = manufacturing profit of 30% × $1,000,000 selling price = $300,000 × 40% remaining to be completed)	(120,000)
		510,000
(c)	Raw materials at current replacement costs	630,000
	Total fair value of inventories acquired assuming full tax basis	2,500,000
	Historical tax basis	2,200,000
	Difference	$ 300,000
	Future tax effect of difference between fair value and tax basis on sale of inventory ($300,000 × 40%, assumed tax rate)	$ 120,000
	Record ($2,500,000 — $120,000)	$2,380,000

Comment: Discounting of the tax effect is not required since the inventories will be sold in the next accounting period.

they were sold. In September 1979 FASB issued Statement of Financial Accounting Standards No 33 (FAS 33), "Financial Reporting and Changing Prices." The Statement requires certain large publicly held companies to report income from continuing operations (1) adjusted for the effects of general inflation (constant dollar accounting) and (2) on a current cost basis (current cost accounting). This requirement will necessitate the remeasurement of inventory and cost of sales on two bases, constant dollar and current cost. The current cost measurements are expected to be similar to the replacement cost of inventory and cost of sales disclosed in accordance with ASR 190. FAS 33 is effective for fiscal years ending on or after December 25, 1979. However, the presentation of current cost information may be postponed until 1980.

In ASR 271 the SEC announced that ASR 190, "Disclosure of Certain Replacement Cost Data," will be repealed when all companies subject to FAS 33 are required to comply with its current cost provisions. In the meantime, an automatic waiver of the ASR 190 requirements will be in effect for those companies which voluntarily comply with the current cost provisions of FAS 33.

COSTS ACCOUNTING STANDARDS

The Defense Production Act of 1970 provided for the creation of the five-member Cost Accounting Standards Board (CASB) as an agent of the Congress and independent of the executive branch of government. The CASB was created in response to testimony before the Congress wherein it was alleged that contractors were making excessive profits on government contracts through manipulation of their costs and profits. The Board consists of the Comptroller General as Chairman, two members from the accounting profession, one representative from industry, and one from a department or agency of the federal government. The Board is authorized to promulgate standards designed to achieve uniformity and consistency in the cost accounting principles followed by defense prime contractors and subcontractors in estimating, accumulating, and reporting costs in connection with the pricing, administration, and settlement of all negotiated prime contract and subcontract national defense procurements in excess of $100,000, except where the price negotiated is based upon (1) established catalog or market prices of commercial items sold in substantial quantities to the general public, or (2) prices set by law or regulation. Initial coverage is established by receipt of a contract of the type covered by CAS in excess of $500,000.

In addition, the enacting legislation directed the CASB to promulgate regulations requiring defense contractors as a condition of contracting to disclose in writing their cost accounting practices. Currently, contractors having received $10 million of CAS covered contracts in any year must file a Disclosure Statement. The Board is authorized to exempt from its standards and regulations certain classes or categories of contractors as it deems appropriate, in addition to those excluded by law. Although the law extends CASB rules only to defense procurements, non-defense agencies of the government have incorporated CASB standards (in whole or in part) in their required accounting practices.

To date the CASB has promulgated the following standards:

APPENDIX A

"Inventory Pricing" by the Committee on Accounting Procedure of the American Institute of Certified Public Accountants

(Chapter 4 of Accounting Research Bulletin No. 43)

Periodic inventories are necessary. 1. Whenever the operation of a business includes the ownership of a stock of goods, it is necessary for adequate financial accounting purposes that inventories be properly compiled periodically and recorded in the accounts.[1] Such inventories are required both for the statement of financial position and for the periodic measurement of income.

Conclusions directed to merchandisers and manufacturers. 2. This chapter sets forth the general principles applicable to the pricing of inventories of mercantile and manufacturing enterprises. Its conclusions are not directed to or necessarily applicable to noncommercial businesses or to regulated utilities.

STATEMENT 1

The term *inventory* is used herein to designate the aggregate of those items of tangible personal property which (1) are held for sale in the ordinary course of business, (2) are in process of production for such sale, or (3) are to be currently consumed in the production of goods or services to be available for sale.

Discussion

Scope of the term "inventory." 3. The term *inventory* embraces goods awaiting sale (the merchandise of a trading concern and the finished goods of a manufacturer), goods in the course of production (work in process), and goods to be consumed directly or indirectly in production (raw materials and supplies). This definition of inventories excludes long-term assets subject to depreciation accounting, or goods which, when put into use, will be so classified. The fact that a depreciable asset is retired from regular use and held for sale does not indicate that the item should be classified as part of the inventory. Raw materials and supplies purchased for production may be used or consumed for the construction of long-term assets or other purposes not related to production, but the fact that inventory items representing a small portion of the total may not be absorbed ultimately in the production process does not require separate classification. By trade practice, operating materials and supplies of certain types of companies such as oil producers are usually treated as inventory.

STATEMENT 2

A major objective of accounting for inventories is the proper determination of income through the process of matching appropriate costs against revenues.

Discussion

Major objective of an inventory is determination of realized income. 4. An inventory has financial significance because revenues may be obtained from its sale, or from the sale of the goods or services in whose production it is used. Normally such revenues arise in a continuous repetitive process or cycle of operations by which goods are acquired and sold, and further goods are acquired for additional sales. In accounting for the goods in the inventory at any point of time, the major objective is the matching of appropriate costs against revenues in order that there may be a proper determination of the realized income.   Thus, the inventory at any given date is the balance of costs applicable to goods on hand remaining after the matching of absorbed costs with concurrent revenues.   This balance is appropriately carried to future periods provided it does not exceed an amount properly chargeable against the revenues expected to be obtained from ultimate disposition of the goods carried forward.   In practice, this balance is determined by the process of pricing the articles comprised in the inventory.

STATEMENT 3

The primary basis of accounting for inventories is cost, which has been defined generally as the price paid or consideration given to acquire an asset.   As applied to inventories, cost means in principle the sum of the applicable expenditures and charges directly or indirectly incurred in bringing an article to its existing condition and location.

Discussion

Definition of "cost" as applied to inventories.   5. In keeping with the principle that accounting is primarily based on cost, there is a presumption that inventories should be stated at cost.   The definition of cost as applied to inventories is understood to mean acquisition and production cost,[2] and its determination involves many problems.   Although principles for the determination of inventory costs may be easily stated, their application, particularly to such inventory items as work in process and finished goods, is difficult because of the variety of problems encountered in the allocation of costs and charges.   For example, under some circumstances, items such as idle facility expense, excessive spoilage, double freight, and rehandling costs may be so abnormal as to require treatment as current period charges rather than as a portion of the inventory cost.   Also, general and administrative expenses should be included as period charges, except for the portion of such expenses that may be clearly related to production and thus constitute a part of inventory costs (product charges).   Selling expenses constitute no part of inventory costs.   It should also be recognized that the exclusion of all overheads from inventory costs does not constitute an accepted accounting procedure.   The exercise of judgment in an individual situation involves a consideration of the adequacy of the procedures of the cost accounting system in use, the soundness of the principles thereof, and their consistent application.

[2] In the case of goods which have been written down below cost at the close of a fiscal period, such reduced amount is to be considered the cost for subsequent accounting purposes.

STATEMENT 4

Cost for inventory purposes may be determined under any one of several assumptions as to the flow of cost factors (such as first-in first-out, average, and last-in first-out); the major objective in selecting a method should be to choose the one which, under the circumstances, most clearly reflects periodic income.

Discussion

Use of identified cost for items sold may not most clearly reflect income. 6. The cost to be matched against revenue from a sale may not be the identified cost of the specific item which is sold, especially in cases in which similar goods are purchased at different times and at different prices. While in some lines of business specific lots are clearly identified from the time of purchase through the time of sale and are costed on this basis, ordinarily the identity of goods is lost between the time of acquisition and the time of sale. In any event, if the materials purchased in various lots are identical and interchangeable, the use of identified cost of the various lots may not produce the most useful financial statements. This fact has resulted in the development of general acceptance of several assumptions with respect to the flow of cost factors (such as *first-in first-out*, *average*, and *last-in first-out*) to provide practical bases for the measurement of periodic income.[3] In some situations a reversed mark-up procedure of inventory pricing, such as the retail inventory method, may be both practical and appropriate. The business operations in some cases may be such as to make it desirable to apply one of the acceptable methods of determining cost to one portion of the inventory or components thereof and another of the acceptable methods to other portions of the inventory.

Benefit of uniformity within an industry. 7. Although selection of the method should be made on the basis of the individual circumstances, it is obvious that financial statements will be more useful if uniform methods of inventory pricing are adopted by all companies within a given industry.

---

[3] Standard costs are acceptable if adjusted at reasonable intervals to reflect current conditions so that at the balance-sheet date standard costs reasonably approximate costs computed under one of the recognized bases. In such cases descriptive language should be used which will express this relationship, as, for instance, "approximate costs determined on the first-in first-out basis," or, if it is desired to mention standard costs, "at standard costs, approximating average costs."

STATEMENT 5

A departure from the cost basis of pricing the inventory is required when the utility of the goods is no longer as great as its cost.   Where there is evidence that the utility of goods, in their disposal in the ordinary course of business, will be less than cost, whether due to physical deterioration, obsolescence, changes in price levels, or other causes, the difference should be recognized as a loss of the current period.   This is generally accomplished by stating such goods at a lower level commonly designated as *market*.

Discussion

Where the utility of goods is less than cost, a loss should be recognized.

8. Although the cost basis ordinarily achieves the objective of a proper matching of costs and revenues, under certain circumstances cost may not be the amount properly chargeable against the revenues of future periods. A departure from cost is required in these circumstances because cost is satisfactory only if the utility of the goods has not diminished since their acquisition; a loss of utility is to be reflected as a charge against the revenues of the period in which it occurs.   Thus, in accounting for inventories, a loss should be recognized whenever the utility of goods is impaired by damage, deterioration, obsolescence, changes in price levels, or other causes.   The measurement of such losses is accomplished by applying the rule of pricing inventories at *cost or market, whichever is lower*.   This provides a practical means of measuring utility and thereby determining the amount of the loss to be recognized and accounted for in the current period.

STATEMENT 6

As used in the phrase *lower of cost or market*[4] the term *market* means current replacement cost (by purchase or by reproduction, as the case may be) except that:

(1) Market should not exceed the net realizable value (i.e., estimated selling price in the ordinary course of business less reasonably predictable costs of completion and disposal); and (2) Market should not be less than net realizable value reduced by an allowance for an approximately normal profit margin.

---

[4] The terms *cost or market, whichever is lower* and *lower of cost or market* are used synonymously in general practice and in this chapter.   The committee does not express any preference for either of the two alternatives.

Discussion

Definition of "market" as applied to inventories.
9. The rule of *cost or market, whichever is lower* is intended to provide a means of measuring the residual usefulness of an inventory expenditure. The term *market* is therefore to be interpreted as indicating utility on the inventory date and may be thought of in terms of the equivalent expenditure which would have to be made in the ordinary course at that date to procure corresponding utility. As a general guide, utility is indicated primarily by the current cost of replacement of the goods as they would be obtained by purchase or reproduction. In applying the rule, however, judgment must always be exercised and no loss should be recognized unless the evidence indicates clearly that a loss has been sustained. There are therefore exceptions to such a standard. Replacement or reproduction prices would not be appropriate as a measure of utility when the estimated sales value, reduced by the costs of completion and disposal, is lower, in which case the realizable value so determined more appropriately measures utility. Furthermore, where the evidence indicates that cost will be recovered with an approximately normal profit upon sale in the ordinary course of business, no loss should be recognized even though replacement or reproduction costs are lower. This might be true, for example, in the case of production under firm sales contracts at fixed prices, or when a reasonable volume of future orders is assured at stable selling prices.

Definition of "market" is not a literal rule.
10. Because of the many variations of circumstances encountered in inventory pricing, Statement 6 is intended as a guide rather than a literal rule. It should be applied realistically in the light of the objectives expressed in this chapter and with due regard to the form, content, and composition of the inventory. The committee considers, for example, that the retail inventory method, if adequate markdowns are currently taken, accomplishes the objectives described herein. It also recognizes that, if a business is expected to lose money for a sustained period, the inventory should not be written down to offset a loss inherent in the subsequent operations.

STATEMENT 7

Depending on the character and composition of the inventory, the rule of *cost or market, whichever is lower* may properly be applied either directly to each item or to the total of the inventory (or, in some cases, to the total of the components of each major category). The method should be that which most clearly reflects periodic income.

Discussion

No absolute
basis for
cost/market
comparison.

11. The purpose of reducing inventory to *market* is to reflect fairly the income of the period. The most common practice is to apply the *lower of cost or market* rule separately to each item of the inventory. However, if there is only one end-product category the cost utility of the total stock—the inventory in its entirety—may have the greatest significance for accounting purposes. Accordingly, the reduction of individual items to *market* may not always lead to the most useful result if the utility of the total inventory to the business is not below its cost. This might be the case if selling prices are not affected by temporary or small fluctuations in current costs of purchase or manufacture. Similarly, where more than one major product or operational category exists, the application of the *cost or market, whichever is lower* rule to the total of the items included in such major categories may result in the most useful determination of income.

Significance
of balanced
inventories.

12. When no loss of income is expected to take place as a result of a reduction of cost prices of certain goods because others forming components of the same general categories of finished products have a market equally in excess of cost, such components need not be adjusted to market to the extent that they are in balanced quantities. Thus, in such cases, the rule of *cost or market, whichever is lower* may be applied directly to the totals of the entire inventory, rather than to the individual inventory items, if they enter into the same category of finished product and if they are in balanced quantities, provided the procedure is applied consistently from year to year.

Cost/market
comparison on
item basis for
excessive
quantities.

13. To the extent, however, that the stocks of particular materials or components are excessive in relation to others, the more widely recognized procedure of applying the *lower of cost or market* to the individual items constituting the excess should be followed. This would also apply in cases in which the items enter into the production of unrelated products or products having a material variation in the rate of turnover. Unless an effective method of classifying categories is practicable, the rule should be applied to each item in the inventory.

Specific
reporting
of unusual
losses.

14. When substantial and unusual losses result from the application of this rule it will frequently be desirable to disclose the amount of the loss in the income statement as a charge separately identified from the consumed inventory costs described as *cost of goods sold.*

STATEMENT 8

The basis of stating inventories must be consistently applied and should be disclosed in the financial statements; whenever a significant change is made therein, there should be disclosure of the nature of the change and, if material, the effect on income.

Discussion

Inconsistency in basis for inventories may improperly affect income statements.
15. While the basis of stating inventories does not affect the overall gain or loss on the ultimate disposition of inventory items, any inconsistency in the selection or employment of a basis may improperly affect the periodic amounts of income or loss. Because of the common use and importance of periodic statements, a procedure adopted for the treatment of inventory items should be consistently applied in order that the results reported may be fairly allocated as between years. A change of such basis may have an important effect upon the interpretation of the financial statements both before and after that change, and hence, in the event of a change, a full disclosure of its nature and of its effect, if material, upon income should be made.

STATEMENT 9

Only in exceptional cases may inventories properly be stated above cost. For example, precious metals having a fixed monetary value with no substantial cost of marketing may be stated at such monetary value; any other exceptions must be justifiable by inability to determine appropriate approximate costs, immediate marketability at quoted market price, and the characteristic of unit interchangeability. Where goods are stated above cost this fact should be fully disclosed.

Discussion

Some inventories may be based on sales prices.
16. It is generally recognized that income accrues only at the time of sale, and that gains may not be anticipated by reflecting assets at their current sales prices. For certain articles, however, exceptions are permissible. Inventories of gold and silver, when there is an effective government-controlled market at a fixed monetary value, are ordinarily reflected at selling prices. A similar treatment is not uncommon for inventories representing agricultural, mineral, and other products, units of which are interchangeable and have an immediate marketability at quoted prices and for which appropriate costs may be difficult to obtain. Where such inventories are stated at sales prices, they should of course be reduced by expenditures to be incurred in disposal, and the use of such basis should be fully disclosed in the financial statements.

STATEMENT 10

Accrued net losses on firm purchase commitments for goods for inventory, measured in the same way as are inventory losses, should, if material, be recognized in the accounts and the amounts thereof separately disclosed in the income statement.

Discussion

Recognition of commitment losses. 17. The recognition in a current period of losses arising from the decline in the utility of cost expenditures is equally applicable to similar losses which are expected to arise from firm, uncancelable, and unhedged commitments for the future purchase of inventory items. The net loss on such commitments should be measured in the same way as are inventory losses and, if material, should be recognized in the accounts and separately disclosed in the income statement. The utility of such commitments is not impaired, and hence there is no loss, when the amounts to be realized from the disposition of the future inventory items are adequately protected by firm sales contracts or when there are other circumstances which reasonably assure continuing sales without price decline.

One member of the committee, Mr. Wellington, assented with qualification, and two members, Messrs. Mason and Peloubet, dissented to adoption of chapter 4.

Points of qualification or dissent by committee members. Mr. Wellington objects to footnote (2) to statement 3. He believes that an exception should be made for goods costed on the *last-in first-out* (LIFO) basis. In the case of goods costed on all bases other than LIFO the reduced amount (market below cost) is cleared from the accounts through the regular accounting entries of the subsequent period, and if the market price rises to or above the original cost there will be an increased profit in the subsequent period. Accounts kept under the LIFO method should also show a similar increased profit in the subsequent period, which will be shown if the LIFO inventory is restored to its original cost. To do otherwise, as required by footnote (2), is to carry the LIFO inventory, not at the lower of cost or current market, but at the lowest market ever known since the LIFO method was adopted by the company.

Mr. Mason dissents from this chapter because of its acceptance of the inconsistencies inherent in *cost or market, whichever is lower.* In his opinion a drop in selling price below cost is no more of a realized loss than a rise above cost is a realized gain under a consistent criterion of realization.

Mr. Peloubet believes it is ordinarily preferable to carry inventory at not less than recoverable cost, and particularly in the case of manufactured or partially manufactured goods which can be sold only in finished form.

He recognizes that application of the *cost or market* valuation basis necessitates the shifting of income from one period to another, but objects to unnecessarily accentuating this shift by the use, even limited as it is in this chapter, of reproduction or replacement cost as *market* when such cost is less than net selling price.

APPENDIX B

International Accounting Standards

INTRODUCTION

1. This statement deals with the valuation and presentation of inventories [1] in financial statements in the context of the historical cost system, which is the most widely adopted basis on which financial statements are presented.

2. The Committee is aware of other systems that are proposed or used in financial statements, including systems that are based on replacement costs or other current values. Inventory valuation and presentation in the context of those other systems are beyond the scope of this Statement. International Accounting Standard 1, *Disclosure of Accounting Policies*, requires that the system adopted must be clearly stated.

3. This Statement does not deal with inventories accumulated under long-term construction contracts and with inventory treatment of by-products.

DEFINITIONS

4. The following terms are used in this Statement with the meanings specified.

Inventories are tangible property (a) held for sale in the ordinary course of business, (b) in the process of production for such sale, or (c) to be consumed in the production of goods or services for sale.

Historical cost of inventories is the aggregate of costs of purchase, costs of

---

[1] The term "inventories" is used throughout this Statement; in some countries inventories are described as "stock and work in progress."

conversion, and other costs incurred in bringing the inventories to their present location and condition.

Costs of purchase comprise the purchase price including import duties and other purchase taxes, transport and handling costs, and any other directly attributable costs of acquisition less trade discounts, rebates, and subsidies.

Costs of conversion are those costs, in addition to the costs of purchase, that relate to bringing the inventories to their present location and condition.

Net realisable value is the estimated selling price in the ordinary course of business less costs of completion and less costs necessarily to be incurred in order to make the sale.

EXPLANATION

5. Inventories comprise a significant portion of the assets of many enterprises. The valuation and presentation of inventories therefore have a significant effect in determining and presenting the financial position and results of operations of those enterprises.

DETERMINATION OF HISTORICAL COST

6. In determining historical cost as defined in paragraph 4, different interpretations arise in practice as regards production overhead, other overheads, and the cost formula to be used.

Production Overhead

7. Production overhead is comprised of costs incurred for production other than direct materials and labour. Examples are indirect materials and labour, depreciation and maintenance of factory buildings and equipment, and the cost of factory management and administration.

8. Production overhead requires analysis to determine the portion related to bringing the inventories to their present location and condition and thus to be included in the costs of conversion when determining the historical cost of inventories.

9. Both fixed and variable production overhead incurred during production are usually allocated to costs of conversion. That practice is based on the view that they are both incurred in putting inventories in their present location and condition. Fixed production overhead is sometimes excluded in whole or in part from costs of conversion on the grounds that it is not considered to relate directly to putting inventories in their present location and condition.

10. In a period of low production or if there is idle plant, it is customary to restrict the allocation of fixed production overhead to the costs of conversion by relating it to the capacity of the production facilities and not to the actual

level of throughput. Capacity of the production facilities is variously interpreted, for example, as the normal production expected to be achieved over a number of periods or seasons or as the maximum production that as a practical matter can be achieved. The interpretation is determined in advance and applied consistently, and is not modified for temporary conditions.

11. Similarly, exceptional amounts of waste—material, labour, or other expenses—which do not relate to bringing the inventories to their present location and condition are excluded from conversion costs.

Other Overheads

12. Overheads other than production overhead are sometimes incurred in bringing inventories to their present location and condition, for example, expenditures incurred in designing products for specific customers. On the other hand, selling expenses, general administrative overheads, research and development costs, and interest are usually considered not to relate to putting the inventories in their present location and condition.

Cost Formula Used

13. Several different formulas with widely different effects are in current use for the purpose of assigning costs, including the following:

    (a) First-in, first-out (FIFO)
    (b) Weighted average cost
    (c) Last-in, first out (LIFO)
    (d) Base stock
    (e) Specific identification
    (f) Next-in, first-out (NIFO)
    (g) Latest purchase price.

14. The FIFO, weighted average cost, LIFO, base stock, and specific identification formulas use costs that have been incurred by the enterprise at one time or another. The NIFO and latest purchase price methods use costs that have not all been incurred and are therefore not based on historical cost.

15. Specific identification is a formula that attributes specific costs to identified items of inventory. This is an appropriate treatment for goods that have been bought or manufactured and are segregated for a specic project. If it is used, however, in respect of items of inventory which are ordinarily interchangeable, the selection of items could be made in such a way as to obtain predetermined effects on profit.

VALUATION OF INVENTORIES BELOW HISTORICAL COST

16. The historical cost of inventories may not be realisable if their selling prices have declined, if they are damaged, or if they have become wholly or

partially obsolete. The practice of writing inventories down below historical cost to net realisable value accords with the view that current assets should not be carried in excess of amounts expected to be realised. Declines in value are computed separately for individual items, groups of similar items, an entire class of inventory (for example, finished goods), or items relating to a class of business, or they are computed on an overall basis for all the inventories of the enterprise. The practice of writing inventories down based on a class of inventory, on a class of business, or on an overall basis results in off-setting losses incurred against unrealised gains.

17. In some countries, writedowns are made which are not based on the practices described in paragraph 16. For example, writedowns below historical cost are arrived at by applying an arbitrary percentage to the amounts otherwise computed or by undisclosed reductions that result in secret reserves; these produce inappropriate effects on financial statements.

PRESENTATION OF INVENTORIES

18. The sub-classification of inventories in financial statements informs readers of the amounts held in different categories and the extent of the changes from period to period. Common sub-classifications are materials, work in progress, finished goods, merchandise, and production supplies.

19. "Inventories" in balance sheets usually consist of items included in the definition of inventories in paragraph 4. Other items are sometimes shown under the heading "Inventories," for example, nonproduction supplies and research and development supplies.

INTERNATIONAL ACCOUNTING STANDARD 2

International Accounting Standard 2 comprises paragraphs 20–36 of this Statement. The Standard should be read in the context of paragraphs 1–19 of this Statement and of the Preface to Statements of International Accounting Standards.

20. Inventories should be valued at the lower of historical cost and net realisable value.

ASCERTAINMENT OF HISTORICAL COST

21. The historical cost of manufactured inventories should include a systematic allocation of those production overhead costs that relate to putting the inventories in their present location and condition. Allocation of fixed production overhead to the costs of conversion should be based on the capacity

of the facilities. If fixed production overhead has been entirely or substantially excluded from the valuation of inventories on the grounds that it does not directly relate to putting the inventories in their present location and condition, that fact should be disclosed.

22. Overheads other than production overhead should be included as part of inventory cost only to the extent that they clearly relate to putting the inventories in their present location and condition.

23. Exceptional amounts of wasted material, labour, or other expenses should not be included as part of an inventory cost.

24. Except as set out in paragraphs 25 and 26, the historical cost of inventories should be accounted for using the FIFO formula or a weighted average cost formula.

25. Inventories of items that are not ordinarily interchangeable or goods manufactured and segregated for specific projects should be accounted for by using specific identification of their individual costs.

26. The LIFO or base stock formulas may be used provided that there is disclosure of the difference between the amount of the inventories as shown in the balance sheet and either (a) the lower of the amount arrived at in accordance with paragraph 24 and net realisable value or (b) the lower of current cost at the balance sheet date and net realisable value.

27. Techniques such as the standard cost method of valuing products or the retail method of valuing merchandise may be used for convenience if they approximate consistently the results that would be obtained in accordance with paragraph 20.

ASCERTAINMENT OF NET REALISABLE VALUE

28. Estimates of net realisable value should be based not on temporary fluctuations of price of cost but on the most reliable evidence available at the time the estimates are made as to what the inventories are expected to realise.

29. Inventories should be written down to net ralisable value item by item or by groups of similar items; whichever method is used should be consistently applied.

30. The net realisable value of the quantity of inventory held to satisfy firm sales contracts should be based on the contract price. If the sales contracts are for less than the inventory quantities held, net realisable value for the excess should be based on general market prices.[2]

31. Normal quantities of materials and other supplies held for incorporation in the production of goods should not be written down below historical cost

---

[2] Firm sales contracts beyond inventory quantities held, and firm purchase contracts are beyond the scope of this Statement.

if the finished products in which they will be incorporated are expected to be realised at or above historical cost. Nevertheless, a decline in the price of materials may indicate that the historical cost of finished products to be produced will exceed net realisable value in which event a writedown of the materials inventories should be made; in this event, replacement cost may be the best available measure of the net realisable value of those materials.

PRESENTATION IN THE FINANCIAL STATEMENTS

32. The profit and loss of the period should be charged with the amount of inventories sold or used (unless allocated to other asset accounts) and with the amount of any writedown in the period to net realisable value.

33. Inventories should be sub-classified in balance sheets or in notes to the financial statements in a manner which is appropriate to the business and so as to indicate the amounts held in each of the main categories.

34. The accounting policies adopted for the purpose of valuation of inventories, including the cost formula used, should be disclosed. A change in an accounting policy related to inventories that has a material effect in the current period or may have a material effect in subsequent periods should be disclosed together with the reasons. The effect of the change should, if material, be disclosed and quantified. (See International Accounting Standard 1, Disclosure of Accounting Policies.)

35. If items are shown under the caption "Inventories" other than those comprehended by the definition in paragraph 4, their nature, amounts and basis of valuation should be disclosed.

EFFECTIVE DATE

36. This International Accounting Standard becomes operative for financial statements covering periods beginning on or after 1 January 1976.

APPENDIX C

United States Internal Revenue Code Provisions with Respect to "Inventories" and Related Regulations

§ 1.471 Statutory provisions; general rule for inventories.

General statutory provision. SEC. 471. *General rule for inventories.* Whenever in the opinion of the Secretary the use of inventories is necessary in order clearly to determine the income of any taxpayer, inventories shall be taken by such taxpayer on such basis as the Secretary may prescribe as conforming as nearly as may be to the best accounting practice in the trade or business and as most clearly reflecting the income.

§ 1.471–1 Need for inventories.

Inventories needed where goods are produced or purchased for sale. In order to reflect taxable income correctly, inventories at the beginning and end of each taxable year are necessary in every case in which the production, purchase, or sale of merchandise is an income-producing factor. The inventory should include all finished or partly finished goods and, in the case of raw materials and supplies, only those which have been acquired for sale or which will physically become a

* The marginal notations are the author's.

377

part of merchandise intended for sale, in which class fall containers, such as kegs, bottles, and cases, whether returnable or not, if title thereto will pass to the purchaser of the product to be sold therein. Merchandise should be included in the inventory only if title thereto is vested in the taxpayer. Accordingly, the seller should include in his inventory goods under contract for sale but not yet segregated and applied to the contract and goods out upon consignment, but should exclude from inventory goods sold (including containers), title to which has passed to the purchaser. A purchaser should include in inventory merchandise purchased (including containers), title to which has passed to him, although such merchandise is in transit or for other reasons has not been reduced to physical possession, but should not include goods ordered for future delivery, transfer of title to which has not yet been effected. (But see § 1.472–1.)

§ 1.471–2   Valuation of inventories.

Inventory rules recognize industry accounting practices.

(a) Section 471 provides two tests to which each inventory must conform:

(1) It must conform as nearly as may be to the best accounting practice in the trade or business, and

(2) It must clearly reflect the income.

(b) It follows, therefore, that inventory rules cannot be uniform but must give effect to trade customs which come within the scope of the best accounting practice in the particular trade or business. In order clearly to reflect income, the inventory practice of a taxpayer should be consistent from year to year, and greater weight is to be given to consistency than to any particular method of inventorying or basis of valuation so long as the method or basis used is in accord with §§ 1.471–1 through 1.471–11.

Inventories may be written down to net realizable values.

(c) The bases of valuation most commonly used by business concerns and which meet the requirements of section 471 are (1) cost and (2) cost or market, whichever is lower. (For inventories by dealers in securities, see § 1.471–5.) Any goods in an inventory which are unsalable at normal prices or unusable in the normal way because of damage, imperfections, shop wear, changes of style, odd or broken lots, or other similar causes, including second-hand goods taken in exchange, should be valued at bona fide selling prices less direct cost of disposition, whether subparagraph (1) or (2) of this paragraph is used, or if such goods consist of raw materials or partly finished goods held for use or consumption, they shall be valued upon a reasonable basis, taking into consideration the usability and the condition of the goods, but in no case shall such value be less than the scrap value. Bona fide selling price means actual offering of goods during a period ending not later than 30 days after inventory date.

The burden of proof will rest upon the taxpayer to show that such exceptional goods as are valued upon such selling basis come within the classifications indicated above, and he shall maintain such records of the disposition of the goods as will enable a verification of the inventory to be made.

Method adopted to be used consistently. (d) In respect of normal goods, whichever method is adopted must be applied with reasonable consistency to the entire inventory of the taxpayer's trade or business except as to those goods inventoried under the last-in, first-out method authorized by section 472 or to animals inventoried under the elective unit-livestock-price method authorized by § 1.471–6. See paragraph (d) of § 1.446–1 for rules permitting the use of different methods of accounting if the taxpayer has more than one trade or business. Where the taxpayer is engaged in more than one trade or business the Commissioner may require that the method of valuing inventories with respect to goods in one trade or business also be used with respect to similar goods in other trades or businesses if, in the opinion of the Commissioner, the use of such method with respect to such other goods is essential to a clear reflection of income. Taxpayers were given an option to adopt the basis of either (1) cost or (2) cost or market, whichever is lower, for their 1920 inventories. The basis properly adopted for that year or any subsequent year is controlling, and a change can now be made only after permission is secured from the Commissioner. Application for permission to change the basis of valuing inventories shall be made in writing and filed with the Commissioner as provided in paragraph (e) of § 1.446–1. Goods taken in the inventory which have been so intermingled that they cannot be identified with specific invoices will be deemed to be the goods most recently purchased or produced, and the cost thereof will be the actual cost of the goods purchased or produced during the period in which the quantity of goods in the inventory has been acquired. But see section 472 as to last-in, first-out inventories. Where the taxpayer maintains book inventories in accordance with a sound accounting system in which the respective inventory accounts are charged with the actual cost of the goods purchased or produced and credited with the value of goods used, transferred, or sold. calculated upon the basis of the actual cost of the goods acquired during the taxable year (including the inventory at the beginning of the year), the net value as shown by such inventory accounts will be deemed to be the cost of the goods on hand. The balances shown by such book inventories should be verified by physical inventories at reasonable intervals and adjusted to conform therewith.

Records to be preserved for investigation. (e) Inventories should be recorded in a legible manner, properly computed and summarized, and should be preserved as a part of the accounting records of the taxpayer. The inventories of taxpayers on whatever basis taken will be subject to investigation by the district director, and the taxpayer must satisfy the district director of the correctness of the prices adopted.

Examples of unapproved methods. (f) The following methods, among others, are sometimes used in taking or valuing inventories, but are not in accord with the regulations in this part:

(1) Deducting from the inventory a reserve for price changes, or an estimated depreciation in the value thereof.

(2) Taking work in process, or other parts of the inventory, at a nominal price or at less than its proper value.

(3) Omitting portions of the stock on hand.

(4) Using a constant price or nominal value for so-called normal quantity of materials or goods in stock.

(5) Including stock in transit, shipped either to or from the taxpayer, the title to which is not vested in the taxpayer.

(6) Segregating indirect production costs into fixed and variable production cost classifications (as defined in § 1.471–11(b)(3)(ii)) and allocating only the variable costs to the cost of goods produced while treating fixed costs as period costs which are currently deductible. This method is commonly referred to as the "direct cost" method.

(7) Treating all or substantially all indirect production costs (whether classified as fixed or variable) as period costs which are currently deductible. This method is generally referred to as the "prime cost" method. [Reg. § 1.471–2.]

§ 1.471–3   Inventories at cost.

Cost means:

Meaning of "cost." (a) In the case of merchandise on hand at the beginning of the taxable year, the inventory price of such goods.

(b) In the case of merchandise purchased since the beginning of the taxable year, the invoice price less trade or other discounts, except strictly cash discounts approximating a fair interest rate, which may be deducted or not at the option of the taxpayer, provided a consistent course is followed. To this net invoice price should be added transportation or other necessary charges incurred in acquiring possession of the goods.

(c) In the case of merchandise produced by the taxpayer since the beginning of the taxable year, (1) the cost of raw materials and supplies entering into or consumed in connection with the product, (2) expenditures for direct labor, and (3) indirect production costs incident to and necessary for the production of the particular article, including in such indirect production costs an appropriate portion of management expenses, but not including any cost of selling or return on capital, whether by way of interest or profit. See § 1.471–11 for more specific rules regarding the treatment of indirect production costs.

(d) In any industry in which the usual rules for computation of cost of production are inapplicable, costs may be approximated upon such basis as may be reasonable and in conformity with established trade practice in the particular industry. Among such cases are: (1) Farmers and raisers of livestock (see § 1.471–6); (2) miners and manufacturers who by a single process or uniform series of processes derive a product of two or more kinds, sizes, or grades, the unit cost of which is substantially alike (see § 1.471–7); and (3) retail merchants who use what is known as the "retail method" in ascertaining approximate cost (see § 1.471–8).

Notwithstanding the other rules of this section, cost shall not include an amount which is of a type for which a deduction would be disallowed under section 162(c), (f), or (g) and the regulations thereunder in the case of a business expense.

§ 1.471–4   Inventories at cost or market, whichever is lower.

Meaning of "market."   (a) Under ordinary circumstances and for normal goods in an inventory, "market" means the current bid price prevailing at the date of the inventory for the particular merchandise in the volume in which usually purchased by the taxpayer, and is applicable in the cases—

(1) Of goods purchased and on hand, and

(2) Of basic elements of cost (materials, labor, and burden) in goods in process of manufacture and in finished goods on hand; exclusive, however, of goods on hand or in process of manufacture for delivery upon firm sales contracts (i.e., those not legally subject to cancellation by either party) at fixed prices entered into before the date of inventory, under which the taxpayer is protected against actual loss, which goods must be inventoried at cost.

(b) Where no open market exists or where quotations are nominal, due to inactive market conditions, the taxpayer must use such evidence of a fair market price at the date or dates nearest the inventory as may be available, such as specific purchases or sales by the taxpayer or others in reasonable volume and made in good faith, or compensation paid for cancellation of contracts for purchase commitments. Where the taxpayer in the regular course of business has offered for sale such merchandise at prices lower than the current price as above defined, the inventory may be valued at such prices less direct cost of disposition, and the correctness of such prices will be determined by reference to the actual sales of the taxpayer for a reasonable period before and after the date of the inventory. Prices which vary materially from the actual prices so ascertained will not be accepted as reflecting the market.

Cost/market comparison for each article.   (c) Where the inventory is valued upon the basis of cost or market, whichever is lower, the market value of each article on hand at the inventory date shall be compared with the cost of the article, and the lower of such values shall be taken as the inventory value of the article.

§ 1.471–5   Inventories by dealers in securities.

Dealers in securities may use market value.   A dealer in securities who in his books of account regularly inventories unsold securities on hand either—

(a) At cost,

(b) At cost or market, whichever is lower, or

(c) At market value,

may make his return upon the basis upon which his accounts are kept, provided that a description of the method employed is included in or attached to the return, that all the securities are inventoried by the same method, and that such method is adhered to in subsequent years, unless another method is authorized by the Commissioner pursuant to a written application therefor filed as provided in paragraph (e) of § 1.446–1. A dealer in securities in whose books of account separate computations of the gain or loss from the sale of the various lots of securities sold are made on the basis of the cost of each lot shall be regarded, for the purposes of this section, as regularly inventorying his securities at cost. For the purposes of this section, a dealer in securities is a merchant of securities, whether an individual, partnership, or corporation, with an established place of business, regularly engaged in the purchase of securities and their resale to customers; that is, one who as a merchant buys securities and sells them to customers with a view to the gains and profits that may be derived therefrom. If such business is simply a branch of the activities carried on by such person, the securities inventoried as provided in this section may include only those held for purposes of resale and not for investment. Taxpayers who buy and sell or hold securities for investment or speculation, irrespective of whether such buying or selling constitutes the carrying on of a trade or business, and officers of corporations and members of partnerships who in their individual capacities buy and sell securities, are not dealers in securities within the meaning of this section.

§ 1.471–6   Inventories of livestock raisers and other farmers.

Use of an inventory method is optional for farmers.   (a) A farmer may make his return upon an inventory method instead of the cash receipts and disbursements method. It is optional with the taxpayer which of these methods of accounting is used but, having elected one method, the option so exercised will be binding upon the taxpayer for the year for which the option is exercised and for subsequent years unless another method is authorized by the Commissioner as provided in paragragh (e) of § 1.446–1.

(b) In any change of accounting method from the cash receipts and disbursements method to an inventory method, adjustments shall be made as provided in section 481 (relating to adjustments required by change in method of accounting) and the regulations thereunder.

Special alternative methods. (c) Because of the difficulty of ascertaining actual cost of livestock and other farm products, farmers who render their returns upon an inventory method may value their inventories according to the "farm-price method," and farmers raising livestock may value their inventories of animals according to either the "farm-price method" or the "unit-livestock-price method."

"Farm-price method." (d) The "farm-price method" provides for the valuation of inventories at market price less direct cost of disposition. If this method of valuing inventories is used, it must be applied to the entire inventory except as to livestock inventoried, at the taxpayer's election, under the "unit-livestock-price method." If the use of the "farm-price method" of valuing inventories for any taxable year involves a change in method of valuing inventories from that employed in prior years, permission for such change shall first be secured from the Commissioner as provided in paragraph (e) of § 1.446–1.

"Unit-livestock-price method." (e) The "unit-livestock-price method" provides for the valuation of the different classes of animals in the inventory at a standard unit price for each animal within a class. A livestock raiser electing this method of valuing his animals must adopt a reasonable classification of the animals in his inventory with respect to the age and kind included so that the unit prices assigned to the several classes will reasonably account for the normal costs incurred in producing the animals within such classes. Thus, if a cattle raiser determines that it costs approximately $15 to produce a calf, and $7.50 each year to raise the calf to maturity, his classifications and unit prices would be as follows: Calves, $15; yearlings, $22.50; 2-year olds, $30; mature animals, $37.50. The classification selected by the livestock raiser, and the unit prices assigned to the several classes are subject to approval by the district director upon examination of the taxpayer's return.

(f) A taxpayer who elects to use the "unit-livestock-price method" must apply it to all livestock raised, whether for sale or for draft, breeding, or dairy purposes. Once established, the unit prices and classifications selected by the taxpayer must be consistently applied in all subsequent taxable years in the valuation of livestock inventories. No changes in the classification of animals or unit prices will be made without the approval of the Commissioner.

Purchased animals to be inventoried at cost. (g) A livestock raiser who uses the "unit-livestock-price method" must include in his inventory at cost any livestock purchased, except that animals purchased for draft, breeding, or dairy purposes can, at the election of the livestock raiser, be included in inventory or be treated as capital assets subject to depreciation after maturity. If the animals purchased are not mature at the time of purchase, the cost should be increased at the end of each taxable year in accordance with the established unit prices, except that no increase is to be made in the taxable year of purchase if the animal is acquired during the last six months of that year. If the records maintained permit identification of a purchased animal, the cost of such animal will be eliminated from the closing inventory in the event of its sale or loss. Otherwise, the first-in, first-out method of valuing inventories must be applied.

Rules for changing inventory method.   (h) If a taxpayer using the "farm-price method" desires to adopt the "unit-livestock-price method" in valuing his inventories of livestock, permission for the change shall first be secured from the Commissioner as provided in paragraph (e) of § 1.446–1. However, a taxpayer who has filed returns on the basis of inventories at cost, or cost or market whichever is lower, may adopt the "unit-livestock-price method" for valuing his inventories of livestock without formal application for permission, but the classifications and unit prices selected are subject to approval by the district director upon examination of the taxpayer's return. A livestock raiser who has adopted a constant unit-price method of valuing livestock inventories and filed returns on that basis will be considered as having elected the "unit-livestock-price method."

Correction of incomplete inventories.   (i) If returns have been made in which the taxable income has been computed upon incomplete inventories, the abnormality should be corrected by submitting with the return for the current taxable year a statement for the preceding taxable year. In this statement such adjustments shall be made as are necessary to bring the closing inventory for the preceding taxable year into agreement with the opening complete inventory for the current taxable year. If necessary clearly to reflect income, similar adjustments may be made as at the beginning of the preceding year or years, and the tax, if any be due, shall be assessed and paid at the rate of tax in effect for such year or years.

§ 1.471–7   Inventories of miners and manufacturers.

Allocation of costs among products.   A taxpayer engaged in mining or manufacturing who by a single process or uniform series of processes derives a product of two or more kinds, sizes, or grades, the unit cost of which is substantially alike, and who in conformity to a recognized trade practice allocates an amount of cost to each kind, size, or grade of product, which in the aggregate will absorb the total cost of production, may, with the consent of the Commissioner, use such allocated cost as a basis for pricing inventories, provided such allocation bears a reasonable relation to the respective selling values of the different kinds, sizes, or grades of product. See section 472 as to last-in, first-out inventories.

§ 1.471–8   Inventories of retail merchants.

"Retail method."   (a) Retail merchants who employ what is known as the "retail method" of pricing inventories may make their returns upon that method, provided that the use of such method is designated upon the return,

that accurate accounts are kept, and that such method is consistently adhered to unless a change is authorized by the Commissioner as provided in paragraph (e) of § 1.446–1. Under the retail method the total of the retail selling prices of the goods on hand at the end of the year in each department or of each class of goods is reduced to approximate cost by deducting therefrom an amount which bears the same ratio to such total as—

(1) The total of the retail selling prices of the goods included in the opening inventory plus the retail selling prices of the goods purchased during the year, with proper adjustment to such selling prices for the mark-ups and mark-downs, less

(2) The cost of the goods included in the opening inventory plus the cost of the goods purchased during the year, bears to (1).

The result should represent as accurately as may be the amounts added to the cost price of the goods to cover selling and other expenses of doing business and for the margin of profit.

(b) For further adjustments to be made in the case of a retail merchant using the last-in, first-out inventory method authorized by section 472, see paragraph (k) of § 1.472–1.

Profit percent-   (c) A taxpayer maintaining more than one department
ages applied by   in his store or dealing in classes of goods carrying different
departments.   percentages of gross profit should not use a percentage of
profit based upon an average of his entire business but should compute and use in valuing his inventory the proper percentages for the respective departments or classes of goods.

Ignoring   (d) A taxpayer (other than one using the last-in, first-out
mark-downs to   inventory method) who previously has determined inven-
approximate   tories in accordance with the retail method, except that, to
lower of cost   obtain a basis of approximate cost or market, whichever is
or market.   lower, has consistently and uniformly followed the practice
of adjusting the retail selling prices of the goods included in the opening inventory and purchased during the taxable year for mark-ups but not for mark-downs, may continue such practice subject to the conditions prescribed in this section. The adjustments must be bona fide and consistent and uniform. Where mark-downs are not included in the adjustments, mark-ups made to cancel or correct mark-downs shall not be included; and the mark-ups included must be reduced by the mark-downs made to cancel or correct such mark-ups.

Computation   (e) In no event shall mark-downs not based on actual
to reflect goods   reduction of retail sale prices, such as mark-downs based
on hand at   on depreciation and obsolescence, be recognized in deter-
selling prices.   mining the retail selling prices of the goods on hand at the
end of the taxable year.

(f) A taxpayer (other than one using the last-in, first-out inventory method) who previously has determined inventories without following the practice of eliminating mark-downs in making adjustments to retail selling prices may adopt such practice, provided permission to do so is obtained in accordance with, and subject to the terms provided by, paragraph (e) of § 1.446–1. A taxpayer filing a first return of income may adopt such practice subject to approval by the district director upon examination of the return.

LIFO users must adjust for mark-downs   (g) A taxpayer using the last-in, first-out inventory method in conjunction with retail computations must adjust retail selling prices for mark-downs as well as mark-ups, in order that there may be reflected the approximate cost of the goods on hand at the end of the taxable year regardless of market values.

§ 1.471–9   Inventories of acquiring corporations.

For additional rules in the case of certain corporate acquisitions specified in section 381 (a), see section 371 (c) (5) and the regulations thereunder.

§ 1.471–10   Applicability of long-term contract methods.

For optional rules providing for application of the long-term contract methods to certain manufacturing contracts, see § 1.451–3.

§ 1.471–11   Inventories of manufacturers.

Mandatory full absorption costing   (a) *Use of full absorption method of inventory costing.* In order to conform as nearly as may be possible to the best accounting practices and to clearly reflect income (as required by section 471 of the Code), both direct and indirect production costs must be taken into account in the computation of inventoriable costs in accordance with the "full absorption" method of inventory costing. Under the full absorption method of inventory costing production costs must be allocated to goods produced during the taxable year, whether sold during the taxable year or in inventory at the close of the taxable year determined in accordance with the taxpayer's method of identifying goods in inventory. Thus, the taxpayer must include as inventoriable costs all direct production costs and, to the extent provided by paragraphs (c) and (d) of this section, all indirect production costs. For purposes of this section, the term "financial reports" means financial reports (including consolidated financial statements) to shareholders, partners, beneficiaries or other proprietors and for credit purposes.

(b) *Production costs*—(1) *In General.* Costs are considered to be production costs to the extent that they are incident to and necessary for production or manufacturing operations or processes. Production costs include direct production costs and fixed and variable indirect production costs.

(2) *Direct production costs.* (i) Costs classified as "direct production costs" are generally those costs which are incident to and necessary for production or manufacturing operations or processes and are components of the cost of either direct material or direct labor. Direct material costs include the cost of those materials which become an integral part of the specific product and those materials which are consumed in the ordinary course of manufacturing and can be identified or associated with particular units or groups of units of that product. See § 1.471–3 for the elements of direct material costs. Direct labor costs include the cost of labor which can be identified or associated with particular units or groups of units of a specific product. The elements of direct labor costs include such items as basic compensation, overtime pay, vacation and holiday pay, sick leave pay (other than payments pursuant to a wage cont'nuation plan under section 105(d)), shift differential, payroll taxes and payments to a supplemental unemployment benefit plan paid or incurred on behalf of employees engaged in direct labor. For the treatment of rework labor, scrap, spoilage costs, and any other costs not specifically described as direct production costs see § 1.471–11 (c)(2).

(ii) Under the full absorption method, a taxpayer must take into account all items of direct production cost in his inventoriable costs. Nevertheless, a taxpayer will not be treated as using an incorrect method of inventory costing if he treats any direct production costs as indirect production costs, provided such costs are allocated to the taxpayer's ending inventory to the extent provided by paragraph (d) of this section. Thus, for example, a taxpayer may treat direct labor costs as part of indirect production costs (for example, by use of the conversion cost method), provided all such costs are allocated to ending inventory to the extent provided by paragraph (d) of this section.

(3) *Indirect production costs*—(i) *In general.* The term "indirect production costs" includes all costs which are incident to and necessary for production or manufacturing operations or processes other than direct production costs (as defined in subparagraph (2) of this paragraph). Indirect production costs may be classified as to kind or type in accordance with acceptable accounting principles so as to enable convenient identification with various production or manufacturing activities or functions and to facilitate reasonable groupings of such costs for purposes of determining unit product costs.

(ii) *Fixed and variable classifications.* For purposes of this section, fixed indirect production costs are generally those costs which do not vary significantly with changes in the amount of goods produced at any given level of production capacity. These fixed costs may include, among other costs, rent and property taxes on buildings and machinery incident to and necessary for manufacturing operations or processes. On the other hand, variable indirect production costs are generally those costs which do vary significantly with changes in the amount of goods produced at any given level of production capacity. These variable costs may include, among other costs, indirect materials, factory janitorial supplies, and utilities. Where a particular cost contains both fixed and variable elements, these elements should be segregated into fixed and variable classifications to the extent necessary under the taxpayer's method of allocation, such as for the application of the practical capacity concept (as described in paragraph (d)(4) of this section).

(c) *Certain indirect production costs*—(1) *General rule.* Except as provided in subparagraph (3) of this paragraph, in order to determine whether indirect production costs referred to in paragraph (b) of this section must be included in a taxpayer's computation of the amount of inventoriable costs, three categories of costs have been provided in subparagraph (2) of this paragraph. Costs described in subparagraph (2)(i) of this paragraph must be included in the taxpayer's computation of the amount of inventoriable costs, regardless of their treatment by the taxpayer in his financial reports. Costs described in subparagraph (2)(ii) of this paragraph need not enter into the taxpayer's computation of the amount of inventoriable costs, regardless of their treatment by the taxpayer in his financial reports. Costs described in subparagraph (2)(iii) of this paragraph must be included in or excluded from the taxpayer's computation of the amount of inventoriable costs in accordance with the treatment of such costs by the taxpayer in his financial reports and generally accepted accounting principles. For the treatment of indirect production costs described in subparagraph (2) of this paragraph in the case of a taxpayer who is not using comparable methods of accounting for such costs for tax and financial reporting, see subparagraph (3) of this paragraph. After a taxpayer has determined which costs must be treated as indirect production costs includible in the computation of the amount of inventoriable costs, such costs must be allocated to a taxpayer's ending inventory in a manner prescribed by paragraph (d) of this section.

(2) *Includibility of certain indirect production costs*—(i) *Indirect production costs included in inventoriable costs.* Indirect production costs which must enter into the computation of the amount of inventoriable costs (regardless of their treatment by a taxpayer in his financial reports) include:

(*a*) Repair expenses,

(*b*) Maintenance,

(*c*) Utilities, such as heat, power and light,

(*d*) Rent,

(*e*) Indirect labor and production supervisory wages, including basic compensation, overtime pay, vacation and holiday pay, sick leave pay (other than payments pursuant to a wage continuation plan under section 105(d)), shift differential, payroll taxes and contributions to a supplemental unemployment benefit plan,

(*f*) Indirect materials and supplies,

(*g*) Tools and equipment not capitalized, and

(*h*) Costs of quality control and inspection,

to the extent, and only to the extent, such costs are incident to and necessary for production or manufacturing operations or processes.

(ii) *Costs not included in inventoriable costs.* Costs which are not required to be included for tax purposes in the computation of the amount of inventoriable costs (regardless of their treatment by a taxpayer in his financial reports) include:

(a) Marketing expenses,

(b) Advertising expenses,

(c) Selling expenses,

(d) Other distribution expenses,

(e) Interest,

(f) Research and experimental expenses including engineering and product development expenses,

(g) Losses under section 165 and the regulations thereunder,

(h) Percentage depletion in excess of cost depletion,

(i) Depreciation and amortization reported for Federal income tax purposes in excess of depreciation reported by the taxpayer in his financial reports,

(j) Income taxes attributable to income received on the sale of inventory,

(k) Pension contributions to the extent that they represent past services cost,

(l) General and administrative expenses incident to and necessary for the taxpayer's activities as a whole rather than to production or manufacturing operations or processes, and

(m) Salaries paid to officers attributable to the performance of services which are incident to and necessary for the taxpayer's activities taken as a whole rather than to production or manufacturing operations or processes.

Notwithstanding the preceding sentence, if a taxpayer consistently includes in his computation of the amount of inventoriable costs any of the costs described in the preceding sentence, a change in such method of inclusion shall be considered a change in method of accounting within the meaning of sections 446, 481, and paragraph (e)(4) of this section.

(iii) *Indirect production costs includible in inventoriable costs depending upon treatment in taxpayer's financial reports.* In the case of costs listed in this subdivision, the inclusion or exclusion of such costs from the amount of inventoriable costs for purposes of a taxpayer's financial reports shall determine whether such costs must be included in or excluded from the computation of inventoriable costs for tax purposes, but only if such treatment is not inconsistent with generally accepted accounting principles.

In the case of costs which are not included in subdivision (i) or (ii) of this subparagraph, nor listed in this subdivision, whether such costs must be included in or excluded from the computation of inventoriable costs for tax purposes depends upon the extent to which such costs are similar to costs included in subdivision (i) or (ii), and if such costs are dissimilar to costs in subdivision (i) or (ii), such costs shall be treated as included in or excludable from the amount of inventoriable costs in accordance with this subdivision. The costs listed in this subdivision are:

(a) *Taxes.* Taxes otherwise allowable as a deduction under section 164 (other than State and local and foreign income taxes) attributable to assets incident to and necessary for production or manufacturing operations or processes. Thus, for example, the cost of State and local property taxes imposed on a factory or other production facility and any State and local taxes imposed on inventory must be included in or excluded from the computation of the amount of inventoriable costs for tax purposes depending upon their treatment by a taxpayer in his financial reports.

(b) *Depreciation and depletion.* Depreciation reported in financial reports and cost depletion on assets incident to and necessary for production or manufacturing operation or processes. In computing cost depletion under this section, the adjusted basis of such assets shall be reduced by cost depletion and not by percentage depletion taken thereon.

(c) *Employee benefits.* Pension and profit-sharing contributions representing current service costs otherwise allowable as a deduction under section 404, and other employee benefits incurred on behalf of labor incident to and necessary for production or manufacturing operations or processes. These other benefits include workmen's compensation expenses, payments under a wage continuation plan described in section 105(d), amounts of a type which would be includible in the gross income of employees under nonqualified pension, profit-sharing and stock bonus plans, premiums on life and health insurance and miscellaneous benefits provided for employees such as safety, medical treatment, cafeteria, recreational facilities, membership dues, etc., which are otherwise allowable as deductions under chapter 1 of the Code.

(d) *Costs attributable to strikes, rework labor, scrap and spoilage.* Costs attributable to rework labor, scrap and spoilage which are incident to and necessary for production or manufacturing operations or processes and costs attributable to strikes incident to production or manufacturing operation or processes.

(e) *Factory administrative expenses.* Administrative costs of production (but not including any cost of selling or any return on capital) incident to and necessary for production or manufacturing operations or processes.

(f) *Officers' salaries.* Salaries paid to officers attributable to services performed incident to and necessary for production or manufacturing operations or processes.

(g) *Insurance costs.* Insurance costs incident to and necessary for production or manufacturing operations or processes such as insurance on production machinery and equipment.

A change in the taxpayer's treatment in his financial reports of costs described in this subdivision which results in a change in treatment of such costs for tax purposes shall constitute a change in method of accounting within the meaning of sections 446 and 481 to which paragraph (e) applies.

(3) *Exception.* In the case of a taxpayer whose method of accounting for production costs in his financial reports is not comparable to his method of accounting for such costs for tax purposes (such as a taxpayer using the prime cost method for purposes of financial reports), the following rules apply:

(i) *Indirect production costs included in inventoriable costs.* Indirect production costs which must enter into the computation of the amount of inventoriable costs (to the extent, and only to the extent, such costs are incident to and necessary for production or manufacturing operations or processes) include:

(*a*) Repair expenses,

(*b*) Maintenance,

(*c*) Utilities, such as heat, power and light,

(*d*) Rent,

(*e*) Indirect labor and production supervisory wages, including basic compensation, overtime pay, vacation and holiday pay, sick leave pay (other than payments pursuant to a wage continuation plan under section 105(d)), shift differential, payroll taxes and contributions to a supplemental unemployment benefit plan,

(*f*) Indirect materials and supplies,

(*g*) Tools and equipment not capitalized,

(*h*) Costs of quality control and inspection,

(*i*) Taxes otherwise allowable as a deduction under section 164 (other than State and local and foreign income taxes),

(*j*) Depreciation and amortization reported for financial purposes and cost depletion,

(*k*) Administrative costs of production (but not including any cost of selling or any return on capital) incident to and necessary for production or manufacturing operations or processes,

(*l*) Salaries paid to officers attributable to services performed incident to and necessary for production or manufacturing operations or processes, and

(*m*) Insurance costs incident to and necessary for production or manufacturing operations or processes such as insurance on production machinery and equipment.

(ii) *Costs not included in inventoriable costs.* Costs which are not required to be included in the computation of the amount of inventoriable costs include:

(*a*) Marketing expenses,

(*b*) Advertising expenses,

(*c*) Selling expenses,

(*d*) Other distribution expenses,

(*e*) Interest,

(*f*) Research and experimental expenses including engineering and product development expenses,

(*g*) Losses under section 165 and the regulations thereunder,

(*h*) Percentage depletion in excess of cost depletion,

(*i*) Depreciation reported for Federal income tax purposes in excess of depreciation reported by the taxpayer in his financial reports,

(*j*) Income taxes attributable to income received on the sale of inventory,

(*k*) Pension and profit-sharing contributions representing either past service costs or representing current service costs otherwise allowable as a deduction under section 404, and other employee benefits incurred on behalf of labor. These other benefits include workmen's compensation expenses, payments under a wage continuation plan described in section 105(d), amounts of a type which would be includible in the gross income of employees under nonqualified pension, profit-sharing and stock bonus plans, premiums on life and health insurance and miscellaneous benefits provided for employees such as safety, medical treatment, cafeteria, recreational facilities, membership dues, etc., which are otherwise allowable as deductions under chapter 1 of the Code,

(*l*) Costs attributable to strikes, rework labor, scrap and spoilage,

(*m*) General and administrative expenses incident to and necessary for the taxpayer's activities as a whole rather than to production or manufacturing operations or processes, and

(*n*) Salaries paid to officers attributable to the performance of services which are incident to and necessary for the taxpayer's activities as a whole rather than to production or manufacturing operations or processes.

(d) *Allocation methods*—(1) *In general.* Indirect production costs required to be included in the computation of the amount of inventoriable costs pursuant to paragraphs (b) and (c) of this paragraph must be allocated to goods in a taxpayer's ending inventory (determined in accordance with the taxpayer's method of identification) by the use of a method of allocation which fairly apportions such costs among the various items produced. Acceptable methods for allocating indirect production costs to the cost of goods in the ending inventory include the manufacturing burden rate method and the standard cost method. In addition, the practical capacity concept can be used in conjunction with either the manufacturing burden rate or standard cost method.

(2) *Manufacturing burden rate method*—(i) *In general.* Manufacturing burden rates may be developed in accordance with acceptable accounting principles and applied in a reasonable manner. In developing a manufacturing burden rate, the factors described in subdivision (ii) of this subparagraph may be taken into account. Furthermore, if the taxpayer chooses, he may allocate different indirect production costs on the basis of different manufacturing burden rates. Thus, for example, the taxpayer may use one burden rate for allocating rent and another burden rate for allocating utilities. The method used by the taxpayer in allocating such costs in his financial reports shall be given great weight in determining whether the taxpayer's method employed for tax purposes fairly allocates indirect production costs to the ending inventory. Any change in a manufacturing burden rate which is merely a periodic adjustment to reflect current operating conditions, such as increases in automation or changes in operation, does not constitute a change in method of accounting under section 446. However, a change in the concept upon which such rates are developed does constitute a change in method of accounting requiring the consent of the Commissioner. The taxpayer shall maintain adequate records and working papers to support all manufacturing burden rate calculations.

(ii) *Development of manufacturing burden rate.* The following factors, among others, may be taken into account in developing manufacturing burden rates:

(a) The selection of an appropriate level of activity and period of time upon which to base the calculation of rates which will reflect operating conditions for purposes of the unit costs being determined;

(b) The selection of an appropriate statistical base such as direct labor hours, direct labor dollars, or machine hours, or a combination thereof, upon which to apply the overhead rate to determine production costs; and

(c) The appropriate budgeting, classification and analysis of expenses (for example, the analysis of fixed and variable costs).

(iii) *Operation of the manufacturing burden rate method.* (a) The purpose of the manufacturing burden rate method used in conjunction with the full absorption method of inventory costing is to allocate an appropriate amount of indirect production costs to a taxpayer's goods in ending inventory by the use of predetermined rates intended to approximate the actual amount of indirect production costs incurred. Accordingly, the proper use of the manufacturing burden rate method under this section requires that any net negative or net positive difference between the total predetermined amount of indirect production costs allocated to the goods in ending inventory and the total amount of indirect production costs actually incurred and required to be allocated to such goods (i. e., the under or over-applied burden) must be treated as an adjustment to the taxpayer's ending inventory in the taxable year in which such difference arises. However, if such adjustment is not significant in amount in relation to the taxpayer's total actual indirect production costs for the year then such adjustment need not be allocated to the taxpayer's goods in ending inventory unless such allocation is made in the taxpayer's financial reports. The taxpayer must treat both positive and negative adjustments consistently.

(b) Notwithstanding subdivision (a), the practical capacity concept may be used to determine the total amount of fixed indirect production costs which must be allocated to goods in ending inventory. See subparagraph (4) of this paragraph.

(3) *Standard cost method*—(i) *In general.* A taxpayer may use the so-called "standard cost" method of allocating inventoriable costs to the goods in ending inventory, provided he treats variances in accordance with the procedures prescribed in subdivision (ii) of this subparagraph. The method used by the taxpayer in allocating such costs in his financial reports shall be given great weight in determining whether the taxpayer's method employed for tax purposes fairly allocates indirect production costs to the ending inventory. For purposes of this subparagraph, a "net positive overhead variance" shall mean the excess of total standard (or estimated) indirect production costs over total actual indirect production costs and a "net negative overhead variance" shall mean the excess of total actual indirect production costs over total standard (or estimated) indirect production costs.

(ii) *Treatment of variances.* (a) The proper use of the standard cost method pursuant to this subparagraph requires that a taxpayer must reallocate to the goods in ending inventory a pro rata portion of any net negative or net positive overhead variances and any net negative or net positive direct production cost variances. The taxpayer must apportion such variances among his various items in ending inventory. However, if such variances are not significant in amount in relation to the taxpayer's total actual indirect production costs for the year then such variances need not be allocated to the taxpayer's goods in ending inventory unless such allocation is made in the taxpayer's financial reports. The taxpayer must treat both positive and negative variances consistently.

(b) Notwithstanding subdivision (a), the practical capacity concept may be used to determine the total amount of fixed indirect production costs which must be allocated to goods in ending inventory. See subparagraph (4) of this paragraph.

(4) *Practical capacity concept*—(i) *In general.* Under the practical capacity concept, the percentage of practical capacity represented by actual production (not greater than 100 percent), as calculated under subdivision (ii) of this subparagraph, is used to determine the total amount of fixed indirect production costs which must be included in the taxpayer's computation of the amount of inventoriable costs. The portion of such costs to be included in the taxpayer's computation of the amount of inventoriable costs is then combined with variable indirect production costs and both are allocated to the goods in ending inventory in accordance with this paragraph. See the example in subdivision (ii) (d) of this subparagraph. The difference (if any) between the amount of all fixed indirect production costs and the fixed indirect production costs which are included in the computation of the amount of inventoriable costs under the practical capacity concept is allowable as a deduction for the taxable year in which such difference occurs.

(ii) *Calculation of practical capacity*—(a) *In general.* Practical capacity and theoretical capacity (as described in (c) of this subdivision) may be computed in terms of tons, pounds, yards, labor hours, machine hours, or any other unit of production appropriate to the cost accounting system used by a particular taxpayer. The determination of practical capacity and theoretical capacity should be modified from time to time to reflect a change in underlying facts and conditions such as increased output due to automation or other changes in plant operation. Such a change does not constitute a change in method of accounting under sections 446 and 481.

(b) *Based upon taxpayer's experience.* In selecting an appropriate level of production activity upon which to base the calculation of practical capacity, the taxpayer shall establish the production operating conditions expected during the period for which the costs are being determined, assuming that the utilization of production facilities during operations will be approximately at capacity. This level of production activity is frequently described as practical capacity for the period and is ordinarily based upon the historical experience of the taxpayer. For example, a taxpayer operating on a 5-day, 8-hour basis may have a "normal" production of 100,000 units a year based upon three years of experience.

(c) *Based upon theoretical capacity.* Practical capacity may also be established by the use of "theoretical" capacity, adjusted for allowances for estimated inability to achieve maximum production, such as machine break-down, idle time, and other normal work stoppages. Theoretical capacity is the level of production the manufacturer could reach if all machines and departments were operated continuously at peak efficiency.

(d) *Example.* The provisions of (c) of this subdivision may be illustrated by the following example:

Corporation X operates a stamping plant with a theoretical capacity of 50 units per hour. The plant actually operates 1960 hours per year based on an 8-hour day, 5 day week basis and 15 shut-down days for vacations and holidays. A reasonable allowance for down time (the time allowed for ordi-nary and necessary repairs and maintenance) is 5 percent of practical capacity before reduction for down time. Assuming no loss of production during starting up, closing down, or employee work breaks, under these facts and circumstances X may properly make a practical capacity computation as follows:

Practical capacity without allowance for down time based on theoretical capacity per hour is (1960 × 50)	98,000
Reduction for down time (98,000 × 5%)	4,900
Practical capacity	93,100

The 93,100 unit level of activity (*i. e.,* practical capacity) would, therefore, constitute an appropriate base for calculating the amount of fixed indirect production costs to be included in the computation of the amount of inven-toriable costs for the period under review. On this basis if only 76,000 units were produced for the period, the effect would be that approximately 81.6 percent (76,000, the actual number of units produced, divided by 93,100, the maximum number of units producible at practical capacity) of the fixed indirect production costs during the year. The portion of the fixed indirect production costs not so included in the computation of the amount of in-ventoriable costs would be deductible in the year in which paid or incurred. Assume further that 7,600 units were on hand at the end of the taxable year and the 7,600 units were in the same proportion to the total units pro-duced. Thus, 10 percent (7,600 units in inventory at the end of the taxable year, divided by 76,000, the actual number of units produced) of the fixed indirect production costs included in the computation of the amount of in-ventoriable costs (the above-mentioned 81.6 percent) and 10 percent of the variable indirect production costs would be included in the cost of the goods in the ending inventory, in accordance with a method of allocation provided by this paragraph.

(e) *Transition to full absorption method of inventory costing*—(1) *In general*—(i) *Mandatory requirement.* A taxpayer not using the full absorp-tion method of inventory costing, as prescribed by paragraph (a) of this section, must change to that method. Any change to the full absorption method must be made by the taxpayer with respect to all trades or businesses of the taxpayer to which this section applies. A taxpayer not using the full absorp-tion method of inventory costing, as prescribed by paragraph (a) of this section, who makes the special election provided in subdivision (ii) of this subparagraph during the transition period described in subdivision (ii) of this subparagraph need not change to the full absorption method of inventory costing for taxable years prior to the year for which such election is made. In determining whether the taxpayer is changing to a more or a less inclusive method of inventory costing, all positive and negative adjustments for all items and all trades or businesses of the taxpayer shall be aggregated. If the net adjustment is positive, paragraph (e)(3) shall apply, and if the net adjustment is negative, paragraph (e)(4) shall apply to the change. The rules otherwise prescribed in sections 446 and 481 and the regulations thereunder shall apply to any taxpayer who fails to make the special election in subdivision (ii) of this subparagraph. The transition rules of this paragraph are available only to those taxpayers who change their method of inventory costing.

(ii) *Special election during two-year-transition period.* If a taxpayer elects to change to the full absorption method of inventory costing during the transition period provided herein, he may elect on Form 3115 to change to such full absorption method of inventory costing and, in so doing, employ the transition procedures and adopt any of the transition methods prescribed in subparagraph (3) of this paragraph. Such election shall be made during the first 180 days of any taxable year beginning on or after September 19, 1973, and before September 19, 1975 (*i. e.*, the "transition period") and the change in inventory costing method shall be made for the taxable year in which the election is made. Notwithstanding the preceding sentence if the taxpayer's prior returns have been examined by the Service prior to September 19, 1973 and there is a pending issue involving the taxpayer's method of inventory costing, the taxpayer may request the application of this regulation by agreeing and filing a letter to that effect with the district director, within 90 days after September 19, 1973 to change to the full absorption method for the first taxable year of the taxpayer beginning after September 19, 1973 and subsequently filing Form 3115 within the first 180 days of such taxable year of change.

(iii) *Change initiated by the Commissioner.* A taxpayer who properly makes an election under subdivision (ii) of this subparagraph shall be considered to have made a change in method of accounting not initiated by the taxpayer, notwithstanding the provisions of § 1.481–1(c)(5). Thus, any of the taxpayer's "pre-1954 inventory balances" with respect to such inventory shall not be taken into account as an adjustment under section 481. For purposes of this paragraph, a "pre-1954 inventory balance" is the net amount of the adjustments which would have been required if the taxpayer had made such change in his method of accounting with respect to his inventory in his first taxable year which began after December 31, 1953, and ended after August 16, 1954. See section 481(a)(2) and § 1.481–3.

(2) *Procedural rules for change.* If a taxpayer makes an election pursuant to subparagraph (1)(ii) of this paragraph, the Commissioner's consent will be evidenced by a letter of consent to the taxpayer, setting forth the values of inventory, as provided by the taxpayer, determined under the full absorption

method of inventory costing, except to the extent that no determination of such values is necessary under subparagraph (3)(ii)(B) of this paragraph (the cut off method), the amount of the adjustments (if any) required to be taken into account by section 481, and the treatment to be accorded to any such adjustments. Such full absorption values shall be subject to verification on examination by the district director. The taxpayer shall preserve at his principal place of business all records, data, and other evidence relating to the full absorption values of inventory.

(3) *Transition methods.* In the case of a taxpayer who properly makes an election under subparagraph (1)(ii) of this paragraph during the transition period—

(i) *10-year adjustment period.* Such taxpayer may elect to take any adjustment required by section 481 with respect to any inventory being revalued under the full absorption method into account ratably over a period designated by the taxpayer at the time of such election, not to exceed the lesser of 10 taxable years commencing with the year of transition or the number of years the taxpayer has been on the inventory method from which he is changing. If the taxpayer dies or ceases to exist in a transaction other than one to which section 381(a) of the Code applies or if the taxpayer's inventory (determined under the full absorption method) on the last day of any taxable year is reduced (by other than a strike or involuntary conversion) by more than an amount equal to $33\frac{1}{3}$ percent of the taxpayer's inventory (determined under the full absorption method) as of the beginning of the year of change, the entire amount of the section 481 adjustment not previously taken into account in computing income shall be taken into account in computing income for the taxable year in which such taxpayer so ceases to exist or such taxpayer's inventory is so reduced.

(ii) *Additional rules for LIFO taxpayers.* A taxpayer who uses the LIFO method of inventory identification may either—

(A) Employ the special transition rules, described in subdivision (i) of this subparagraph. Accordingly, all LIFO layers must be revalued under the full absorption method and the section 481 adjustment must be computed for all items in all layers in inventory, but no pre-1954 inventory balances shall be taken into account as adjustments under section 481; or

(B) (1) Employ a cut-off method whereby the full absorption method is only applied in costing layers of inventory acquired during all taxable years beginning with the year for which an election is made under subparagraph (e)(1)(ii).

(2) In the case of a taxpayer using dollar value LIFO, employ a cut-off method whereby the taxpayer must use, for the year of change, the full absorption method in computing the base year cost and current cost of a dollar value inventory pool for the beginning of such year. The taxpayer shall not be required to recompute his LIFO inventories based on the full absorption method for a taxable year beginning prior to the year of change to the full absorption method. The base cost and layers of increment previously computed shall be retained and treated as if such base cost and layers of increment had been computed under the method authorized by this section. The

taxpayer shall use the year of change as the base year in applying the double extension method or other method approved by the Commissioner, instead of the earliest year for which he adopted the LIFO method for any items in the pool.

(4) *Transition to full absorption method of inventory costing from a method more inclusive of indirect production costs*—(i) *Taxpayer has not previously changed to his present method pursuant to subparagraphs (1), (2), and (3) of this paragraph.* If a taxpayer wishes to change to the full absorption method of inventory costing (as prescribed by paragraph (a) of this section) from a method of inventory costing which is more inclusive of indirect production costs and he has not previously changed to his present method by use of the special transition rules provided by subparagraphs (1), (2) and (3) of this paragraph, he may elect on Form 3115 to change to the full absorption method of inventory costing and, in so doing, take into account any resulting section 481 adjustment generally over 10 taxable years commencing with the year of transition. The Commissioner's consent to such election will be evidenced by a letter of consent to the taxpayer setting forth the values of inventory, as provided by the taxpayer determined under the full absorption method of inventory costing, except to the extent that no determination of such values is necessary under subparagraph (3) (ii) (*b*) of this paragraph, the amount of the adjustments (if any) required to be taken into account by section 481, and the treatment to be accorded such adjustments, subject to terms and conditions specified by the Commissioner to prevent distortions of income. Such election must be made within the transition period described in subparagraph (1)(ii) of this paragraph. A change pursuant to this subparagraph shall be a change initiated by the taxpayer as provided by § 1.481–1(c)(5). Thus, any of the taxpayers "pre-1954 inventory balances" will be taken into account as an adjustment under section 481.

(ii) *Taxpayer has previously changed to his present method pursuant to subparagraphs (1), (2) and (3) of this paragraph or would satisfy all the requirements of subdivision (i) of this subparagraph but fails to elect within the transition period.* If a taxpayer wishes to change to the full absorption method of inventory costing (as prescribed by paragraph (a) of this section) from a method of inventory costing which is more inclusive of indirect production costs and he has previously changed to his present method pursuant to subparagraphs (1), (2), and (3) of this paragraph or he would satisfy the requirements of subdivision (i) of this subparagraph but he fails to elect within the transition period, he must secure the consent of the Commissioner prior to making such change. [Reg. § 1.471–11.]

§ 1.472   Statutory provisions; last-in, first-out inventories.

LIFO statutory provisions. Sec. 472. *Last-in, first-out inventories*—(a) *Authorization.* A taxpayer may use the method provided in subsection (b) (whether or not such method has been prescribed under section 471) in inventorying goods specified in an application to use such method filed at such time and in such manner as the Secretary may prescribe. The change to, and the use of, such method shall be in accordance with such regulations as the Secretary may prescribe as necessary in order that the use of such method may clearly reflect income.

(b) *Method applicable.* In inventorying goods specified in the application described in subsection (a), the taxpayer shall:

(1) Treat those remaining on hand at the close of the taxable year as being: First, those included in the opening inventory of the taxable year (in the order of acquisition) to the extent thereof; and second, those acquired in the taxable year;

(2) Inventory them at cost; and

(3) Treat those included in the opening inventory of the taxable year in which such method is first used as having been acquired at the same time and determine their cost by the average cost method.

(c) *Condition.* Subsection (a) shall apply only if the taxpayer establishes to the satisfaction of the Secretary that the taxpayer has used no procedure other than that specified in paragraphs (1) and (3) of subsection (b) in inventorying such goods to ascertain the income, profit, or loss of the first taxable year for which the method described in subsection (b) is to be used, for the purpose of a report or statement covering such taxable year—

(1) To shareholders, partners, or other proprietors, or to beneficiaries, or

(2) For credit purposes.

(d) *Preceding closing inventory.* In determining income for the taxable year preceding the taxable year for which the method described in subsection (b) is first used, the closing inventory of such preceding year of the goods specified in the application referred to in subsection (a) shall be at cost.

(e) *Subsequent inventories.* If a taxpayer, having complied with subsection (a) uses the method described in subsection (b) for any taxable year, then such method shall be used in all subsequent taxable years unless—

(1) With the approval of the Secretary a change to a different method is authorized; or,

(2) The Secretary determines that the taxpayer has used for any such subsequent taxable year some procedure other than that specified in paragraph (1) of subsection (b) in inventorying the goods specified in the application to ascertain the income, profit, or loss of such subsequent taxable year for the purpose of a report or statement covering such taxable year (A) to shareholders, partners, or other proprietors, or beneficiaries, or (B) for credit purposes; and requires a change to a method different from that prescribed in subsection (b) beginning with such subsequent taxable year or any taxable year thereafter.

If paragraph (1) or (2) of this subsection applies, the change to, and the use of, the different method shall be in accordance with such regulations as the Secretary may prescribe as necessary in order that the use of such method may clearly reflect income.

§ 1.472–1   Last-in, first-out inventories.

Any taxpayer may elect LIFO as of close of any year.   (a) Any taxpayer permitted or required to take inventories pursuant to the provisions of section 471, and pursuant to the provisions of §§ 1.471–1 to 1.471–9, inclusive, may elect with respect to those goods specified in his application and properly subject to inventory to compute his opening and closing inventories in accordance with the method provided by section 472, this section, and § 1.472–2. Under this last-in, first-out (LIFO) inventory method, the taxpayer is permitted to treat those goods remaining on hand at the close of the taxable year as being:

(1) Those included in the opening inventory of the taxable year, in the order of acquisition and to the extent thereof, and

(2) Those acquired during the taxable year.

The LIFO inventory method is not dependent upon the character of the business in which the taxpayer is engaged, or upon the identity or want of identity through commingling of any of the goods on hand, and may be adopted by the taxpayer as of the close of any taxable year.

Matched purchases and sales for future delivery may be treated as completed transactions.   (b) If the LIFO inventory method is used by a taxpayer who regularly and consistently, in a manner similar to hedging on a futures market, matches purchases with sales, then firm purchases and sales contracts (i.e., those not legally subject to cancellation by either party) entered into at fixed prices on or before the date of the inventory may be included in purchases or sales as the case may be, for the purpose of determining the costs of goods sold and the resulting profit or loss, provided that this practice is regularly and consistently adhered to by the taxpayer and provided that, in the opinion of the Commissioner, income is clearly reflected thereby.

LIFO may be applied to only material in inventory costs.   (c) A manufacturer or processor who has adopted the LIFO inventory method as to a class of goods may elect to have such method apply to the raw materials only (including those included in goods in process and in finished goods) expressed in terms of appropriate units. If such method is adopted, the adjustments are confined to costs of the raw material in the inventory and the cost of raw material in goods in process and in finished goods produced by such manufacturer or processor and reflected in the inventory. The provisions of this paragraph may be illustrated by the following examples:

Example (1). Assume that the opening inventory had 10 units of raw material, 10 units of goods in process, and 10 units of finished goods, and that the raw material cost was 6 cents a unit, the processing cost 2 cents a unit, and overhead cost 1 cent a unit. For the purposes of this example, it is assumed that the entire amount of goods in process was 50 percent processed.

Opening Inventory

	Raw material	Goods in process	Finished goods
Raw material	$0.60	$0.60	$0.60
Processing cost	—	.10	.20
Overhead	—	.05	.10

In the closing inventory there are 20 units of raw material, 6 units of goods in process, and 8 units of finished goods and the costs were: Raw material 10 cents, processing cost 4 cents, and overhead 1 cent.

Closing Inventory

(Based on cost and prior to adjustment)

	Raw material	Goods in process	Finished goods
Raw material	$2.00	$0.60	$0.80
Processing costs	—	.12	.32
Overhead	—	.03	.08
Total	2.00	.75	1.20

There were 30 units of raw material in the opening inventory and 34 units in the closing inventory. The adjustment to the closing inventory would be as follows:

Closing Inventory As Adjusted

	Raw material	Goods in process	Finished goods
Raw material:			
20 at 6 cents	$1.20	—	—
6 at 6 cents	—	$0.36	—
4 at 6 cents	—	—	$0.24
4 at 10 cents [1]	—	—	.40
Processing costs	—	.12	.32
Overhead	—	.03	.08
Total	1.20	.51	1.04

[1] This excess is subject to determination of price under section 472(b) (1) and § 1.472–2. If the excess falls in goods in process, the same adjustment is applicable.

The only adjustment to the closing inventory is the cost of the raw material; the processing costs and overhead cost are not changed.

Example (2). Assume that the opening inventory had 5 units of raw material, 10 units of goods in process, and 20 units of finished goods, with the same prices as in example (1), and that the closing inventory had 20 units of raw material, 20 units of goods in process, and 10 units of finished goods, with raw material costs as in the closing inventory in example (1). The adjusted closing inventory would be as follows in so far as the raw material is concerned:

Raw material, 20 at 6 cents	$1.20
Goods in process:	
15 at 6 cents	.90
5 at 10 cents [1]	.50
Finished goods:	
None at 6 cents	.00
10 at 10 cents [1]	1.00

[1] This excess is subject to determination of price under section 472(b) (1) and § 1.472–2.

The 20 units of raw material in the raw state plus 15 units of raw material in goods in process make up the 35 units of raw material that were contained in the opening inventory.

LIFO comparisons to be by similar types of materials.   (d) For the purposes of this section, raw material in the opening inventory must be compared with similar raw material in the closing inventory. There may be several types of raw materials, depending upon the character, quality, or price, and each type of raw material in the opening inventory must be compared with a similar type in the closing inventory.

Groupings in cotton textile industry.   (e) In the cotton textile industry there may be different raw materials depending upon marked differences in length of staple, in color or grade of the cotton. But where different staple lengths or grades of cotton are being used at different times in the same mill to produce the same class of goods, such differences would not necessarily require the classification into different raw materials.

Primal cuts from hogs may be grouped.   (f) As to the pork packing industry a live hog is considered as being composed of various raw materials, different cuts of a hog varying markedly in price and use. Generally a hog is processed into approximately 10 primal cuts and several miscellaneous articles. However, due to similarity in price and use, these may be grouped into fewer classifications, each group being classed as one raw material.

Each raw material must be identified.   (g) When the finished product contains two or more different raw materials as in the case of cotton and rayon mixtures, each raw material is treated separately and adjustments made accordingly.

Material-content method can be elected at any time.

(h) Upon written notice addressed to the Commissioner of Internal Revenue, Attention T:R, Washington 25, D.C. by the taxpayer, a taxpayer who has heretofore adopted the LIFO inventory method in respect of any goods may adopt the method authorized in this section and limit the election to the raw material including raw materials entering into goods in process and in finished foods. If this method is adopted as to any specific goods, it must be used exclusively for such goods for any prior taxable year (not closed by agreement) to which the prior election applies and for all subsequent taxable years, unless permission to change is granted by the Commissioner.

Material-content method can be limited to basic processing.

(i) The election may also be limited to that phase in the manufacturing process where a product is produced that is recognized generally as a salable product as, for example, in the textile industry where one phase of the process is the production of yarn. Since yarn is generally recognized as a salable product, the election may be limited to that portion of the process when yarn is produced. In the case of copper and brass processors, the election may be limited to the production of bars, plates, sheets, etc., although these may be further processed into other products.

All materials need not be on LIFO.

(j) The election may also apply to any one raw material, when two or more raw materials enter into the composition of the finished product; for example, in the case of cotton and rayon yarn, the taxpayer may elect to inventory the cotton of section only. However, a taxpayer who has previously made an election to use the LIFO inventory method may not later elect to exclude any raw materials that were covered by such previous election.

LIFO may be used with the retail method.

(k) If a taxpayer using the retail method of pricing inventories, authorized by § 1.471–8, elects to use in connection therewith the LIFO inventory method authorized by section 472 and this section, the apparent cost of the goods on hand at the end of the year, determined pursuant to § 1.471–8, shall be adjusted to the extent of price changes therein taking place after the close of the preceding taxable year. The amount of any apparent inventory increase or decrease to be eliminated in this adjustment shall be determined by reference to acceptable price indexes established to the satisfaction of the Commissioner. Price indexes prepared by the United States Bureau of Labor Statistics which are applicable to the goods in question will be considered acceptable to the Commissioner. Price indexes which are based upon inadequate records, or which are not subject to complete and detailed audit within the Internal Revenue Service, will not be approved.

LIFO may be used with the dollar-value method.   (1) If a taxpayer uses consistently the so-called "dollar-value" method of pricing inventories, or any other method of computation established to the satisfaction of the Commissioner as reasonably adaptable to the purpose and intent of section 472 and this section, and if such taxpayer elects under section 472 to use the LIFO inventory method authorized by such section, the taxpayer's opening and closing inventories shall be determined under section 472 by the use of the appropriate adaptation. See § 1.472–8 for rules relating to the use of the dollar-value method.

§ 1.472–2   Requirements incident to adoption and use of LIFO inventory method.

General requirements for adoption of LIFO.   Except as otherwise provided in § 1.472–1 with respect to raw material computations, with respect to retail inventory computations, and with respect to other methods of computation established to the satisfaction of the Commissioner as reasonably adapted to the purpose and intent of section 472, and in § 1.472–8 with respect to the "dollar-value" method, the adoption and use of the LIFO inventory method is subject to the following requirements:

(a) The taxpayer shall file an application to use such method specifying with particularity the goods to which it is to to be applied.

(b) The inventory shall be taken at cost regardless of market value.

(c) Goods of the specified type included in the opening inventory of the taxable year for which the method is first used shall be considered as having been acquired at the same time and at a unit cost equal to the actual cost of the aggregate divided by the number of units on hand. The actual cost of the aggregate shall be determined pursuant to the inventory method employed by the taxpayer under the regulations applicable to the prior taxable year with the exception that restoration shall be made with respect to any writedown to market values resulting from the pricing of former inventories.

(d) Goods of the specified type on hand as of the close of the taxable year in excess of what were on hand as of the beginning of the taxable year shall be included in the closing inventory, regardless of identification with specific invoices and regardless of specific cost accounting records, at costs determined pursuant to the provisions of subparagraph (1) or (2) of this paragraph, dependent upon the character of the transactions in which the taxpayer is engaged:

(1) (i) In the case of a taxpayer engaged in the purchase and sale of merchandise, such as a retail grocer or druggist, or engaged in the initial production of merchandise and its sale without processing, such as a miner selling his ore output without smelting or refining, such costs shall be determined—

(*a*) By reference to the actual cost of the goods most recently purchased or produced;

(*b*) By reference to the actual cost of the goods purchased or produced during the taxable year in the order of acquisition;

(*c*) By application of an average unit cost equal to the aggregate cost of all of the goods purchased or produced throughout the taxable year divided by the total number of units so purchased or produced, the goods reflected in such inventory increase being considered for the purposes of section 472 as having been acquired all at the same time; or

(*d*) Pursuant to any other proper method which, in the opinion of the Commissioner, clearly reflects income.

(ii) Whichever of the several methods of valuing the inventory increase is adopted by the taxpayer and approved by the Commissioner shall be consistently adhered to in all subsequent taxable years so long as the LIFO inventory method is used by the taxpayer.

(iii) The application of subdivisions (i) and (ii) of this subparagraph may be illustrated by the following examples:

Example (1). Suppose that the taxpayer adopts the LIFO inventory method for the taxable year 1957 with an opening inventory of 10 units at 10 cents per unit, that it makes 1957 purchases of 10 units as follows:

January	1 at $0.11 =	$0.11
April	2 at .12 =	.24
July	3 at .13 =	.39
October	4 at .14 =	.56
Totals	10	1.30

and that it has a 1957 inventory of 15 units. This closing inventory, depending upon the taxpayer's method of valuing inventory increases, will be computed as follows:

(*a*) Most recent purchases—

	10 at $0.10	$1.00
	4 at .14 (October)	.56
	1 at .13 (July)	.13
Totals	15	1.69

or

(*b*) In order of acquisition—

	10 at $0.10	$1.00
	1 at .11 (January)	.11
	2 at .12 (April)	.24
	2 at .13 (July)	.26
Totals	15	1.61

or

(c) At an annual average—

	10 at $0.10	$1.00
	5 at 13 (130/10)	.65
Totals	15	1.65

Example (2). Suppose that the taxpayer's closing inventory for 1958, the year following that involved in example (1) of this subdivision, reflects an inventory decrease for the year, and not an increase; suppose that there is, accordingly, a 1958 closing inventory of 13 units. Inasmuch as the decreased inventory will be determined wholly by reference to the 15 units reflected in the opening inventory for the year, and will be taken "in the order of acquisition" pursuant to section 472(b)(1), and inasmuch as the character of the taxpayer's opening inventory for 1958 will be dependent upon its method of valuing its 5-unit inventory increase for 1957, the closing inventory for 1958 will be computed as follows:

(a) In case the increase for 1957 was taken by reference to the most recent purchase—

	10 at $0.10 (from 1956)	$1.00
	1 at .13 (July 1957)	.13
	2 at .14 (October 1957)	.28
Totals	13	1.41

or

(b) In case the increase for 1957 was taken in the order of acquisition—

	10 at $0.10 (from 1956)	$1.00
	1 at .11 (January 1957)	.11
	2 at .12 (April 1957)	.24
Totals	13	1.35

or

(c) In case the increase for 1957 was taken on the basis of an average—

	10 at $0.10 (from 1956)	$1.00
	3 at .13 (from 1957)	.39
Totals	13	1.39

(2) In the case of a taxpayer engaged in manufacturing, fabricating, processing, or otherwise producing merchandise, such costs shall be determined:

(i) In the case of raw materials purchased or initially produced by the taxpayer, in the manner elected by the taxpayer under subparagraph (1) of this paragraph to the same extent as if the taxpayer were engaged in purchase and sale transactions; and

(ii) In the case of goods in process, regardless of the stage to which the manufacture, fabricating, or processing may have advanced, and in the case of finished goods, pursuant to any proper method which, in the opinion of the Commissioner, clearly reflects income.

Interim statements need not reflect LIFO, and market values may be used in annual statements. (e) The taxpayer shall establish to the satisfaction of the Commissioner that the taxpayer, in ascertaining income, profit, or loss for the taxable year for which the LIFO inventory method is first used or for any subsequent taxable year, for credit purposes or for the purpose of reports to shareholders, partners, or other proprietors, or to beneficiaries, has not used any inventory method other than that referred to in § 1.472–1 or at variance with the requirement referred to in paragraph (c) of this section. The taxpayer's use of market value in lieu of cost or his issuance of reports or credit statements covering a period of operations less than the whole of the taxable year is not considered at variance with this requirement.

Starting inventory to be at cost. (f) Goods of the specified type on hand as of the close of the taxable year preceding the taxable year for which this inventory method is first used shall be included in the taxpayer's closing inventory for such preceding taxable year at cost determined in the manner prescribed in paragraph (c) of this section.

Conditions for change from LIFO. (g) The LIFO inventory method, once adopted by the taxpayer with the approval of the Commissioner, shall be adhered to in all subsequent taxable years unless—

(1) A change to a different method is approved by the Commissioner; or

(2) The Commissioner determines that the taxpayer, in ascertaining income, profit, or loss for the whole of any taxable year subsequent to his adoption of the LIFO inventory method, for credit purposes or for the purpose of reports to shareholders, partners, or other proprietors, or to beneficiaries, has used any inventory method at variance with that referred to in § 1.472–1 and requires of the taxpayer a change to a different method for such subsequent taxable year or any taxable year thereafter.

Records to be preserved for verification. (h) The records and accounts employed by the taxpayer in keeping his books shall be maintained in conformity with the inventory method referred to in § 1.472–1; and such supplemental and detailed inventory records shall be maintained as will enable the district director readily to verify the taxpayer's inventory computations as well as his compliance with the requirements of section 472 and §§ 1.472–7 through 1.472–7.

Use of LIFO may be required for all similar goods. (i) Where the taxpayer is engaged in more than one trade or business, the Commissioner may require that if the LIFO method of valuing inventories is used with respect to goods in one trade or business the same method shall also be used with respect to similar goods in the other trades or businesses if, in the opinion of the Commissioner, the use of such method with respect to such other goods is essential to a clear reflection of income.

§ 1.472–3   Time and manner of making election.

LIFO election and supporting data to be filed with tax return.   (a) The LIFO inventory method may be adopted and used only if the taxpayer files with his income tax return for the taxable year as of the close of which the method is first to be used a statement of his election to use such inventory method. The statement shall be made on form 970 pursuant to the instructions printed with respect thereto and to the requirements of this section, or in such other manner as may be acceptable to the Commissioner. Such statement shall be accompanied by an analysis of all inventories of the taxpayer as of the beginning and as of the end of the taxable year for which the LIFO inventory method is proposed first to be used, and also as of the beginning of the prior taxable year. In the case of a manufacturer, this analysis shall show in detail the manner in which costs are computed with respect to raw materials, goods in process, and finished goods, segregating the products (whether in process or finished goods) into natural groups on the basis of either (1) similarity in factory processes through which they pass, or (2) similarity of raw materials used, or (3) similarity in style, shape, or use of finished products. Each group of products shall be clearly described.

Other data may be requested.   (b) The taxpayer shall submit for the consideration of the Commissioner in connection with the taxpayer's adoption or use of the LIFO inventory method such other detailed information with respect to his business or accounting system as may be at any time requested by the Commissioner.

Use of LIFO may be required for other goods.   (c) As a condition to the taxpayer's use of the LIFO inventory method, the Commissioner may require that the method be used with respect to goods other than those specified in the taxpayer's statement of election if, in the opinion of the Commissioner, the use of such method with respect to such other goods is essential to a clear reflection of income.

LIFO procedures subject to review.   (d) Whether or not the taxpayer's application for the adoption and use of the LIFO inventory method should be approved, and whether or not such method, once adopted, may be continued, and the propriety of all computations incidental to the use of such method, will be determined by the Commissioner in connection with the examination of the taxpayer's income tax returns.

§ 1.472–4   Adjustments to be made by taxpayer.

Objective is to reflect true income.
A taxpayer may not change to the LIFO method of taking inventories unless, at the time he files his application for the adoption of such method, he agrees to such adjustments incident to the change to or from such method, or incident to the use of such method, in the inventories of prior taxable years or otherwise, as the district director upon the examination of the taxpayer's returns may deem necessary in order that the true income of the taxpayer will be clearly reflected for the years involved.

§ 1.472–5   Revocation of election.

Election is irrevocable.
An election made to adopt and use the LIFO inventory method is irrevocable, and the method once adopted shall be used in all subsequent taxable years, unless the use of another method is required by the Commissioner, or authorized by him pursuant to a written application therefor filed as provided in paragraph (e) of § 1.446–1.

§ 1.472–6   Change from LIFO inventory method.

Procedure for changing from LIFO.
If the taxpayer is granted permission by the Commissioner to discontinue the use of LIFO method of taking inventories, and thereafter to use some other method, or if the taxpayer is required by the Commissioner to discontinue the use of the LIFO method by reason of the taxpayer's failure to conform to the requirements detailed in § 1.472–2, the inventory of the specified goods for the first taxable year affected by the change and for each taxable year thereafter shall be taken—

(a) In conformity with the method used by the taxpayer under section 471 in inventorying goods not included in his LIFO inventory computations; or

(b) If the LIFO inventory method was used by the taxpayer with respect to all of his goods subject to the inventory, then in conformity with the inventory method used by the taxpayer prior to his adoption of the LIFO inventory method; or

(c) If the taxpayer had not used inventories prior to his adoption of the LIFO inventory method and had no goods currently subject to inventory by a method other than the LIFO inventory method, then in conformity with such inventory method as may be selected by the taxpayer and approved by the Commissioner as resulting in a clear reflection of income; or

(d) In any event, in conformity with any inventory method to which the taxpayer may change pursuant to application approved by the Commissioner.

§ 1.472–7   Inventories of acquiring corporations.

For additional rules in the case of certain corporate acquisitions specified in section 381(a), see section 381 (c) (5) and the regulations thereunder.

§ 1.472–8   Dollar-value method of pricing LIFO inventories.

Mechanics of "dollar-value" method.   (a) *Election to use dollar-value method.* Any taxpayer may elect to determine the cost of his LIFO inventories under the so-called "dollar-value" LIFO method, provided such method is used consistently and clearly reflects the income of the taxpayer in accordance with the rules of this section. The dollar-value method of valuing LIFO inventories is a method of determining cost by using "base-year" cost expressed in terms of total dollars rather than the quantity and price of specific goods as the unit of measurement. Under such method the goods contained in the inventory are grouped into a pool or pools as described in paragraphs (b) and (c) of this section. The term "base-year cost" is the aggregate of the cost (determined as of the beginning of the taxable year for which the LIFO method is first adopted, i.e., the base date) of all items in a pool. The taxable year for which the LIFO method is first adopted with respect to any item in the pool is the "base year" for that pool, except as provided in paragraph (g) (3) of this section. Liquidations and increments of items contained in the pool shall be reflected only in terms of a net liquidation or increment for the pool as a whole. Fluctuations may occur in quantities of various items within the pool, new items which properly fall within the pool may be added, and old items may disappear from the pool, all without necessarily effecting a change in the dollar value of the pool as a whole. An increment in the LIFO inventory occurs when the end of the year inventory for any pool expressed in terms of base-year cost is in excess of the beginning of the year inventory for that pool expressed in terms of base-year cost. In determining the inventory value for a pool, the increment, if any, is adjusted for changing unit costs or values by reference to a percentage, relative to base-year cost, determined for the pool as a whole. See paragraph (e) of this section. See also paragraph (f) of this section for rules relating to the change to the dollar-value LIFO method from another LIFO method.

Manufacturers and processors may use one LIFO pool for each natural business unit.   (b) *Principles for establishing pools of manufacturers and processors*—(1) *Natural business unit pools.* A pool shall consist of all items entering into the entire inventory investment for a natural business unit of a business enterprise, unless the taxpayer elects to use the multiple pooling method provided in subparagraph (3) of this paragraph. Thus, if a business enterprise is composed of only one natural business unit, one pool shall be used for all of its inventories, including raw materials, goods in process, and finished goods. If, however, a business enterprise is actually composed of more than one natural business unit, more than one pool is required. Where similar types of goods are inventoried in two or more natural business units of the taxpayer, the Commissioner may apportion or allocate such goods among the various natural business units, if he determines that such apportionment or allocation is necessary in order to clearly reflect the income of such taxpayer. Where a manufacturer or processor is also engaged in the wholesaling or retailing of goods purchased from others, any pooling of the LIFO inventory of such purchased goods for the wholesaling or retailing operations shall be determined in accordance with the rules of paragraph (c) of this section.

Considerations in establishing natural business units.   (2) *Definition of natural business unit.* (i) Whether an enterprise is composed of more than one natural business unit is a matter of fact to be determined from all the circumstances. The natural business divisions adopted by the taxpayer for internal management purposes, the existence of separate and distinct production facilities and processes, and the maintenance of separate profit and loss records with respect to separate operations are important considerations in determining what is a business unit, unless such divisions, facilities, or accounting records are set up merely because of differences in geographical location. In the case of a manufacturer or processor, a natural business unit ordinarily consists of the entire productive activity of the enterprise within one product line or within two or more related product lines including (to the extent engaged in by the enterprise) the obtaining of materials, the processing of materials, and the selling of manufactured or processed goods. Thus, in the case of a manufacturer or processor, the maintenance and operation of a raw material warehouse does not generally constitute, of itself, a natural business unit. If the taxpayer maintains and operates a supplier unit the production of which is both sold to others and transferred to a different unit of the taxpayer to be used as a component part of another product, the supplier unit will ordinarily constitute a separate and distinct natural business unit. Ordinarily, a processing plant would not in itself be considered a natural business unit if the production of the plant, although saleable at this stage, is not sold to others, but is transferred to another plant of the enterprise, not operated as a separate division, for further processing or incorporation into another product. On the other hand, if the production of a manufacturing or processing plant is transferred to a separate and distinct division of the taxpayer, which constitutes a natural business unit, the supplier unit itself will ordinarily be considered a natural business unit. However, the mere fact that a portion of the production of a manufacturing or processing plant may be sold to others at a certain stage of processing with the remainder of the production being further processed or incorporated into another product will not of itself be determinative that the activities devoted to the production of the portion sold constitute a separate business unit. Where a manufacturer or processor is also engaged in the wholesaling or retailing of goods purchased from others, the wholesaling or retailing operations with respect to such purchased goods shall not be considered a part of any manufacturing or processing unit.

Examples of natural business units.   (ii) The rules of this subparagraph may be illustrated by the following examples:

Example (1).   A corporation manufactures, in one division, automatic clothes washers and driers of both commercial and domestic grade as well as electric ranges, mangles, and dishwashers. The corporation manufactures, in another division, radios and television sets. The manufacturing facilities and processes used in manufacturing the radios and television sets are distinct from those used in manufacturing the automatic clothes washers, etc. Under these circumstances, the enterprise would consist of two business units and two pools would be appropriate, one consisting of all of the LIFO inventories entering into the manufacture of clothes washers and driers, electric ranges, mangles, and dishwashers and the other consisting of all of the LIFO inventories entering into the production of radio and television sets.

Example (2).   A taxpayer produces plastics in one of its plants. Substantial amounts of the production are sold as plastics. The remainder of the production is shipped to a second plant of the taxpayer for the production of plastic toys which are sold to customers. The taxpayer operates his plastics plant and toy plant as separate divisions. Because of the different product lines and the separate divisions the taxpayer has two natural business units.

Example (3).   A taxpayer is engaged in the manufacture of paper. At one stage of processing, uncoated paper is produced. Substantial amounts of uncoated paper are sold at this stage of processing. The remainder of the uncoated paper is transferred to the taxpayer's finishing mill where coated paper is produced and sold. This taxpayer has only one natural business unit since coated and uncoated paper are within the same product line.

Multiple pools may be used.   (3) *Multiple pools*—(i) *Principles for establishing multiple pools*. (a) A taxpayer may elect to establish multiple pools for inventory items which are not within a natural business unit as to which the taxpayer has adopted the natural business unit method of pooling as provided in subparagraph (1) of this paragraph. Each such pool shall ordinarily consist of a group of inventory items which are substantially similar. In determining whether such similarity exists, consideration shall be given to all the facts and circumstances. The formulation of detailed rules for selection of pools applicable to all taxpayers is not feasible. Important considerations to be taken into account include, for example, whether there is substantial similarity in the types of raw materials used or in the processing operations applied; whether the raw materials used are readily interchangeable; whether there is similarity in the use of the products; whether the groupings are consistently followed for purposes of internal accounting and management; and whether the groupings follow customary business practice in the taxpayer's industry. The selection of pools in each case must also take into consideration such factors as the nature of the inventory items subject to the dollar-value LIFO method and the significance of such items to the taxpayer's business operations. Where similar types of goods are inventoried in natural business units and multiple pools of the taxpayer, the Commissioner may apportion or allocate such goods among the natural business units and the multiple pools, if he determines that such apportionment or allocation is necessary in order to clearly reflect the income of the taxpayer.

Pooling of
raw materials.
(b) Raw materials which are substantially similar shall be pooled together in accordance with the principles of this subparagraph. However, inventories of raw or unprocessed materials of an unlike nature may not be placed into one pool, even though such materials become part of otherwise identical finished products.

Pooling of
finished and
in-process
inventories.
(c) Finished goods and goods-in-process in the inventory shall be placed into pools classified by major classes or types of goods. The same class or type of finished goods and goods-in-process shall ordinarily be included in the same pool. Where the material content of a class of finished goods and goods-in-process included in a pool has been changed, for example, to conform with current trends in an industry, a separate pool of finished goods and goods-in-process will not ordinarily be required unless the change in material content results in a substantial change in the finished goods.

Pool for
miscellaneous
items.
(d) The requirement that pools be established by major types of materials or major classes of goods is not to be construed so as to preclude the establishment of a miscellaneous pool. Since a taxpayer may elect the dollar-value LIFO method with respect to all or any designated goods in his inventory, there may be a number of such inventory items covered in the election. A miscellaneous pool shall consist only of items which are relatively insignificant in dollar value by comparison with other inventory items in the particular trade or business and which are not properly includible as part of another pool.

Raw materials
and material-
content pool.
(ii) *Raw materials content pools.* The dollar-value method of pricing LIFO inventories may be used in conjunction with the raw materials content method authorized in § 1.472–1. Raw materials (including the raw material content of finished goods and goods-in-process) which are substantially similar shall be pooled together in accordance with the principles of subdivision (i) of this subparagraph. However, inventories of materials of an unlike nature may not be placed into one pool, even though such materials become part of otherwise identical finished products.

Pools for
wholesalers,
retailers, etc.
(c) *Principles for establishing pools for wholesalers, retailers, etc.* Items of inventory in the hands of wholesalers, retailers, jobbers, and distributors shall be placed into pools by major lines, types, or classes of goods. In determining such groupings, customary business classifications of the particular trade in which the taxpayer is engaged is an important consideration. An example of such customary business classification is the department in the department store. In such case, practices are relatively uniform throughout the trade, and departmental grouping is peculiarly adapted to the customs and needs of the business. However, in appropriate cases, the principles set forth in paragraphs (b) (1) and (2) of this section, relating to pooling by natural business

units, may be used, with permission of the Commissioner, by wholesalers, retailers, jobbers, or distributors. Where a wholesaler or retailer is also engaged in the manufacturing or processing of goods, the pooling of the LIFO inventory for the manufacturing or processing operations shall be determined in accordance with the rules of paragraph (b) of this section.

If found appropriate, pooling may not be changed. (d) *Determination of appropriateness of pools.* Whether the number and the composition of the pools used by the taxpayer is appropriate, as well as the propriety of all computations incidental to the use of such pools, will be determined in connection with the examination of the taxpayer's income tax returns. Adequate records must be maintained to support the base-year unit cost as well as the current-year unit cost for all items priced on the dollar-value LIFO inventory method, regardless of the method authorized by paragraph (e) of this section which is used in computing the LIFO value of the dollar-value pool. The pool or pools selected must be used for the year of adoption and for all subsequent taxable years unless a change is required by the Commissioner in order to clearly reflect income, or unless permission to change is granted by the Commissioner as provided in paragraph (e) of § 1.446–1. However, see paragraph (h) of this section for authorization to change the method of pooling in certain specified cases.

Alternatives to "double-extension" method of computation. (e) *Methods of computation of the LIFO value of a dollar-value pool*—(1) *Methods authorized.* A taxpayer may ordinarily use only the so-called "double-extension" method for computing the base-year and current-year cost of a dollar-value inventory pool. Where the use of the double-extension method is impractical, because of technological changes, the extensive variety of items, or extreme fluctuations in the variety of the items in a dollar-value pool, the taxpayer may use an index method for computing all or part of the LIFO value of the pool. An index may be computed by double-extending a representative portion of the inventory in a pool or by the use of other sound and consistent statistical methods. The index used must be appropriate to the inventory pool to which it is to be applied. The appropriateness of the method of computing the index and the accuracy, reliability, and suitability of the use of such index must be demonstrated to the satisfaction of the district director in connection with the examination of the taxpayer's income tax returns. The use of any so-called "link-chain" method will be approved for taxable years beginning from December 31, 1960, only in those cases where the taxpayer can demonstrate to the satisfaction of the district director that the use of either an index method or the double-extension method would be impractical or unsuitable in view of the nature of the pool. A taxpayer using either an index or link-chain method shall attach to his income tax return for the first taxable year beginning after December 31, 1960, for which the index or link-chain method is used, a statement describing the particular link-chain method or the method used in computing the index. The statement shall be in sufficient detail to facilitate the determination as to whether the method used meets the standards set forth in this subparagraph. In addition, a copy of the statement shall be filed with the Commissioner of Internal Revenue, Attention: T:R, Washington 25, D.C. The taxpayer shall submit such other information as may be requested with respect to such index or link-chain method. Adequate records must be maintained by the taxpayer to support the appropriateness, accuracy, and reliability of an index or link-chain method. A taxpayer may request the Commissioner to approve the appropriateness of an index or link-chain method for the first taxable year beginning after December 31, 1960, for which it is used. Such request must be submitted within 90 days after the beginning of the first taxable year beginning after December 31, 1960, in which the taxpayer desires to use the index or link-chain method, or on or before May 1, 1961, whichever is later. A taxpayer entitled to use the retail method of pricing LIFO inventories authorized by paragraph (k) of § 1.472–1 may use retail price indexes prepared by the United States Bureau of Labor Statistics. Any method of computing the LIFO value of a dollar-value pool must be used for the year of adoption and all subsequent taxable years, unless the taxpayer obtains the consent of the Commissioner in accordance with paragraph (e) of § 1.446–1 to use a different method.

Mechanics of double-extension method.   (2) *Double-extension method.* (i) Under the double-extension method the quantity of each item in the inventory pool at the close of the taxable year is extended at both base-year unit cost and current-year unit cost. The respective extensions at the two costs are then each totaled. The first total gives the amount of the current inventory in terms of base-year cost and the second total gives the amount of such inventory in terms of current-year cost.

(ii) The total current-year cost of items making up a pool may be determined—

(*a*) By reference to the actual cost of the goods most recently purchased or produced;

(*b*) By reference to the actual cost of the goods purchased or produced during the taxable year in the order of acquisition;

(*c*) By application of an average unit cost equal to the aggregate cost of all of the goods purchased or produced throughout the taxable year divided by the total number of units so purchased or produced; or

(*d*) Pursuant to any other proper method which, in the opinion of the Commissioner, clearly reflects income.

(iii) Under the double-extension method a base-year unit cost must be ascertained for each item entering a pool for the first time subsequent to the beginning of the base year. In such a case, the base-year unit cost of the entering item shall be the current-year cost of that item unless the taxpayer is able to reconstruct or otherwise establish a different cost. If the entering item is a product or raw material not in existence on the base date, its cost may be reconstructed, that is, the taxpayer using reasonable means may determine what the cost of the item would have been had it been in existence in the base year. If the item was in existence on the base date but not stocked by the taxpayer, he may establish, by using available data or records, what the cost of the item would have been to the taxpayer had he stocked the item. If the base-year unit cost of the entering item is either reconstructed or otherwise established to the satisfaction of the Commissioner, such cost may be used as the base-year unit cost in applying the double-extension method. If the taxpayer does not reconstruct or establish to the satisfaction of the Commissioner a base-year unit cost, but does reconstruct or establish to the satisfaction of the Commissioner the cost of the item at some year subsequent to the base year, he may use the earliest cost which he does reconstruct or establish as the base-year unit cost.

(iv) To determine whether there is an increment or liquidation in a pool for a particular taxable year, the end of the year inventory of the pool expressed in terms of base-year cost is compared with the beginning of the year inventory of the pool expressed in terms of base-year cost. When the end of the year inventory of the pool is in excess of the beginning of the year inventory of the pool, an increment occurs in the pool for that year. If there is an increment for the taxable year, the ratio of the total current-year cost of the pool to the total base-year cost of the pool must be computed. This ratio when multiplied by the amount of the increment measured in terms of base-year cost gives the LIFO value of such increment. The LIFO value of each such increment is hereinafter referred to in this section as the "layer of increment" and must be separately accounted for and a record thereof maintained as a separate layer of the pool, and may not be combined with a layer of increment occurring in a different year. On the other hand, when the end of the year inventory of the pool is less than the beginning of the year inventory of the pool, a liquidation occurs in the pool for that year. Such liquidation is to be reflected by reducing the most recent layer of increment by the excess of the beginning of the year inventory over the end of the year inventory of the pool. However, if the amount of the liquidation exceeds the amount of the most recent layer of increment, the preceding layers of increment in reverse chronological order are to be successively reduced by the amount of such excess until all the excess is absorbed. The base-year inventory is to be reduced by liquidation only to the extent that the aggregate of all liquidation exceeds the aggregate of all layers of increment.

Examples of double-extension method.   (v) The following examples illustrate the computation of the LIFO value of inventories under the double-extension method.

Example (1). (*a*) A taxpayer elects, beginning with the calendar year 1961, to compute his inventories by use of the LIFO inventory method under section 472 and further elects to use the dollar-value method in pricing such inventories as provided in paragraph (a) of this section. He creates Pool No. 1 for items A, B, and C. The composition of the inventory for Pool No. 1 at the base date, January 1, 1961, is as follows:

Items	Units	Unit cost	Total cost
A	1,000	$5	$ 5,000
B	2,000	4	8,000
C	500	2	1,000
Total base-year cost at Jan. 1, 1961			$14,000

(*b*) The closing inventory of Pool No. 1 at December 31, 1961, contains 3,000 units of A, 1,000 units of B, and 500 units of C. The taxpayer computes the current-year cost of the items making up the pool by reference to the actual cost of goods most recently purchased. The most recent purchases of items A, B, and C are as follows:

Item	Purchase date	Quantity purchased	Unit cost
A	Dec. 15, 1961	3,500	$6.00
B	Dec. 10, 1961	2,000	5.00
C	Nov. 1, 1961	500	2.50

(*c*) The inventory of Pool No. 1 at December 31, 1961, shown at base-year and current-year cost is as follows:

Item	Quantity	Dec. 31, 1961, inventory at Jan. 1, 1961, base-year cost		Dec. 31, 1961, inventory at current-year cost	
		Unit cost	Amount	Unit cost	Amount
A	3,000	$5.00	$15,000	$6.00	$18,000
B	1,000	4.00	4,000	5.00	5,000
C	500	2.00	1,000	2.50	1,250
Total			$20,000		$24,250

(*d*) If the amount of the December 31, 1961, inventory at base-year cost were equal to, or less than, the base-year cost of $14,000 at January 1, 1961, such amount would be the closing LIFO inventory at December 31, 1961. However, since the base-year cost of the closing LIFO inventory at December 31, 1961, amounts to $20,000, and is in excess of the $14,000 base-year cost of the opening inventory for that year, there is a $6,000 increment in Pool No. 1 during the year. This increment must be valued at current-year cost, i.e., the ratio of 24,250/20,000, or 121.25

per cent. The LIFO value of the inventory at December 31, 1961, is $21,275, computed as follows:

Pool No. 1

	Dec. 31, 1961, inventory at Jan. 1, 1961, base-year cost	Ratio of total current-year cost to total base-year cost	Dec. 31, 1961, inventory at LIFO value
		Per cent	
Jan. 1, 1961, base cost	$14,000	100.00	$14,000
Dec. 31, 1961, increment	6,000	121.25	7,275
Total	$20,000		$21,275

Example (2). (*a*) Assume the taxpayer in example (1) during the year 1962 completely disposes of item C and purchases item D. Assume further that item D is properly includible in Pool No. 1 under the provisions of this section. The closing inventory on December 31, 1962, consists of quantities at current-year unit cost, as follows:

Items	Units	Current-year unit cost Dec. 31, 1962
A	2,000	$6.50
B	1,500	6.00
D	1,000	5.00

(*b*) The taxpayer establishes that the cost of item D, had he acquired it on January 1, 1961, would have been $2.00 per unit. Such cost shall be used as the base-year unit cost for item D, and the LIFO computations at December 31, 1962, are made as follows:

Items	Quantity	Dec. 31, 1962, inventory at Jan. 1, 1961, base-year cost Unit cost	Amount	Dec. 31, 1962, inventory at current-year cost Unit cost	Amount
A	2,000	$5.00	$10,000	$6.50	$13,000
B	1,500	4.00	6,000	6.00	9,000
D	1,000	2.00	2,000	5.00	5,000
Total			$18,000		$27,000

(c) Since the closing inventory at base-year cost, $18,000, is less than the 1962 opening inventory at base-year cost, $20,000, a liquidation of $2,000 has occurred during 1962. This liquidation is to be reflected by reducing the most recent layer of increment. This LIFO value of the inventory at December 31, 1962, is $18,850, and is summarized as follows:

Pool No. 1

	Dec. 31, 1962, inventory at Jan. 1, 1961, base-year cost	Ratio of total current-year cost to total base-year cost	Dec. 31, 1962, inventory at LIFO value
		Per cent	
Jan. 1, 1961, base cost	$14,000	100.00	$14,000
Dec. 31, 1961, increment	4,000	121.25	4,850
Total	$18,000		$18,850

Change from another LIFO procedure to dollar-value method requires advance permission if pools are changed.   (f) *Change to dollar-value method from another method of pricing LIFO inventories*—(1) *Consent required.* Except as provided in § 1.472–3 in the case of a taxpayer electing to use a LIFO inventory method for the first time, or in the case of a taxpayer changing to the dollar-value method and continuing to use the same pools as were used under another LIFO method, a taxpayer using another LIFO method of pricing inventories may not change to the dollar-value method of pricing such inventories unless he first secures the consent of the Commissioner in accordance with paragraph (e) of § 1.446–1.

Mechanics of change to dollar-value method.   (2) *Method of converting inventory.* Where the taxpayer changes from one method of pricing LIFO inventories to the dollar-value method, the ending LIFO inventory for the taxable year immediately preceding the year of change shall be converted to the dollar-value LIFO method. This is done to establish the base-year cost for subsequent calculations. Thus, if the taxpayer was previously valuing LIFO inventories on the specific goods method, these separate values shall be combined into appropriate pools. For this purpose, the base year for the pool shall be the earliest taxable year for which the LIFO inventory method had been adopted for any item in that pool. No change will be made in the overall LIFO value of the opening inventory for that year of change as a result of the conversion, and that inventory will merely be restated in the manner used under the dollar-value method. All layers of increment for such inventory must be retained, except that all layers of increment which occurred in the same taxable year must be combined. The following examples illustrate the provisions of this subparagraph:

Example (1). (i) Assume that the taxpayer has used another LIFO method for finished goods since 1954 and has complied with all the requirements prerequisite for a change to the dollar-value method. Items A, B, and C, which have previously been inventoried under the specific goods LIFO method, may properly be included in a single dollar-value LIFO pool. The LIFO inventory value of items A, B, and C at December 31, 1960, is $12,200 computed as follows:

Year	Base quantity and yearly increments	Unit cost	Dec. 31, 1960, inventory at LIFO value
Item A			
1954 (base year)	100	$ 1	$ 100
1955	200	2	400
1956	100	4	400
1960	100	6	600
Total	500		$ 1,500
Item B			
1954 (base year)	300	6	1,800
1955	100	8	800
1960	50	10	500
Total	450		$ 3,100
Item C			
1954 (base year)	1,000	4	4,000
1955	200	6	1,200
1956	300	8	2,400
Total	1,500		$ 7,600
LIFO value of items A, B, and C at Dec. 31, 1960			$12,200

There were no increments in the years 1957, 1958, or 1959.

(ii) The computation of the ratio of the total current-year cost to the total base-year cost for the base year and each layer of increment in Pool No. 1 is shown as follows:

Item	1954 base-year unit cost	Year 1954	Increments		
			1955	1956	1960
A					
Base-year cost	$1.00	$ 100	$ 200	$ 100	$ 100
LIFO value		100	400	400	600
B					
Base-year cost	6.00	1,800	600	—	300
LIFO value		1,800	800	—	500
C					
Base-year cost	4.00	4,000	800	1,200	—
LIFO value		4,000	1,200	2,400	—
Total—base-year cost		$5,900	$1,600	$1,300	$ 400
Total—LIFO value		5,900	2,400	2,800	1,100
Ratio of total current-year cost to total base-year cost (per cent)		100.00	150.00	215.38	275.00

(iii) On the basis of the foregoing computations, the LIFO inventory of Pool No. 1, at December 31, 1960, is restated as follows:

	Dec. 31, 1960, inventory at base-year cost	Ratio of total current-year cost to total base-year cost	Dec. 31, 1960, inventory at LIFO value
		Per cent	
1954 base cost	5,900	100.00	$ 5,900
1955 increment	1,600	150.00	2,400
1956 increment	1,300	215.38	2,800
1960 increment	400	275.00	1,100
Total	9,200		$12,200

Example (2). Assume the same facts as in example (1) and assume further that the base-year cost of Pool No. 1 at December 31, 1961, is $8,350. Since the closing inventory for the taxable year 1961 at base-year cost is less than the opening inventory for that year at base-year cost, a liquidation has occurred during 1961. This liquidation absorbs all of the 1960 layer of increment and part of the 1956 layer of increment. The December 31, 1961, inventory is $10,131, computed as follows:

	Dec. 31, 1961, inventory at base-year cost	Ratio of total current-year cost to total base-year cost	Dec. 31, 1961, inventory at LIFO value
		Per cent	
1954 base cost	$5,900	100.00	$ 5,900
1955 increment	1,600	150.00	2,400
1956 increment	850	215.38	1,831
Total	$8,350		$10,131

Pooling treated as a method of accounting.   (g) *Transitional rules*—(1) *Change in method of pooling.* Any method of pooling authorized by this section and used by the taxpayer in computing his LIFO inventories under the dollar-value method shall be treated as a method of accounting. Any method of pooling which is authorized by this section shall be used for the year of adoption and for all subsequent taxable years unless a change is required by the Commissioner in order to clearly reflect income, or unless permission to change is granted by the Commissioner as provided in paragraph (e) of § 1.446–1. Where the taxpayer changes from one method of pooling to another method of pooling permitted by this section, the ending LIFO inventory for the taxable year preceding the year of change shall be restated under the new method of pooling.

Changing pools will not change previously established costs.   (2) *Manner of combining or separating dollar-value pools.* (i) A taxpayer who has been using the dollar-value LIFO method and who is permitted or required to change his method of pooling, shall combine or separate the LIFO value of his inventory for the base year and each yearly layer of increment in order to conform to the new pool or pools.

Each yearly layer of increment in the new pool or pools must be separately accounted for and a record thereof maintained, and any liquidation occurring in the new pool or pools subsequent to the formation thereof shall be treated in the same manner as if the new pool or pools had existed from the date the taxpayer first adopted the LIFO inventory method. The combination or separation of the LIFO value of his inventory for the base year and each yearly layer of increment shall be made in accordance with the appropriate method set forth in this subparagraph, unless the use of a different method is approved by the Commissioner.

Mechanics of separating pools.   (ii) Where the taxpayer is permitted or required to separate a pool into more than one pool, the separation shall be made in the following manner: First, each item in the former pool shall be placed in an appropriate new pool. Every item in each new pool is then extended at its base-year unit cost and the extensions are totaled. Each total is the amount of inventory for each new pool expressed in terms of base-year cost. Then a ratio of the total base-year cost of each new pool to the base-year cost of the former pool is computed. The resulting ratio is applied to the amount of inventory for the base year and each yearly layer of increment of the former pool to obtain an allocation to each new pool of the base-year inventory of the former pool and subsequent layers of increment thereof. The foregoing may be illustrated by the following example of a change for the taxable year 1961:

Example. (*a*) Assume that items A, B, C, and D are all grouped together in one pool prior to December 31, 1960. The LIFO inventory value at December 31, 1960, is computed as follows:

	Pool ABCD		
	Dec. 31, 1960, inventory at Jan. 1, 1956, base-year cost	Ratio of total current-year cost to total base-year cost	Dec. 31, 1960, inventory at LIFO value
		Per cent	
Jan. 1, 1956, base cost	$10,000	100	$10,000
Dec. 31, 1956, increment	1,000	110	1,100
Dec. 31, 1958, increment	5,000	120	6,000
Dec. 31, 1960, increment	4,000	125	5,000
Total	$20,000		$22,100

(*b*) The extension of the quantity of items A, B, C, and D at respective base-year unit costs is as follows:

Item	Quantity	Base-year unit cost	Amount
A	2,000	$2	$ 4,000
B	1,000	3	3,000
C	1,000	5	5,000
D	4,000	2	8,000
Total			$20,000

(*c*) Under the provisions of this section the taxpayer separates former Pool ABCD into two pools, Pool AB and Pool CD. The computation of the ratio of total base-year cost for each of the new pools to the base-year cost of the former pool is as follows:

Item	Total base-year cost	Ratio
Pool AB:		
A	$ 4,000	
B	3,000	
	7,000	7,000/20,000
Pool CD:		
C	$ 5,000	
D	8,000	
	$13,000	13,000/20,000
Total for pool ABCD	$20,000	

(d) The ratio of the base-year cost of new Pools AB and CD to the base-year cost of former Pool ABCD is 7,000/20,000 and 13,000/20,000, respectively. The allocation of the January 1, 1956, base cost and subsequent yearly layers of increment of former Pool ABCD to new Pools AB and CD is as follows:

	Base-year cost to be allocated	Pool	
		AB	CD
Jan. 1, 1956, base cost	$10,000	$3,500	$ 6,500
Dec. 31, 1956, increment	1,000	350	650
Dec. 31, 1958, increment	5,000	1,750	3,250
Dec. 31, 1960, increment	4,000	1,400	2,600
Total	$20,000	$7,000	$13,000

(e) The LIFO value of new Pools AB and CD at December 31, 1960, as allocated, is as follows:

	Dec. 31, 1960, inventory at Jan. 1, 1956, base-year cost	Ratio of total current-year cost to total base-year cost	Dec. 31, 1960, inventory at LIFO value
Pool AB			
		Per cent	
Jan. 1, 1956, base cost	$ 3,500	100	$ 3,500
Dec. 31, 1956, increment	350	110	385
Dec. 31, 1958, increment	1,750	120	2,100
Dec. 31, 1960, increment	1,400	125	1,750
Total	$ 7,000		$ 7,735
Pool CD			
Jan. 1, 1956, base cost	$ 6,500	100	$ 6,500
Dec. 31, 1956, increment	650	110	715
Dec. 31, 1958, increment	3,250	120	3,900
Dec. 31, 1960, increment	2,600	125	3,250
Total	$13,000		$14,365

Mechanics of combining pools.   (iii) Where the taxpayer is permitted or required to combine two or more pools having the same base year, they shall be combined into one pool in the following manner: The LIFO value of the base-year inventory of each of the former pools is combined to obtain a LIFO value of the base-year inventory for the new pool. Then, any layers of increment in the various pools which occurred in the same taxable year are combined into one total layer of increment for that taxable year. However, layers of increment which occurred in different taxable years may not be combined. In combining the layers of increment a new ratio of current-year cost to base-year cost is computed for each of the combined layers of increment. The foregoing may be illustrated by the following example:

Example. (a) Assume the taxpayer has two pools at December 31, 1960. Under the provisions of this section the taxpayer combines these pools into a single pool as of January 1, 1961. The LIFO inventory value of each pool at December 31, 1960, is shown as follows:

	Dec. 31, 1960, inventory at Jan. 1, 1957, base-year cost	Ratio of total current-year cost to total base-year cost	Dec. 31, 1960, inventory at LIFO value
Pool No. 1			
		Per cent	
Jan. 1, 1957, base cost	$10,000	100	$10,000
Dec. 31, 1957, increment	2,000	110	2,200
Dec. 31, 1960, increment	1,000	120	1,200
Total	$13,000		$13,400

	Dec. 31, 1960, inventory at Jan. 1, 1957, base-year cost	Ratio of total current-year cost to total base-year cost	Dec. 31, 1960, inventory at LIFO value
Pool No. 2			
		Per cent	
Jan. 1, 1957, base cost	$5,000	100	$5,000
Dec. 31, 1960, increment	3,000	140	4,200
Total	$8,000		$9,200

(*b*) The computation of the ratio of the total current-year cost to the total base-year cost for the base year and each yearly layer of increment in the new pool is as follows:

		Increments	
Pool	Base year 1957	Dec. 31, 1957	Dec. 31, 1960
No. 1:			
Base-year cost	$10,000	$2,000	$1,000
LIFO value	10,000	2,200	1,200
No. 2:			
Base-year cost	5,000	—	3,000
LIFO value	5,000	—	4,200
Total, base-year cost	$15,000	$2,000	$4,000
Total, LIFO value	15,000	2,200	5,400
Ratio of total current-year cost to total base-year cost (percent)	100	110	135

(*c*) On the basis of the foregoing computations, the LIFO inventory of the new pool at December 31, 1960, is restated as follows:

	Dec. 31, 1960, inventory at Jan. 1, 1957, base-year cost	Ratio of total current-year cost to total base-year cost	Dec. 31, 1960, inventory at LIFO value
		Per cent	
Jan. 1, 1957, base cost	$15,000	100	$15,000
Dec. 31, 1957, increment	2,000	110	2,200
Dec. 31, 1960, increment	4,000	135	5,400
Total	$21,000		$22,600

(iv) In combining pools having different base years, the principles set forth in subdivision (iii) of this subparagraph are to be applied, except that all base years subsequent to the earliest base year shall be treated as increments, and the base-year costs for all pools having a base year subsequent to the earliest base year of any pool shall be redetermined in terms of the base cost for the earliest base year. The foregoing may be illustrated by the following example:

Example. (*a*) Assume that the taxpayer has two pools at December 31, 1960. Under the provisions of this section the taxpayer combines these pools into a single pool as of January 1, 1961. The LIFO inventory value of each pool at December 31, 1960, is shown as follows:

	Dec. 31, 1960, inventory at Jan. 1, 1956, base-year cost	Ratio of total current-year cost to total base-year cost	Dec. 31, 1960, inventory at LIFO value
Pool No. 1			
		Per cent	
Jan. 1, 1956, base cost	$ 7,000	100	$ 7,000
Dec. 31, 1956, increment	1,000	105	1,050
Dec. 31, 1957, increment	500	110	550
Dec. 31, 1958, increment	500	110	550
Dec. 31, 1960, increment	1,000	120	1,200
Total	$10,000		$10,350

	Dec. 31, 1960, inventory at Jan. 1, 1958, base-year cost		
Pool No. 2			
Jan. 1, 1958, base cost	$ 3,500	100	$ 3,500
Dec. 31, 1958, increment	1,000	110	1,100
Dec. 31, 1959, increment	500	115	575
Total	$ 5,000		$ 5,175

(*b*) The next step is to redetermine the 1958 base-year cost for Pool No. 2 in terms of 1956 base-year cost. January 1, 1956, base-year unit cost must be reconstructed or established in accordance with paragraph (e) (2) of this section for each item in Pool No. 2. Such costs are assumed to be $9.00 for item A, $20.00 for item B, and $1.80 for item C. A ratio of the 1958 total base-year cost to the 1956 total base-year cost for Pool No. 2 is computed as follows:

Item	Quantity	Jan. 1, 1956, base-year unit cost	Jan. 1, 1956, base-year cost
A	250	$ 9.00	$2,250
B	75	20.00	1,500
C	500	1.80	900
Total			$4,650

Item	Quantity	Jan. 1, 1958, base-year unit cost	Jan. 1, 1958, base-year cost
A	250	$10.00	$2,500
B	75	20.00	1,500
C	500	2.00	1,000
Total			$5,000

(*c*) The ratio of the 1956 total base-year cost to the 1958 total base-year cost for Pool No. 2 is 4,650/5,000 or 93 per cent. The January 1, 1958, base cost and each yearly layer of increment at 1958 base-year cost is multiplied by this ratio. Such computation is as follows:

	Dec. 31, 1960, inventory at Jan. 1, 1958, base-year cost	Ratio	Dec. 31, 1960, inventory restated at Jan. 1, 1956, base-year cost
		Percent	
Jan. 1, 1958, base cost	$3,500	93	$3,255
Dec. 31, 1958, increment	1,000	93	930
Dec. 31, 1959, increment	500	93	465
Total			$4,650

(*d*) The computation of the ratio of the total current-year cost to the total base-year cost for the base year (1956) and each yearly layer of increment in the new pool is as follows:

Pool	Base year 1956	Increments				
		Dec. 31, 1956	Dec. 31, 1957	Dec. 31, 1958	Dec. 31, 1959	Dec. 31, 1960
No. 1:						
Base-year cost	$7,000	$1,000	$ 500	$ 500	—	$1,000
LIFO value	7,000	1,050	550	550	—	1,200
No. 2:						
Base-year cost as restated	—	—	3,255	930	$465	—
LIFO value	—	—	3,500	1,100	575	—
Total, base-year cost	$7,000	$1,000	$3,755	$1,430	$465	$1,000
Total, LIFO value	7,000	1,050	4,050	1,650	575	1,200
Ratio of total current-year cost to total base-year cost (percent)	100.00	105.00	107.86	115.38	123.66	120.00

(e) On the basis of the foregoing computation, the LIFO inventory of the new pool at December 31, 1960, is restated as follows:

	Dec. 31, 1960, inventory at Jan. 1, 1956, base-year cost	Ratio of total current-year cost to total base-year cost	Dec. 31, 1960, inventory at LIFO value
		Percent	
Jan. 1, 1956, base cost	$ 7,000	100.00	$ 7,000
Dec. 31, 1956, increment	1,000	105.00	1,050
Dec. 31, 1957, increment	3,755	107.86	4,050
Dec. 31, 1958, increment	1,430	115.38	1,650
Dec. 31, 1959, increment	465	123.66	575
Dec. 31, 1960, increment	1,000	120.00	1,200
Total	$14,650		$15,525

An authorized dollar-value computation method must be used for years beginning after Dec. 31, 1960.

(3) *Change in methods of computation of the LIFO value of a dollar-value pool.* For the first taxable year beginning after December 31, 1960, the taxpayer must use a method authorized by paragraph (e) (1) of this section in computing the base-year cost and current-year cost of a dollar-value inventory pool for the end of such year. If the taxpayer had previously used any methods other than one authorized by paragraph (e) (1) of this section, he shall not be required to recompute his LIFO inventories for taxable years beginning on or before December 31, 1960, under a method authorized by such

paragraph. The base cost and layers of increment previously computed by such other method shall be retained and treated as if such base cost and layers of increment had been computed under a method authorized by paragraph (e) (1) of this section. The taxpayer shall use the year of change as the base year in applying the double-extension method or other method approved by the Commissioner, instead of the earliest year for which he adopted the LIFO method for any items in the pool.

Right to change pooling in first year ending after April 15, 1961.   (h) *Change without consent in method of pooling—* (1) *Authorization.* Notwithstanding the provisions of paragraph (g) of this section, a taxpayer, for his first taxable year ending after April 15, 1961, may change from one method of pooling authorized by this section to any other method of pooling authorized by this section provided the requirements of subparagraph (2) of this paragraph are met. Also, for such year, if a taxpayer is currently using only a method of pooling authorized by this section, or a method of pooling which would be authorized by this section if additional items were included in the pool, and could change to the natural business unit method, except for the fact he has not inventoried all items entering into the inventory investment for such natural business unit on the LIFO method, he may change to the natural business unit method if he elects under the provisions of § 1.472–3 to extend the LIFO election to all items entering into the entire inventory investment for such natural business unit, provided the requirements of subparagraph (2) of this paragraph are met. The method of pooling adopted shall be used for the year of change and for all subsequent taxable years unless a change is required by the Commissioner in order to clearly reflect income, or unless permission to change is granted by the Commissioner as provided in paragraph (e) of § 1.446–1.

(2) *Requirements.* A statement shall be attached to the income tax return for the year of change referred to in subparagraph (1) of this paragraph setting forth, in summary form, the following information:

(i) A description of the new pool or pools,

(ii) The basis for selection of the new pool or pools,

(iii) A schedule showing the computation of the LIFO value of the former pool or pools, and,

(iv) A schedule showing the transition from the former pool or pools to the new pool or pools.

In addition, a copy of the statement shall be filed with the Commissioner of Internal Revenue, Attention: T:R, Washington 25, D.C. The taxpayer shall submit such other information with respect to the change in method of pooling as may be requested.

APPENDIX D

Proposed Rules on LIFO Conformity Requirement

SUMMARY: This document contains proposed amendments to the regulations relating to the financial reporting conformity requirement incident to the use of the last-in, first-out (LIFO) method of inventory accounting. The proposed amendments would provide the public with guidance needed to comply with that requirement and would affect taxpayers using the LIFO method for Federal income tax purposes.

DATES: Written comments and requests for a public hearing must be mailed or delivered by September 17, 1979. Except as otherwise provided, the amendments are proposed to be effective for taxable years beginning after December 31, 1953, and ending after August 16, 1954.

ADDRESS: Send comments and requests for a public hearing to: Commissioner of Internal Revenue, Attention: CC:LR:T, (LR–84–77), Washington, D.C. 20224.

FOR FURTHER INFORMATION CONTACT: Geoffrey B. Lanning of the Legislation and Regulations Division, Office of the Chief Counsel, Internal Revenue Service, 1111 Constitution Avenue, N.W., Washington, D.C. 20224, Attention: CC:LR:T, 202–566–3909, not a toll-free call.

SUPPLEMENTARY INFORMATION: Background. This document contains proposed amendments to the Income Tax Regulations (26 CFR Part 1) under section 472 of the Internal Revenue Code of 1954. The proposed regulations are to be issued under the authority contained in section 7805 of the Internal Revenue Code of 1954 (68A Stat. 917:26 U.S.C. 7805).

EXPLANATION OF PROPOSED REGULATIONS

Section 472 provides taxpayers with an election to account for inventories on the last-in, first-out (LIFO) method of inventory accounting. Section 472(c) and (e) generally provide that taxpayers using the LIFO method for Federal income tax purposes must not use any other inventory method for purposes of reporting income, profit, or loss in credit statements or financial reports to shareholders, partners, other proprietors, or beneficiaries. This requirement is the so-called LIFO conformity requirement.

The proposed amendments to the regulations would provide that supplemental or explanatory financial disclosures issued after the proposed amendments are filed by the Federal Register do not violate the LIFO conformity requirement. The proposed amendments would provide rules for determining whether a disclosure is supplemental or explanatory.

Section 1.472-2 (e) of the Income Tax Regulations currently provides that the LIFO conformity requirement is not violated if a taxpayer uses market value rather than cost for financial reporting purposes or issues reports or credit statements that cover a period of operations less than the whole of a taxable year.

The proposed amendments to the regulations would provide that the use of market value in lieu of cost for financial reporting purposes is not a violation of the LIFO conformity requirement only if the market value used is less than the LIFO cost of the inventory items.

The proposed regulations would also provide that credit statements or financial reports that cover a one-year period of operations overlapping two taxable years are subject to the conformity requirement.

The proposed amendments to the regulations would also provide that internal management reports are not reports to shareholders within the meaning of section 472 (c) and (e) and are not subject to the LIFO conformity requirement. In addition, the proposed amendments would provide that balance sheet reports of the value of taxpayers' inventories on hand are not reports of income, profit, or loss and are not subject to the LIFO conformity requirement.

RELIANCE ON PROPOSALS

Pending the adoption of final regulations, taxpayers may rely on these proposed rules in preparing financial reports, credit statements, or other reports.

If any provisions of the final regulations are less favorable to taxpayers than these proposed rules, those provisions will be effective only after the date of adoption.

COMMENTS AND REQUESTS FOR A PUBLIC HEARING

Before adopting these proposed regulations, consideration will be given to any written comments (preferable six copies) that are submitted to the Commissioner of Internal Revenue. All comments will be available for public inspection and copying. A public hearing will be held upon written request to the Commissioner by any person who has submitted written comments. If a public hearing is to be held, notice of the time and place will be published in the Federal Register.

DRAFTING INFORMATION

The principal author of these proposed regulations is Geoffrey B. Lanning of the Legislation and Regulations Division of the Office of Chief Counsel, Internal Revenue Service. However, personnel from other offices of the Internal Revenue Service and Treasury Department participated in developing the regulations, both on matters of substance and style.

Proposed Amendments to the Regulations

The proposed amendments to 26 CFR Part 1 are as follows:
Section 1.472–2 (e) is revised to read as follows:

§ 1.472–2 **Requirements incident to the adoption and use of LIFO inventory method.**

* * *

(e) *LIFO conformity requirement*—(1) *In general.* The taxpayer must establish to the satisfaction of the Commissioner that the taxpayer, in ascertaining the income, profit, or loss for the taxable year for which the LIFO inventory method is first used or for any subsequent taxable year, for credit purposes or for purposes of reports to shareholders, partners, or other proprietors, or to beneficiaries, has not used any inventory method other than that referred to in § 1.472–1 or at variance with the requirement referred to in § 1.472–2 (c). For this purpose, the following are not considered at variance with the requirement of this paragraph:

(i) The taxpayer's use of an inventory method for purposes of ascertaining information reported after July 17, 1979, a a supplement to or explanation of the taxpayer's primary presentation in financial statements of the taxpayer's income, profit or loss for a taxable year. See paragraph (e) (2) of this section for rules relating to the reporting of supplemental and explanatory information ascertained by the use of an inventory method.

(ii) The taxpayer's use of an inventory method to ascertain the value of taxpayer's inventory of specified goods on hand for purposes of reporting such value on the taxpayer's balance sheet.

(iii) The taxpayer's use of an inventory method for purposes of ascertaining information reported in internal management reports.

(iv) The taxpayer's issuance of reports or credit statements covering a single continuous period of operations that is both less than the whole of a taxable year and less than twelve months. See paragraph (e)(3) of this section for rules relating to a series of interim reports.

(v) The taxpayer's use of market value each year in lieu of LIFO cost assigned to the items of inventory for Federal income tax purposes, where market value is less than such LIFO cost.

(2) *Supplemental and explanatory information*—(i) *Face of the income statement.* Information reported on the face of a taxpayer's financial income statement for a taxable year is not considered a supplement to or explanation of the taxpayer's primary presentation in financial statements of the taxpayer's income, profit, or loss for the taxable year. For example, information reported in a parenthetical statement on the face of a taxpayer's income statement is not considered supplemental or explanatory for purposes of this paragraph. For purposes of paragraph (e)(2) of this section, the face of an income statement does not include footnotes to the statement.

(ii) *Notes to the income statement.* Information reported in notes to a taxpayer's financial income statement for a taxable year is considered a supplement to or explanation of the taxpayer's primary presentation of income, profit, or loss for the taxable year if the notes accompany the income statement in a single report. If notes to an income statement are issued in a report that does not include the income statement, the question of whether the information reported therein is supplemental or explanatory is determined under the rules in paragraph (e)(2)(iv) of this section.

(iii) *Appendices and supplements to the income statement.* Information reported in an appendix or supplement to a taxpayer's financial income statement for a taxable year is considered a supplement to or explanation of the taxpayer's primary presentation of income, profit, or loss for the taxable year if the appendix or supplement accompanies the income statement in a single report and the information reported in the appendix or supplement is clearly identified as a supplement to or explanation of the taxpayer's primary presentation of income, profit, or loss for the taxable year as reported on the face of the taxpayer's income statement. If an appendix or supplement to an income statement is issued in a report that does not include the income statement, the question of whether the information reported therein is supplemental or explanatory is determined under the rules in paragraph (e)(2)(iv) of this section.

(iv) *Other reports.* Information reported in a news release, letter to shareholders, letter to creditors, or other report (other than a taxpayer's income statement or accompanying notes, appendices, or supplements) is considered a supplement to or explanation of the taxpayer's primary presentation of income, profit, or loss for the taxable year if the supplemental or explanatory information is clearly identified as a supplement to or explanation of the taxpayer's primary presentation of income, profit, or loss for the taxable year as reported on the face of taxpayer's income statement for the taxable year and the specific item of information being explained or supplemented, such as the cost of goods sold, net income, or earnings per share, ascertained using the LIFO method, is also reported in the news release, letter, or other report.

(3) *Series of interim reports.* For purposes of paragraph (e) (1) (iv), a series of credit statements or financial reports is considered a single statement or report covering a single continuous period of operations if the statements or reports in the series are prepared using a single inventory method and can be combined to disclose the income, profit, or loss for the continuous period.

JEROME KURTZ,
Commissioner of Internal Revenue.

APPENDIX E

State (City) Corporate Tax Requirements Where LIFO Adopted, Readopted, Etc. for Federal Income Tax Purposes

CONFORMITY WITH THE FEDERAL CALCULATION OF TAXABLE INCOME

Many states conform with federal taxable income as the base or as the base with adjustments for calculating the state tax liability. In the majority of states the initial adoption of LIFO for state purposes is automatic where LIFO has been adopted for federal income tax purposes. Also in the majority of states if LIFO is readopted, changed, or terminated for federal purposes, such change is automatic for state purposes. In other cases an initial federal LIFO election is automatically allowed for state purposes, but the termination, change, or readoption of LIFO is not similarly automatic for state purposes. Even in the cases requiring that state approval be obtained, it is generally granted where federal approval has been obtained. This is so because most states are interested in federal-state conformity.

STATE REQUEST UNTIMELY FILED

The desire for conformity is often extended to an approval of a state change (where a federal change has been approved) even though the state request is not timely filed. Though state law would empower the state to reject an untimely application, the desire for conformity is generally given great weight. If a state change is not timely, it should be ascertained if the state desires that a formal request be filed. Where a late request is filed, the state is in a delicate position—the law would reject the request as untimely, but the tax commission would rather approve the change in the interests of conformity. In such cases it may be advisable to merely attach copies of the federal document to the state return as is often indicated in the attached schedule in column IV, D. In cases where an election is untimely and the appropriate documents are attached to the return there can be no certainty that the state will accept the change on audit. Therefore, the comments in column IV, D of the attached can only be relied on as guidelines involving apparent state practices at the time this release was updated (February 1979). Persons faced with an untimely state request for change, might consult with Price Waterhouse & Co. to determine if there has been a change in state policy, since such policy is often informal and subject to change.

EXPLANATION OF THE SCHEDULES

Certain abbreviations have been used in the attached schedules. For instance, the time limitation in column IV, A is often stated as "90 days after beginning of taxable year," etc.; this should be interpreted to mean within 90 days. . . .

Footnotes one to six indicate attachments to the state returns. These footnotes are only concerned with the attachment to state returns of Form 970 and copies of federal approvals for changes. Therefore, they should not be taken to mean that other federal schedules, etc., should not be attached to state returns as required. The scope of this release is only directed to situations where LIFO elections (or rulings) must be singularly attached or attached as part of a general state requirement of filing a copy of the complete federal return with the state return.

* * *

Where the word "state" is used in the above commentary the word "city" may be substituted when applicable.

LIFO

State (City) Corporate Tax Requirements Where LIFO Adopted, Readopted, Etc. for Federal Income Tax Purposes

I	II	III	IV			
	Initial adoption	Readoption, alteration or termination of LIFO and changes requiring federal approval	If state (city) approval not automatic what form must it take either for initial adoption (I) or for a change (C)?			
			A	B	C	D
State or city	Is adoption automatic for state (city) purposes if adopted for federal purposes?	Is state (city) approval automatic without any action by taxpayer?	Time limitation	Information required	Address of state (city) authority	Situation if state (city) request not timely filed
Alabama	No (1)	No (1)	(I & C) Before filing return	(I & C) Letter describing change	(I & C) Walter Cronier; Alabama Department of Revenue; Income Tax Division; Montgomery, Alabama 36130	(I & C) Generally accepted within reasonable period of time after federal approval received
Alaska	Yes (1)	Yes (1)	N/A	N/A	N/A	N/A

I	II	III	IV A	IV B	IV C	IV D
Arizona	Yes (7)	No	(C) 90 days after beginning of taxable year	(C) Letter request for change	(C) Arizona Department of Revenue; P.O. Box 29002; Phoenix, Arizona 85038	(I & C) Generally accepted if filed within reasonable period of time after federal approval received
Arkansas	No	No	(I) 60 days prior to year end	(I) Letter request for change accompanied by Form 970 and statement that IRS permits such a change	(I & C) Income Tax Director; Department of Finance and Administration; P.O. Box 1272-CT; Little Rock, Arkansas 72203	(I & C) Generally accepted if filed 60 days prior to due date (including extensions) of state return
			(C) As above	(C) Statement that IRS approved change		
California	Yes (7)	No (8)	(C) 180 days after beginning of taxable year	(C) Letter request	(C) Franchise Tax Board; Sacramento, California 95857	(C) Generally accepted if filed within reasonable period of time after federal approval received

State					
Colorado	Yes	Yes	N/A	N/A	N/A	N/A
Connecticut	Yes	Yes	N/A	N/A	N/A	N/A
Delaware	Yes (1)	Yes (1)	N/A	N/A	N/A	N/A
District of Columbia	No	No	(I & C) 2 to 3 weeks prior to due date (including extensions) of tax return	(I) Form 970 and an explanatory letter (C) Explanatory letter and copy of federal approval	(I & C) Director of Department of Finance and Revenue; 300 Indiana Avenue, N.W.; Washington, D.C. 20001	(I & C) N/A
Florida	Yes (1)	Yes (1)	N/A	N/A	N/A	N/A
Georgia	Yes (1)	Yes (1)	N/A	N/A	N/A	N/A
Hawaii	Yes (5)	No (5)	(C) First 90 days of taxable year	(C) Copy of federal request, later copy of federal approval	(C) Director of Taxation; State Department of Taxation; 425 Queen Street; Honolulu, Hawaii 96813	(C) File copy of federal approval with return, do same where timely
Idaho	Yes (1)	Yes (1)	N/A	N/A	N/A	N/A
Illinois	Yes	Yes	N/A	N/A	N/A	N/A
Indiana (10) Gross income tax	No (9)	No (9)	N/A	N/A	N/A	N/A
Adjusted gross income tax	Yes	Yes	N/A	N/A	N/A	N/A

441

I	II	III	IV A	IV B	IV C	IV D
Supplemental net income tax	Yes	Yes	N/A	N/A	N/A	N/A
Iowa	Yes (5)	Yes (5)	N/A	N/A	N/A	N/A
Kansas	Yes (1)	Yes (1)	N/A	N/A	N/A	N/A
Kentucky	Yes (2)	Yes (2)	N/A	N/A	N/A	N/A
Louisiana	Yes (5)	No (5)	(C) 90 days after beginning of taxable year	(C) Copy of federal request, later copy of federal approval	(C) Collector of Revenue; P.O. Box 201; Baton Rouge, Louisiana 70821	(C) File copy of federal approval with return, do same where timely
Maine	Yes	Yes	N/A	N/A	N/A	N/A
Maryland (10)	Yes (1)	Yes (1)	N/A	N/A	N/A	N/A
Massachusetts	Yes (1)	Yes (1)	N/A	N/A	N/A	N/A
Michigan (10)	Yes	Yes	N/A	N/A	N/A	N/A
Detroit	Yes (2)	Yes (2)	N/A	N/A	N/A	N/A
Other cities (15)	Yes	Yes	N/A	N/A	N/A	N/A

	No	No	(I) File as soon as possible after deciding to adopt LIFO (C) As above	(I) File copy of Form 970 with return and a copy of Form 970 with a letter request to adopt LIFO (C) File letter request including same information as required for federal purposes	(I) Minnesota Department of Revenue; Corporate Income Tax Division; Centennial Office Bldg., St. Paul, Minnesota 55145 (C) As above	N/A
Minnesota	No	No	(I) File as soon as possible after deciding to adopt LIFO / (C) As above	(I) File copy of Form 970 with return and a copy of Form 970 with a letter request to adopt LIFO / (C) File letter request including same information as required for federal purposes	(I) Minnesota Department of Revenue; Corporate Income Tax Division; Centennial Office Bldg., St. Paul, Minnesota 55145 / (C) As above	N/A
Mississippi	Yes (6)	Yes (6)	N/A	N/A	N/A	N/A
Missouri	Yes (1)	Yes (1)	N/A	N/A	N/A	N/A
Kansas City	Yes	Yes	N/A	N/A	N/A	N/A
St. Louis	Yes	Yes	N/A	N/A	N/A	N/A
Montana	Yes (1)	Yes (1)	N/A	N/A	N/A	N/A
Nebraska	Yes (1)	Yes (1)	N/A	N/A	N/A	N/A
New Hampshire	Yes	Yes	N/A	N/A	N/A	N/A
New Jersey (11)	Yes	Yes	N/A	N/A	N/A	N/A
New Mexico	Yes	Yes	N/A	N/A	N/A	N/A

I	II	III	IV A	B	C	D
New York	Yes (12)	Yes (12)	N/A	N/A	N/A	N/A
New York City	Yes	Yes	N/A	N/A	N/A	N/A
North Carolina	Yes (3)	Yes	N/A	N/A	N/A	N/A
North Dakota	Yes (3)	Yes (5)	N/A	N/A	N/A	N/A
Ohio (13)	Yes	Yes	N/A	N/A	N/A	N/A
Akron	Yes (4)	Yes	N/A	N/A	N/A	N/A
Cincinnati	Yes (4)	Yes	N/A	N/A	N/A	N/A
Cleveland	Yes (4)	Yes	N/A	N/A	N/A	N/A
Columbus	Yes	Yes	N/A	N/A	N/A	N/A
Dayton	Yes	Yes	N/A	N/A	N/A	N/A
Toledo	Yes	Yes	N/A	N/A	N/A	N/A
Oklahoma	Yes	Yes	N/A	N/A	N/A	N/A

Oregon	Yes (1 & 16)	No (1)	(C) Within first 180 days of taxable year	(C) Letter request for change	Department of Revenue; Salem, Oregon 97310	(C) State will accept if federal accepts change. State will issue a confirming letter if requested. Complete copy of federal return required to be attached to state return
Pennsylvania	Yes (1)	Yes (1)	N/A	N/A	N/A	N/A
Rhode Island	Yes (6)	Yes (6)	N/A	N/A	N/A	N/A
South Carolina	Yes (3 & 14)	Yes (14)	N/A	N/A	N/A	N/A
Tennessee	Yes (5)	Yes (5)	N/A	N/A	N/A	N/A
Utah	Yes (3)	Yes	N/A	N/A	N/A	N/A
Vermont	Yes (1)	Yes (1)	N/A	N/A	N/A	N/A
Virginia	Yes (1)	Yes (1)	N/A	N/A	N/A	N/A
West Virginia	Yes (4)	Yes	N/A	N/A	N/A	N/A
Wisconsin	Yes (5)	Yes (5)	N/A	N/A	N/A	N/A

FOOTNOTES

[The word "city" may be substituted for "state" in footnotes 1–5]

1. Complete copy of federal return attached to state return. "Complete" is defined to include a copy of Form 970 or federal ruling, where applicable.
2. Complete copy of federal return attached to state return in lieu of filling in certain state detail schedules.
3. Form 970 required to be attached to state return.
4. Form 970 requested by state to be attached to state return.
5. Form 970 required to be attached to state return and IRS approval for changes (e.g., readoption of LIFO, alteration of LIFO election, or termination of LIFO) required to be attached, each where applicable.
6. Form 970 requested by state to be attached to state return and, where applicable, the state requests that a copy of IRS approval for changes (examples as in #5 above) be attached to state return.
7. *Arizona* and *California* require that Form 970 be filed, in triplicate, with the franchise or income tax return.
8. *California* requires permission to terminate LIFO or readopt LIFO. Alteration of existing election may require advance approval if considered a change in accounting method. Change to dollar value from specific goods not considered a change. Redesignation of previously selected LIFO pools considered a change in method.
9. *Indiana* does not permit use of LIFO for gross income tax purposes unless tax computed on gross earnings method. No need to file Form 970 with state return if valid election made for federal purposes.
10. LIFO not allowed to be used for personal property tax purposes.
11. *New Jersey* requires that for purposes of the portion of the tax measured by net worth an adjustment is required to increase LIFO to FIFO. Courts have allowed such adjustment on a net of federal tax basis.
12. *New York State* requires that a complete copy of federal return be attached to state Form CT-3 when used.
13. *Ohio* assesses the franchise tax as the higher of the tax on income or the tax on net worth. Where the net worth method is used the Commissioner may disallow the LIFO reserve; however, if books are on LIFO (i.e., a reserve is not booked) he cannot adjust LIFO to FIFO. Additionally, LIFO cannot be used for Ohio personal property tax purposes.
14. *South Carolina* does not require advance permission to readopt LIFO, to alter an existing LIFO election, or to terminate LIFO. In adopting LIFO, the taxpayer, in effect, agrees to notify the state in writing of any change or proposal to change by the IRS of the inventory computed under LIFO within 30 days of receipt of IRS notice of change or proposal to change. Notification to state should be in the form of a letter to the Income Tax Division, South Carolina Tax Commission, P. O. Box 125, Columbia, South Carolina 29214.

15. The following Michigan cities, in addition to Detroit, have adopted the Michigan Uniform City Income Tax Ordinance:

Albion	Hudson
Battle Creek	Jackson
Big Rapids	Lansing
Flint	Lapeer
Grand Rapids	Pontiac
Grayling	Port Huron
Hamtramck	Saginaw
Highland Park	

Depending on each city's filing requirements, all or certain designated pages of the federal return may be attached to the city income tax return in lieu of certain information required on the respective forms.

16. *Oregon* will follow the federal LIFO election in the interest of conformity though automatic acceptance is contrary to existing state regulations requiring application for accounting changes within 180 days after the beginning of the taxable year. State will issue a confirming letter, if requested.

Index